Hortense Allart

The Woman and the Novelist

Helynne Hollstein Hansen

University Press of America,® Inc.
Lanham • New York • Oxford

Copyright © 1998
University Press of America,® Inc.
4720 Boston Way
Lanham, Maryland 20706

12 Hid's Copse Rd.
Cummor Hill, Oxford OX2 9JJ

Library of Congress Cataloging-in-Publication Data

Hansen, Helynne Hollstein.
Hortense Allart : the woman and the novelist / Helynne Hollstein
Hansen.
p.   cm.
Includes bibliographical references.
1. Allart de Méritens, Hortense, 1801-1879. I. Title
PQ2152.A7Z73 1998   843'.7—dc21   98-29734 CIP

ISBN 0-7618-1213-X (cloth: alk. ppr.)

™ The paper used in this publication meets the minimum
requirements of American National Standard for Information
Sciences—Permanence of Paper for Printed Library Materials,
ANSI Z39.48—1984

Elle ne veut pas éteindre les foyers qu'elle a allumés, elle les respecte et elle les entretient comme des autels.

She does not wish to extinguish the fires that she has lighted, she respects them and maintains them as though they were altars.

George Sand, 1872

To my family—those by my side and those scattered far and wide—for your constant encouragement and support.

Also, it is to Hortense Allart herself and in memory of her life as a serious woman of letters that this work is lovingly dedicated.

Sophie and Hortense Allart, c. 1814

Hortense Allart (painting by her sister, Sophie Allart Gabriac), c. 1829

Contents

Chronology of Hortense Allart[1]

1764   Birth in Paris of Nicolas-Jean-Gabriel Allart, father of Hortense Allart.

1765   Dec. 3. Birth in Lyon of Marie-Françoise Gay, mother of Hortense Allart.

1798   Dec. 9 (19 frimaire, year VII). Marriage in Paris of Nicolas-Jean-Gabriel Allart and Marie-Françoise Gay, at the Mairie of the 2nd arrondissement.

1801   Sept. 7 (30 fructidor, year IX). Birth in Milan of Hortense-Thérèse-Sigismonde-Sophie Alexandrine Allart.

1804   Feb. 28. Birth in Paris of Sophie-Marie-Gabrielle Allart, sister of Hortense Allart and future Madame Pierre Gabriac.

1817   June 15. Death of Nicolas-Jean-Gabriel Allart.

1821   Jan. 8. Death of Marie-Françoise Gay Allart.
—   Summer. Hortense visits her godmother, the Duchess of Raguse, then the Countess Régnault of Saint Jean-d'Angély ("Laure").
—   December. Publication of *La Conjuration d'Amboise* at A. Marc of Paris, Allart's first published work.

1822   Hortense becomes a tutor for the children of
               General and Madame Bertrand, who reside at 6,
               rue de la Victoire. She will hold this position for two
               years.

1823   Summer. At Val, Hortense makes the
               acquaintance of Anthony Sampayo.

1824   September. Journey to the château of Laleuf,
               residence of Madame Bertrand.

—   October. Hortense moves to a residence in Paris,
               where she receives Sampayo, Béranger, Thiers,
               Mignet.

1825   March. *Lettres sur les ouvrages de Madame de
               Staël* published at Bossange, Paris.
—   Summer. Voyage to Vitry-sur-Seine at the
               residence of the Duchesse de Raguse.
—   Nov. 1. Hortense leaves Paris for Italy. She is
               welcomed in Geneva by Sismondi and
               Bonstetten. Visits Coppet.
—   Late November through February 1826. She resides
               in Milan.

1826   February. Hortense leaves Milan and arrives in
               Florence towards the end of February or early
               March.
—   May. Hortense moves into an apartment at the
               palais Carraresi. She visits often with Libri and
               Capponi.
—   June 16. Birth of Marcus-Napoléon Allart.
—   Summer. Hortense moves to an apartment,
               Piazza Santa Croce.

1827   Spring. Sojourn at Casentino.
—   Summer. Hortense moves to the villa della
               Pace, at the Roman gate of Florence.
—   Autumn. Trips to Pisa and Livourne.
—   Returning to Florence, she moves to an
               apartment at Casa Rossi, via della Scala.
—   October. Hortense makes the acquaintance of
               Stendhal, who is passing through Florence.

1827
—   November. *Gertrude* is published by Ciardetti
            in Florence.

1828   Jan. 27. Hortense leaves Florence for Rome,
            where she will remain until April.
—   April 24-May 24. Sojourn at Albano.
—   Summer Sojourn at Castellammare.
—   October. Trip to the valley of Chiana.
—   Oct. 25. *Gertrude* is published in Paris by
            Dupont.
—   Nov. 1. *Gertrude* appears in a second edition.
—   Early November. Return to Florence, residence
            at via della Scala.

1829   Early April. Hortense leaves Florence for Rome.
            She moves into 17, via Quattro Fontane, in the
            apartment of her sister, Sophie Allart.
—   April 18. Hortense meets René de
            Chateaubriand, ambassador to Rome
—   May. Hortense leaves Rome for Paris, where
            she moves into a residence on the rue d'Enfer,
            near Chateaubriand.
—   July 18-19. Hortense and Chateaubriand pass
            together the "night at Étampes."
—   July 19. Hortense leaves her residence at rue
            d'Enfer for one at the Rue Godot.
—   Sept. 12. *Jérôme, ou le jeune prélat* is
            published by Ladvocat.
—   Oct. 15. Hortense moves into a residence at 32,
            rue de l'Université.

1830   Jan. 29. Beginning of Hortense's collaboration
            with the *National*.
—   April-May. Trip to London and visit with
            Madame Hutchinson, Grosvenor Street West,
            where she meets Henry Bulwer-Lytton.
—   June. Returning to Paris, Hortense lodges near
            the Jardin des Planètes.
—   July. Stay at Montlignon, near Montmorency.
—   Late August. Hortense and Bulwer meet at
            Saint-Valéry-sur-Somme.

1830
— July. Stay at Montlignon, near Montmorency.
— Late August. Hortense and Bulwer meet at Saint-Valéry-sur-Somme.
— September. Hortense et Bulwer leave for England.
— October. Hortense and Bulwer leave for Belgium, which is, at that time, experiencing a violent insurrection. They return to London at the end of this month.

1831   End of February. Hortense leaves London for Paris.
— Late March-early April. Béranger introduces Hortense to Sainte-Beuve.
— May-early June. Hortense and Bulwer spend time in Saint-Germain and Paris.
Bulwer returns to London on June 14.
— Late June. Hortense stays at Montlignon.
— July-October. Hortense stays four months in London with Bulwer. She lives at 3, Upper Eaton, Street, Grosvenor Place, then moves on Aug. 1 to 17 Ranelagh Street, Belgrave Square.
— Late October. Hortense and Bulwer have a short stay at Boulogne. Bulwer leaves again for London.
— November. Hortense moves to 19, rue Bleue, Paris.

1832   March. *Sextus ou le Romain des Maremmes* is published at Heidelof et Campe. Hortense's correspondence with Sainte-Beuve begins.
— Spring. Hortense and Bulwer stay four months in England at London and Hastings. Hortense returns to Paris in June.
— August. Hortense arranges to meet Bulwer at Beauvais. They travel together to Paris. Bulwer leaves for London in September.
— November. Hortense moves into a small, two-room apartment at 3, rue Mondovi.
— December. *L'Indienne* is published at Vimont.
— Late December. Hortense meets George Sand.

1833 Spring. Hortense moves to the village of
Herblay. She will return there numerous times
until 1850.

— Autumn. Hortense and Bulwer stay in
Versailles.

— December. Hortense and Bulwer move to an
apartment, rue Basse-du-Rempart, Paris.

1834 Feb. 10. Bulwer leaves Paris for London.
Hortense moves back to her Apartment at 3,
Rue Mondovi.

— Summer. Sojourn at Herblay.

1835 February-June. Sojourn of Hortense and Bulwer
in England at London and at Putney.

— June. Hortense leaves London for Paris.

— July 28. Hortense leaves Paris for England.
After a three-month stay in Putney,
Hortense and Bulwer return to Paris in October.
This is the end of her English Channel crossings.

1836 January. *La Femme et la démocratie de nos
temps* is published by Delaunay et Pinard

— Feb. 10. Marriage of Sophie Allart, sister of
Hortense Allart, and Pierre Gabriac, in Rome.

— April. *Settimia* is published by Arthus Bertrand.

— Summer-autumn. Stay at Herblay.

— August. Beginning of the contributions by
Hortense of articles for the *Gazette des Femmes.*

— Autumn. Hortense participates actively in the
feminist movement in Paris begun by Flora
Tristan.

— Dec. 10. Hortense returns from Herblay to Paris,
rue Mondovi.

1837 April. *Histoire de la République de Florence,*
T.I., is published at Moutardier.

— May. Hortense leaves Paris for Florence, and
arrives there June 14.

— Summer-autumn. Stay at Arricia and at Arezzo.
Dec. 15-March 1838. Stay in Florence, via
Melaranccio.

1838   Spring-summer. Stay at the villa Belvédère, near
      Sienna.
—   October. In Florence, Hortense makes the
      acquaintance of Marie d'Agoult and Franz Liszt.

1839   March 21. Birth in Florence of Henri-Marcus-
      Diodati Allart, son of Hortense Allart and Jacopo
      Mazzei.
—   Summer-autumn. Stay in Scarperia

1840   Late May. Hortense leaves Florence for Paris.
—   Early June. She moves back to Herblay.
—   November. She moves to Paris, 4, rue
      Trudaine.

1841   April 7. Death of Anthony Sampayo in Paris.
—   August. Probable beginning of the brief sexual
      liaison between Hortense Allart and Sainte-Beuve
      ("le clou d'or").

1842   April 11. Charles Didier, during a visit to
      Hortense, finds there Chateaubriand "assez
      embarrassé de sa contenance."

1843   February. *Histoire de la République de Florence*
      is published by Delloye et Garnier.
—   March 30. Hortense is married at Herblay to
      Napoléon-Louis-Frédéric de Méritens.
—   Early April. The newlyweds leave for
      Montauban in southwestern France.

1844   Late March. Hortense leaves Montauban, taking
      her son Henri, but leaving her husband. She
      arrives in Paris at the Hôtel du Rhône in early
      April and is met at the coach by Marcus and
      Sainte-Beuve.
—   June. Hortense returns to Herblay.

1845   Feb. 28. Hortense is accorded a yearly literary
      indemnity by the Ministère de l'Instruction
      publique.
—   Marie d'Agoult becomes Hortense's neighbor at
      Herblay.

1846　　Marie d'Agoult returns for a second summer at
　　　　　Herblay.
　　　　　Hortense becomes a grandmother as Anthony
　　　　　Allart is born to Marcus Allart and his mistress.

1847　　March. *Lettre à Abdel-Kader*, brochure on the
　　　　　government of France, is published.
—　　　　October. Hortense moves to Passy, 1, rue de la
　　　　　Glacière.

1848　　Late March. Trip to Burgundy.
—　　　　Late April-early May. Hortense and
　　　　　Chateaubriand meet in person for the last time.
—　　　　July 4. Death of Chateaubriand.
—　　　　Dec. 9. Marriage of Henry Bulwer-Lytton to
　　　　　Georgina-Charlotte-Mary Wellesley.

1850　　May. Hortense moves to Bezons (Seine-et-
　　　　　Oise), settles in a country home.
—　　　　May 20. Hortense and Sainte-Beuve meet for the
　　　　　last time.
—　　　　August. *Premier Petit Livre, Etudes Diverses*
　　　　　published by Renault.
—　　　　September. Hortense moves to a country home
　　　　　at Coulanges-la-Vineuse (Yonne).
—　　　　November. *Second Petit Livre, Etudes Diverses*
　　　　　published by Renault.

1851　　April *Troisième petit Livre, Etudes Diverses*
　　　　　published by Renault.
—　　　　October. Hortense leaves Coulanges-la-Vineuse
　　　　　for Ville-neuve-le-Roi, near Sens. She stays
　　　　　until September 1853.

1853　　October. Hortense moves to Thiais (Seine).

1854　　October. Hortense moves to Chilly-Mazarin
　　　　　(Seine-et-Oise).

1855　　October. Hortense moves to Monthléry.

1857　　June. *Essai sur l'histoire politique* published by
　　　　　Just Rouvier et Dentu.

1857   September. *Novum organum* published by
            Garnier.

1859   May. Hortense moves to Bourg-la-Reine on the
            outskirts of Paris.

1860   October. Hortense moves to Monthléry.
—   November. *Extrait de mémoires inédits,*
            the story of the relationship between Hortense
            Allart and Chateaubriand, is published
            by Sainte-Beuve in *Chateaubriand et son
            groupe littéraire.*

1862   July 19. Death of Henri Allart.
—   December. Publication of *Nouvelle concorde
            des quatre évangélistes.*

1863   Aug. 22. Marriage of Marcus Allart and Berthe
            Vernier.

1864   March. Publication of *Essai sur la religion
            intérieure.*
—   June. Publication of *Lettres choisies de
            Béranger à Mme Hortense Allart de Méritens.*

1865   Spring. Publication of *Clémence,* novella, by
            Sceaux.
—   Autumn. Publication of *Première [-Troisième]
            Lettre de Mme Hortense A. de Méritens au Lord
            Comte Henry W.*

1866   September. Publication of *Histoire de la
            République d'Athènes.*

1869   Oct. 13. Death of Sainte-Beuve.

1870   January. Publication of *Lettres de Mme
            Prudence de Saman et de Lord Walter North.*
—   September. Hortense moves to 14, rue
            Castellane, Paris.

1872   August. Publication of *Les Enchantements
            de Mme Prudence de Saman l'Esbatx* by
            Sceaux.

1873 April. *Les Enchantements du Prudence* (2nd edition with a preface by George Sand), published by Michel Lévy. A third edition will appear this same year.

— July. *Les Nouveaux Enchantements* published by Michel Lévy.

1874 November. *Derniers Enchantements* published by Michel Lévy.

1876 September. Publication of *Timide Essai sur la correspondance sublime de Cicéron.*

1877 *Les Enchantements de Prudence* (new edition) published by Calmann Lévy.

1879 Feb. 28. Hortense Allart dies at Monthléry. She is interred at the cemetery at Bourg-la-Reine.

1882 *Les Nouveaux Enchantements* (new edition) published by Calmann Lévy.

— *Derniers Enchantements* (new edition) published by Calmann Lévy.

1901 Jan. 12. Death of Marcus Allart. He is buried next to his mother at the cemetery in Bourg-la-Reine.

1908 *Lettres inédites à Sainte-Beuve (1841-1848)* published by Léon Séché.

— *Hortense Allart de Méritens dans ses Rapports avec Chateaubriand, Béranger, Lamennais, Sainte-Beuve, G. Sand, Mme D'Agoult,* published by Léon Séche, Société de Mercure de France.

1940 June 1 and 15; Aug. 15 and Sept. 1. Certain letters from Hortense Allart to Sainte-Beuve are published in the *Revue de Deux-Mondes* by Marie-Louise Pailleron.

1957   *The Life and Writings of Hortense Allart (1801-
                  1879),* unpublished dissertation, is written by
                  Lorin A. Uffenbeck and submitted in partial
                  fulfillment of a Ph.D. degree at the University
                  of Wisconsin.

1961   *Lettere inédite a Gino Capponi*   published by
                  M. Petre Ciureanu.

—   *Hortense et ses Amants* published by André
                  Billy, Flammarion, Paris.

—   *Hortense Allart de Méritens et Henri Bulwer-
                  Lytton* published by Juliette Decreus, J.J.
                  Minard, Paris.

1965   *Nouvelles Lettres à Sainte-Beuve (1832-1864),*
                  compiled and annotated by Lorin A. Uffenbeck,
                  published by Librairie Droz S.A., Geneva.

1973   *The Other Side of the Ideal: Women Writers of
                  Mid-Nineteenth-Century France (George Sand,
                  Daniel Stern, Hortense Allart, and Flora Tristan),*
                  unpublished dissertation, is written by Leslie
                  Rabine and submitted in partial fulfillment of a
                  Ph.D. degree at Stanford University.

[1]Dates and events on this list were drawn and translated, in part, from
the chronology listed in *Nouvelles Lettres à Sainte-Beuve (1823-1864):   Les
lettres de la collection Lovenjou* , Lorin A. Uffenbeck, ed. (Geneva: Librairie
Droz S.A.,   1965) xiii-xvii.

Preface

The complexity of the interweaving of Romanticism, intellectualism, and feminism that characterized the lifetime and the writings of Hortense Allart might best be examined through the paradox through which her friend, George Sand once viewed her.

The friendship and correspondence between the two writers, which went on for more than 40 years, consisted of a prickly, but ultimately warm rapport that culminated in Sand's highest praise of her colleague. The uneasiness that characterized the early years of their relationship is not difficult to understand when seen in the light of an era in which genuine solidarity between women writers was fraught with suspicion and mistrust. A sense of sisterhood among female writers and their common struggle to create a gynocentric language and purpose would not be sought after and valued until more than a century later.

Therefore, Allart's secure place in Sand's heart was not only long in coming, but also well-earned and hard-won. It took Sand a long while not only to feel comfortable with a fellow female novelist but also to reconcile herself to what she considered a confusing contradiction in her friend's literary works, that is, a too traditionally feminine persona and an overly masculine bent in her writing style.

Soon after she met Allart, Sand, who had fought hard to avoid the connotation of a certain silliness, or at best, a lack of literary seriousness that surrounded women novelists of the time, wrote their mutual friend, Sainte-Beuve, referring to Allart pejoratively as *une écriveuse.* [1] The use of a feminine form of *écrivain,* which does not really exist, marked Sand's determination to separate herself from the "women authors" of her time of whom she feared Allart was a part.

Sand further criticized her new acquaintance and her writing style in an April 1833 letter to a friend, Laure Decerfz, calling Allart "pédante . . . tranchante, politique, hommasse, femme auteur comme tous les diables."[2]

Sand does not make clear how a *femme auteur* could also be called *hommasse*—defined by the Larousse dictionary as "une femme dont l'aspect, la voix, les manières tendent de l'homme." However, at a point early in her career when she herself was being labeled "lesbian," "man-eater," and other unpleasant epithets by her critical public, Sand seemed almost ready to join the ranks that were against *her*.

Interestingly, Sand was not the first to notice a certain "male" bent to Allart's works (although she was the first to deem it offensive). Allart had been cited at least twice for having a "male mind" — but in a more flattering manner, and by men. In her last major work, her eclectic autobiography, *Les Enchantements de Prudence,* she noted that when her first novel, *Gertrude,* was published in 1827, it was praised by critics as "un ouvrage *mâle.*"[3] Later, in *Les Enchantements de Prudence,* she describes how Chateaubriand first read her manuscript of her second novel, *Jérôme* (1829), and declared that "j'avais l'esprit mâle, qu'il fallait faire un ouvrage sérieux" (*EP* 187).

Allart's life was as unconventional as Sand's own. Independent, candid, and scrupulously honest about her multitude of lovers—who comprised several prominent French male writers, including Chateaubriand and Sainte-Beuve—and her unwed motherhood, she blissfully refused to see her chosen lifestyle as scandalous. She was, however, of a different image than the top-hatted, waistcoated, cigar-smoking Sand when it came to physical appearance.

The idea of Allart's "male mind" is particularly intriguing as one begins to picture the young writer in the prime of her career between the 1820s and 1840s—lovely and petite, demurely dressed, her blond hair tidily coiffed. She was blessed with an easy charm, vivaciousness, enthusiasm and natural intelligence, but even as she campaigned courageously through her novels, scholarly tracts and personal correspondence for equal legal rights and greater respect for women and protection for families, her demeanor was subdued, respectful, scholarly, controlled.

Another vivid image is that of Allart at age 41, finally marrying amid all the hopes and dreams of a new wife, but staying in that union just one year, escaping the estate of a domineering, brutal mate, tossing her wedding ring from the window of the carriage as she flees. Although Allart's character wouldn't allow her to tolerate the stereotypical demands placed on a submissive wife, she nevertheless championed a kinder, idealized family life, was a devoted mother to her two out-of-wedlock sons, and strove through the touching stories of the heroines of her novels to create the hope that happy marriages somehow might be possible for intelligent, independent women.

Realizing, though, that she herself could not—in late 20th-century feminist parlance—"have it all," Allart realistically and philosophically opted to spend the remaining 35 years of her life without romantic love and marriage, but with the blessings of scholarly solitude with her writing, her sons, her grandchildren, and a core of unfailing inner serenity.

If Sand had difficulty with the dichotomy that was Allart as the latter produced, in equal measure, Romantic novels, scholarly and religious essays, and histories on civilizations and governments, she was to grow more understanding and charitable through the years. Sand came to admire simultaneously Allart's intensely Romantic sensitivity and her amazingly broad-based intellectuality that set her apart from virtually any other of France's *femmes auteurs* of the time. Sand also could not fail to praise—and even envy—Allart's uncommon lack of even the slightest enmity or resentment toward each of the friends and lovers who had crossed her path, then moved on.

Indeed, it was Sand, who, toward the end of both women's rich and productive lives, called her friend, "a very great lady," and praised her for not wishing ever to "extinguish the home fires that she has kindled."[4]

The enigma of the *"femme auteur"* with the *"esprit mâle"* that was a source of bewilderment and suspicion during the 19th century, is the basic *pâte* that late 20th-century critics love to mold in to the most convoluted and intriguing of critical studies. Nonetheless, the relative paucity of scholarship on Allart during the past few decades, particularly in the English language, indicates that she and her works have all but fallen through the cracks of the feminist criticism movement begun about 1968.

Until 1908, when Léon Séché published the biography *Muses romantiques: Hortense Allart de Méritens dans ses rapports avec Chateaubriand, Béranger, Lamennais, Sainte-Beuve, G. Sand, Mme Agoult,* the only accounting of Allart's life was her own 1872 *Les Enchantements de Prudence.* The most recent books written about her life were both published in 1961 and in French—*Hortense et ses Amants* by André Billy and *Hortense Allart et Henry Bulwer-Lytton* by Juliette Decreus—and are detailed biographical studies rather than critiques of her literary works.

The only other commentaries on her works in the latter half of this century, aside from a minuscule number of short articles (virtually all of them in French), are two unpublished English-language doctoral dissertations—Lorin A. Uffenbeck's exhaustive and meticulously documented "The Life and Writings of Hortense Allart," written in

1957, and Leslie Rabine's "The Other Side of the Ideal: Women Writers of Mid-Nineteenth-Century France: (George Sand, Daniel Stern, Hortense Allart, Flora Tristan)," produced in 1973, which devotes one chapter to Allart.

This study sheds not only more light on the character and the novels of Hortense Allart for English-speaking scholars of 19th-century French literature, but also delves into the modernity of her works and her "male mind" that is a counterpart to her intellectualism and her Romanticism. Most important, this work traces the step-by-step progress of the courageous, uncompromising feminism of an uncommonly gifted writer and scholar who has too long remained undeservedly obscure and underappreciated.

Notes

[1] "Sauf à passer pour une écriveuse comme Madame A[llart], je veux vous faire l'injure d'un billet." Letter to Sainte-Beuve, March 10, 1833. *Correspondence de George Sand,* George Lubin, ed., (Paris; Classiques Garnier, 1967) 2:276.

[2]*Correspondance de George Sand ,* 2:291.

[3]Mme P[rudence] de [Hortense Allart de Méritens] Saman l'Esbatx, *Les Enchantements de Prudence.* (Paris: Typographie de E. Dépée, mai 1872) 88 (Allart's italics).

[4]George Sand, *Préface, Les Enchantements de Prudence,* 2nd ed., (Paris: [Michel Lévy Frères, Libraire nouvelle, 1873), my translation.

Chapter 1

An Unconventional Life
(1801-1825)

If ever there was a mélange of philosophical contradictions in both the life and the writings of a French writer, it must be in those of Romantic feminist Hortense Allart (1801-1879), an indefatigable novelist, scholar and historian whose relentless search for exalted love paralleled a stark awareness of women's problems of the day and pleadings for society's sympathy and reform.

As devoted as she was to France and to the betterment of its future for women and for mankind in general, Allart was really the product of two countries, two cultures and two sources of flourishing Romanticism. Born in Italy of French parents, then raised in the environs of Paris, Allart was to return to Italy for two extended stays in her adult life. She wrote eloquently of nature's beauties in both France and Italy as she sought numerous times in her life and writings the ideal love, and often longed to be her own Romantic heroine.

Although she based her often heady emotions upon a profound and mystic Christianity, she boldly charted her own moral course, bore two sons from different liaisons, and wrote at the end of her life an autobiographical work looking back on her many experiences in love and describing them as "enchantments."

To study her life and read her personal letters is to perceive a complete absence of resentment or bitterness as each of her relationships, including one disastrous marriage, comes to an end. Her lifetime is chronicled by a wealth of candid, guileless correspondence with the men whom she had loved and lost (or loved and left), and with some of the women who were her victorious competition for these men's devotion.

As the colorful portrait of this woman unfolds, she stands courageous and lucid in the face of the inequalities crushing down upon Frenchwomen of the day, including the injustices meted out by individual husbands and sanctioned by the *Code Napoléon.* She was a constant example of the lifestyle she wished to procure for all women as she quietly led her life according to her own goals and conscience, refusing to be fettered by anyone else's—including her most passionate lover's— determination to chart the course of her life.

There was much in Allart that was typical of her adored predecessor, Madame de Staël, about whose writings Allart wrote her first major work, and also typical of her friend and correspondent George Sand, who eventually was to admire Allart as much as Allart admired her. Like these other women writers, Allart was a gifted intellectual, given to in-depth study and discussion of literary and philosophical masters from Plato through her own time. She was uncommonly creative and prolific, writing almost constantly throughout her 77-year lifetime, even in the midst of her most unsettling personal traumas, and producing an *œuvre* that consisted of several well-received novels, numerous scholarly essays, political tracts, and exhaustive histories of Florence and Athens.

If Allart's works in general and her novels in particular—now all long out of print and sometimes difficult to procure—have not endured as well as those of her peers, it may be because her own unflagging optimism about life and love may have painted scenarios for at least some of her heroines that were ultimately too simplistic or insufficiently tragic to capture the attention of the more hard-core, long-suffering Romantics or of the militant feminists of her day and of the future.

Three of Allart's novels and her short novella, which end in a happy marriage, do so with a one-sentence wrap-up: *Gertrude, Sextus, Settimia, and Clémence* all conclude with a sentence such as "And so they were married" with no complicated intrigue surrounding their rapport, no dramatic revelations, no Romantic descriptions of their reunion and conversation as they resolve to be together forever (*à la Mauprat*), not even a simple, tender, gratifying embrace (*à la La Mare au Diable*), no glance into their happy future (*à la La Petite Fadette*).

Of course, Allart hardly can be faulted for not anticipating the development of 20th-century entertainment media, and their propensity for turning literary classics into costume dramas in the form of film extravaganzas and elongated TV mini-series. Furthermore, though most modern producers might not consider her fiction as quite the stuff of Romantic visual drama for the large or small screen, her novels, nevertheless, contain sufficient compelling narration and scope as well as viable commentaries on the situation of women of her day to warrant more modern-day scrutiny and respect than they heretofore have received.

Her work that retains the most interest today is her semi-fictionalized autobiography, *Les Enchantements de Prudence de Saman D'Esbatx,* originally published in 1872 when she was 71. Although the narrative uses pseudonyms for some of the real-life characters it describes, it is the summary of her life's events and her less-than-idealized struggles to maintain independence and control as she sought both love and professional respect. Since Allart's life was characterized by a continuous uphill battle for women's rights, it is not surprising that the feminist underpinnings are the clearest and the most bold in this culmination of her 10 novels. The work contains an unusual potpourri of period Romanticism and personal actions and commentaries describing the horrors that many women—wives in particular—were forced to endure, and a call for social awareness and action.

The novel's Romantic voice is traditional and rich, with extensive descriptions of nature and of exhilarating emotion. It includes the novella *Marpé,* which Allart originally published in 1851 as part of her *Troisième Petit Livre.* Also, certain passages from several of her other earlier novels are reproduced verbatim in this book. The work also contains original poetry and original maxims and ends with the author's religious philosophies and her own sentimental and devoted Christian prayers.

The counterpoint to the Romanticism in the novel is equally sanguine, and its call to social action is punctuated with a bold and unapologetic feminist voice that one would be more likely to associate with a "self-actualized" woman of the late 20th century.

For all her detailed description of her major life events and emotions in *Les Enchantements de Prudence,* Allart declines to fill the reader in on many details about her childhood and adolescence. It is mostly through the research of biographer Léon Séché (*Hortense Allart de Méritens dans ses Rapports avec Chateaubriand, Béranger, Lamennais, Sainte-Beuve, G. Sand, Mme D'Agoult,* 1908) that readers first learn of the first 20 years of a courageous and uncommonly productive life. Unless otherwise noted, the following early biographical information comes from both the Séché book and from André Billy's 1961 *Hortense et ses Amants.*

Hortense-Thérèse-Sigismonde-Sophie-Alexandrine Allart was born on Sept. 7, 1801, in Milan, the daughter of Nicolas-Jean-Gabriel Allart and Marie-Françoise Gay. Her birth was recorded in the *état civil* in Milan in terms of the Revolutionary calendar, 30 fructidor, year IX.

In an interesting coincidence of dates, records from the Auberge de la Ville show that just after her baptism on Sept. 19, the French diplomat Henri Beyle, who would become the novelist Stendhal and Allart's trusted friend and mentor, had just returned to Milan, where he would continue his service in Napoleon's army, and later spend a significant portion of his diplomatic life.

Her first name came from her godmother, wife of General Marmont. Sigismonde was given in honor of her maternal uncle and godfather, Sigismond Gay, who married a famous beauty named Sophie Nichault de la Vallette. Their daughter, the vivacious Delphine Gay, three years Hortense's junior, would make a mark on Parisian high society a few years later as the dashing wife of Emile de Girardin, and as a poet in her own right.

All the women in Hortense's immediate family were of the same superior and independent ilk, patterning themselves deliberately after Madame de Staël, for whom Hortense would show an early admiration and fascination.   Billy states, "Hortense, sa mère, sa tante Sophie et sa cousine Delphine, appartenaient à la même espèce de femmes, vraies descendantes de Mme de Staël, libres, intelligentes et ambitieuses." [1]

Hortense's mother, Marie-Françoise Gay, herself an unusually talented young scholar, was born Dec. 3, 1765, in Lyon, the eldest of six children of a family that was noble, but penniless. Her father, Josèph Gay, who was born in Aix-les-Bains in 1724, was ennobled by Victor Amadeus II of Sardinia in 1782, but died impoverished a few years later. Her mother, Marie-Claudine-Louise Galy, was the daughter of a merchant of Lyon who was ruined by the Revolution.   As an adolescent, Marie-Françoise served as president of the *Société philanthropique des dames de Chambéry,* to the satisfaction of the supervising Abbé Grégoire,   before leaving for Paris to seek her fortune.   Orphaned in 1783, when she was but 17, Marie-Françoise left her native region of Savoie some 10 years later "en pleine Terreur," states Séché, "n'ayant pour tout bien que sa beauté et l'exellente éducation que lui avaient donnée ses parents,"[2]   taking along her younger brother, Sigismond, and younger sister, Anne-Sophie.

Marie-Françoise Gay's informal, but thorough education, backed by letters of recommendation from the Abbé Grégoire and her own confidence and enthusiasm, soon gained her a respected position in the Parisian intellectual society, and a job as translator of the works of English writer Anne Radcliffe, which were gaining popularity in the capital at the time.   In an unedited letter to her cousin in Aix-les-Bains dated 23 vendémaire, year VI (Nov. 18, 1797), she spoke of local social events, and asked if he had read her recent translation of the seven-volume *Eléonore de Rosalba, ou le confessional des pénitents noirs,* asking "Sont-ils suffisants pour endormir le lecteur?"[3]   In 1799, she published *Les Secrets de Famille,* a five-volume translation of a novel by Samuel Jackson Pratt.[4] Marie-Françoise also wrote original works, including a novel, *Ablation,* that was mostly autobiographical.[5]

A few years later, thanks to her connections and her talents, she met and wed Nicolas-Jean-Gabriel Allart, son of a clerk in the Parisian parliament.   Allart's father was also a financial counselor in such major cities as Lyon, Toulouse and Aix-la-Chapelle.   The younger Allart himself became an independent businessman, practicing *l'usure,* or money-lending on the Rue Chapon.   Tall and handsome, Allart had a reputation as a ladies' man who loved the theater, occasionally appearing on the stage himself.   From about 1795 to 1797 he played the title role in various productions of *La mort de César.*[6]   In the summer of 1797 he played Caesar at Udine before an audience that included Napoleon Bonaparte and Josephine, who had been married for a year and a half.

At the home of his friend, Talma, a fellow dilettante actor with whom he had appeared in *La mort de César,* Allart met a certain Mademoiselle Desgarcins, an actress of the Comédie-Française, who specialized in roles of the tragic, love-struck victim. Her fondness for such roles carried into her personal life as she became Allart's mistress. One morning, devastated by her suspicions of Allart's infidelity (actually, her rivals for his attentions were many), she appeared at his home, demanded an explanation, then stabbed herself three times in the chest.

Her guilty lover, who was shaken more by fear and remorse than by tenderness, nevertheless nursed his histrionic actress back to health before leaving her forever.   Mademoiselle Desgarcins, though not seriously wounded, was sufficiently traumatized by the incident to give up the theater. She retired to the countryside, was terrorized by bandits one night (tied up, then locked in her basement with her servants), and died insane just a few months later.

As for Allart, the whole incident only served to enhance his reputation among the *parisiennes.*   Whether or not this brought him to the attention of Marie-Françoise Gay, when she was age 33, and he 34, can only be imagined. However, after their marriage in Paris on 19 frimaire, year VII (Dec. 9, 1798), Allart settled down and became a faithful husband and devoted father to Hortense, and to her younger sister Sophie-Marie-Gabrielle Allart, who was born in Paris on Dec. 28, 1804.   Sophie would later become a respected artist who exhibited her paintings in professional salons from 1827 to 1834.   "Quelle famille, adonnée aux arts libéraux!"[7]

Not long after his marriage, Allart fell out of favor with the First

Consul, but thanks to the proper connections, soon obtained a prosperous position in Milan working for the French government in the liquidation of Austrian assets. This post lasted about three years, then the family returned to Paris when Hortense was still small, and Sophie not yet born. Here, Gabriel Allart maintained a prestigious *cabinet d'affaires* that governed the financial management of cities such as Lyon, Toulouse, Marseilles, Anvers, and Liège.

In the early pages of *Les Enchantements de Prudence,* Hortense states that she and her sister were "élévées dans les plaisirs et la prospérité."[8] Her mother, whom she described as "très jolie," aided her husband in his work by maintaining a salon that was frequented by "une société spirituelle et distinguée" (*EP* 7-8). Among the sparse iconography of Hortense Allart is a portrait of her, at about age 14, with small Sophie, the younger sister's arms tenderly placed around the slightly taller shoulders of the elder (see iconography). Hortense wears a chignon augmented with large, lovely curls, framing a "profile pure, profile grec."[9] At this point, Hortense, who was already unusually studious, was so frail of health and so nervous that her physician, Dr. Bourdais, counseled her parents to burn her numerous notebooks. He later would recant, however, and suggest that study would be the best remedy to calm her intense sensibilities and her tendency even to faint in the streets.

Although she had been a very pious child in the family's Protestant faith, her father, once finding his two daughters together in prayer, had her read selections from Rousseau as well as the correspondence between Voltaire and King Frederick of Prussia. After this study, Hortense retained her belief in God, but not her literal belief in the Bible, taking on, it would seem, the Voltairian view that worship and belief were matters of the most deeply personal interpretation. In *Les Enchantements de Prudence,* she mentions other areas of study undertaken in her youth, which included Latin, philosophy, history, French poetry, physics, algebra and astronomy. "Toute sa vie nous la verrons lire, lire, lire," states Billy. "Elle fut le type même de l'autodidacte, servi par une mémoire exceptionnelle et un dévorant appétit de connaissances . . . . Le besoin d'apprendre fut avec l'ambition le principal ressort de sa conduite" (29).

By the time Hortense was 14, her father, who, unfortunately, was already beginning to lose money and status in his business dealings due to the demise the First Empire, began to host dances for young people on Sundays. Observing that "Hortense portait dans ces bals innocents un cœur brûlant,"[10] Gabriel Allart began to consider marrying off his elder daughter as soon as possible. Billy speculates, however, as do several others who have written on Hortense's life and character, that an early marriage, even to a man she loved, would not have been a viable course for her. "On doute que, même mariée jeune à un garçon qu'elle aurait aimé, elle eût été une épouse de tout repose" (16).

Gabriel Allart's plan was never put into effect, for in 1817, financially ruined by the final fall of Napoleon, he died, leaving a grieving wife who followed him to the grave four years later. Madame Allart's brother, Sigismond Gay, who also had been impoverished since 1811, died soon after as well.

Hortense, thus orphaned at age 20, was melancholy, but nonetheless, filled with a spirit of adventure and a passionate desire for a literary career. "Plus qu'indépendante: Elle avoue avoir été aventureuse, pleine d'audace et d'élans vers l'avenir. Elle n'aurait pas voulu d'une vie obscure. Dès sa prime jeunesse elle rêva de gloire littéraire" (Billy 17).

Although Hortense's writings do not make it clear what her 17-year-old sister did at this time, one may surmise that Sophie Allart was already developing her talent and her passion for painting. Shortly after finding herself on her own, Sophie began to study with the painting master Ingres. She exhibited paintings in salons of 1827, 1831, 1833 and 1834. Sophie's portrait of her sister painted in Italy c. 1829, is in the collection of Dr. H. Le Savoureux at La Vallée-aux-Loups (see iconography).

During a stay in Rome to perfect her knowledge of certain art masterpieces, Sophie met a French merchant, Pierre Gabriac. He fell in love with the pretty young artist, and Ingres was a witness at their wedding on Feb. 10, 1836. After her marriage, Sophie Allart no longer painted professionally, but turned her attention to art appreciation, and to the raising of three children (Uffenbeck, 11, n. 35).

As for Hortense herself, soon after her mother's death, she turned for comfort and moral support to her godmother, the Duchess of Raguse, a spirited woman with a taste for adventure, who noticed the same tendencies in her young visitor. Hortense was already beginning to bloom with her famous enthusiasm and fervor of mind and spirit, as well as a bold Bonapartist patriotism. In 1819, four years after the disaster of Waterloo and the second exile of the emperor, during a short summer excursion at the home of her uncle Sigismond in Aix-la-Chapelle, she had the temerity to write to Czar Alexander and to beg him "in the name of the youth of France" to mollify the treatment of Bonaparte at Sainte-Hélène. Two years earlier, hearing that the famous prisoner was ill, she had already written to General Bertrand at Sainte-Hélène, volunteering to travel to the isolated island in the South Atlantic to nurse the fallen dictator back to health.

This simple love and dedication was not lost on the general, nor on

military officer, Amable de G . . . , who later would serve as a model for the character of Alphonse de Sernine in her first novel, *Gertrude.*

Typically, though, during her visits to Val, Hortense contented herself with her friendship with the countess, and with the occasions to lose herself in the nearby forests to dream of love and of glory. Also, with Laure, who had an uncharacteristically violent hatred of the Bourbons, and for the current reign of Louis XVIII, Hortense would sing the anti-monarchist songs of the poet Pierre-Jean de Béranger, (whom Hortense would soon meet in person, and with whom she would become lifelong friends.)

Most of Laure's guests loved to gather and discuss the possible overthrow of the Bourbons. According to Laure, all the young men who came to Val did so mostly for the purpose of seeing Hortense. She also gently reproached Hortense for being too much the coquette. "L'étais-je? Je n'y songeais pas. J'étais très heureuse, très animée, très amusée."[12]

Among the guests at Val were two brothers, François-Antoine and Hippolyte Passy. The first was a botanist and geologist and a member of the *Académie des Sciences,* the second was, at first, a cavalry officer, then a government administrator. The Passy brothers were to remain long-time friends of Hortense, and would be helpful to her later in life as well.

Far from spending these agreeable days at Laure's residence entirely in flirtations and patriotic and sentimental conversations, Hortense was diligently at work on her first original literary effort. Her book, *La Conjuration d'Amboise,* which she called simply "un ouvrage historique, très favorable aux protestants," was a 251-page tome analyzing the Huguenots' violent struggles as they strove for religious liberty during the Reformation in mid-16th-century France. Though the author noted later that her work did not ever see a second printing, at its first appearance, "On le loua beaucoup pourtant" (*EP* 65).

Laure heard the study read aloud by its author as it took form, and offered suggestions and encouragement before the manuscript was sent off to A. Marc, an author and book seller, whose store was located in the Palais-Royal area of Paris. The book was published in 1822 under the name Mlle Hortense Allart. The author was not yet 23 years old.

The talent and sophistication of the young and fledgling writer in this early effort could not be denied. "Ce serait peut-être un chef-d'œuvre si l'on savait exactement le sens de ce terme. A vingt-deux ans, Hortense y montrait déjà les qualités d'un écrivain de métier. Le récit est bien conduit, le détail sobre, sans digressions inutiles, entremêlé de portraits" (Billy 27).

Billy praises, in particular, Hortense's portrait of Catherine de

Medici, quoted, in part:

> Son caractère fut un mélange de vanité, de faiblesse et de despotisme; de là l'incertitude de sa conduite, la versatilité de ses idées. Elle voulut dominer les partis, et, confiant l'authorité tantôt à l'un, tantôt à l'autre, elle crut être toujours maîtresse de tout en se rendant tour à tour l'esclave de chacun. Le peuple rendit ses efforts inutiles; c'est un torrent qui, retenu par les travaux que dirige une main habile, entraîne et déracine les faibles digues, et qui, croissant toujours, entraîne enfin tout et roule tumultueusement au loin jusqu'à de qu'il se soit frayé un lit pour y couler à jamais, libre, fier et paisible.[13]

Her Protestant sympathies aside, the young author's sensitivity to the character of a fearsome, but vulnerable queen from several centuries past indicated a mind that was sharply in tune with the events and personae in her country's history, and a taste for educated speculation as to their impact on the political scenarios of her own day. Furthermore, *La Conjuration d'Amboise* testifies of Allart's patience, diligence and thoroughness in historical research (which would serve her well in more lengthy writing projects in the future), her psychoanalytical spirit, and her specific interest in the role of women in the moving forth of her country's saga.

Hortense's sensitivity to people and happenings of her day, specifically, her sincerity in wishing to nurse the dying Napoleon, had stayed in the mind of General Bertrand and of his wife, the Countess Bertrand, *née* Dillon, who were now returned to Paris from Sainte-Hélène, and lodged with their children on the rue Chantereine, in a former home of Bonaparte. Hortense's reputation for courageous sincerity, backed by a recommendation from the Duchess of Raguse that assured the general of the young scholar's impressive intellectuality, secured Hortense a position as a tutor of the Bertrands' young daughter. She would serve the Bertrand family for the next two years.

Madame Bertrand had given birth to 18 children, five of whom were surviving, when Hortense began her responsibilities with the family. The new young tutor, who loved children, was particularly delighted when the general's wife was delivered of another son not long after her arrival, and fascinated to observe how the experienced mother cared for the baby. "Madame Bertrand était une créole élégante et gracieuse, avec beaucoup de naturel, mais aussi de la fierté. Elle avait une taille élevée, de petites mains et de petits pieds. Elle représentait pour Hortense l'idéal féminin" (Billy 29). After a few months of service, Hortense was given a month of vacation by Madame Bertrand, who departed for the family estate in the Berry region.   She passed most of the free time in Val at the château of a certain Madame de Surpré, and it was here that she met in person, the poet Béranger, who impressed her with his volatile personality—a hardy zest for life, love of jokes and jests, and a surprising timidity that she found endearing. The two would be friends until his death in 1857, quickly rallying to one another's help and defense and bolstering each other in times of crisis, each one never hesitating to use his/her various influences to smooth the personal or professional road of the other.

In 1824, Laure sold her home in Val to put her late husband's estate in better order.   Even with the house gone, Hortense and Laure continued to meet each Sunday to dine together, and to frequent a liberal and Protestant salon hosted by Madame Davilliers on Boulevard Poisonnière.   During this time, toward the end of her service to the Bertrands, Hortense found herself in a period of vacillating emotions, which began pulling her into the maelstrom of a burgeoning Romantic spleen.   "Ennui profound.   Regret amer et douloureux, besoin des affligés de répandre des larmes.   Puis tranquillité douce et parfaite, contentement passager" (Billy 31).   Her moods were often such to make Madame Bertrand fear for her young tutor's life.

Hortense's doldrums were, as she herself recognized, "simple affaire de nerfs et d'imagination" (Billy 31).   Some months earlier she had been introduced to the 24-year-old nephew of Madame de Surpré, the Count Anthony Teixeira Sampayo, a young Englishman of Portuguese-Irish descent, who, though she would make of him in her writings thereafter a "prelate priest," was actually a married man.   He had wed, at age 20, the niece of the Countess Regnault of Saint-Angély, and settled in Paris.   The son of a Portuguese immigrant who was principal agent of the Royal Company of Wines from Oporto, then later general consul from Portugal in London, the young Sampayo was visiting with the priest of l'Isle-Adam when he first met Hortense at the abbey at Val.

Hortense's dramatic and detailed account of her first love affair and the man who never ceased to touch her heart would be revealed in arduous Romantic detail in her second novel, *Jérôme ou le jeune prélat* (1829), as well as in *Les Enchantements de Prudence* (in which the pseudonym for Sampayo—"Jérôme"— is retained).

In *Les Enchantements*, she describes her impressions of "Jérôme" during their long walks and discussions together.   His skin was of an olive tone, his face reflected a melancholy beauty, his smile was gracious, but his black eyes were lacking in expression.   He had both an English accent, and "English phlegm," or an attitude of calm, sometimes supercilious self-possession. "Jérôme réveilla mon attention et mon courage. Je ne trouvais pas en lui l'esprit français, l'esprit leger et riant où j'étais habituée, mais quelque chose de nouveau, de grandiose, de grave, d'ironique pourtant, d'amer même; mais le tout si haut, si fier, si à part, que sans m'expliquer, j'en étais complètement frappée et séduite" (*EP* 29).

Hortense herself was blossoming into ripe and beautiful young womanhood at this time. In addition to her delicate physical beauty, she was caught up in the romantic excesses of the period to the point of being perhaps too naive, and too easy a target of such a type as Sampayo. "Hortense fut aussi tendre que belle, avec de longs yeux languissants, un teint de fleur, une bouche ronde et fraîche, par-dessus tout une vivacité naive qui enflammait le cœur des jeunes hommes."[14]

Sampayo, despite his charm, also possessed a coldness and a bitterness that made him somewhat singular among young men of his station. "Ce jeune sage avait quelque chose de glacé, d'ironique et d'amer, qui le situait à part. Il s'intérressait d'autant moins aux intrigues ourdies au Val qu'il était étranger et que sa pensée planait sur les hauteurs" (Billy 31).

Neither Laure nor Béranger nor Madame Hamelin, another close friend who would later serve as Hortense's link to Chateaubriand, held a good opinion of the haughty young Englishmen who was suddenly frequenting their milieu and their young *protegée*. "Laure avait de la sensibilité et Sampayo en était dépourvu, ce qui explique le désir qu'elle avait de rendre [Hortense] sensible" (Billy 36).

Hortense, however, was so admiring of Sampayo, whom she considered superior to any of the other young male visitors to Val, that she began to contemplate a future in which she would marry some other man simply for the sake of respectability, then devote the rest of her life to this young foreigner, "jeune penseur, explorateur d'un univers inconnu."[15]

Her sentiments left her vulnerable. "On voit que la jeune fille ne fut pas armée pour lutter avec un Jérôme. Patiemment, sans hâte, celui-ci poursuivait ses desseins" (Pailleron 68).

Sampayo had Hortense read Adam Smith and a variety of other political and philosophical writers. The two of them clashed on political opinions (he did not hesitate to tell her how much he hated Bonaparte), and yet, no indication of their obvious incompatibility nor the impracticality of their union, nor the fact that others disapproved of their liaison, could discourage Hortense's flourishing infatuation. "Il était un dieu pour moi . . . il était beau . . . mais je n'osais voir sa beauté, je ne voyais que son mérite" (*EP* 38).

Their relationship was one of high drama. Numerous times, one or the other would swear to break off the liaison. Tears and reconciliations would follow, and Laure's wise counsel about how no good could come of such a union fell on deaf ears.

Hortense would write extensively about every new heartbeat in the progression and demise of this tumultuous relationship a few years later. However, at the time the liaison was going on, she was hard at work on a writing project completely unrelated, but equally challenging to a young mind that was at once absorbed with the search for an ideal love and the quest to be taken seriously as a literary scholar. Her *Lettres sur les ouvrages de Mme de Staël*, produced during her two years of service at the Bertrands as well as during the affair with Sampayo, were published at the Parisian printers of Bossange in March 1825, when she was 24.

A short time prior to the publication of the work, with Sampayo, the Bertrand children, and her writing making increasingly heavy demands on her time, Hortense decided to leave Madame Bertrand's employ to establish herself independently as a *femme de lettres*. Etienne de Jouy had promised to take her on as a researcher at *Biographie des contemporains.* From this point on, she lived on her own.

With the publication of the *Lettres sur les ouvrages de Mme de Staël*, the subsequent attention they received, and the controversy they sparked, Hortense no doubt quickly became Jouy's best-known employee.

Looking back on the influence that Madame de Staël held over the generation of young female Romantics who would follow her, the literary critic and author Charles Augustin Sainte-Beuve, in a letter about Allart written in 1860, stated, "Mme de Staël était l'astre de ce temple là qui donnait des coups de soleil ou des coups de lune rousse sur les têtes blondes de femmes."[16]

Of all the blond heads that were turning at this time to the varied writings of Madame de Staël, Allart's must have been the most sensitively in tune with her works in their entirety, and the most dedicated in delving into and offering commentary on the best-known pieces. Her 150-page collection contains seven separate letters on Staël's *Des Lettres sur Rousseau, De l'influence des passions sur le bonheur, De la Littérature, Delphine, Corinne,* and *De l'Allemagne.* The concluding letter is entitled simply "Sur Madame de Staël."

More than anything, the *Lettres* are a glowing tribute to Staël, and a testament to the intellectual and emotional rapport that existed between two women who had never actually met. In her last letter "Sur Madame de Staël," Hortense states, "Au moment de parler d'elle, nous éprouvons cette émotion et cet ébranlement qu'on éprouve en

abordant ce qui est sacré."[17]
Yet, Hortense's goal was to analyze, not merely to praise. "In her criticism, she attempted to behave like a judge, not an acolyte" (Uffenbeck 31). For example, in the same letter, the young critic expressed her desire to be wise in expressing her admiration and prudent in containing her superlative evaluations. ". . . j'ai contenu des paroles trop vives; mais quelquefois cet enthousiasme contenu se ranime dans toute sa puissance, et me reproche une modération si pénible" ("Lettre sur Madame de Staël" 125).

While establishing her opinion that Staël was a great writer, Allart also attempted to make political commentaries on the texts, sliding in her own. In the letter on *De l'Allemagne,* she supports Staël's idea that northern countries with their sombre climates foster greater imagination in the human spirit, but hastens to add that *any* existence would be enriched under governments that accorded people greater liberties. ". . . mais tout climat devient beau avec la liberté; toute existence s'anime et s'agrandit par elle. Il est juste, il est doux de compter sur une autre vie; mais le jour est arrivé où la morale publique doit rendre le bonheur possible aussi sur terre" (*Lettres* 123). In other words, though the Romantics may look towards an idealized afterlife, the moral ambiance established by society ought to permit a greater happiness in the here and now. She concludes with the admonition to encourage more practical and fewer esoteric solutions to the human condition. "Les peuples ne sont plus au temps où il ne leur fallait que des idées qui les aidassent à supporter leurs misères" (*Lettres* 123).

Allart is also laudatory of Staël's two principal novels and her philosophy that "un roman doit être une révélation des passions du cœur humain." She adds, "le travail de l'écrivain est de retracer ce que la vie enseigne, en s'aidant à la foi de la raison, du sentiment et de l'imagination," and assures her readers that Staël has succeeded in that goal. "Madame de Staël a prouvé dans son ouvrage que tout ce qu'elle demande aux romanciers était possible à elle, sinon à tous" ("Lettre sur le Roman de *Delphine*" 29-30).

As Staël was a fellow Protestant, Allart is particularly supportive of the pleas for legalized divorce that are entwined throughout *Delphine.* (By 1802, when *Delphine* was published, divorce had become virtually impossible in France under the *Code Napoléon*). Hortense expresses pity for the character of Thérèse, who was mired in an unhappy marriage, then opted to enter a convent even after she was free to marry the man she adored, because she felt he loved her less than she loved him (*Lettres* 46). Hortense admires the character M. Lebensei, who married a divorced woman, and who stands up for the right of all unhappy spouses to end unsatisfactory marriages. She also cites Delphine's letter on divorce written to persuade Léonce to leave Mathilde. "Il se fonde sur cette idée que le but et le moyen de la nature, nous menant à l'accomplissement de nos premiers devoirs par l'instinct et la tendresse même, n'a pas pu vouloir l'indissolubilité de liens qui ne commanderaient ni l'amour ni l'affection" (*Lettres* 53).

The "Lettre sur le Roman de *Corinne*" cites how the 1807 novel indicates Staël's unmistakable superiority as a novelist and as a woman. "[C'est] l'ouvrage de Madame de Staël qui a eu le plus d'éclat, de celui où elle a mis toute son âme. Ici son talent est plus formé . . . tout est admirable" (*Lettres* 67). Allart does pinpoint, however, certain aspects of the novel that she finds lacking in naturalness, truth and imagination. For example, Allart finds Corinne's dancing, pantomimes, etc., though decent, to be unworthy of a gifted intellectual. "[Ils] ne sont point dans la dignité d'une femme qui s'élève aux plus hautes méditations de la pensée" (*Lettres* 93).

Allart identifies the moral of *Corinne* as a lesson to women not to become attached to a man whom one loves more than she is loved by him. She compares *Delphine* and *Corinne,* citing different strengths of each one. "Celui-ci [*Corinne*] est utile comme un guide pour les personnes qui entrent dans le monde avec une âme exaltée et de l'indépendance d'esprit: celui-là [*Delphine*] vous soutient dans la solitude" (*Lettres* 101). She notes the evidence that Staël's attitude aged noticeably during the five years between the production of *Delphine* and *Corinne.* Therefore, the second novel contains stronger passions, but less confidence and joy. "L'âme de *Delphine* est nouvelle à toutes les impressions. *Corinne* n'ignorait que les profondeurs du sentiment, six anneés d'une vie indépendante avaient éclairé son esprit et calmé dans son cœur tout ce qui était irréfléchi" (*Lettres* 102).

The tenor of the last letter is boldly feminist, although Allart limits her sympathy, as did Staël herself, mostly to the "superior woman." Interestingly, in this last essay, Allart praises Staël as she herself would be praised just a few years later, first by the Count Saint Leu, who was speaking of *Gertrude* (see Chapter 2), then by Chateaubriand, who was referring to *Jérôme* (see Chapter 3). That is, she credits Staël with having a "male mind." Allart also cites the unfortunate side of the phenomenon—women who possess the wisdom to think as a man are forbidden by society to act viably upon such wisdom: "Femme, elle a eu l'esprit d'un homme; et cette énérgie de pensée réunie à l'impossibilité d'agir est un supplice, quand une raison forte qui n'est pas du domaine de la jeunesse, ne règle pas les mouvements de l'âme" (*Lettres* 129-30).

Allart expands on her sympathy towards Staël's struggles, and towards the plight of the superior woman in general whose gifts are suppressed by a society that imposes upon her a preconceived role, and gives her insufficient vent for creative expression:

> Elle a beaucoup souffert d'être femme; mais elle a dû peut-être à son organisation même cette excessive sensibilité et cette délicatesse qui, unies à tant de vigeur d'idées, en font un être unique . . . ce qui fait le malheur des femmes supérieures, c'est ce peu de proportions entre les devoirs qu'on leur a assignées, dès leur première jeunesse, et ce besoin progressif des grandes facultés que se déploient (*Lettres* 130-31).

Again, reminiscent of René, she identifies the plight of superior woman who finds herself tragically alone in a sea of lesser companions who lack her complete understanding of great truths:

> Elles seules ne trouvent pas leur pareils, elles seules les cherchent, elles seules souffrent cruellement de l'absence, et tourmentées par leur élevation même, ne peuvent pas remplacer qui les abandonne . . . Plaignons profondément les femmes supérieures, qui s'égarent, car les femmes supérieures seules comprennent avec l'âme et l'esprit les vérités morales . . . (*Lettres* 131-32).

The similarities between Staël's and Allart's philosophies toward women were not lost on the reviewers who began publishing opinions on *Lettres sur les ouvrages de Mme de Staël* during the spring of 1825. The *Courier français*, in its April 8 issue described the new, mostly unknown author as a new Madame de Staël. Describing Allart's writing as "d'un style formé et plein d'éclat," the reviewer noted a resemblance between the young author's lettres and those of Staël herself on Rousseau . . . "non par la ressemblance du travail, mais par celle du talent."[18]

On May 2, the *Constitutionnel*, then the most powerful newspaper in France, called Allart's letters "un ouvrage de critique très remarquable . . . [avec] une sagacité et une fermeté d'esprit rares." The reviewer credited Allart for understanding the subject and spirit of *Delphine* as well as did Staël herself.[19]

Not nearly so complimentary was a third review that appeared in the *Globe* on May 19. The reviewer criticized not only the letters, but also the previous reviews, and was particularly displeased with the comparison of Allart to Staël. The reviewer also mentions Allart's obvious youth and naiveté, intimating that she had not had enough experience in life or in the literary world to comment with any value on Staël's letters, and that she was merely copying Staël's writing style rather than equaling it.[20]

However, most of the surviving members of Madame de Staël's coterie (she had been dead only eight years when the letters on her works were published), sided with the positive reviews, and adored Allart for her efforts.   The Duchess of Broglie, formerly Albertine de Staël, the late author's only surviving daughter, sought out Allart, and dined with her first at the home of the Duchess de Raguse then in her own home (Uffenbeck 26).

Sismondi, who had been part of Staël's circle of friends at Coppet, was particularly touched. "J'ai vu naître ces ouvrages que vous analyzez avec tant d'âme et de talent . . ." [21]   Henri de Latouche, in his article in the *Mercure du dix-neuvième siècle* in October 1825, described how Juliette Récamier, a friend of Madame de Staël's from the days when the two of them were blacklisted by an indignant Napoleon, was filled with emotion upon reading Hortense's *Lettres*. "Si vous avez vu trembler la main qui vous offrait ce livre par l'émotion que venaient de lui donner ses souvenirs."   Latouche, who also credited Allart for being even younger than she was, ("L'auteur a dix-neuf ou vingt ans"), had seen her in public, and contrasted her fresh, young appearance with the sophistication of her writings. "Observez ce juge en robe couleur de rose; et l'expression pensive de ses yeux et de son front, vous verrez se mêler tout-à-coup un naïf sourire qui creusera deux fossettes enfantines dans des joues couleur de sa robe."

As did the two earlier reviewers, Latouche also compared Allart to Staël herself, particularly in the writing style of Staël's *Lettres sur Rousseau,* then called for respect and encouragement of Allart's Staëlian-style enthusiasm. "Il ne faut point le décourager; il faut le respecter, même quand on s'apercevrait de ses erreurs. L'enthousiasme ne se rencontre jamais que dans les esprits qui seront un jour capables de l'inspirer."[22]

Likewise, Bonstetten, also a former member of the group at Coppet, wrote to Allart, praising her talent and superiority. "Hortense avait, disait encore Bonstetten, un aplomb, une fermeté dans le style qui contrastait avec son âge et sa personne. Son style, brillant sans être brillanté, et d'un éclat qui venait du fond, avait souvent beaucoup de rapports avec celui de Mme de Staël."[23]

The comparison between Staël's early style and that of Allart in her own *Lettres* evidently stemmed from each young woman's *attitude* and *élan* rather than from her exact subject matter or writing patterns. Both writers, with a zest and ebullience for which each would become well-known as her career progressed, had a talent for *relishing* the object of her analysis, and at the same time *down-playing* in the gentlest possible manner any kind of negativity that she felt toward the subject.

Just as Allart was cited—even in her own time—for an overwillingness to praise and adore Madame de Staël, so has Staël puzzled critics—especially modern ones—for her sometimes illogical verve in honoring Rousseau. He, after all, was no champion of equality for women, even those of Staël's caliber. The impetuosity that characterized Allart's letters is evident in Staël's first *Lettre sur Rousseau* in which she apologizes for his rather blatant attitude about female inferiority. Staël focuses, rather, on her enthusiasm for Rousseau's emphasis on exhilarating romantic love:

> Enfin, il croit à l'amour, sa grâce est obtenue; qu'importe aux femmes que sa raison leur dispute l'empire, quand son cœur leur est soumis? qu'importe même à celles que la nature a douées d'une âme tendre, qu'on leur ravisse le faux honneur de gouverner celui qu'elles aiment? Non, il leur est plus doux de sentir sa supériorité, de l'admirer, de le croire mille au-dessus d'elles, de dépendre de lui, parce qu'elles l'adorent . . . . [24]

The *Lettres sur Rousseau,* although they were published anonymously in 1788, were well-received by patrons of pre-Revolutionary Parisian salons, who knew perfectly well who the 22-year-old author was. They established the initial literary reputation of the young Anne-Louise Germaine Necker, who, just two years earlier had become Madame de Staël. Therefore, much as Staël was able to sweep aside Rousseau's obviously patriarchal attitude about women and love, and to emphasize the portion of his philosophy that she adored, so was Allart adept at glossing over such negative observations on Staël's work—such as the inconsistency of Corinne's talents and her character—in favor of what she saw as the vitality and intensity of the novel's overall value. As we have seen, this positive vehemence in the style of both young authors received more accolades than it did criticism.

Amid this mostly laudatory reaction to her work and to her writing style, Allart remained humble, matter-of-fact, and kept her feet firmly planted on what she knew was the tenuous and fickle ground of Parisian literary criticism. She never attempted to capitalize on the comparisons of herself to Staël, for she felt they were not exact. Furthermore, imitating the other woman's style never had been her intention. She admired Staël without ever trying to emulate her or to be her equal. This attitude, says Billy was typical throughout the life of Allart, who never considered herself a woman "à la Staël" (44).

Nevertheless, Allart was sufficiently encouraged by the positive feedback from both *La Conjuration d'Amboise* and *Lettres sur les ouvrages de Madame de Staël* to begin thinking of producing her first novel. First, however, there were concerns in her personal life that needed to be tended to.

Her relationship with Sampayo was becoming less and less a romantic hotbed of happiness and exaltation for her than it was a source of heartbreak and stress. At one point, she shed heartbroken tears in front of Sampayo because of their difficulties together. His response was derisive laughter. "Elle s'effrayait d'une tendresse qu'elle ne parvenait pas à modérer, d'une âme qui ne lui avait été donnée que pour être donnée. Cela le fit rire " (Billy 40).

Looking back on this period of her life, beginning about March 1825, Allart writes journal-style in *Les Enchantements de Prudence* as she confides each conversation between her and Sampayo/Jérôme on topics both personal and intellectual, each visit, each quarrel, each exchange of letters, each traumatic adieu, each tearful reconciliation. (Although the 1829 novel *Jérôme ou le jeune prélat* and the verbatim portions of it that are reprinted *Les Enchantements de Prudence* and *Les Nouveaux Enchantements* has some fictionalized aspects, generally it is an accurate rendering of the events and emotions in her own life at that time).

Even before the Staël letters were published, a difficult dispute had begun between the two. Hortense wrote, "Jérôme dédaigneux de l'amour développa un caractère nouveau, plein d'amertume et presque méchant, et moi, confondue de cette conduite, je résistai avec fermeté et sagesse aux pressions dangereuses qu'il me causait" (*EP* 60).

Although Sampayo frequently renewed his declarations of love, he also applied certain manipulations, at one point telling her that his love was responsible for her genius. She quotes his words: "Si vous cessiez de m'aimer, Prudence ne serait Prudence, vous n'auriez plus de génie. . . votre génie est au cœur. Je l'ai vu croître avec votre amour. Vous étiez prédéstinée à m'aimer." Hortense/Prudence confided to her readers, "Son esprit intimidait le mien" (*EP* 63).

Amid descriptions of more ruptures and rapprochements, and letters full of spleen and typical *mal de siècle,* Hortense's writings about Sampayo/Jérôme are discreetly devoid of any mention of their physical love or hints as to when it first occurred. She reveals, however, that during the fall of 1825, she knew that she was with child. "Il revient de la compagne, et en me voyant souffrante, il croit que je serai mère . . . Cependant, j'éprouvais les éclairs d'une nouvelle tendresse et je voulais créer une âme forte. Il disait qu'il aimait déjà cet enfant" (*EP*   79).

Naturally, marriage was not an option in either the actual situation or in its fictional recreation.   In the future novel, Jérôme was a novice priest.   In real life, the Count Sampayo was already married.   (He and his wife later had five sons, all of them French citizens) (Billy 45).

Weary of the quarrels, the frustration, and the uncertainty, Hortense, already ill with the pregnancy,   indicated in *Les Enchantements*   her plans to leave for Italy, despite Jérôme's protests, and await his decision about his future, that is, whether he would find a space in his life for Hortense and for their child.   "Je partais, car je ne pouvais plus supporter une vie si tourmentée. J'allais me calmer, attendre, voir ce que Jérôme déciderait, ce qu'il saurait faire.   Je restais maîtresse de revenir ou de l'oublier.   Je me sentais forte, je sentais que s'il savait se guérir, moi je saurais l'oublier" (*EP*   79).

Billy speculates on the sort of man that was Sampayo: "Un Tartufe [sic]? Un sot? Un débile? Un maladroit? Un beau ténébreux à prétentions mystiques?"   Regardless of how one judges Sampayo, one must certainly feel some sympathy for Hortense, at this point the dupe of an intelligent, though emotionally paralyzed and confused man. "Belle intelligence, peut-être, mais faux génie paralysé par le sentiment de son impuissance et des ses contradictions" (Billy 45).   As for Hortense, she still felt herself a sort of virgin. Sampayo's austerity had left her still ignorant of *volupté* or sensual pleasure.

Hortense left Paris for Milan on Nov. 1, 1825.   Although her heart was no doubt heavy from the apparent failure of her first experience in love, she would never reproach Sampayo for what was in the past.   This first affair set a pattern that would be repeated through her numerous future experiences in love, for Hortense had one of those rare souls that never harbored bitterness, and could console itself with happy memories.

"Elle était," said Séché, "de ces âmes foncièrement bonnes qui ne connaissent pas la rancune et se consolent avec le souvenir. Le bonheur qu'elle avait goûté dans les bras d'un amant le sacrait, en quelque sorte, pour toujours a ses yeux" (47).

Upon hearing of the death of Sampayo in 1844, some 19 years after she had left him, Hortense still felt a tender regard for the father of her first child.   In a letter to Sainte-Beuve March 2, 1844, she wrote, "La mort de Sampayo m'a fait croire qu'il serait mieux où il allait qu'ici-bas, et ce chagrin-là se trouvait ainsi compensé."[25]

Although Hortense did head for Italy with the goal of concealing her pregnancy from those left behind in Paris, she did not go with any sense of shame or despair at her condition.   On the contrary, she felt on the verge of a new life, feeling the possibilities of a new and exciting future surging through her veins. "Je me sentais pourtant un courage, une ardeur qui devaient triompher des ennuis. La terre était à moi; j'avais en moi le sentiment d'une force brillante" (*EP* 79).

As had been typical of Allart up to this point, and as would be typical throughout her life, she was ready to turn a difficult situation into a personal and professional bonanza.

Notes

[1]André Billy. *Hortense et ses Amants.* (Paris: Flammarion, Editeur, 1961) 2.

[2]Léon Séché. *Hortense Allart de Méritens dans ses Rapports avec Chateaubriand, Béranger, Lamennais, Sainte-Beuve, G. Sand, Mme D'Agoult.* (Paris: Société de Mercure de France, 1908) 33-34.

[3] Séché 35.

[4]Lorin A. Uffenbeck *The Life and Writings Hortense Allart (1801-79).* (Diss. U. of Wisconsin, 1957) 10.

[5]André Beaunier. *Trois Amis de Chateaubriand.* (Paris: Charpentier, 1910) 238.

[6]Uffenbeck 7.

[7]Beaunier 238.

[8] Mme, P[rudence] de [Hortense Allart de Méritens] Saman l'Esbatx. *Les Enchantements de Prudence.* (Paris: Typographie de E. Dépée, first ed., mai 1872)   8.   (Subsequent references to this work will appear in parentheses after the quotation, and will be indicated by the abbreviation *EP*).

[9]Billy 15.

[10]Billy 15.

[11]René de Chateaubriand. *Atala, René, Le dernier Abencérage.* (Paris: Editions Garnier Frères, 1962)   203.

[12] *Les Enchantements de Prudence,*   quoted by Billy 26.

[13]Hortense Allart, *La Conjuration d'Amboise.* (Paris: A. Marc, Libraire, 1922), page number not given; quoted by Billy 27.

[14]Marie-Louise   Pailleron. "Hortense Allart et Chateaubriand," *La Revue des Deux Mondes,*   CX (Jan 1, 1940): 67.

[15]*Les Enchantements de Prudence,*   quoted by Billy 35.

[16]Charles Augustin Sainte-Beuve, in a letter to Madame de Solms, dated October 27, 1860, in the MS Archives in Mariemont (Belgium) folio 4612, quoted by Uffenbeck ii.

[17]Hortense Allart. *Lettres sur les ouvrages de Mme de Staël.* (Paris: Bossange Père, Libraire, 1824) 124. (Subsequent references to this collection will appear in parentheses after the quotation, and will be indicated by the word *Lettres*).

[18]*Le Courier français,* No. 98 (vendredi, le 8 avril 1825), p. 3, column 1, quoted by Uffenbeck 32.

[19]*Le Constitutionnel, journal du commerce, politique, et littéraire,* No. 122 (Lundi, 2 mai 1825), p. 3, column 2, quoted by Uffenbeck 33.

[20]*Le Globe, journal littéraire,* No. 109 (jeudi, le 19 mai, 1825) 551-52, quoted by Uffenbeck 34-35.

[21]Uffenbeck notes that this letter, loaned by Allart to Sainte-Beuve, was published in the latter's *Chateaubriand et son groupe littéraire sous l'Empire, cours professé à Liège, 1848-1849,* nouvelle édition annotée par Maurice Allem (Paris: 1949), I: 56; Uffenbeck 37.

[22]H[enri de Latouche], "Mademoiselle Hortense Allard [sic]" *Le Mercure du dix-neuvième siècle,* XI (1825) 128; quoted by Uffenbeck 38-39.

[23]Lettre inédite. Collection Lovenjoul. Dossier Hortense Allart, folio 254; quoted by Billy 43.

[24]Madame de Staël. *Lettres sur les Ecrits et le Caractère de J.J. Rousseau. Œuvres Complètes de Madame de Staël,* 2 vols. (Paris: Firmin Didot Frères et Cie, Librairies, 1826) 1: 4-5.

[25]Hortense Allart de Meritens. *Lettres Inédites à Sainte-Beuve: 1841-1848.* (Paris: Société de Mercure de France, 1908) 85.

Chapter 2

Gertrude: The Young Writer Acts Out (1825-1828)

Hortense's story as she left France and headed for Italy via Switzerland was as far from the stereotypical tale of the shamed and banished unwed mother as Hortense herself was from the prototype of the Frenchwoman living under the *Code Napoléon.* Although the weather was glum (she missed enjoying the Alps because a heavy fog accompanied her on her route), her spirits were high, especially as she found along the way that her reputation as an up-and-coming literary critic had proceeded her. She was feted from Dijon to Milan—and particularly during a two-week stay in Geneva— by acquaintances and strangers who, having no idea she was pregnant, had read and loved her *Lettres sur les Ouvrages de Mme de Staël.* "Mes lettres sur Madame de Staël m'attiraient la bienveillance de tout le monde à Genève" (*EP* 81).

Furthermore, upon making her acquaintance, her well-wishers were even more impressed to find that the young author possessed beauty and charm as well as literary talent. "Partout elle eut le plaisir d'entendre l'éloge de son livre. Sa joliesse, sa jeunesse, son esprit, son intelligence contribuèrent autant que ses *Lettres* à son succès" (Billy 48). Hortense also visited Coppet, which already stood as a visitors' attraction and monument to the life and writings of Madame de Staël, as it does today.

Near the Swiss-Italian border she became acquainted with a cultured, rich, and handsome Englishman of about 40, who, feeling a young woman should not travel through the Alps alone, offered her a seat in his carriage. She accepted, and after a few days of travel together, and a week's stay in Turin, with him pressing his suit assiduously upon her, she felt it necessary to tell him the truth about her pregnancy. His reaction was to propose that they retire to the countryside together until she gave birth, after which they would marry, and no one would suspect the truth about her past. She politely refused, and traveled on to Milan without the gallant friend.

Arriving in November 1825, in the city that was her birthplace, Hortense was invited to stay at the home of a friend of her late mother, and soon began surrounding herself with the local literary intelligentsia. In the Staëlian tradition, she found herself enchanted with Italy. She first grew to love Milan, as her mother's friend introduced her to operas at La Scala, as well as theater and salons. A few months later she began to revel in the opulent cultures of Florence and Rome.

Soon after she arrived in Florence in February 1826, she was presented to the Marquis de Terrigiani, who offered a reception in her honor. Although 100 persons arrived to meet her, the marquise, who had heard of Hortense's pregnancy, declined to attend. Undaunted and unembarrassed, Hortense gently refused the marquis' offer to seek out his wife and introduce the two. "Je voulais une position sincère et non pas étonner les dames de l'Italie" (quoted by Billy 52). Thus, in typical Allart tradition, she favored complete honesty about her condition, but remained unoffended by those who might find the situation uncomfortable. In the meantime, she met with pleasure the other 100 guests who were presented to her.

The marquis de Terrigiani also introduced her to another Tuscan marquis, Gino Capponi, a writer, journalist, and brilliant figure in Florentine society. Capponi, whom she mentions in *Les Enchantements* under the pseudonym the Marquis Camillo, had been impressed with her *La Conjuration d'Amboise,* and encouraged her to study history, and to write about great men. As fervent as her love was for history, it was really the men of the present, not the past, who captured her interest. "Ce n'étaient pas les grands hommes du passé qu'allait aimer la douce et vive Hortense, avec un zèle, avec une patience admirables, mais les grands hommes de son temps, eux-mêmes, pour leurs exploits, et pour leurs livres, et pour eux-mêmes" (Beaunier 242).

Other acquaintances she mentions during this time were the young count Guillaume (Gulielmo)-Brutus-Icilius-Timoléon Libri Carrucci della Sommaia, Antonio Bargagli, and Swiss poet Charles Didier. Probably, each of these three, as well as Capponi, was her lover at some time following the birth of her son. "Mon histoire à Florence s'est borné à ceci: Un homme m'a ravie (Libri) un homme m'a plu (Antonio Bargagli), un homme a touché mon âme (Charles Didier); aucun l'a su (*EP* 89).

Such an exciting new life was almost enough to take Sampayo off her mind. "Si Jérôme eut un vrai rival, ce fut ce pays, cette musique . . . . Je vivais dans une exaltation extraordinaire" (*EP* 83). Her passion for him did not flag in the first months in Italy, however, as she imagined him at her side as she traveled to the points of interest and wrote him of her many impressions. Giuseppe Longhi, a famous artist and engraver, completed her portrait, which she sent back to Sampayo in Paris.

Regrets never weighed upon her, though, as, buoyed by the ambiance of Italy as well as the positive reception of her letters on Madame de Staël, she spent the balance of her pregnancy working on her first novel, *Gertrude,* which she completed at about the same time as the birth of her son, Marcus-Napoléon Allart, on June 16, 1826.

The production of this rather lengthy and convoluted novel, which was originally published in Florence in November 1827 in four volumes, covered a period her life that she was to recall with fondness. "Je me rappelle ce temps avec plaisir, j'aimais ce roman; je l'avais fait avec passion; il ne vaudra jamais le plaisir qu'il m'a causé. Quel temps agréable, égal, doux, indépendant! Je regrettais les passions, mais mon fils m'occupait" (*EP* 88).

Miffed at Sampayo for not coming to Milan for their child's birth as he had promised, she sent no word, but left him to find out about his son from others. Later, she would speculate that she was probably wrong to indulge in this uncharacteristic, if understandable, snit. After all, Sampayo was a married man, and perhaps not at liberty to break away and travel to Italy with the right amount of discretion. In any case, she ended up giving him the benefit of the doubt. ("Aujourd'hui je trouve que j'avais tort. Pouvait-il changer son caractère? . . . . pouvait-il se changer et ne le connaissais-je pas?" [*EP* 86]). Hortense eventually would bring her young son to meet his father, and she would correspond with and see her former lover (platonically) at sporadic intervals for the rest of Sampayo's life, avoiding any mention of rancor, and admitting his continued effect upon her heart.

Lest one think too ill of Sampayo, there exists a letter from Hortense at this time to a bank in Paris, indicating her confusion over a rent check that was sent to the landlord of an apartment in Florence that she no longer inhabited.[1] Apparently, Sampayo was a little behind on her comings and goings, but was making a token monetary attempt to aid the mother of his child.

She chose to nurse the baby herself, continued to receive company at her apartment, and accepted philosophically any moral judgments about her situation that came her way. Libri visited often, dazzling her with his handsomeness and intelligence. "Il semblait que la terre tremblât sous ses pas. Son visage était beau et régulier, ses yeux noirs très beaux, plein de flammes" (*EP* 86).   He would sit upon her bed, talking of all sorts of great things, much in the manner of Sampayo, but with more selflessness and finesse. "Un homme à comparer à Jérôme, mais bien différent. Il pensait à la gloire " (*EP* 85).

She also received the visit of Louis Bonaparte, the former king of Holland, who, likely knowing of her admiration for his late brother, wooed her with gifts. "Malade, il lui fit timidement la cour, lui envoya des fruits, des fleurs, des vers et son ouvrage sur la Hollande . . . " (Billy 56).

Hortense soon found that motherhood and authorship agreed with her much more than did preoccupation with a lost romance, and that her newfound independence was bringing her more satisfaction than did her love affair. "Je regrettais l'amour pour lequel j'étais faite, mais une vie si forte, si studieuse, me charmait. Je n'y sacrifiais rien, je crois, à la vanité, à l'erreur, je vivais autant que je pouvais avec la vérité" (*EP* 89).

Word about her motherhood was not long in finding its way back to Paris.   The news probably originated with Hortense's cousin, Delphine Gay, and quickly reached Madame de Récamier, who was a flippant, though perhaps not a malicious, gossip.   Délécluze reported in his *Journal* dated March 8, 1827, that the word through Madame Récamier (whom he calls only by the name of "Louise"), was that Hortense had "produced something in Italy."   He continued, "Car il est bon de savoir que la pauvre Mlle Allart a fait à Paris un petit poupon qu'elle élève et nourrit elle-même à Florence ouvertement." He also named the married Sampayo as the father. He noted, however, that Hortense "a pris tout cela très philosophiquement."[2]

Indeed, she was so calm over the whole matter that she sent back one of Sampayo's letters unopened and continued to receive Libri nearly every evening.   The faithful, non-judgmental Béranger, who was also apprised of the birth of baby Marcus, wrote to Hortense, urging her to simplify her tastes in men. "Rallumez votre lanterne, si vous l'aviez éteinte; mais soyez moins difficile dans vos recherches, ne demandez pas tant de vertus, tant de gloires.   Contentez-vous de beaucoup d'amabilité, de beaucoup de bonté, de beaucoup d'attachement, et surtout de beaucoup de jeunesse."[3]

Apparently, Béranger, then 46 years old, did not see himself as a candidate for Hortense's more intimate affections, nor did she, although she had invited him to come join her in Italy to partake of the poetic inspiration there.

Curiously, Hortense opted not to mention in *Les Enchantements de Prudence* or elsewhere in her writings her friendship with Stendhal, which began while they were both residing in Florence, and which was of considerable importance to her career during this time. Likewise, Stendhal made no mention of her in his autobiography, and there is little evidence as to whether the two of them met later in Paris. That their friendship was important to each on a personal and professional level, is evident, however, in Stendhal's positive reaction to *Gertrude* immediately after its first printing in Florence, as well as in the ensuing few years of warm, friendly correspondence between them. In addition to the forthright writing style of *Gertrude,* which Stendhal praised, the novel contains a brief comparison of Racine and Shakespeare, which the scholar, who had already published an essay on that topic (*Racine et Shakespeare,* 1823-25), could not have failed to notice and appreciate. Certain critics also have suggested that Hortense's influence on Stendhal is evident in *Le Rouge et le Noir.* [4]

The two writers met in Florence just as *Gertrude* was about to appear for the first time from the Florentine publisher Ciardetti in four tomes. Most likely, they were presented to each other at the famous *cabinet de lecture* of Vieusseux, a scholar associated with the Italian liberal movement, whose salon attracted the most elite literati who resided in or passed through Florence.

In *Gertrude,* the story of a young woman who marries the wrong man, but eventually is united with her true love, is seen Hortense's perceptive indulgence in a French literary tradition—that of careful psychological analysis and insight. It involves the same kind of realistic, unabashed self-scrutiny that Stendhal had used in *Armance,* which was published that same year, and in *Le Rouge et le Noir,* which would appear in 1830.

Hortense herself described her intention in writing her first novel. "J'achevais *Gertrude,* où j'avais voulu exposer plusieurs idées morales" (*EP* 87). Later in *Les Enchantements,* she stated that the novel was an effort on behalf of women in general. "Je voulais beaucoup d'abord dans *Gertrude* traiter de la morale, améliorer le sort des femmes. Je l'ai toujours voulu" (*EP* 271).

The title character in *Gertrude,* an evident representation of the author herself, analyses throughout the narrative her progressive realization that she originally allowed herself to be taken in by a man who possessed abundant charm, but insufficient character. Her quest to understand herself as woman as well as to create a happy future for herself that is above and beyond what Parisian society would wish to accord her is the essence of the intrigue, which also contains an array of other characters—mostly female—and subplots.

Gertrude, which was published under the partial pseudonym Madame Hortense Allart de Thérase, was already enjoying its initial success when Hortense met Stendhal. "*Gertrude* paraissait et reçut bon acceuil," she said of its first printing. "Le comte Saint-Leu la loua beaucoup, on disait que c'était un ouvrage *mâle*" (*EP* 88, Allart's italics).

After the second printing of *Gertrude* in Florence later in 1827, Stendhal reviewed it in the *New Monthly Magazine* on April 20, 1828, citing the novel as "Une œuvre où il y a beaucoup de talent et même du génie," and stating that it offered an accurate depiction of the prejudices operating among the upper classes of contemporary Parisian society.[5] Stendhal's review also stated that parts of *Gertrude* were more powerful than anything that had been written since the death of Madame de Staël in 1817. (Perhaps it is worth noting that George Sand would not publish her first novel until 1832).

With such an encouraging response, Hortense felt an urgency to have her novel published in Paris, and turned to Stendhal for help. According to letter that she wrote to him in Paris from Rome on March 10, 1828, the diplomat had already offered his services for obtaining a publisher in Paris. She did not take him up on the offer immediately because she thought Béranger already was finding her a publisher in the capital. However, Béranger's efforts, although sincere, were quickly scotched by Sampayo, who had read *Gertrude,* no doubt recognized the less-than-flattering characterization of himself in the plot, and was not amused. Hortense, then, knew Béranger was no longer of use to her in the face of such direct adversity. "[Béranger] a cessé de s'en occuper," she wrote to Stendhal, "étant comme vous savez d'un caractère faible et timide."[6]

She had already picked out the Parisian publisher she wished for *Gertrude,* and asked only that Stendhal go to the offices and put in a good word:

> Vous devriez seulement parler de l'ouvrage et dire au libraire qu'il peut le prendre en sûreté puisqu'il a réussi en Italie et s'est très bien vendu . . . . Veuillez me rendre ce service qui ne vous coûtera que quelques mots et qui m'obligerait inifiniment, car je veux absolument que *Gertrude* soit imprimée à Paris . . . un mot de vous fera tout.[7]

She ended the letter by telling Stendhal of the success of *Gertrude* in Rome, and that she was receiving letters eight pages long from enthusiastic readers. The Romans, however, were reading the book *"en secret."* Although all the female characters were chaste, the novel dared speak of divorce, and was, therefore, forbidden reading in Rome, banned by the Maître du Sacro Palazzo. Thus, another reason that

Hortense desired a Parisian printing. (Interestingly, Stendhal's *Armance,* although it hints of Œdipal feelings, escaped the Catholic blacklist).

Stendhal's efforts were indeed influencial in getting *Gertrude* published by Ambroise Dupont et Cie in Paris in 1828. His praises of the novel also are recorded in a letter to Marc-Antoine Jullien, director of the *Revue Encyclopédique,* to whom he sent two copies of *Gertrude.* Stendhal wrote, "Je ne crois pas qu'il y ait aucune femme vivante capable d'écrire avec cette originalité et cette profondeur. *L'auteur ose être soi-meme.* Rien de plus rare par le temps qui court."[8] He was impressed, then, not only by Allart's novel, but also by the uncompromising sincerity of her lifestyle and persona as reflected in her development of the plot.

His *New Monthly Magazine* review had observed, "Peu de romans, même ceux de Mme de Staël, contiennent des descriptions aussi curieuses et cependant aussi parfaitement vraies que celle qui nous montre comment l'amant de Gertrude parvient tout d'abord à faire une impression favorable sur sa maîtresse."[9]

To Jullien, Stendhal continued, "La séduction de Gertrude par l'homme qu'elle épouse me semble un chef-d'œuvre de vérité . . . C'est la société telle que nous la faisons tous les jours. Voilà une mérite bien rare et auquel il n'est pas facile d'atteindre."

The story of how Gertrude falls in love with the charming, though shallow, Alphonse de Selmire is a transluscent, if not transparent, rendering of Hortense's own epiphany about her relationship with Sampayo. Bertelà notes how such sophistication in writing is rare in a first novel. "Le récit de l'amour entre Gertrude et Alphonse montre une expérience d'écrivain achevé étonnante dans un premier ouvrage romanesque. Allart montre ici, une capacité remarquable de pénétration psychologique outre une exquise sensibilité d'artiste" (Bertelà 97).

Uffenbeck dismisses *Gertrude* rather quickly as a fairly typical example of popular women's fiction of the day.[10] However, in her dissertation, Rabine examines in detail the lucidity of Allart's self-analysis through the title character, and the ways in which her narrative stands out as a momument of feminist writing that is decades ahead of its time. The modernity of the novel stems from the near-effortless way in which it is able to transcend the stereotype of the Romantic heroine.

It is easy to take issue with the idea that *Gertrude* is too much a novel *à la Staël,* since Allart's title character is a heroine who is more self-confident and independent than either Delphine or Corinne, and, unlike *any* of Staël's female protagonists, ends up happily with the right man. (The same contrast can be made with most of Sand's early heroines—the title characters of *La Marquise, Lavinia, Indiana* [in its original ending], *Valentine, Lélia*—who all come to unrewarding, if not tragic, ends). As do her fellow female novelists, Allart creates heroines who struggle with the usual aspects of a woman's lot in early 19th-century life. She is different, though, in her determination to allow her protagonists the will and the discernment ultimately to triumph by finding a way out.

In the first pages, Gertrude, a lovely 18-year-old orphan and heiress, who lives with her uncle and cousins, Hedwige and Eléanore, muses as to why her mood, which used to be more lighthearted, recently has become somber. Allart's own dichotomy of male/female sentiments is evident as Gertrude states, "Je ne suis plus ferme, intrépide, et moi qui me croyais le courage et les vertus d'un homme, je me sens femme."[11] She feels heaven has destined her to these "vertus de femme" that she has long abhorred. She would rather direct herself and feel independent, but feels a loss of control. Gertrude, however, can recognize her problem, and although she makes an error in judgment in choosing her husband, she is courageous enough to rise above the usual restrictions on women, and rectify the wrong.

"Hortense Allart understands too intuitively well this phenomenon of the romantic hero and heroine to believe in it," states Rabine. ". . . Allart was never the prisoner [of the romantic heroine] . . . . Perhaps it was because she made herself so much of an idealogical misfit, and because she so acutely cut to the core of the romantic myth, that she escaped the rivalries and jealousies of her circle."[12]

Therefore, Gertrude, unlike the Staëlian and Sandian heroines, is exceptional, not in being regarded as superior to other women, but in "risking centure for her inability to conform to the 19th-century ideal" (Rabine 189).

In the first chapter, the reader learns that Gertrude has already turned down several young men whom her uncle has introduced as prospective husbands. "Je ne trouvais rien de supérieur à eux" (*Ger.* Chp. I, Tome 1; Chp. I, 4). She particularly admires the love between Hedwige and her fiancé, Charles, a political refugee from a dangerous mission for an unnamed eastern European country. "Votre amour m'a donné l'idée d'une félicité que je n'avais jamais imaginée . . . J'ai vu là seulement cette ferme union de deux personnes devant laquelle les biens de la terre ne sont rien." She dreams of a husband who could understand her unique soul, "mais le trouverais-je?" (*Ger.* Chp. I, Tome I; Chp. 1, 5).

It is not suprising when Gertrude declines to consider marriage to M. Muller, an older gentleman whom her uncle introduces to her.

First, she knows that he, as well as other men of her acquaintance, are more concerned with her wealth than they are with her as an individual. "Jugez donc de quel œil je contemple ces genes qui viennent ici briguer ma main dans la seule idée que je suis une riche heritière" (*Ger.* Chp. I, Tome I; Chp. I, 6). Secondly, whereas the 16-year-old Eléonore (she is called Léonore in the original version) dreams only of placid domesticity, Gertrude and Hedwige aspire to a combination of love, passion, and independence. "Hedwige et Gertrude se livraient à des rêveries romanesques, Eléonore rêvait une vie paisible et concentré dans les affections de famille " (*Ger.* Chp. II, Tome I; Chp. II, 11).

The eventual marriage of Eléonore to M. Muller, the embodiment of the condescending, dominating husband that is sanctioned by the *Code Napoléon,* is predictable. Gertrude's capitulation to Alphonse de Selmire, Muller's nephew, is less understandable. Alphonse, who already has enough reputation for frivolity that his uncle is ready to send him off to America, admits to Muller that his attentions toward Gertrude are materialistic in nature. "Elle est riche, ce mariage arrangerait mieux que vous mes affaires" (*Ger.* Chp. VI, Tome I; Chp. VI, 24). However, Alphonse ignites Gertrude's romantic imagination by dancing with her incognito two nights in a row at a Parisian ball, then ingratiates himself to the family by aiding Charles with a failed political mission. Eventually, she succumbs to Alphonse's charm. "Cependant comment se défendre d'un homme si plein de charme . . . comment s'en défendre avec ce cœur de Gertrude, porté à l'amour, sensible depuis longtemps, qui cherchait un enivrement?" (*Ger.* Chp. , Tome I; Chp. VIII, 38).

Gertrude observes the wedding of Muller and Eléonore with sadness that there seems to be a lack of love between the two. ("Gertrude, mécontente, cherchait en eux quelque émotion vive, et s'indignait de tant de calme" (*Ger.* Chp. X, Tome I; Chp. VI 27).

Whereas Eléonore is the ideal Romantic heroine, the other women are not, preferring to chose their mates with at least some measure of intellectual reasoning. "In fact, the novel concerns a multitude of relations among people, very few of whom fulfill romantic stereotypes, as they seek the individual of the opposite sex who best matches their own qualities" (Rabine 191).

As she embarks on marriage to Alphonse, Gertrude is grateful for an abundant outpouring of romantic love that guides her. Nonetheless, her feelings will not control her. "Gertrude . . . se distinguait surtout par un air plein de naturel et une âme indépendante en dehors de toute influence" (*Ger.* Chp. 12, 54).

Fortunately, Allart is not mired in or limited by male-structured language, as has been identified by contemporary feminist critics as an unavoidable weakness of 19th-century female writers. Her use of Gertrude as a straighforward, omnicient, third-person narrator lets the reader see through a woman's vantage point the tragically bogus characteristics of society and of certain men that confound and manipulate unsuspecting young women.

For example, three years into Gertrude's marriage (the beginning of the second tome, or Chapter 15 of the later version), as the initial delight sours in the face of Alphonse's infidelities and pursuit of pleasure, Gertrude/Allart analyzes carefully the attitudes and mores in society that have brought her to this point. First of all, she realizes that female physical passions usually develop *after* the age at which Gertrude and most young women of the day contract what they believe will be an eternal union. Gertrude entered the marriage with unlimited confidence, enthusiasm, and hope, yet was unaware of and unprepared for the realities ahead.

And yet, the narrator asks, how can women of the tender age and with the naïveté of the average bride be expected to choose a mate with sufficient sophistication to guarantee a happy future? "Devons-nous la condamner pour ce mariage funeste? Pouvait-elle se défendre à la fois de la nature et de la société? Quoi! Gertrude à dix-huit ans aurait su attendre? Gertrude aurait su l'avenir? . . . Elle aurait attendu, pour aimer, de rencontrer un être en harmonie avec des sentiments qu'elle n'avait pas encore?" (*Ger.* Chp. I, Tome II; Chp. 15, 62).

After Gertrude has fallen in love with Alphonse's charm, the narrator asks, how she could find the strength to push him away or to cope with the sadness and discouragement in her soul? "Quand a-t-on vu l'humanité sortir ainsi de ses lois?" (*Ger.* Chp. 15, 63).

Such a candid, unapologetic analysis of a love gone wrong is a major literary step beyond Madame de Staël's courageous, yet veiled, protests of the unhappy fates, which she suggests were inevitable for her Delphine and Corinne. Staël was wont outwardly in her novels to pay perfunctory tribute to male values, and to disguise cleverly her pleas for reform under the most humble of speeches from her heroines.

"[Staël] understood that in order to forge a woman's language, she would have to engage in the most fundamental linguistic activity, that of nomination. She would have to make her own meanings, to call the world by her own names."[13]

For example, in the following excerpt from the concluding pages of *Corinne,* one perceives a seeming tone of self-deprecation as, on her deathbed, Corinne bids her final farewell to Oswald and to Rome: "Si j'obtiens encore quelques larmes, si je me crois encore aimée, c'est parce que je vais disparaître, mais si je resaisissais la vie, elle retournerait bientôt contre moi tous ses poignards . . . N'importe, obéissons.

J'avais choisi sur la terre, et mon cœur n'a plus d'asile. Vous décidez pour moi; mon sort en vaudra mieux."[14]

In this passage, Corinne seems resigned to society's destructive power over her, and she acknowledges her choice in the matter, and the consequences it has wrought. Of course, perceptive readers of *Corinne* know the heroine is not truly recanting the path she followed in life. Since women in the post-Revolutionary and Napoleonic years were virtually barred from the world of discourse and action, Staël was proceeding with caution, avoiding terms that were too direct.

Hogsett states that language in Staël's time was always an inadequate instrument for women, since it is too straightforward and too subject to male restrictions.

> [Woman] is a secondary being who depends on the male mind for her existence. Every word she speaks travels out of her contingent place, its route to the listener inevitably indirect, distorted. The primary, fundamental role belongs to man. It is he who substantiates, who defines, who decides on and imposes meanings. He insists that she function in his world, where he has established the links between signifier and signified (26).

With such fearsome restrictions on a woman writer's basic mode of expression, one can see how Staël tended in her writing, particularly in her fiction, to be "deeply intimidated, potentially crippled with guilt, cowed by threatening voices and disapproving looks" (Hogsett 27). The measure of Staël's courage is that she did indeed continue to write, and to write with a self-perception, and, eventually to confront the opposing forces as she does in *Corinne,* albeit in a round-about manner that would bring upon her the least suspicion and criticism.

"Certainly [Staël] is chafing at the restrictions placed on women writers, tapping along the walls, in search of a way out," says Hogsett (65).

In the above passage in which Corinne might seem to be regretting or recanting the values she espoused in life, she surely is aware of the fact that her chosen path as scholar, artist, poet, performer, and independent woman has led her away from the man she loved, and is now leading her to death. Yet, just a few lines later in the text, after Corinne has dismissed Oswald and now speaks only to Lucile, she says of Oswald, "Je lui pardonne d'avoir déchiré mon cœur, les hommes ne savent pas le mal qu'ils font, et la société leur persuade que c'est un jeu de remplir une âme de bonheur, et d'y faire ensuite succéder le désespoir" (*Cor.* 2:367). She later tells a priest, "Je ne me suis jamais vengée du mal qu'on m'a fait; jamais une douleur vraie ne m'a trouvé insensible, mes fautes ont été celles des passions . . . J'ai vécu pour aimer, et sans vous je mourrais seule" (*Cor.* 2:368).

Staël's Corinne, then, eventually does speak honestly of the injustices in society that have led to her demise.   The speech can be accomplished, however, only after the author has paid lip service to the status quo, accepted her fate, and seemingly acknowledged it as the only course that a woman of her attitude and actions could have expected.   In other words, Staël makes a concession to Christian humility and meekness, and puts on a display of traditional feminine delicacy and submissiveness in order to mollify her feminist indignation against society and to mold it into language that will set more easily (perhaps) with a male-dominated literary world.

With Allart there is no such "tapping along the walls in search of a way out," but rather, a forthright, matter-of-fact rendering of Gertrude's unfortunate situation with no attempt at mitigation or concession to authority in the telling.   The same unapologetic, straight-shooting style would typify Allart's writings for the rest of her life.

After explaining Gertrude's disillusionment in marriage—which has occurred through no fault of her own—the narrator assures the readers that, as a married woman, Gertrude has continued to study and improve her mind, and has refused to go down into the mental oblivion of domesticity.   She also maintains a respected salon in her Parisian home.

> Depuis son mariage, elle n'avait pas cessé de cultiver son esprit comme aux jours de sa solitude, et elle avait trouvé dans son existence actuelle une heureuse instruction.   Esprit curieux, ambitieux, esprit inquiet, actif; esprit hardi, esprit flottant   . . . esprit qui savait juger ce qui était au-dessous de lui et en rester indépendant, mais qui agrandissait ce dont il ne savait pas bien la mesure . . . esprit dont la progression continuelle modifia parfois l'opinion (*Ger.* Chp. 2, Tome II; Chp. XV, 64-65).

This strength of mind, serenity of spirit, mobility, individuality, freedom in society and decision-making power that Gertrude retains in her marriage help her bear the disillusionment of Alphonse's infidelities, and to continue learning from her error in judgment as well as from those of other women.

Through Muller, an austere husband to Eléonore, Allart illustrates how the stereotyping of marriage and women through society's preconceived roles is disastrous. "It is only the laws of marriage that force Muller into egotism and injustice towards his wife, for according to law and custom, she has no internal life except the one he molds" (Rabine 195).

As if his own extra-marital dalliances were not despicable enough, Alphonse encourages his friend Pélage, a Romantic poet infatuated with Eléonore, to entice the young wife away from her husband. Gertrude sees through the shallowness and destructiveness of Pélage's particular brand of romanticism, and spells it out. "On l'avait vu suivre en tous lieux des femmes seulement pour leur visage . . . et aussitôt il croyait lire dans cet assemblage la tendresse et l'amour" (*Ger.* Chp. 8, Tome II; Chp. XVIII, 79).

Allart's plainspoken descriptions of Pélage's attitude is a warning to young female readers everywhere to beware of men who equate a pretty face with eternally destined love, and place an attractive lady into their own pre-conceived notions of the Ideal Woman. "[Pélage] se dit qu'Eléonore était destinée à lui par le ciel, qu'elle était la femme qu'il avait imaginée dans ses poétiques rêveries . . . " (*Ger.* Chp. 8 Tome II; Chp XVIII, 81).

Whereas Gertrude is too strong a person to be taken in by Pélage's rhetoric and histrionic declarations, the younger, weaker Eléonore becomes his victim. "Gertrude learns more about the impossible situation of the romantic heroine caught in the trap of romantic love . . . The women strong enough for romantic love are never chosen as its object. The ideal is inevitably too weak to fulfill the role" (Rabine 197). Staël's, and later, Sand's first few female protagonists will perpetuate the idea of romantic heroine as both the desirable recipient of romantic love and its inevitable victim. The iconoclastic Allart shows such a woman as a person to be pitied, not emulated, and a person who should rebel against such a trend, not bow before it.

The aforementioned comparison of Racine and Shakespeare—a tibit in the narrative that shows Allart's broad-based literary acquaintance—is worked into a scene in which Gertrude, Eléonore, Muller and Pélage attend the theater in Paris to watch the actress Juliane play the title role in *Phèdre.* As they are all enthralled with the performance, the narrator comments on how Racine revamped the idea of passion without using overly passionate characters. "En cela il est l'opposé de Shakespeare." Unlike Hamlet, whose passions are a static and innate part of his character, Phèdre represents the dynamic development of guilty passions through intense self-analysis. "L'Anglais part d'un objet partiel pour vous mener à l'idée générale, et c'est là comment instruit l'univers; l'autre [Racine] part d'une idée générale pour arriver à l'individu, c'est là le trait de la pensée humaine" (*Ger.* Chp. XXI, Tome II; Chp. XXII, 95).

Unaware that Juliane is one of Alphonse's former lovers, who had come to the Paris theater to try to win him back, Gertrude insists on visiting the talented actress, and learning of the sad events of her life.

(An autobiographic note is evident here, as perhaps Allart was recalling the story of her late father's difficulty with an adoring actress.) Juliane, another embodiment of the romantic heroine gone overboard, is an actress who not only plays dramatic roles, but also lives them.   As Juliane reveals her past history with Alphonse, Gertrude is less shocked than she is touched with pity for the other woman.   "Elle pensa à Juliane, et elle plaignit profondément cette femme dont les accents révélaient une âme accessible à tous les sentiments qui déchirent" (*Ger.* Chp. V, Tome III; Chp. XXIII, 99).

Juliane, in turn, admires Gertrude's ability to have developed her mind instead of just her emotions.   "Vous avez cultivé votre intelligence et votre moralité; je n'ai rien cultivé, j'ai souffert. J'ai eu deux maladies, la fierté et l'amour: ce sont deux maladies cruelles" (*Ger.* Chp. V, Tome III;   Chp. XXVI, 119).   Despite Gertrude's attempts to convince Juliane that her life is worth living, the actress soon departs for Switzerland, and is not heard from again.   Gertrude searches for her in vain, fearing that Juliane ended her own life, as she had threatened, or at least, went down into a quick annihilation as had the real-life Mademoiselle Desgarcins, the unfortuate lover of Gabriel Allart, a generation earlier.

The story of Eléonore and Pélage is resolved in an atypical twist— and, for this period of time, a very courageous one to include in a novel—as they are allowed to pursue their love after the granting of a divorce.   Muller allows his wife her freedom, and escorts her to Germany to put a legal end to their marriage.   Since Pélage is German and Protestant, he will be permitted to marry the divorced Eléonore. Allart probably realized the potentially dangerous position into which this piece of writing was placing her in Italy as well as in her own country, where the constitutional monarchy under Charles X was still under the strict anti-divorce laws of the *Code Napoléon.*

Furthermore, it was only 26 years earlier that Madame de Staël had found herself banished 40 lieues from Paris by Bonaparte after the publication of *Delphine* (1802), partly because the novel dared advocate through Delphine's Protestant friends, the Lebenseis, the sanity and morality of legalized divorce.[15]

The volatile nature of this plot point did not seem to faze Hortense, however, as she used the events and conversations that occur before the divorce as a bold forum for her opinions on the corrupt attitudes about marriage that abounded in French society.   She describes Muller's condescending attitude toward his wife: he berates Eléonore for her leniency toward their children and treats her as though she were a child herself.   "Enfant vous-même, reprit-il avec un tendre accent, que je devrais gronder, et qui m'inspirez la même faiblesse que ceux-ci vous inspirent" (*Ger.* Chp. 13, Tome III; Chp. XXXIII, 150).

Later, when Alphonse warns Muller about Pélage's attentions to Eléonore, Muller smugly laughs him off, claiming that he controls his wife, even though he does not love her. [Eléonore] me respecte, elle me craint, elle a une haute idée de mon authorité, de ma bonté . . . . Elle a passé de l'autorité de son père sous la mienne. Je suis son affection première, ses enfants viennent après . . . . hors de là il n'est rien pour elle (*Ger.* Chp. XV, Tome III; Chp. XXIV, 161).

Through Alphonse's gloating reaction to this statement, Allart observes that most husbands have the same self-satisfied attitude as does Muller: "Cette confiance commençait à amuser beaucoup Alphonse. Il l'avait observé chez tous les maris de sa société" (*Ger.* Chp. XV, Tome III; Chp. XXIV, 161).

The credibility of Muller's change of heart and his willingness to grant Eléonore a divorce just a short while later may be somewhat strained. Nevertheless, Allart unhesitatingly opts to show him humbled and repentant about the way his country and religion allow men to treat their wives. "O sages lois de mon pays! ô ma sage religion! s'écria-t-il d'une voix altérée, je suis tout près de maudire le pouvoir que vous me laissez! Je voudrais que Dieu et la loi m'ayant imposé une union éternelle, me permissent de prendre mon intérêt pour mon devoir!" (*Ger.* Chp. XVIII, Tome III; Chp. XXXVIII, 176).

As the Mullers and Pélage head for Germany for the divorce, the last fourth of *Gertrude* focuses primarily upon resolving the relationship that has been developing between the heroine and Rodrigue de Valdivia, who was introduced at about the same time that Gertrude was beginning to admit to herself her disillusionment about her husband. Rodrigue, named for the hero in Corneille's *Le Cid,* has arrived recently in France from his native South America, where he was engaged in military and civil service. One sees in Rodrigue, who is of Hispanic heritage, but raised in England, some direct parallels to Count Sampayo. Solemn, pompous, and seemingly devoid of charm, Rodrigue appears the exact opposite of Alphonse. Both characters, however, are representations of Sampayo as Allart criticizes the irresponsible side of her former lover through Alphonse and creates a wise and admirable Sampayo through Rodrigue.

As Alphonse becomes increasingly inconstant, and even proud to be so, Gertrude admits to herself, "Le développement inattendu de ses facultés lui apportait des lumières qu'elle n'avait pas prévues, et avec la même bonne foi qu'elle avait cru M. de Selmire digne d'elle, elle s'étonnait aujourd'hui de le trouver si médicore, et de se sentir isolée" (*Ger.* Chp. XIV, Tome II, 101; quote is not in later edition). On the other hand, Gertrude's initial conversations with Rodrigue open before her a whole new universe of ideas, as well as a kind of mental rapport with a man that she had not thought was possible. "Il lui faisait aborder un ordre d'idées inconnues; il l'associait à ses découvertes sur cette terre où l'homme trouve en lui seul la puissance" (*Ger.* Chp. XIV, Tome II; Chp. XVII, 77).

The friendship between these protagonists initially is purely cerebral, lacks the passion for which the Gertrude longs, and is not always harmonious. Before the Mullers' divorce, for example, Rodrigue piques Gertrude with his authoritarian view that a "wife's duty" is to be uncompromisingly forebearing and virtuous regardless of her husband's conduct. Gertrude takes issue, "Vous la condamnerez, donc . . . à un isolement éternel" (*Ger.* Chp. XXII, Tome II; Chpt. XXIII, 101). She is also vexed over Rodrigue's rather sanctimonious judgment that Juliane's profession took her away from her "duty as a woman" (*Ger.* Chp. VII, Tome III; Chp. XXVIII, 129).

Rodrigue's further philosophizing about what should constitute a more ideal society prefigures Allart's 1836 brochure *La Femme et la Démocratie de Nos Temps,* in which she would advocate a kind of oligarchic government in which intellectually superior men and women would be a country's leaders and decision-makers. "Tandis que les multitudes, fidèles à la loi et à l'ordre établi, montrent leur vertu par leur respect, l'homme supérieur, instruit de ce que cette vertu leur coûte, et prévoyant les besoins d'une époque plus avancée, perfectionne, améliore et change la loi" (*Ger.* Chp IX, Tome III; Chp. XXX, 137).

Though she finds her mind stimulated by Rodrigue, Gertrude still dreams of another power—love and passion—which surely must equal any intellectual ideas. "La passion de l'amour, la passion en un mot, lui semblait seule équivaloir cette pensée qu'elle admirait . . . . ou plutôt par moments elle croyait pressentir que cet autre monde, vaste, infini, que révélait la passion, devait tout surpasser" (*Ger.* Chp. XI, Tome III; Chp. XXXII, 141).

She continues to long for greater passion in Rodrigue—"Si son âme s'élévait jamais à la hauteur de son intelligence! Gertrude mettrait des années à cet ouvrage" (*Ger.* Chp. XI, Tome III; Chp. XXXII, 142)—but is nevertheless delighted to be seduced by his fine mind, which contrasts with Alphonse's shallow charm. "Non, rien n'est à comparer à ce qu'elle éprouvait en écoutant des idées, des paroles si élevés, sortir d'une bouche si jeune, d'une tête si belle. Jamais séduction plus noble et plus puissante ne s'était plus justement adressée" (*Ger.* Chp. XI, Tome III; Chp. XXXII, 143).

After the bewilderment she feels from the Muller's divorce and during a temporary separation from Rodrigue, Gertrude finds solace in the works of a great woman.   Although she does not specifically name Madame de Staël, the description is clear:

> Les ouvrages d'une femme dont la réputation grandira avec les âges, et qui sera d'autant mieux comprise que le genre humain prendra plus d'élévation et de délicatesse, la calmaient par leur sensibilité, supérieure, pour Gertrude, à toutes les sensibilités connues . . . . et elle pensait que la plus digne reconnaissance pour cette femme unique était le bien même qu'on recevait d'elle (*Ger.* Chp. I, Tome IV; Chp. XL, 179).

Gertrude's sexual awakening, which occurs only through the course of her burgeoning, but still chaste, relationship with Rodrigue, leaves her with a feeling of loss of control, followed by loss of self as she feels herself becoming possessed by such an intense male presence. "C'était comme un tourment à la fois moral et physique et un grand trouble, une intelligence bouleversée. Tout lui semblait sombre et effrayant: il n'y avait plus pour elle que de l'horreur et du désordre" (*Ger.* Chp. XLIV, 205).   The atypical aspect of such an epiphany is Allart's/Gertrude's unreserved willingness to articulate such feelings.

To cope with the bewilderment, Gertrude begins to discipline herself in a commitment to calmness and study.   She feels seized by a feminist call to action and stung by the limitations placed upon her sex.   "Une intrépidité, une audace, un courage, qui appealient des épreuves, des actions; le regret que son sexe l'empêchât de laisser à ce caractère son plein essor" (*Ger.* Chp. I, Tome IV; Chp. XL, 179).

As she succeeds step-by-step in her quest to overcome her own passions and follow Rodrigue's example of temperance and reserve, he arrives, announcing that he has decided he must follow *her* example—listen to his heart, give more vent to his passions, and strive, thereby, to become more worthy of her. Filled with emotion, he begs, "Loin de vouloir être convertie à mes leçons, faites que mon cœur apprenne de vous ce qu'il ignore. Que je sois digne de vous mériter! C'est là cette grande pensée qui m'occupe!" (*Ger.* Chp II, Tome IV; Chp. XLI, 183).

Thrilled with his declaration—"Rodrigue m'aime! Moi, Rodrigue!" (184)—Gertrude quickly revives the passions she was trying to supress, yet reciprocates his feelings in a restrained, intellectual manner. "Je crois qu'être aimée de vous doit m'élever à la plus grande hauteur morale où il me soit permis d'atteindre. J'attends de vous le perfectionnement et l'estime de moi-même; formez-moi pour vous; faites-moi femme de l'homme que vous êtes, et je serai ce que j'espère " (*Ger.* 187).

It is the two kinds of love depicted in *Gertrude*—the rudimentary passion that arises between Pélage and Eléonore (and, to a slightly superior extent, between Hedwige and Charles), and the combination of passion and thought that develops between Gertrude and Rodrigue—that might have influenced Stendhal as he embarked on *Le Rouge et le Noir.* Bertelà says of *Gertrude*:

> Cette distinction qu'Allart fait, dans son roman, entre un amour passion tout naturel, tel celui de Léonore et de Pélage, et un amour passion soutenu toutefois par la pensée, avec toutes les difficultés que cela crée, ici l'amour de Gertrude et de Rodrigue, ne fait-elle pas penser elle aussi, que Stendhal . . . ait put trouver dans ce roman un exemple et quelques idées pour les deux amours de Julien Sorel, Mme de Rênal and Mathilde de la Mole? (Bertelà 108).

Allart's idea that love could take such distinctly different forms apparently intrigued Stendhal, although he and Allart arrived at opposite conclusions—she favoring the more cerebral love between Gertrude and Rodrigue, and he ultimately sustaining the sentimental ideal between Julien and Mme de Rênal. "Sans donc vouloir comparer *Gertrude* et *Le Rouge et le Noir,* nous croyons toutefois que la lecture de *Gertrude* a été fertile pour notre grand écrivain et que s'il loue le roman, ce n'est pas une louange de circonstance" (Bertelà 108).

Through Rodrigue, Allart adds another subtle plea for legalized divorce. He muses on his frustrations over loving a married woman: "Non que la loi du mariage ne me semble admirable . . . elle est bien noble quand elle consacre ainsi les affections et l'élévation de l'homme." However, says Rodrigue, when difficulties and inequalities arise within marriage, "La loi du divorce naquit pour ces circonstances. Elle est la loi de l'homme comme le mariage. Lui seul entre les créatures juge et dispose des instincts de la nature" (*Ger.* Chp II, Tome IV; Chp. XLI, 189).

As Gertrude and Rodrigue dream of running away together to America, Alphonse returns ill from a stay with his latest mistress in Switzerland. Gertrude faithfully nurses her husband for the next few months, while passionate letters from Rodrigue continue to arrive. Although she and Alphonse entertain visitors from Paris, Gertrude is tormented with the awareness of how shallow her life is, and she is overcome with a wish to transcend the ordinary.

> Elle rêvait un avenir tout semblable à ses impressions du moment: souffrir, mais s'ennoblir, mais exister au-delà de l'existence ordinaire . . . Rodrigue lui avait donné une idée de la passion qui lui faisait dédaigner les amours passagers, et il lui

avait fait comprendre une pensée qui la détachait de toutes les pensées des hommes (*Ger.* Chp. V, Tome IV;   Chp. XLV, 216; 217-18).

When Alphonse dies, calling out the names of his former mistresses,   Gertrude, though free, still fears the self-annihilation that may be the result of giving oneself over to a man of passion.   Again, she resolves to elevate her heart with the sort of study and reason that Rodrigue had inspired in her.   She prays for strength to steel herself against Rodrigue's love, feeling that women never can be permitted to indulge their passions even with the most superior of men:

> Qu'est-ce donc que cette fierté fatale que le ciel donna aux femmes avec des âmes passionées?   Oh! à genoux devant Rodrigue ou pressant sur son sein sa noble tête, que Gertrude eût voulu s'abandonner à cette impérieuse tendresse qu'elle contenait avec tant de souffrance! Oh! l'adorer librement . . . . confondre enfin son âme avec cette âme à laquelle sa vie est attachée, ainsi Gertrude eût voulu témoigner sa passion (*Ger.* Chp. 16, Tome IV; quote not in later edition).

The constant tension in the relationship between Gertrude and Rodrigue as each one attempts to surmount passion in favor of reason before coming to terms with a happy combination of both, has seemed to more than one reader to be just a bit long. "Je dois avouer que le récit de ces luttes me paraît montrer quelques longueurs," says Bertelà (100). Entire chapters are devoted to Rodrigue's philosophizing and Gertrude's inward struggles with how to school or to liberate her own feelings.

What lifts *Gertrude* out of the stream of other similar romantic novels of the day are Allart's candid lamentations about how the question of love typically brings women, particularly intelligent women with more than simple domestic goals in life, to the necessity of making a tragic choice—either love without a sense of self or self-actualization without love.   As usual, the author will not pull punches or mitigate the sorry state of society's double standard.

"Hommes! Hommes! vous seuls, vous pouvez aimer! à vous seuls il est permis d'exprimer tout ce que vous sentez!" (*Ger.* Chp 16, Tome IV, 200; quote not in later edition). As for gifted women: "Le ciel voulut douer quelques femmes, mais voulant aussi, dans ses décrets cachés, leur faire payer chers ses présens [sic]." Gertrude imagines a voice from heaven telling such women to cultivate their mental gifts, but to renounce the possibility of love, which can only enslave them emotionally to the detriment of their potential:

> Allez, leur dit-il, en les envoyant ici-bas, allez, soyez femmes
> supérieures, ayez des intelligences fortes, ayez une sensibilité
> profound . . . mais je vous condamne à la nécessité d'aimer; toutes
> nos facultées dépendront de l'amour . . . . Je vous attache par les
> liens de fer à ce sexe plus indépendent que vous . . . je vous attache
> aux hommes, vous les aimerez avec une puissance qui ne vous
> laisserez ni liberté ni repos; . . . vous aimerez pour vivre . . . vous
> aimerez ou vous mourrez; allez, soyez femmes supérieures, allez!
> (*Ger.* Chp. 16, Tome IV, 200-2, quote not in later edition).

Interestingly, as Allart deplores this plight of women, she never identifies it as a conflict or contention *between women and men.* The problem is, rather, society's corruption of the natural progress of love, which should allow equality between the sexes. Society has skewed the process to make women fatally vulnerable in a men's world.

Amid such a traumatic analysis of the choices before her, Gertrude hears from Rodrigue of the death of Hedwige, who had followed Charles to the battlefields of Greece, and perished from disease. Rodrigue includes Hedwige's last letters to Gertrude that speak of her exalted love for Charles, and her happiness with him, even in the face of death. "J'ai payé cher ce bonheur," Hedwige writes, "et je le paie aujourd'hui de la vie. J'ai été aimée comme je voulais l'être et j'ai aimé comme je voulais aimer! La femme qui trace de telles lignes, n'est-elle pas heureuse entre les femmes heureuses?" (*Ger.* Chp. 13, Tome IV; Chp. XLVI, 229).

Months pass; just before his planned departure to America, Rodrigue visits Gertrude. As they ride horses together, he envisions her as the ideal he might have had, but cannot: "Vous voilà, une héroïne, lui dit-il; c'est ainsi que je vous voyais déjà m'accompagner en Amérique et courir les périls avec moi; mais ce temps, mais ce rêve est passé" (*Ger.* Chp. XLVII, 234).

Rodrigue departs, only to be called back on the road to Paris by a letter from Gertrude, who, in a burst of passionate idealism and newfound confidence, has vowed to create with him a transcendent happiness, and to exalt her calling as woman to make it so. "Je vous montrerai que cette création de femme est sublime puisque la femme peut seule donner la félicité à qui elle adore. Là, la divinité se livra et se révéla" (*Ger.* Chp. 19, Tome IV; Chp. XLVII, 240).

In a technique that will be typical of Allart's future novels as well, she declines to give a detailed description of her protagonists' passionate reunion in the vein that her future 20th-century readers might expect.

The last paragraph reveals only that Rodrigue retraced his steps to Gertrude's house, and "se mit aux genoux de celle qui allait devenir sa femme" (*Ger.* Chp. 19, Tome IV; Chp. XLVII, 241), declaring that such a love as theirs was the product of 6,000 years of humanity in the making.

If *Gertrude* is not a great first novel, the consensus of critics is generally that it is an ambitious and sincere one with a courageous bent and a no-nonsense rendering of the author's life, times, and turmoil. If certain dialogues in the novel are ponderous, they are realistic etchings of specific prejudices and inequities that Allart expects her society—or at least its most intelligent women—to recognize, protest and rectify. If Allart makes Gertrude and Eléonore pitiable victims of men, she also makes a concession to society by having them remain chaste and behave properly towards their husbands as long as they remain married. If the resolution of two bad marriages seems a little too pat—Eléonore can get a divorce, while Gertrude is conveniently widowed—Allart is bolstering French women everywhere with faith in themselves as individuals, and hope for happier and more equitable future relationships with men.

The novel's writing style is one of more sophistication than one would expect of someone of Allart's age and experience. The chapters are brief and usually pithy, and each episode has an element of surprise that leads one to believe the author is more experienced at compelling writing techniques than she really is. "Si Allart n'en était pas à son premier roman, il faudrait penser à un art déjà mûr," says Bertolà. "Allart unit ici une sensibilité toute romantique à une écriture qui ressent, dans les clauses finales, de la rhétorique classique, dans le sens meilleur du terme. Dans ces clauses finales, c'est l'écrivain qui révèle directement sa pensée, sa sensibilité ou son expérience" (Bertolà 106-107).

Billy identifies Allart's writing style as an elegy to the passion of Chateaubriand's *René,* softened by a woman's sensitivity, as well as a precursor to the emotive poignancy of Alfred de Musset. "C'est le 'Levez-vous, orages désirés!' adouci par la sensibilité d'une femme. Ailleurs, on pense à une *Confession d'un enfant du siècle* où ce serait le père, ou un frère aîné" (Billy 64).

In what sense, then, is *Gertrude*, as at least one of her contemporary critics said, "un ouvrage mâle"? No doubt it is her psychoanalytic bent combined with her straightforward style with its refusal to attenuate her opinions on society and on women's lot, or to cloak her feelings behind seeming proprieties. Certainly *Gertrude* is a feminist novel, but one that ushers in a new kind of unmannered feminism, an attitude that bursts forth undisguised, and confident that it has nothing it must hide.   "Pour son idée du monde féminin, il faut bien dire qu'Allart, écrivaine sûrement féministe, est toutefois une féministe atypique" (Bertolà 108).

Allart's first novel is a work in which the feminism tempers the romanticism, and in which the romanticism tempers the feminism, and each is bolstered by her exceptional self-confidence and honesty that surpass in their boldness even the brave, but diplomatic expressions of Madame de Staël.   Even as Allart the novelist soon would be all but eclipsed by the quickly rising star of George Sand, and even by such lesser luminaries as Marie d'Agoult (who wrote under the name of Daniel Stern) and Flora Tristan, her first novel would stand out from the works of these others as a uncompromising work of feminist romanticism in its most direct and candid form.

As her reputation as a talented young novelist thus was growing, Hortense's personal life was on a verge of a new and infamous adventure as well.   During her publication efforts for *Gertrude,* she had made a trip to Rome, and it was here that she first made the acquaintance of René de Chateaubriand.

Notes

[1]Letter from Hortense Allart to the Banque Caccia Frères, rue des Petits-Champs in Paris, quoted by Billy 58.

[2]Quoted by Billy 54-55.

[3]Quoted by Billy 56.

[4]Maddelena Bertelà.   "*Gertrude,* Un roman qui plaisait à Stendhal," *Francophonia* VI, 11 (autunno 1986): 87-109.   Bertelà states, "Mais voyons de plus près cette écriture d'Allart que Bonnéfon, cité, a défini à la Stendhal,' sans dire que *Gertrude* est contemporain *d'Armance* mais précède *Le Rouge et le Noir:* et c'est ici qu'à notre avis Stendhal porte à un haut degré de perfection quelques idées déjà présentes dans le roman que nous allons analyser" 91.   More on Bertelà's analysis of *Gertrude* in a short while.

[5]Review quoted by Billy 60-61.

[6]Letter from Allart to Stendhal, March 10, 1828, quoted by Billy 61.

[7]Same letter quoted by Billy 61.

[8]Quoted by Bertelà 88-89, her italics.

[9]Quoted by Billy 60.

[10]Uffenbeck cites an unfavorable 1828 review from *Le Mecure de France au dix-neuvième siècle* that reproaches Allart for what the reviewer saw as the hermetic character of the novel, and assigned it to an "effeminate" literature of the period: "D'une civilisation efféminée est sortie

une littérature bizarre qu'on a nommée *l'école du cœur"* (89). He also cites an early assessment of *Gertrude* by Sainte-Beuve (from the Spoelberch de Lovenjoul collection) that calls Allart's novel "bon roman de la famille de *Corinne, Delphine,* d'une morale de sentiment" (91). Uffenbeck himself concludes by agreeing that *Gertrude* "appears to be no more than one of those novels meant to capture the popular imagination for a moment and then fall from sight" (91).

[11]Madame Hortense Allart de Thérase. *Gertrude,* 4 vols. (Paris: Ambroise Dupont et Cie., 1828), Chp. I, Tome 1, 4-5.

Mme P. de Saman. *Derniers Enchantements.* (Paris: Michel Lévy frères, 1874), Chp. I, 2-3. As the original 1828 Parisian edition of *Gertrude* can be found now only on microfiche at the Bibliothèque Nationale in Paris, and is more readily accessible in its slightly expurgated form as part of *Les Derniers Enchantements* (1-241), I will include the chapter and volume number from which each quotation is found in the 1828 edition (whenever possible), and the chapter and page number from the later printing.

(Subsequent references to this work will appear in parentheses after the quotation and will be indicated by the abbreviation *Ger.*).

[12]Leslie Rabine. *The Other Side of the Ideal: Women Writers of Mid-Nineteenth-Century France (George Sand, Daniel Stern, Hortense Allart, and Flora Tristan)* (Diss. Stanford U, 1973) 165.

[13]Charlotte Hogsett. *The Literary Existence of Germaine de Staël* (Carbondale and Edwardsville, Ill: Southern Illinois University Press, 1987) 154.

[14]Madame de Staël. *Corinne ou l'Italie,* 2 vols. (Paris: Garnier Frères, Librairie-Editeurs, no date) 2:366. (Subsequent references to this work will appear in parentheses after the quotation and will be indicated by the abbreviation *Cor.*)

[15]Madame de Staël. *Delphine,* 2 vols. (Paris: Editions des Femmes, 1981). Lébensei's famous letter to Delphine states, in part, "Ceux qui condamnent le divorce prétendent que leur opinion est d'un moralité plus parfait . . . mais je veux examiner, avec vous si les principes qui me font approuver le divorce sont d'accord avec la nature de l'homme, et avec les intentions bienfaisantes que nous devons attribuer à la Divinité" (Lettre XVII, Part 4, 2:71).

Chapter 3

Jérôme: The Modernity of a Romantic Heroine (1829-1830)

The years 1827 and 1828 were exciting for Hortense not only because of the publication and success of *Gertrude* in two different countries, but also because of the travels she was able to make throughout central Italy. While Florence remained her *pied à terre*, she traveled to Pisa, Livourne, Naples, and three times to Rome, sometimes staying for several months at a time.

She spent a month in the spring of 1828 in Albano on the outskirts of Rome, and the entire summer at Castellammare, where she began to outline her second novel, *Jérôme ou le jeune prélat.* This work would be a more literal rendering of her relationship with Sampayo than was reflected in *Gertrude,* although she would choose Roman Catholic upper-crust society as the setting, make the hero a novice priest, and base several other characters on individuals she met in Rome.

Les Enchantements de Prudence abounds with *Corinne*--like descriptions of the ancient charm of Italy, and its eternal intrigue and significance for mankind. "L'Italie séduit dans son malheur, parce que sa destinée ressemble à celle de l'homme. Quel être a vécu et souffert, qui ne sente que le sort de l'Italie est d'accord avec le sien?" (*EP* 92).

Of all her sojourns, Rome was the spot that moved her the most—the majesty of the city, the nostalgic ambiance of the nearby countryside, the ruins everywhere of an earlier splendor. "Mais Rome, mais son histoire, mais ses musées, mais ses paysages, mais ses collines, mais cette impression de majestueuse noblesse, tout cela composait un cadre idéal pour la vie d'un être intelligent et passioné comme elle" (Billy 69).

She visited the Forum, the Coliseum, and other historic sites, took in all the ancient and Renaissance artwork she could absorb, read assiduously, studied Italian literature, attended classical plays at the theater, took copious notes from interviews with Roman scholars and archeologists, and began to write about the ancient history of all of Italy, emphasizing the civilization's inspirational effect on the human spirit.

> L'homme indépendant, que les sociétés de l'Europe fatiguant, respire en Italie.   Il est libre, et réfléchissant et régnant sur les faits, il lui semble participer au pouvoir qui fut si longtemps l'apanage de ce pays.   La nature y conserve les caractères qui le peuplèrent de dieux, qui rendirent les forêts prophétiques, qui inspirèrent Virgile; quelques monuments semblent rivaliser de durés avec elle, et tout fait rêver, jusqu'à la poussière.   Terre de Saturne! Terre antique, berceau de tant de républiques . . . lieux mythologiques . . . (*EP* 92).

During Easter week in Rome, 1828, she was thrilled by the festivities of the carnival.   The Count Giovanni Giraud, a French actor and dramatic director of the Italian theater, who lived in a lovely palace on the Corso, offered her a seat at his windows to view the parade.   At his home, she met numerous Italian noblemen, including two Roman princes, Don Michelangelo Caetani, and his brother Don Filippo Caetani, descendants of the family of Boniface VIII (a pope from the 13th century).   She received the visit of Monsignor Piccolomini, a young prelate from a noble family, whom she recreated in *Jérôme* under the name Dom Clément.

Typical at every point in her travels were visits from friends, some of whom would stay up talking with her until 2 or 3 a.m.   At this time, Libri and Capponi were rivals for her affections, although it was Libri who usually won out.   Back in Florence during October 1828, "Elle retrouva Libri et Capponi, le premier brillant, éloquent, le second cédant dédaigneusement l'avantage à son rival" (Billy 72).   Charles Didier was still part of her life as well, and their liaison would not end until 1832, when each would meet George Sand.

There is evidence that Hortense and Capponi still were lovers during the early months of 1829, but her letter to him dated March 25 of that year indicates that her ardor was on the wane.   After all, he was content to see her but once a week!   Her letter recalls fondly their first meetings and some of their good times, and how she appreciated his praises of *Gertrude*.   She informed him, however, that "vous n'étiez ni assez indépendant, ni assez passioné pour moi; vous avez été heureux en voyant votre maîtresse une fois tous les huit jours; moi voir mon amant une fois tous les huit jours, et pas plus, c'en serait assez pour me faire vivre désespérée." She asked that they strive henceforth for "l'amitié-affection," between themselves, rather than "l'amitié-passion."[1]

Her desire for ongoing friendship with Capponi was sincere, as evidenced by their correspondence that continued throughout the next few years, and how she valued his opinion on some of her subsequent writings.[2]

On the other hand, Hortense's relationship with Libri, who filled the roles of both lover and mentor, was flourishing up through the early months of 1829. The young writer and scholar, who had earned a degree in law at age 17, authored two papers on mathematical theory, and been a professor of mathematics at the University of Pisa when he was but 20, continued to enthrall her with his vast knowledge and vivacity. From Florence he wrote her lengthy letters that urged her to set goals to receive the loftiest inspiration and to achieve the most grandiose projects.

In *Les Enchantements,* she quotes Libri at length. "D'ailleurs peu importe à la fin la manière dont on est inspiré, pourvu qu'on ait de grandes inspirations. Ainsi que ce soit la gloire, ou la religion, ou la patrie, ou vos amis, ou l'amour, ou la philanthropie qui vous animent, tout cela c'est bien égal pourvu que l'on soit animé aux grandes actions" (*EP* 98).

Speaking to her of her studies, Libri urged her to strive for excellence in a few things rather than to become mediocre in many. "Songez qu'il faut bien faire ou ne rien faire, que la médiocrité en beaucoup de choses, fait briller en société, mais que pour se rendre illustre, il faut bien savoir une chose" (*EP* 98).

He also had opinions on society's double standard toward male and female writers, believing the public condescended to female authors and expected too little quality from them. "On gâte les femmes, en général, parce que les hommes les considèrent comme une classe inférieure, et tous les éloges qu'on donne à leurs essais, quelquefois très faibles, démontrent le peu de cas qu'on en fait" (*EP* 99). Hortense, who was already straining towards goals that most of her society would insist were beyond a woman's reach, must have been pleased with Libri's egalitarian views regarding the sexes, and particularly, with his faith in her potential to compete in a man's world. Libri's letter continues:

> Moi, je pense, au contraire, que les femmes peuvent parvenir à tout; mais qu'il leur faut beaucoup de force pour s'élever à travers tous les obstacles et les dangers qui les entourent . . . Les femmes

qui vous ont précédée se sont arrêtées à moitié chemin. Voulez-
vous de cette gloire? Elle est facile à cueiller et vous l'avez déjà;
mais ce n'est pas ce que je veux pour vous. . . . je vous trouve un
caractère extraordinaire, et je pense qu'avec cela, vous pouvez aller
où vous voudrez, car la première qualité d'un caractère c'est la
fermeté (*EP* 99).

Continuing his letter, Libri counseled Hortense to stay true to her
already-proven work ethic and to seek only a few trusted friendships.
"Sachez vous-même ce que vous valez, ayez deux ou trois personnes qui
vous comprennent, et méprisez le reste du monde, la postérité saura
bien vous comprendre" (*EP* 99).

Early in April 1829, Hortense left Florence for her third stay in
Rome and took up a more long-term residence with her sister, Sophie
Allart, who was as passionately involved in her painting as Hortense
was in her literature. This third sojourn truly marked Hortense's
destiny.

She had in her possession a letter of introduction from Madame
Hamelin, a friend in Paris, who also was a close acquaintance of His
Excellency the ambassador of France to Rome, the vicomte François-
René de Chateaubriand. Madame Hamelin, who had once been on
friendly terms with both Napoleon and Josephine, had met
Chateaubriand in Paris some years earlier, probably at the salon of
Madame de Récamier. Against the wishes of his wife, the ambassador
was himself still corresponding with Madame Hamelin at the time he
met Hortense.

The mutual friend had suggested that Hortense call on the
ambassador sometime while in Rome, and Hortense, before she
summoned sufficient courage to do so, prepared herself by reading
Atala. She was enthralled with the novel, which describes the heady
emotions of an Indian woman in the wilderness of America. Thus awed
by the reputation and works of the famous writer, who was now 60
years old, she still hesitated to call. "Oserais-je aller le voir?" (*EP*
117).   (Contrary to her practice regarding Sampayo and Henry
Bulwer-Lytton, Hortense does *not* fictionalize Chateaubriand's name
in *Les Enchantements de Prudence).*

Chateaubriand, who was disappointed that Charles X had passed
him over for the appointment to the presidency of the Conseil, had
accepted the ambassadorship to Rome as a kind of retreat where he could
rest on his political and literary reputation in semi-exile. At age 60,
he still fancied himself very much the ladies' man, and was always on
the lookout for new conquests. The long-suffering Madame de
Chateaubriand, who, though exhausted with his infidelities, stood by

her husband through the years, had joined him in Rome. Other women who came, went, and wrote regularly in his life were legion. He had wished for the devoted, but independent Madame de Récamier to come to Rome as well. Although he wrote that his heart was still galvanized in her favor ("Ne craignez rien, je suis cuirassé"[3]), she declined to make the trip from Paris. (Chateaubriand's heart was never one to be truly galvanized). To the Romantic writer who also was known as the Enchanter, life at the palais Simonetti, aside from the usual parties and receptions, was lacking in excitement and in the spontaneous, "laissant insatisfait l'insatiable sexagénaire" (Billy 74).

Therefore, it was a somewhat bored and frustrated Chateaubriand, most eager for just such charms as the 27-year-old Hortense could offer, who received a note one spring day from the young novelist, mentioning the name of Madame Hamelin, and asking if she could call. "Sait-on jamais? Elle est peut-être jeune et jolie, cette femme de lettres. Le lendemain, la voici! Jeune et jolie, elle l'est! Et non seulement jolie, non seulement jeune, mais charmante, mais intelligente, mais pleine d'esprit. . . . Dix ans lui sont à l'instant même enlevés des épaules" (Billy 75).

Although Chateaubriand ultimately did not make more than a perfunctory mention of Allart as he wrote his *Mémoires d'Outre-Tombe* some 18 years later, there is evidence nearly everywhere else— particularly in the numerous biographies on the Enchanter—that she marked his life in a profoundly touching way. She was able to uncover a new side of the middle-aged writer—a spontaneity and a *joie de vivre* that had been lacking in his life for years. "Elle a libéré une part de sa nature, un être vif, presque joueur, presque résigné, ne dédaignant aucune des savoureuses réalités terrestres, spontané dans ses appétits et dans ses abdications."[4]

Furthermore, with her laughter, optimism, and gaiety, she was able to sustain his interest for many months, and even to divert his attention from richer and grander ladies. " . . . il aima Hortense qui l'aima: cette personne vive, complaisante et qui avait, avec un esprit de philosophie et de littérateur, un cœur de grisette, le divertit des grandes dames" (Beaunier 231).

No doubt aware of the rejuvenating effect her presence had on the stately diplomat, the "grisette" (which is defined roughly as a sprightly, independent working girl) herself related, "Il me reçut avec coquetterie, et se montra charmant et charmé. Son beau visage et sa bonne grâce me le firent trouver agréable. Il me traita avec beaucoup de distinction, et parla de nous revoir" (*EP* 117). In short, their first meeting was delightful for both. Hortense chatted excitedly to her sister Sophie about the visit. "Je disais mille choses de M. de Chateaubriand, et j'en étais ravie" (*EP*   117).

Hortense was surprised at just how soon he returned her visit. The next day, Easter Sunday, she took a walk in the area of Sainte-Marie-Majeure.   When she returned home, she learned that the ambassador had visited.   She wrote expressing disappointment that she had missed him, and inviting him to return.   He called again, a flower in his lapel, and returned many times after that.   Even several decades in retrospect, Hortense's awe over the romantic master is superlative. "Il revient plusieurs fois, il commença une sorte de cour; j'en étais surprise, j'en étais flattée, son ton plein de grâce m'était des plus agréables; son âge s'oubliait, et son beau et noble visage me plaisait" (*EP*   117).

Also, his sophistication and experience in life and literature made him compare most favorably even to her favorites among her former lovers. "C'est un homme déjà arrivé, déjà au bout de ces rêves, que Jérôme, que Libri m'avait tant exprimés. L'homme d'action, l'homme politique, l'écrivain, je l'abordais ici, c'était lui-même qui venait me parler d'action et de gloire" (*EP*   117-18).

Naturally, her infatuation was not only for the man himself, but also for the legend that surrounded him. "Du reste, cette jeune femme, qui éprouvait une tendresse véritable pour un illustre vieillard, aimait en lui, autant que lui, sa légende et le grand poème de son œuvre" (Beaunier 233).

Although she admitted that she still had some feelings for both Sampayo and Libri, her interest in other men seemed to diminish during this time—at least for the most part. Capponi visited and gave her a cameo ring with the figure of a dog running, and claimed he was running away as well. Chateaubriand entered as she was dispatching the servant to return the ring to its sender. "Vous voyez une femme bien mécontente," she told him. "C'est Italiens ne savent pas aimer" (*EP* 118).

The ambassador visited every day thereafter, his courtship becoming increasingly intense and possessive. One afternoon he became angry and stomped out when Hortense arrived home on the arm of another man, Don Michelangelo Caetani.

As always, Hortense is vague as to when their relationship was consummated physically, and gives no specific accounting thereof.[5] Chateaubriand's renewed and invigorated attitude, however, was a tell-tale sign to those who knew him. ". . . déjà on parlait dans Rome de sa gaité nouvelle" (*EP* 118).

In addition to the tenderness and passion, their relationship had its intellectual side. They adored stimulating conversation together on the current events of the day, although they disagreed on such fundamentals as politics and religion. Hortense dared to tell him she disagreed with him about his support of the war in Spain, and on his fervent Catholicism. Fortunately, she found his mind open enough that they could converse on just about any subject. Credit must be given to her own broad-minded attitude as well. "D'ailleurs il avait un esprit si vaste, si tolérant, une âme si élévée, si accessible, et un caractère si aimable, et si doux, qu'excepté sur la religion catholique, on pouvait toujours s'entendre avec lui. Je comprenais sa doctrine de la liberté unie à sa grandeur" (*EP* 120).

Chateaubriand was also valuable to her as a literary adviser and catalyst for her work. He read her manuscript of *Jérôme,* declared that the author had "du génie, que c'était admirable" (*EP* 118). Later, she would reflect, "M. de Chateaubriand m'excitait à des études fortes; il me disait que j'avais l'esprit mâle, qu'il fallait faire un ouvrage sérieux. Béranger me disait la même chose" (*EP* 187).

Many Chateaubriand biographers mention that the ambassador's interest in her novel was more gallantry and a desire for her person than true regard for her work. Hortense herself was sufficiently wise and realistic not to need a Chateaubriand biographer to point this out to her. She also suspected that, because of the many differences between them, their relationship could be of only limited duration:

> Un homme trouve du génie à la femme dont il est amoureux . . .
> Pouvait-il s'éprendre si vite? Et moi, devais-je le croire sincère?
> Pourquoi si peu de réflextion de mon côté? Pourquoi me laisse-je
> m'entraîner par un homme dont je n'aimais ni la religion ni la
> politique? Pouvions-nous jamais nous entendre avec cette distance
> d'âge et d'expérience? Ce ne pouvait être ici qu'une liaison
> passagère (*EP* 118-19).

Their differences notwithstanding, events in Italy soon were to bring Hortense and Chateaubriand to a more committed decision about their future together. Pope Leo XII had died Feb. 10, 1829. Chateaubriand, whose task it was to influence the appointment of a successor who would favor France's interests, was pleased with the appointment of Castiglioni, who, in April, became Pope Pius VIII. The ambassador was less satisfied with the appointment of the papal secretary, and—perhaps feeling a little jaded with diplomacy, anyway— asked for a leave of absence to be spent in Paris while he decided whether or not to tender his resignation as ambassador.

He hesitated for a short time, though. Since Madame de Chateaubriand was planning a trip to Paris herself, he considered staying behind in Rome—with Hortense. He wrote to to M. de

Marcellus on April 29, "Si Mme de Chateaubriand veut aller à Paris toute seule, je pourrais bien passer ici mon été. Je regrette Rome."[6] His wife thought better of this arrangement, and persuaded him to accompany her. "Mais 'la Chatte' ne se souciait pas de laisser 'le Chat' derrière elle: elle avait peur des petites souris . . . " (Séché 108-9). However, before leaving for Paris with Madame, he exacted from Hortense a promise that she would follow soon.

Back in Florence before her departure, she received visits from Libri, Capponi and Bargagli, all of whom knew why she was going to Paris.   Although Libri watched her leave with regret, he took scant satisfaction in the fact that it was Chateaubriand whom she preferred to him, and not Capponi.

With three-year-old Marcus in tow, Hortense left for Paris, not far behind Chateaubriand's departure.   Although her original intention was to stay for only three months, then return to Florence, she would not see Italy for several more years, as both France and England soon would claim a large portion of her destiny.   For the next few months of 1829, this new chapter in her relationship with Chateaubriand was a particularly glorious one.   She took lodgings on the Rue d'Enfer in the area of the Observatoire, near the Infirmerie Marie-Thérèse, where he and his wife had taken an apartment.   Céleste Chateaubriand busied herself with charity work at the infirmary, thus freeing the errant husband from her watchful eye and leaving him at liberty to pursue his new infatuation.

> . . . son époux, délivré de son regard perçant et de sa présence importune, courait allègrement retrouver Hortense. On le voit pendant que sa femme discute et s'efforce de ramener l'ordre dans sa 'fondation' ménacée, sortant par la petite porte de son jardin, fermant avec précaution la barrière de bois et s'éloignant pour rejoindre sa belle au Pont d'Austerlitz.[7]

Hortense and René spent every possible moment together.   ". . . et alors commencèrent pour eux des jours délicieux"   (Billy 78). Together, they corrected the galley proofs of her second novel, a skill in which she had lacked such expert guidance when she had published her previous works.   Chateaubriand had secured a publishing contract for *Jérôme* with Ladvocat, and predicted for it a great success.   As had Capponi, he counseled her to abandon novels in favor of history. "Il me disait souvent que j'étais observatrice. Il me conseillait les études sérieuses, me disait de laisser les romans pour l'histoire, que j'avais un talent fait pour paraître et un caractère fait pour dominer" (*EP* 124). (Although she would later pen lengthy histories of Florence and

Athens, Hortense never gave up fiction writing for historical research). Their rendez-vous were rich in emotion as well as in professional discussion. The aging author of *René* seemed to be, from the start, a victim of the *coup de foudre,* or love at first sight. "René de plus en plus épris, me disait qu'il n'avait jamais été aimé d'une femme si tendre" (*EP* 124). Furthermore, she was pleased at how favorably he compared in kindness and sensitivity to Sampayo:

> C'était la première fois que je trouvais dans un homme tant de grâce et de tendresse. Rien ici des façons dures ou amères de Jérôme. C'était en tout une bienveillance, une bonté, une égalité parfaite, une gaîté innocente, une moquérie inoffensive, toute l'amabilité de l'esprit unie à la grâce et à la politesse . . . . Il louait beaucoup, s'étonnait de mes idées . . . . Je recevais de lui, dans ce culte des muses, cette education *toute divine* qu'il a peinte dans la Grèce. (*EP* 124, Allart's italics).

The pair's rendezvous on July 18, 1829, at Étampes near Paris when Chateaubriand was on his way to the Pyrénées to take the waters at Cauterets has become a well-known moment of Romantic idyll. "Nous y dînâmes comme cachés au désert . . . Jamais plus élégante, plus gracieuse nature [de Chateaubriand] ne peut se rencontrer. Moi, j'étais très éprise . . . Nous étions vrais chacun, et charmés l'un de l'autre . . . Nous ne nous hâtions pas, nous aurions voulu retenir les heures" (*EP* 125).

They took drives in the countryside outside of Paris. In the area of Champ-de-Mars, rough and sandy terrain made them think of Roman fields. They returned there several times, making friends with a peasant woman who tended cows and offered them fresh milk. "Nous causions longuement en allant et revenant, sur mille sujets, moi mêlant beaucoup de gaité et de folies à mes propos" (*EP* 131).

There were other excursions outside of Paris, plus walks down the Champs-Elysées, dinner at the Jardin-des-Plantes, and rendez-vous on the bridge Austerlitz. Sometimes Marcus would come along, his governess keeping him a short distance away. "Mon amour prit un nouvel éveil, il fut vif, continuel . . . . Sa pensé, son génie, son visage, son amour s'emparèrent de ma vie; toutes mes impressions, depuis mon lever jusqu'à mon coucher, furent pleines de douceur et d'un enchantement croissant" (*EP* 130).

Years later, it was the description of their relationship in *Les Enchantements de Prudence* that would cause the work to be vilified by critics such as Barbey D'Aurevilly, who was scandalized at seeing a literary master in what he considered an undignified light (see Chapter

9).   Hortense, however, had no such sense of scandal   as her liaison
with the Enchanter continued in Paris through summer and fall 1829.
Earlier, she had written to Laure:

> Vous dites que la morale est absolue, mais rien n'est absolu.
> Vous la mesurez sur la perfection ou la modération. Ne vaudrait-il
> pas mieux le mesurer à l'espèce humaine? Je crois que la vertu
> même est relative, et que le seul vrai précepte est de faire, dans
> tous les temps, le plus de bien et le moins de mal qu'il est possible
> (*EP* 30).

Thus emboldened with her own charted moral course regarding the
pursuit of happiness, Hortense was not chagrined either during or
decades after her liaison with Chateaubriand. Furthermore, she was
feeling some reawakening of her feelings for another married man—
Sampayo.

Soon after her arrival in Paris, Hortense thought one day that she
saw her former lover pass by in a carriage. She was shaken. "Je restai
bouleversée . . . je connus d'abord le danger où j'étais venue" (*EP* 122).
A few days later, Sampayo contacted Hortense, asking to see Marcus
without having to see her.   Grateful for this attitude, knowing how
emotionally vulnerable she might be in Sampayo's presence,   she
arranged for father and son to meet for the first time—then left the
premises. She took advantage of the time alone to pay a visit to
Béranger, who had been jailed at La Force for nine months for the
publication of his anti-monarchist poem *Sacre,* which had run afoul of
Charles X.

She deliberately returned late, but not quite late enough, for
Sampayo was still there. "Il me demanda si j'avais toujours *confiance*
en lui.   Question inoüie!   Comment pouvait-il la faire?" (*EP* 122,
Allart's italics).   Not wishing to deal with what must have been a
troubling and bewildering question for someone who never wished to
let go completely of any of her former loves, she did not reply, and he
left.

She was tempted, however, even in the midst of her gratifying
relationship with Chateaubriand, to revive what she and Sampayo had
once had together. "Je songeai tout à coup de le revoir, rétablir ce qui
avait été malheureusement brisé, et cette fois, à jouer ma vie, à atteindre
ce but ou à mourir. S'il eût senti la moitié de ce que j'éprouvais, nous
nous étions liés encore, et mieux que jamais . . . cette passion existait
plus fort que jamais" (*EP* 127).

The idea of a second chance to transcend the less-than-perfect past
and to approach an ideal love with one's original beloved was dear to

Hortense, but she knew it was not to be. She and Sampayo did meet on occasion to discuss Marcus' future, but she kept her hopes and feelings to herself. *Jérôme ou le jeune prélat* was published anonymously, but Hortense's acquaintances, including the real-life "Jérôme," knew from whom it came. Once again, Sampayo was less than pleased about how Hortense had depicted him in a novel. More than one critic opted not to write a review of the book for fear of incurring his wrath. Although Hortense admitted to herself that she still loved the man who inspired her title character, she was relieved when he left for England shortly after the novel appeared (*EP* 127).

For reasons that are not clear, *Jérôme* is now the most difficult of all Allart's novels to acquire. Some original copies of the 1829 *Jérôme* may well exist in certain libraries or in private collections. However, the Bibliothèque Nationale in Paris has no catalogue listing for the novel, and research materials there indicate that it exists now only as part of *Les Enchantements de Prudence*.[8] This fact, however, is in no way a reflexion on the quality or readability of Allart's second novel.

In *Jérôme,* the author combines an accurate emotional depiction of her real-life experience with Sampayo in Paris with her newfound awe and respect for Roman and Catholic culture, which, despite her own Protestantism, truly fascinated her and commanded her respect. Even as Allart lambastes Catholic orthodoxy, use of the church for political gain, traditions of the priesthood, convent life, and the church's restrictions on individuals' freedoms, one senses in *Jérôme* the underpinnings of grudging admiration for Roman Catholicism as an administrative model and a world power, if not as a way to worship Christ. If only such a model could be placed in the hands of superior intellectuals, and not in those of ambitious, often corrupt clergymen!

> Although she rejects the Catholic Church as a religious institution, she . . . admires it as a worldly power . . . . In the realm of political theory, Hortense Allart believes that her feminist ideas could best be realized modeled after the Catholic Church. One could simply replace the hierarchy based on wealth and brutality by a hierarchy based on talent, as if by an act of will. If she could will herself to be whatever she wanted, could not whole peoples and governments do the same?" (Rabine 169).

Again, this question would be treated in more detail in her 1836 *La Femme et la Démocratie de Nos Temps.*

The principal theme of *Jérôme,* however, involves less emphasis on Catholic politics than on the author's feminist concern—that is, her unapologetic assertion that the strong, independent woman is held in unfair disrepute, and that a weak man who lets himself be manipulated by society's traditional expectations should not be allowed—as he was, tragically, in every one of Madame de Staël's fictional works—to be the heroine's undoing.

The first-person narrator is Hortense's young self—this time named Elisabeth—in the guise of a young orphan recently arrived in Rome from England. She describes her childhood as marked by a certain hardness, replaced at age 20 by a sadness and boredom. " . . . mon enthousiasme se changea en douleur; l'ennui s'empara de ma vie, et elle devint par moments si sombre, que je songeais presque à y mettre fin."[9] Certain other characters in the novel were based on Hortense's real-life acquaintances as well. Besides the depiction of Monsignor Piccolomini as Dom Clément, Capponi appears as the Toscan nobleman Torelli, Filippo Caetani is recreated as the Prince Caïus, and Libri is represented as Giampaolo. Regrettably, these last three characters are absent from the shortened version of *Jérôme* in *Les Nouveaux Enchantements.*

Since the death of Elisabeth's tutor, she has taken her inheritance, and, bolstered by her own independence and initiative, has made her way to Italy. Again, in the Staëlian tradition, the transition from English to Italian culture was singularly exhilarating for the heroine, and her melancholia has given way to a delicious reawakening of the soul. "Le passé me sembla rapproché de moi; les siècles et les distances s'effaçaient" (*Jér.* 244).

The transition, however, also entails a certain amount of negative cultural shock, as the heroine realizes the overweening power of Catholicism on the society. "Je me trouvais dans un pays séparé du mien par des siècles, dans un pays dont les mœurs, les idées, la grossièreté monastique rappellent trop à une protestante de longs malheurs et le gouvernement de l'Eglise" (*Jér.* 244).

Elisabeth arrives in Italy with a letter introducing her to Sir John Erval, a well-to-do English Catholic. She is eager to meet Sir John's 26-year-old son, Jérôme, a prelate and poet, who is touted as having one of the finest creative minds in Italy. Jérôme might be seen as a kind of a male Corinne, as his father is a staid Englishman, and his mother an Italian princess. However, despite his artistic gifts, Jérôme seems to have a preponderance of British austerity in his character, and is given to the same bursts of bitterness and mockery that characterized Sampayo.

Elisabeth soon learns that Jérôme's family has slated him for a powerful future in the church—to be a cardinal, or even the pope. He reveals that his ambitions are less for religious goals than a desire for political power (and that, in his country, Catholic power and political influence go hand-in-hand). "Je ferai tout pour être pape; mais si le sort me le refuse, on a vu des cardinaux governer le pape et l'état, et c'est là où j'aspire" (*Jér.* 249).

However, Jérôme, who is handsome, delicate, and in tenuous health, has not yet taken his final vows. When he and Elisabeth meet, a special closeness unites them immediately. ". . . nos esprits s'entendaient, une douce intimité s'établissait entre nous. Nous devinions nos pensées avant de les exprimer" (*Jér.* 247). As their relationship develops, Elisabeth feels its transcendent, romantic power. " . . . j'avais quitté la terre; j'étais entrée dans un monde, dans une existence inconnue; j'avais pris une autre âme" (*Jér.* 255).

Jérôme, who is experiencing passion for the first time, is swept along to the point that he promises to abandon the church for her and leave Italy. "Dans ces élans de la passion, nous nous abandonnions à la destinée; la passion était pour nous la loi suprême: l'instinct, la nature, nos cœurs, tout nous défendait de la combattre . . . [Jérôme] répondait que son amour ne s'éteindrait qu'avec lui, que c'était son souffle de vie" (*Jér.* 260).

The progress of their relationship—set against the backdrop of glorious Roman ruins—the yearly carnival (which combines Catholic traditions with ancient Roman mythology), the pope blessing the crowd from the Vatican, hell-fire sermons delivered during Lent, Easter Mass at Saint Peter's, and other such morsels of ethnic richness—is an emotional roller coaster consisting mostly of Jérôme's vacillating exhilaration, guilt, and fear of his father's fierce authority over him. Elisabeth worries that his love ultimately will be too compromised by these other concerns: ". . . il me semble qu'il y avait de l'hésitation dans son amour, et que sa douleur lui faisait entrevoir avec effroi ce qu'il faisait" (*Jér.* 259).

Jérôme reneges on his promise to leave the priesthood for her, she gives him his liberty, they agree to part, they cry, reconcile, and the conflict goes on, as Allart takes the opportunity to insert her admiration as well as her criticism about another aspect of Catholic orthodoxy. Jérôme's cousin, Don Clément, also a prelate, wishes for his 18-year-old sister, Settimia, a novice nun, to take her final vows, although she has doubts about making the lifetime commitment. While Jérôme defends convent life to Elisabeth with traditional platitudes ("Croyez-vous que ces femmes soient malheureuses? Elles échappent aux mille peines de la vie" [*Jer.* 267]), Elisabeth finds the idea repugnant—especially for their modern and enlightened times:

J'étais révoltée. Un Anglais! dans le XIX^em siècle! faire des
discours et amener une scène qu'on trouve dans les romans qui
peignent les mœurs des anciens temps. . . . La vie de ces femmes,
la savez-vous? Quand j'ai entendu parler d'elles, inquiète de leur
sort, j'ai consulté à Rome leurs confesseurs et leurs médecins . . . .
elles meurent dans de lentes souffrances et dans le désespoir, ou
bien enfin que la nature s'égare et qu'elles tombent dans le dernier
degré de l'avalissement (*Jer.* 267-68).

When Elisabeth continues to denounce the families of young
women who force them into convent life, Jérôme agrees to persuade his
father (Settimia's uncle) not to force her to take her final vows, but to
give her a dowry instead.   Sir John acquiesces, but is suspicious of
why Jérôme acted in such a way for Settmia, and begins to be afraid of
the power Elisabeth has over his son.   As for Elisabeth, she is worried
about this new indication of how weak Jérôme is—particularly before
his father. "Je me rappelai les discours de son père; incapable de
comprendre entièrement son fils, il en savait assez pour le dominer"
(*Jer.* 274).
    Sir John, in turn, speaks with contempt about the strong,
independent woman that Elisabeth is.   "Cette femme est une femme
forte, dites-vous; laissez-la donc triompher d'un sentiment si nouveau;
qu'elle aille dans son pays trouver un mari et suivre sa carrière de femme
et de mère" (*Jer.* 276).   Despite a recent audience with the pope, and
his visions of a great clerical career, Jérôme still hesitates between
ambition and love.   His father tells him to beware of Elisabeth's
power.   "C'est une femme, lui dit-il, qui voudra vous gouverner,
directement d'abord parce qu'elle est hautaine, et aussi indirectement
parce qu'elle est femme.   Prenez-y garde. . . . Elle a un pouvoir plus
grand, fondé sur ses charmes" (*Jer.* 280).
    Despite Elisabeth's passion for Jérôme, her lover's weakness in the
face of his father's authoritarianism begins to wear down her devotion.
"Une sorte de dégoût, de toutes les impressions la plus insupportable, la
plus redoutable, la plus terrible, naquit en moi et se soutint quelques
jours" (*Jer.* 281).   His lack of resolve seems to allow every influence
to militate against their love.   "Tantôt amant passionné, tantôt fils
repentant, il me désolait sans me détacher" (*Jer.* 285).
    It is at this point that Allart's departure from the typical fate that
Madame de Staël heaped upon all the heroines of her novellas and
novels is most evident.   Rather than allow Elisabeth slowly to
crumble before the forces of Roman Catholic tradition as well as the
power of a disdainful patriarch, and to be devastated by the weakness of
a lover who lacks the desire and the will to stand up to such forces,

Allart gives us a heroine who, blithely unaware that *she really should not be able to do this in her time and place*, takes command of her own fate.

"Her oblivion to the realities of her society reveals itself most precisely in her views of religion and politics," says Rabine (169). "She writes as if she is totally unaware of doing or thinking anything out of the ordinary, unaware of the type of society she lived in, even unaware of the attitude a serious rebel was supposed to assume . . . . Hortense Allart's heroines take it for granted that societal restrictions cease to exist for anyone who simply refuses them" (160-61).

Allart's Elisabeth, frustrated though she might be by Jérôme's ultimate inability to throw off age-old religious and political shackles and make her romantic dreams come true, simply will not be destroyed by the restrictions and the prejudices of the status quo. Furthermore, she is sufficiently self-analytical, even in the depths of an intense emotional relationship, to realize that Jérôme's weakness is as much—or more—to blame for their problem as is her unconventional nature. The knowledge that his paralyzing indecisiveness is proving him unworthy of her will allow her eventually to let him go with a minimum of personal trauma. "Sa faiblesse seule, et non pas mon courage, m'inspirait ce dessein; il m'eût tuée si j'avais toujours cru Jérôme tel qu'il m'avait paru d'abord" (*Jér.* 281).

Instead of accepting Jérôme's lifelong devotion to his priesthood as something by which she must be hopelessly victimized, Elisabeth looks squarely at his attitude as an unfair inconvenience which she should not and *cannot* tolerate. Whereas he regards their love not as something natural and good, but as an infraction of his principles, she sees love as a right, and not as something that goes against duty and virtue.

As Jérôme's vacillation between love and his religious calling continues through the waning pages of the novel, Elisabeth, though still devoted to him, begins to dream of a man with a stronger will and a truer capacity for love. "Mécontente, indignée, exaltée, je rêvais un autre amour, je rêvais un homme qui sût aimer; et honteuse alors de cette sorte d'infidélité, je me méprisais moi-même, *quand tout le tort était à lui*" (*Jér.* 288, my emphasis).

Far from considering—or even conceiving of—self-destruction in the vein of Delphine and Corinne, Elisabeth resolves, with surprisingly little emotional agony, to return to England and to leave behind all hopes of a future with Jérôme. "Je voyais l'homme qui m'avait séduite disparaître: je ne songeais qu'à fuir et à l'oublier" (*Jér.* 292). She is happy to be with child, and the thought of motherhood gives her courage. Elisabeth claims that she hopes to pass on to her child only *male* qualities. "Je voulais ne passer à mon enfant que des qualités mâles; je repoussais les larmes et la faiblesses" (*Jér.* 292). Interestingly, though, these so-called "male" traits no doubt will be passed to the child from Elisabeth herself, and not from the father, for it is only she who possesses strength and resolve.

Elisabeth's story ends with her realization that she never should have left the decision-making power to Jérôme, who was incapable of such a responsibility. "Ainsi je le quittai après avoir toujours fait avec lui, depuis le commencement jusqu'à la fin, le contraire de ce qu'il fallait faire. Il avait besoin qu'on le prît par sa bonté, qu'on le guidât fermement et doucement; j'avais au contraire tout laissé dépendre de lui" (*Jér.* 293).

She concludes by speculating on the value of publishing her story as a caveat for other young women in a similar position. "Je pensai seulement qu'il ne serait peut-être pas sans utilité qu'une femme donnât un pareil exemple. Une faute pareille n'offense pas la loi éternelle . . . . trop de femmes en ont souffert, et trop d'enfants en ont péri" (*Jér.* 293).

Allart is quick to assure readers that her heroine, in her moment of self-discovery, can and will learn from her mistakes and build upon her experience to become a stronger, better person. Already, she speaks of a new relationship that is beckoning: " . . . un nouveau lien m'offrit comme un appui et un droit . . . " (*Jer.* 293). Once again, contrary to Madame de Staël's literary alter-egos, Allart's protagonist will not allow her moment of truth to be her downfall or society's triumphant "I told you so."

Thus, *Jérôme* was published, and, whether future readers were to know or not that it was a tale based on a true experience, it did stand as just what Allart intended—as a warning to young women about the heartache that would result from involvement with indecisive and unworthy men.

Although the novel circulated well among Hortense's friends ("J'en reçus beaucoup de compliments," [*EP* 129]), published reviews of *Jérôme* were few. This was due partly to Sampayo's influence in suppressing them, and partly because the novel enjoyed only modest sales to the general public. Also, as an anonymous review in the December 23, 1829, issue of *Le Temps* attests, most of Parisian literary society was ready to accept neither such an independent and strong-willed heroine as Elisabeth, nor the straightforward writing style of an author who championed the superior woman:

> Il est à remarquer en outre que les femmes qui veulent s'affranchir des strictes lois de leur sexe par une résolution d'éclat,

n'ont pas assez réfléchi que c'était la chose du monde la plus banale, et qu'il fallait plutôt baisser les yeux que les lever pour voir un très grand nombre d'antécédens de ce genre, antécédens sur lesquels il faut jeter un voile pudique. A quoi servira le génie, s'il ne nous enseigne qu'à descendre?[10]

The reviewer also urges the author not to "be an attorney for the seven deadly sins," although he does not give a synopsis of the plot of *Jérôme*, or point out where and how such sins are described or defended. He takes the opposing view of Allart on superior women, claiming that female genius needs to be subdued rather than kindled, heartened, and judged by rigorous standards. The review continues, "Plus on y trouve de supériorité réelle et de talent, plus nous devons engager son auteur à mieux comprendre sa vocation, à tirer meilleur parti de sa plume. Ajoutez à cela qu'il est d'une femme, comme le trahit ça et là cette finesse de perspicacité, ce coloris passioné."

Finally, however, the reviewer concedes that the author of *Jérôme* had an admirable writing style. "Du reste, coloris brillant, tableaux variés, style pur et suave, telles sont les principales qualités de cet ouvrage. Les caractères ne nous semblent pas être expliqués par les faits avec autant d'énergie que sous la plume de l'auteur . . ." (quoted by Uffenbeck 131).

This review angered Béranger, who wrote to Hortense, "Quelle est la personne de votre connaissance qui s'est avisée de vous juger ainsi, et de parler de votre héros d'une si singulière manière? Cet article ne m'a pas satisfait."[11]

Hortense most likely took such reviews in her usual stride. It is not known, however, if she ever knew about Stendhal's quiet defection from support of her literary efforts. Although there is no record of what he himself may have said about *Jérôme*, he lent his copy of the book to a friend, Madame Virginie Ancelot, who returned it to him with a deprecating note:

Voici *Jérôme*. Je suis désolée de le trouver très inférieur à *Gertrude*. Il y a encore moins de variété; c'est toujours *elle,* et comme *elle,* est une exception, l'ouvrage ne peut avoir un succès de vogue, car il ne sympathisera avec personne. Ce n'est pas comme cela que l'on sent et que l'on pense généralement. Tous les personnages du roman ne sont connus que dans leurs rapport avec l'héroïne . . . . Il n'y a pas assez de réalité dans tout cela; les sentiments sont exaltés et se perdent dans le vague.[12]

This letter is the last of any known correspondence between or about the friendship of Allart and Stendhal. He would soon leave Paris and not return until 1833, and Hortense's personal interests would be sustained by Chateaubriand until such as time as she made her first trip to England in spring 1830, when they would be focused on Bulwer-Lytton.

In the meantime, Chateaubriand lavished attention upon her. Although she missed Italy as the summer of 1829 turned into fall, she still reveled in her numerous getaways with Chateaubriand, and in her ever-growing attachment to him. "Je l'aimais, certes, et parfaitement. J'en étais amoureuse, doucement, heureusement, sans crainte, sans trouble, et c'était lui qui modérait mon cœur" (*EP* 133).   She also reported with pleasure that Chateaubriand, in his *Mémoire*, would say of the year 1829, *"cette année fut la plus heureuse de ma vie"* (*E P* 130, Allart's italics).

If Chateaubriand was a little amused at his own sudden passion for a young, fledging writer, so was all of Paris. "L'auteur du *Génie du Christianisme,* le restaurateur de la religion catholique en France, l'ancien ministre, le plus illustre soutien de la monarchie légitime, le représentant du roi de France auprès du successeur de Sainte-Pierre, faisait des folies pour une petite femme de lettres! . . . Et, si Chateaubriand s'amusait, Paris aussi" (Beaunier 253).

With Madame de Chateaubriand busy with her charity work at the Infirmerie Marie-Thérèse, and Madame de Récamier occupied, as always, with her elegant salon at the Abbaye-au-Bois, the unlikely lovers were free to spend long periods of time in each other's company.   Their attachment was not a secret for long.   One of Chateaubriand's contemporaries, the Count de Rémusat, wrote to his friend, the baron de Barante, in a letter dated Oct. 25, 1929, "M. de Chateaubriand . . . est généralement fort découragé, il s'est avisé d'être l'amant de mademoiselle Allart (vous savez qui c'est) qui cherche à se faire ici une certaine existence et un salon de gens d'esprit. Elle vient de Rome où elle a fait un roman intitulé *Jérôme* sur son aventure avec M. Sampayo."[13]

The Enchanter's feelings for Hortense were more melancholic that they had been for almost any other woman . . . "et la mélancholie était le sentiment qui entrait le plus loin dans l'âme ardente et triste de René" (Beaunier 254).   He was not delusional, however, about what likely would be the outcome of their relationship. Though Hortense pledged her fidelity, he replied, "que j'étais trop jeune pour en répondre, que je ne savais pas ce qui m'attendait" (*EP* 131). He also had a rather morbid preoccupation with old age and death. "Si j'oubliais son âge, lui ne l'oubliait pas, il me parlait souvent de sa mort, et il aimait de voir mes yeux se mouiller de larmes" (*EP* 131).   Furthermore, Hortense was aware that the two other women (Madame de Chateaubriand and Madame de Récamier) had a far stronger hold on him than she—"il était tenu chez lui et dans le monde par des liens tyranniques; deux femmes âgées, dont je n'étais pas jalouse (la sienne et une autre)" (*EP* 130)— but she refused to let this trouble their happiness.

One day in the countryside, Chateaubriand dictated to her the passage from his *Etudes Historiques,* which would appear in print in April 1831: "Je mourrai sur ton sein, tu me trahiras, et je te le pardonnerai" (*EP* 133). Often he would have her read aloud to him passages from his own works. Her elocution of his *Le Martyr d'Eudore* made him weep. "Il ne pouvait retenir ses larmes, un jour, il pleurait, je lisais toujours, il allait jusqu'aux sanglots" (*EP* 134).

She also read to him frequently the poetry and songs of Béranger. Chateaubriand, who also had penned songs in his career, listened to the sentimental, patriotic ballads with rapt admiration "Il l'écoutait, ravi de cette belle poésie, attendri, touché, exalté" (Billy 89).

The year 1830 began amid rumblings of political upheaval and an uncertain future for Charles X. In January, Hortense began her collaboration with *La Nationale,* writing articles on Rome, Milan, Florence and Naples. A few weeks earlier, she had broken into the Parisian free-lance writing scene with a piece entitled "Des Femmes" for another journal, *Keepsake Français, ou souvenir de littérature contemporaine.* Her two-page article, a defense of the "femme supérieure, " echoed and built upon Libri's idea that society expects too little out of intelligent women, judges them by an inferior standard, and therefore, stifles their potential. "[C]e qui fait le malheur des femmes supérieures, c'est le peu de proportion entre les devoirs qu'on leur a assignés dès leur première jeunesse, et ce besoin progressif des grandes facultés qui se déploient . . . . Entourées d'êtres dignes d'elles, de quelle pure et austère félicité ne seraient-elles pas capables."[14]

During the first weeks of 1830, Hortense also was working on a history of Italy, and beginning to write a new novel, to be called *Sextus ou le Romain des Maremmes,* which would be published in 1832.

As soon as Béranger was released from La Force in early 1830, Hortense began immediate plans to get him together with Chateaubriand. These two particular Frenchmen were unlikely mutual admirers. Each was a master of literary sentimentality (Séché dares to call Béranger "le père de romantisme," admitting that this title is usually credited to Chateaubriand [96]), but their political positions were hardly in sync. Chateaubriand had been serving loyally in Charles X's diplomatic corps, while Béranger was riding a crest of popularity with the ever-growing, anti-Charles X contingent. Although Béranger's songs and poetry are not read or sung much in France today, it was his poetic spirit that spurred the July Monarchy. " . . . il représente mieux que personne l'esprit fondeur et libéral qui détermina la Révolution de Juillet. "[15]

At Hortense's arrangement, Chateaubriand paid Béranger a visit, asking the poet to write a song just for him. He also offered to use his influence to get the his new friend appointed to the *Académie Française.* The gentle, always self-effacing Béranger, who had a special affinity for Chateaubriand's *Le Génie du christianisme,* was overwhelmed. He modestly refused the chance for the *Académie,* and agonized as to whether he was talented enough or sensitive enough to the Enchanter's point of view to do justice to a song in his honor. "J'ai eu beau être élevé à l'école de M. de Chateaubriand et lui avoir les plus grandes obligations littérairement parlant," he wrote to Hortense. "J'ai fait de mon talent un usage si opposé à cette education qu'il n'est pas possible que le maître puisse en faire un grand cas."[16]

Three weeks later, bolstered by Hortense's encouragement and by the fact that Chateaubriand could recite from memory some of his songs, Béranger had gained self-confidence. In another letter, he thanked Hortense for bringing the two of them together. "J'aurais dû au moins lui répondre que, si vous ne m'aviez pas prédit sa visite, je n'aurais osé croire qu'il me fît cet honneur."[17] By early 1831, and after the July Monarchy had sent Chateaubriand to Switzerland in an indignant, self-imposed exile, Béranger had produced the commissioned *chanson,* entitled "A M. de Chateaubriand: Air d'Octavie." Although Béranger was in a tight spot with the task of honoring a writer whose political views were so far from his own, his effort proved that he could be a diplomat in literary matters. His poem begins and ends with the stanza:

> Chateaubriand, pourquoi fuir ta patrie,
> Fuir notre amour, notre encre et nos soins?
> N'entends-tu pas la France qui s'écrie:
> "Mon beau ciel pleure une étoile de moins?"

The poem also credited Chateaubriand for devotion to freedom and service to humanity. Both the exilee and the French public were pleased with the poet's efforts. Henceforth, Béranger and Chateaubriand would be lifelong friends.

The poem's literary merit was less important than its ultimate effect on its subject. "C'est mal écrit, mais l'idée est bonne" (Beaunier 273). The verses had evoked much regret about Chateaubriand's exil, as seen printed in various newspapers. The Enchanter was flattered enough to take the poem literally and return to France by October 1831 (although other political intrigues would send him back to Switzerland for another short-term exile in summer 1832).

Late in January 1830, Hortense, who had already inhabited three different apartments since her arrival in Paris, was about to rent another lodging for herself and Chateaubriand, when she received a letter from a friend in England—described in *Les Enchantements de Prudence* as a certain "madame M.," (*EP* 142)—inviting Hortense to visit her in London.   She arranged to leave Marcus behind, and to make the trip.

Chateaubriand, at the time caught up in a whirlwind of activity, was rash enough to encourage her to go—"à passer un ou deux mois à courir" (*EP*   142).   It was a fatal idea.   Hortense would return to Paris in less than six months, but the bloom would be off the rose of their love.   ". . . mais quand elle revint, le charme était rompu, elle avait trouvé une nouvelle chaussure à son pied" (Séché 129).

Hortense's swift and fervent plunge into her relationship with English parliamentarian Henry Bulwer-Lytton would open an entirely new vista in her quest for exhilaration in love.   Although Sampayo would remain the most emotional love of her life, Bulwer would be her greatest passion.   "Sampayo a bien été l'homme d'Hortense, celui qui a marqué le plus fortement sa vie sentimentale, si sa vie intellectuelle a subi d'autre influence et si, physiquement, c'est Bulwer qui a compté le plus" (Billy 85).

Hortense explains that, up until this moment, she had not experienced the kind of sensual delight she was about to discover in England.   "Je partis sans avoir jamais connu ce qu'on appelle vraiment *l'amour* (her italics).   Jamais je n'avais le moindre idée de volupté. J'étais entrainée comme malgré moi vers une contrée que j'avais parfois rêvée en Italie, et où la curiosité et la politique m'attiraient" (*EP* 142).

She also put some of the blame for her future infidelity on Chateaubriand.   When he encouraged her to go to England, he should have guessed what was likely to happen!   "Ce fut son imprudence s'il m'aimait.   Chateaubriand eût dû savoir comment il était dangereux d'envoyer la jeunesse errer à l'aventure, surtout dans les langeurs du printemps" (*EP*   142).

Her caring and her devotion to Chateaubriand would never be over, but the ardor would be forever replaced by a new man and a new adventure that would take her to the zeniths of happiness and to the depths of frustration in a maelstrom of travel, danger, and reinvigorated literary productivity.

Notes

[1]Ciureanu, Petre. "Lettere di Hortense Allart à Gino Capponi," *Studi Francesi,* 1 (1957): 245.

[2]Cirueanu 246-49. In another letter printed in this collection, dated March 31, 1830, Allart wrote from Paris, and mentioned sending Capponi a copy of her latest novel *Sextus,* which she says he inspired. In another letter from Paris, dated Feb. 7, 1836, she sent Capponi a copy of her brochure *La Femme et la Démocratie de Nos Temps,* and solicited his comments on it.

[3]Quoted by Billy 74.

[4]Marie-Jeanne Durry. *La Vieillesse de Chateaubriand,* 2 vols. (Paris: Le Divan, 1933) 1:509.

[5]At least there is no mention of this delicate topic that made it into the final printings of any of the editions of *Les Enchantements de Prudence.* Uffenbeck mentions (107), that in the original manuscript, preserved in the Spoelberch de Lovenjou collection (D 583, folios 263-97), there appears in the discussion of Chateaubriand a marginal notation: "Il me demande une autre preuve encore—qui lui fut alors accordée." Uffenbeck says this "preuve," if it indeed refers to consummation, would place the act somewhere between May 7, the date Chateaubriand announced his imminent return to Paris, and May 16, the date of his actual departure from Rome. Of course, the "preuve" might also refer to his request that Hortense follow him to Paris.

[6] From*Mémoires d'Outre-Tombe.* quoted by Séché 108.

[7]Marie-Louise Pailleron. "Hortense Allart et Chateaubriand I," *La Revue des Deux Mondes.* CX (Jan. 1, 1940) 76.

[8]A kind and very patient man working in the reference section of the Bibliothèque Nationale helped me search at length for a call number or any reference to an exisiting copy of *Jérôme.* Whereas copies of all of Allart's other fictional works exist there either as original books or on microfiche or microfilm, no copy or reproduction of *Jérôme* in its original 1829 published form is available for perusal. One reference book the employee finally found indicated that *Jérôme* exists now only as a part of *Les Enchantements de Prudence* (in which the whole novel is not told, and the Roman setting is not evident). Fortunately, Allart included a more thorough, though still expurgated, form of *Jérôme* in her 1873 *Les Nouveaux Enchantements,* 243-93, which still can be found in hard-copy form. It is from this copy that I will quote.

[9]Mme P. de Saman *Jérôme ou le jeune prélat, Les Nouveaux Enchantements.* (Paris: Calmann Lévy, Editeur, 1882) 243-44. (Subsequent references to this work will appear in parentheses after the quotation and will be indicated by the abbreviation *Jer.*)

[10]Review printed in the *feuilleton* of *Le Temps, journal des progrès politiques, scientifiques, littéraires et industriels,* Dec. 23, 1829, cols. 821-828, quoted by Uffenbeck 130.

[11]Letter from Béranger to Hortense Allart dated Jan. 8, 1830, quoted by Séché 275.

[12]Letter from Madame Virginie Ancelot, dated "1830", by Henri Martineau, has been published in *Cent soixante lettres à Stendhal (1810-1842),* ed. Henri Martineau (Paris, 1947), I, 213-14, quoted by Uffenbeck 132, and by Beaunier 251, Ancelot's italics.

[13]*Souvenirs du baron de Barante de l'Académie française (1782-1866),* ed. Claude de Barante (Paris, 1892), III, 523-24, quoted by Uffenbeck 138.

[14] Quoted by Uffenbeck 142.

[15]Séché 80. (In this same paragraph, Seché lapses into first person in his enthusiasm over the friendship that Hortense helped spark between Chateaubriand and Béranger: "C'est en 1830, que ces deux homes se lièrent ensemble, et comme, à mon avis, elle n'a rien fait de plus glorieux en ce monde, je suis heureux de dire tout de suite que c'est Hortense Allart qui leur servit de trait d'union.")

[16]Quoted by Séché 116.

[17]Quoted by Séché 122.

Chapter 4

Sextus: The Channel Crossings (1830-1832)

When Hortense departed for England for the first time, she had no idea that the trip, intended originally to be merely a short visit with a woman friend, would be the first step in a stormy, often frenzied five-year attachment to Henry Bulwer-Lytton. Amid the numerous ruptures, reconciliations, adieux, and tearful reunions, their relationship eventually would cause her to cross the English Channel 14 times.

This tumultuous, yet tender and passionate liaison is the subject of an entire 1961 book, *Hortense Allart et Henry Bulwer-Lytton* by Juliette Decreus. The author meticulously traces the events leading up to and running throughout the relationship and its aftermath, and also speculates on the great question about these two gifted, vivacious young people who were so enthralled with one another: Why did they never marry?

William Henry Lytton-Earle Bulwer, later the first Baron of Wood and Dalling, was handsome and charming, but not one to rest solely on his more superficial endowments, for he was also brilliant and driven. At the time Hortense met him in August 1830, when he was 29, and she just a few weeks short of that birthday, he already had begun a career in international diplomacy and was being groomed by his family and by his own heady ambition for distinguished service in the British Parliament. He had already run unsuccessfully for a seat in the House of Commons, and was about to present himself as a candidate for the next elections.

Hortense herself first described Bulwer, to whom she refers in *Les Enchantements de Prudence* by the pseudonym "M. Henry Warwick," as "un ambitieux, mais un dandy" (*EP* 144). She adds that he was "occupé de la mode et des chevaux" (*EP* 144).   Involved though he was with fashion, horses, and women, it was his love of politics, and his affinity for other countries, their cultures and their governments that always would win out in any conflict of interests in his life.   At the age of 22, he had left England, and shown a courageous and distinctly non-dandified side of his character by taking part in the Greek war of independence, although a case of malaria sent him back to England before he had seen much action. (Hortense would later note that this decision to leave Greece when he fell ill, was a mark of his good sense—even more admirable than the actions of Lord Byron, who had died fighting for Greece in 1824, shortly before Henry's arrival there.   She states,   "Cet héroïsme et cette sagacité firent [Henry] beaucoup valoir à mes yeux" (*EP*   145).

Bulwer's political aspirations and lust for adventure were only a part of his character, for, at the time that Hortense met him, he was already a published poet and author.   Amid his interest in other countries, he particularly adored France and Bonaparte.   His *Ode on the death of Napoleon; lines on the Neapolitan Revolution and other poems,* had been printed by London, Gossling and Egley in 1822.

Decreus calls his poetry "l'œuvre d'un jeune homme cultivé et non d'un poète."[1] Nonetheless, his verses, which consist of the two poems in the title, plus a second poem on Napoleon, another poem dedicated to his mother, another dedicated to his brother Edward, and eight love poems ("ou pour parler plus justement, de poèmes galants, petites chansons ou guitares, bien scandées [Decreus 19]), are sincere and sentimental, and adequately mirror the Romantic style of the day set by such English contemporaries as Percy Bysshe Shelley.

In his *Ode on the death of Napoleon* Bulwer speculates on why the emperor was punished for his ambition, and wonders why he did not seek death at Waterloo rather than to allow himself to be exiled and mocked by other nations. He ends the poem by describing a Bonaparte still admired in France:

> Oh! 'tis a blessed thing to know,
> Tho' but beloved by few,
> That there is one in weal or woe,
> Who will remember *you.* [2]

Also, at about this same time, Henry had already become the subject of someone else's novel. Hortense noted in *Les Enchantements de Prudence* that, at the time that she met him, he was "un jeune homme dont le caractère à la foi léger, aimable et ambitieux, avait déjà fait le sujet d'un très joli roman en deux volumes qui avait eu un grand

Henry Bulwer-Lytton at age 24
(From the Cabinet of Estampes, British Museum, London)

succès" (*EP* 143). (She does not, however, mention the title or author of this novel).

If all this were not enough to attract Hortense to him, Bulwer also belonged to the oldest artistocracy in England, and she was always one to be impressed by venerable genealogy. She noted that his lineage could be traced back to the first Normans to invade England in 1066, and at his birth, the family still possessed lands that had been given to their ancestor Turold Bulwer, who had fought with William at the Battle of Hastings (*EP* 143-44).

Henry was born at 31 Bakerstreet in London, the second of three sons of General William-Earle Bulwer and Elisabeth-Barbe Lytton, on Feb. 13, 1801.   His mother, herself the descendant of ancient Welsh and British royalty, was a proud aristocrat who was determined to impress upon her three sons, William, Henry, and Edward (the last, a successful novelist, would become the most famous in the family), a notion of their superior status and potential.

> Elle continua de les diriger, de les cultiver, de les modeler non en obscurs seigneurs terriens, soucieux seulement de la prospérité de leur domaine, mais en hommes distingués qui jouassent un rôle dans le monde, l'état, la société, les lettres, les sciences ou les arts . . . . de véritables Lytton pour tout dire, imprégnés de ses propres goûts et de ses propres ambitions (Decreus 30).

Elisabeth-Barbe Lytton, who was fortified with a background in *belles lettres* that surpassed that of most young women of her station, had begun writing poetry at age 14, and by 1826, she consented to a private publication of her poems. She also drew, painted, and played guitar, and wished to instill in her sons the same talents and refinement, as well as a respect for religion.   (In this last quest, she was successful with both her eldest and youngest offspring, but not with Henry).

Widowed at age 31, when Henry was but six years old, Mrs. Bulwer turned to her mother for help with the education of her lively, headstrong middle son.   The grandmother, who soon made Henry her favorite, was responsible for teaching her grandson his elegant manners, which Hortense was to admire in him,   as well as his special charisma—"cet art si difficile de briller sans se faire remarquer, de se faire valoir par une réflexion pertinente glissée à propos et ce souci de plaire sans paraître s'y efforcer" (Decreus 31).

Henry was sent to a school at Sunbury in Middlesex, where his brother Edward joined him two years later, then to the prestigious school of Harrow. Young Edward, who proved too delicate to withstand the rigors of Harrow, was placed with a tutor at Ealing. He and Henry would not become close until the two studied together at Cambridge (where their elder brother, William, had preceded them).

At the university, Henry read voraciously and with much enthusiasm. However, according to Edward, who himself was preparing more conscientiously for a parliamentary career, Henry read "au hasard et sans méthode" (Decreus 20). Upon the death of his grandmother and his inheritance of her considerable fortune, Henry left Cambridge, and turned his attention to serious studies on his own. He soon published his *Lines on the Neopolitan Revolution,* which quickly gave him the reputation as a champion of underdog nations and peoples, and, in his aristocratic milieu, made him a controversial figure. "[Les vers] posaient leur auteur en ennemi des nations opprimées et en avocat de l'indépendance des peuples" (Decreus 21). He became involved with a London society that espoused Greek philosophy, and soon gained an irresistible desire to go fight in the homeland of Homer.

Just before leaving for the war zone in 1824, he published with Chiswick a second work in verse, a satire entitled *Today and Yesterday.* The verses included quotations that showed Henry an apt disciple of Horace, Euripides, Samuel Johnson, Rousseau, Voltaire, and others. These last two sources were favorites of his late grandfather, Richard Warburton Lytton, an erudite, liberal Englishman who had hobnobbed with French Revolutionary philosophers at his estate in Boulogne before the Reign of Terror forced him to flee back to England. Of course, Rousseau and Voltaire were dear to Hortense as well. "Ici encore les deux futurs amoureux tombaient admirablement d'accord" (Decreus 21). Furthermore, Bulwer's satire also contained a philosophy that was special to Hortense—an anticlericalism that took to task first the Roman ecclesiastics, then the Anglicans. Some of Bulwer's verses were comparable to Hortense's sentiments about Catholic orthodoxy and corruption that she had developed during her stay in Rome. His attitude, however, was more audacious and caustic than Hortense's ever could be:

> And if you've no objection to degrees
> In vice, become a bishop when you please . . . .
>
> Rome still held sacred for her ancient dust
> And now the Emporium of each modern lust;
> Where pimps are found in every priest you meet,
> And lechery lounges in religious seat.[3]

Today and Yesterday concludes with a tribute to Henry's brother Edward, and reveals that the poet is about to embark on a long voyage.

Although Henry was at first awed by the prospect of fighting for Greece, upon his arrival in the country he began to wonder if the Greeks were sufficiently mature to govern themselves. He treated this question in a letter he sent to C.B. Herdian, and from this was born his first prose work, *An Autumn in Greece,*[4] which would be published in 1826, a few months after his return to England in 1825.

Feeling somewhat at odds as to what to do with himself when he again reached English soil, Henry considered both Parliament and the diplomatic corps, but realized these were professions in which he could hardly start in a desirable position without the proper influence behind him.   His connections were better in the military, where his father had been one of four generals called to defend England in case of invasion. General William-Earle Bulwer had commanded the Third Midland Regiment, and had formed and financed by himself two regiments abroad—the 106th Norfolk Rangers, sent to serve in the West Indies, and another destined for service in the east. Henry, then, chose service in the army, and on Nov. 19, 1825, was named Cornette in the 2nd Regiment of Guards in the cavalry.

He left this post behind almost immediately, however, when he came upon an opportunity to serve a diplomatic mission to France. He arrived in Paris, and was soon joined by his brother Edward, both of them carrying letters of introduction for several houses at the Faubourg Saint-Germain.   A young Irish Jesuit priest, the Abbé Kinsela, the confessor of the Duchess de Polignac, wife of the minister to Charles X, took the two young Englishmen under his wing and introduced them into the highest echelons of Parisian society.   Although the brothers circulated through numerous aristocratic homes, the salons of various wealthy French royalists did not suit Henry's tastes for long. Leaving Edward behind, he soon returned to England, and to the army. On June 26, 1826, he became an officer in the 58th Regiment.

Bulwer continued to parlay his military position into more diplomatic opportunities, and by January 1829, he was named attaché at the British Embassy in Berlin. He later served in Vienna and in The Hague, espousing principles of liberty and championing the cause of oppressed nations.   He became particularly attached to the quest for independence in Belgium, an attitude that foreshadowed his ill-fated trip to that country with Hortense and young Marcus a few years later.

Between his diplomatic assignments, Henry continued to inch his way toward the opportunity to obtain a seat in Parliament. He and Edward, whose political ambitions equaled his devotion to literary output, both supported the Radical movement in English politics, shunning the Tories, and finding a compromise by working with the section of the Whigs that embraced liberalism.   Their political ideas were far more radical than those of Hortense, who did not advocate extended suffrage or recommend changes in the economy, but rather, believed that all government problems would be solved if the reins were in the hands of an elite, intellectual aristocracy. Also, the Bulwer brothers never even had considered the idea of women's rights, a subject precious to Hortense.

Early in 1830, Edward planned to pose his candidacy for the House of Commons representing the Hertforshire district, the ancestral domain of the Lyttons. He sent Henry to the district, armed with the proper letters of recommendation, but Henry, who, probably believing that since he was the elder brother by two years, he was the more likely man for the post, used the letters to his own advantage, and presented himself as the candidate instead. A short while later, when he learned that Tom Duncombe, another liberal aristocrat, was running for the same seat, Henry withdrew his candidacy so as not to divide the liberal vote.

Aside from what Edward Bulwer must have thought of or said to his brother about this affair, the unpleasantness was just beginning. Word circulated that Henry had accepted a bribe from Lord Salisbury to withdraw, and to assure the election of Duncombe. Lord Glengall, a close friend of King George IV, published the accusation, and public rumor speculated that the second Bulwer son could not possibly have a promising career ahead of him. However, the Bulwer family—especially the ill-used Edward—rallied together in the face of the scandal. Edward took his brother's part and demanded a retraction of Lord Glengall's accusation, which was accomplished. Henry rushed to his own defense, but his honor already had been saved. Mrs. Bulwer's reaction was to welcome Edward, whom she had refused to receive for three years because of her disapproval of his marriage, back into her good graces.

It was into this atmosphere that Hortense first entered Henry's life. She depicted him in at difficult point in his career, describing him as being in a "position comme des plus désespérées, engagé dans une crise de fortune et d'élection" (*EP*, cited by Decreus 28). As soon as Hortense arrived in London, Madame M., who was at that time alone in the city, gave to her friend Bulwer the task of showing the newcomer about the town. Madame M. was amused at how fast Bulwer became smitten with the pretty French visitor—"Elle s'amusa de le voir s'éprendre dès le premier jour. . . ." Hortense herself, though no doubt flattered by his quick devotion, was not unaware of Henry's reputation with the ladies: " . . . mais ne passait-il pas sa jeunesse dans les amours?" (*EP* 143).

Together, they visited Westminster Abbey, the houses of

Parliament, the Tower of London, various museums and galleries, and the countryside of Richmond. During the evening, Henry would stay chatting at Madame M.'s home until 2 or 3 a.m. If Henry was the victim of the *coup de foudre,* Hortense was not far behind. Her first descriptions of Bulwer indicate her confusion as to whether, despite his ambitions, he was more serious or more light-minded. "Il me sembla l'opposé d'un esprit sérieux: très spritiuel, très fin, parfois même profond, et pourtant léger; très ambitieux, très oocupé de son pays et des hommes d'action, mais sans projet arrêté; il était aussi très porté au plaisir et fait pour toutes les séductions qui s'offraient sur sa route" (*EP* 143).

At first, they spoke only of politics, as Henry dismissed certain politicians of his day as being "hommes de bureau," crushed by their preoccupation with details and pedantry, and claimed that one need not be ponderous to be intelligent. "Il disait qu'il faut savoir agir en riant . . . . il avait les idées éclairées d'un Anglais" (*EP* 144).

Before long, Hortense was entranced, focusing first on Henry's impressive heritage and intellectuality, and then on his personal appearance and charms:

> Son visage était noble et régulier, mais sans éclat, parce qu'il était un peu marqué de la petite vérole; sa bouche, belle, ornée de perles, avec des lèvres bien dessinées et légèrement épaisses; sa taille haute, très mince, élégante; ses manières étaient parfaites, naturelles, gracieuses, distinguées; un charme extrême régnait dans toute sa personne (*EP* 144).

She was perceptive enough to recognize that such a charm as his could be perilous for a woman with a heart as romantic as her own. "Ce charme est ce qu'on peut rencontrer de plus entraînant et de plus dangereux dans un homme. A ceux qui en sont doués, le poète qui a chanté *l'art d'aimer,* a dit; 'Je vous fais rois de l'Empire amoureux'" (*EP* 144, Allart's italics).

Despite Hortense's reservations, the two were inseparable, and their love and passion grew steadily in the first few weeks of their acquaintance. The time for her departure back to France arrived, but she changed her plans. She left Madame M.'s house and rented an apartment nearby, waiting for Henry to declare his love. Not much time passed before he did so. He visited "sans cesse" (*EP* 147), admitted his passion and his love for her, and asked her to remain in England and to share his life. He spoke of marriage, although he did not press her for a legal commitment, knowing the stir this would cause with his mother.

His proposal might be seen as a romantic dream come true, but for Hortense, the future was not quite so simple. Although she desired to be his lover, there were a number of reasons for which she hesitated to plunge into a new relationship and eventual marriage, either at this early stage of their courtship, or in the months and years to come. One of the most irksome was her genuine dislike of England and her inability to tolerate its climate for more than a few months at a time.

Soon after Henry had begun to show her the sights of the city, she had written, "Londres ne me plaisait point," and agreed with Chateaubriand's statement that *"L'Angleterre manque de grandeur"* (*EP* 144, her italics). She continues her complaint that England was scarcely the misty northern locale and culture of mystical and Romantic inspiration that she once had imagined it would be. Rather, France in its rainy moments better fulfilled that role:

> Le ciel était bas, étroit, terne, odieux, l'air pesant; les galeries, les tableaux me semblaient horribles; les palais, ou plutôt les maisons, ignobles et mesquines; les promenades arrangées, ridicules, la verdure et les eaux de la Tamise, noirs et hidieuses . . . . Non! L'Angleterre n'était pas ce pays mélancholique, mais beau et inspirateur que je rêvais en Italie; La Gaule seule, dans ses jours de pluie est telle (*EP* 145-46).

Hortense also was hesitant about marriage because of her lingering feelings for Sampayo. "Je lui répondis que je craindrais un mariage à cause de Jérôme, que cette passion était mal éteinte" (*EP* 147). She also feared that, as in the case of her first lover, Henry might have his priorities out of the order she desired. Where would he place love among his myriad of other concerns and interests? Already, she perceived that his passion for his professional ambitions equaled or surpassed his devotion to her. "Il ne voulait au monde que le Parlement et l'amour, je ne lui verrais d'autre passion; sa vie serait consacrée à moi et à cette ambition politique qui était aussi le mien" (*EP* 147).

Another reason for her uncertainty was her knowledge that the haughty and domineering Mrs. Bulwer-Lytton would not approve of her son's marriage to a French bluestocking of bourgeois background, who also had an illegitimate child—hardly the proper mold for the wife of a Parliamentarian. Furthermore, Mrs. Bulwer-Lytton already had been vocal, even melodramatic, about her disapproval of her other two sons' choices of wives. Neither of these daughters-in-law could equal Hortense in personal independence or non-conformity.

On the question of marriage, Mrs. Bulwer-Lytton believed that marrying according to one's station in life was far more important a factor than was love.   In her youth, she had almost married a man whom she loved, but who was beneath her in social rank. Her father had forbidden the union, calling down upon her the vision of her noble ancestors and her responsibility to their legacy.   Several years later, after a long hesitation, and under the persuasion of her mother, she had married Colonel Bulwer, 20 years her senior, whom she did not love. She endured the unhappy union with the cantankerous, dispassionate military commander until his death liberated her. She expected the same kind practical choice and Christian forbearance from her sons when they married.

Nevertheless, Edward braved his mother's fierce disapproval, and married in 1827 the beautiful niece of an Irish general.   He was so much in love that he took his chances with Mrs. Bulwer-Lytton's ultimatum that she would break off all contact with him if he married the young lady.   She made good on her threat, and forbade Edward and his bride entrance to her house, sent back his all his letters unopened, and mailed to him every small souvenir that could remind her of his existence.   Although she did unbend temporarily when Edward came to Henry's defense in the candidacy matter, her stern tactics eventually were the ruin of what would have been, under more tolerant circumstances, a compatible couple and a happy marriage. "L'intrasigeance de la grande dame envenima et finit par briser ignominieusement l'union passionnée de deux êtres beaucoup mieux assortis aux yeux du monde que ne l'eussent été Henry et Hortense" (Decreus 29).

The eldest son, William, also had married for love and against the wishes of his mother.   By 1830, then, Mrs. Bulwer-Lytton was looking to Henry to contract a marriage of which she could be proud. Not wishing to cause her a third displeasure, Henry proposed to Hortense in the only way that he though he was able—he promised marriage at a future date when his mother would be deceased, and suggested that they cohabitate discreetly in the meantime. Even to marry in secret while his mother was still alive might be too risky.

"S'imagine-t-on, à la suite d'une possible indiscrétion, le mariage clandestin d'Henry et d'Hortense porté devant le tribunal familial sous la juridiction d'une telle mère?" asks Decreus (34).   Thus dominated by such a mother, none of the three Bulwer-Lytton sons were ever to allow passion to triumph completely over their sense of filial duty.

Henry's passion for Hortense was sincere, or at least one that he lived out with a maximum of semi-convincing histrionics.   She writes, "Son amour le faisait souffrir; c'était comme un supplice, une maladie. Il perdait la tête; il était au deséspoir (ou il feignait de l'être). Il me causait des impressions semblables; à côté de lui je perdais la raison" (*EP* 147). His offer of a life together embroiled in politics, intellectuality and love was tempting—in fact, the very thing of which she had always dreamed. "Ce Parlement pour lequel elle avait passé la Manche et une vie toute de politique, d'étude et d'amour. Son rêve!" (Billy 100).

She promised to tie up her loose ends in France, then return to England as soon as possible, and become his mistress, "et de vivre pour l'amour et la politique" (*EP* 148). Bulwer, however, was loathe to let her go, even to the point of taking her passport away on the pretext of obtaining a visa for her, and refusing to give it back. After two agitated days, however, Henry relented and let her depart, on condition that she would return as soon as possible to become his wife, or at least, his mistress.

In the midst of her liaison with Bulwer was Allart's ongoing correspondence and occasional meetings with a jealous and devastated Chateaubriand, who was mortified that she could have left him for "un Anglais" (*EP* 150). Although ever solicitous of his feelings, she never agreed to leave Henry and resume their past rapport.

Stopping at Calais after her first return from England in early summer 1830, she penned a rhyming verse to Chateaubriand telling him their intimate relationship was over. However, she had mixed feelings about ending a liaison that had given each of them so much joy. After meeting with Chateaubriand again in Paris, she reflected, "Il voyait que je l'aimais, il sentait son pouvoir, il laissa sa fierté inutile. Comment moi, en le voyant si bon, si pressant, et en l'aimant si tendrement, me sentais-je si liée en Angleterre que l'idée de revenir à lui ne s'offrit même pas?" (*EP* 149).

As for Chateaubriand, he told her he would not ask what went on between her and the Englishman, but exhorted her to remain in France. She softened her rebuff by assuring him—and he actually believed her—that Bulwer had been only her third lover after Sampayo and himself. (In reality, there had been at least three others—Libri, Capponi, and Didier). At her gentle, but determined refusal to stay with Chateaubriand, "Il sortit irrité mais sans adieu," slamming the door behind him (*EP* 150).

He wrote the next day telling her that she would lose her talent if she went to England, and that it was he alone who could help her cultivate and develop her gift: " . . . que lui seul saurait le soigner, le développer" (*EP* 150). He continued his arguments as to why she should never return to England, even stating that if it was marriage she wanted, he would marry her and take her back to Italy as soon as he was free. (Madame de Chateaubriand would live another 17 years. She would not die until February 1847, a year and five months before her

husband's death at age 80).   He spoke of suicide, claiming he had just
loaded a pistol for the deed.   He wrote, "Hortense, vous m'avez trahi!
Je n'avais rien fait pour vous perdre!" (quoted by Billy 102).

She responded to all this with tenderness, but still refused to
renounce her plans with Bulwer.   Chateaubriand found this sincerity
terrible, and claimed he would rather be deceived with lies than hear of
her forthright opinions and decisions.   Finally, he demanded that she
return all of his letters.   She complied, but not before carefully making
copies of each one.   He returned most of her letters, as well, but kept
some of his favorites that testified that her now-spent passion for him
had been only recently very much alive.[5]

In July 1830, Paris was warming for a revolution.   Hortense
wondered what would happen to Chateaubriand if France were left
without Charles X, whom he had served with so much loyalty and
enthusiasm.   With a hint of retrospective guilt, she later mused, "Je
l'avais donc quitté quand tout le quittait!" (*EP* 151).

Soon after the July Monarchy, he and Béranger both wrote to her
saying they each refused to have a part in whatever the government of
Louis-Philippe might offer them.   Béranger warned that Chateaubriand
was so disenchanted with the situation in France that he was about to
leave the country, although Béranger was trying to dissuade him.
Chateaubriand would soon go into exile in Switzerland, and not return
to France until summer 1832, and then, only briefly.

Hortense was not without sympathy for her friends, or without her
own disdain for the new regime.   "Le mot *démocratie* ouvrait la carrière
aux basses classes ou plutôt aux ambitieux qui les trompent.   M. de
Chateaubriand et les royalistes virent seuls les périls où nous courions"
(*EP* 153-54, Allart's italics).   Hortense quit Paris just before the rise of
the July Monarchy.   After a brief stay in Montlignon, near
Montmorency, she received word that Bulwer had just been named to
the House of Commons.   Hortense's conscience about Chateaubriand
did not sting sufficiently to prevent her from rushing off to meet the
new Parliamentarian at Saint-Valéry in Picardie in late August.

Four-year-old Marcus accompanied his mother as she hastened to
meet Bulwer-Lytton in Saint-Valéry in late August 1830.   The small
town in the Somme was a "pays désert, primitif, 'vaste et original,'"
states Billy, noting that it would have been more convenient for her to
meet Henry in Calais or Boulogne, but not nearly as romantic, for
someone for whom "exaltation c'était son climat naturel" (103-4).

Although Hortense candidly described her son as "méchant et
gâté," she noted that Henry treated the little boy with "la plus grande
tendresse" (*EP* 153).   Mother and son traveled with Bulwer on the
first leg of the journey back to England.   They parted briefly near Saint-

Valéry, with Hortense once again fearing for her personal freedom. "Ici j'aurais pu comprendre ce qu'allait être cet homme dans ma vie, et combien, il devait dominer . . . ." (*EP* 156). She noticed that she had been happy in Saint-Valéry, and Henry had been miserable. As they drew nearer toward England, his mood became light-hearted, and hers began to sink. She reflected upon how their future plans for a life in England would favor his interests, and not hers, and wondered if their love might weather such a storm. "J'avais connu jusqu'ici un amour intellectuel où les sens, détournés et combattus, avaient langui sans s'éveiller. Aujourd'hui j'abordais la Vénus antique, mais la Vénus sacré, ou plutôt j'abordais ce sacrement de l'amour dont les prêtres ont fait le sacrement du mariage" (*EP* 156).

Despite these reservations, as soon as she received word that Henry was ill in Boulogne, she and Marcus joined him there, then left for London with him that September. They spent two weeks in Hampstead, where he traveled often to London, while she stayed behind and finished her novel *Sextus,* as well as some studies on Italy that would be incorporated into it. They rented a house, and Henry began to speak again of marriage. "Il parlait d'un temps ou nous serions mariés, ne comprenait pas mes craintes, me reprochait de n'être pas confiante" (*EP* 157).

In October 1830, Lord Aberdeen, minister of foreign affairs, sent Henry on a diplomatic trip to Brussels, while Hortense moved into the same London apartment where they had begun their love. She was aware that he was sent to survey France's activities in Belgium, and felt uncomfortable with the situation. "Mr. Warwick n'allait en Belgique que pour surveiller la France et agir contre nous. Je le savais, mais en aimant un Anglais j'avais dû savoir qu'il servirait au besoin contre nous" (quoted by Billy 105). Henry returned soon and, even though Belgium was then embroiled in a violent insurrection in its break from the Netherlands, he asked Hortense to go back to Brussels with him. They departed with Marcus later that month.

In Gand, protests by French supporters penetrated the auberge at which they were staying. Although Bulwer attempted to speak diplomatically with them, a fearful Hortense burned all of his papers, and they left in haste. Along the road, the Vicount de Pontécoulant, a pro-Bonapartist adventurer recently returned from Brazil, where he had been sentenced to death, and who was now head of a Parisian contingent to save Belgium, accosted Bulwer and Hortense. Fortunately, Hortense recognized his name because she had known his family. She told the viscount her name and stopped Henry from brandishing his pistols. Pontécoulant confiscated the guns and escorted the fugitives back to the auberge. To a man in the entourage whom Henry had already wounded in the arm with his pistol, the parliamentarian promised half his fortune to make amends. Hortense settled the affair with two louis.

The next morning Pontécoulant thought it prudent to accompany the pair back to Brussels. However, when they arrived, chaos reigned. "A Bruxelles, ils s'aimèrent au bruit du tambour et des cris" (Billy 106). Whereas Henry was in his element dispatching diplomatic messages to and from his government, Hortense was unhappy in her position, feeling she was not being treated as well as she might have been if she were Mrs. Bulwer-Lytton. "Cette situation lui plaisait, mais non à elle qui, au regard du monde, souffrait de ne pas être sa femme" (Billy 106).

Anvers was burning, and as it capitulated before the advancing Dutch, Bulwer and Hortense, with Marcus clinging to her skirts, traveled towards the doomed city. Once there, Henry stayed, but arranged for Hortense and Marcus to leave with a group of fleeing peasants. After a frightening night in a terrible auberge, Henry found her, and took her and Marcus back to Brussels, then to London.

They took an apartment, where Hortense tried to resume her writing. However, still shaken by the harrowing experiences in Belgium, she felt herself in a creative and emotional slump. "Et arrive alors pour moi un temps de désespoir stupide" (*EP* 161). Henry was "passioné" by night, but gone all day and every day. The solitude as well as the dank December weather made her miserable. "Je commence à subir sur moi de ce pays qui m'a toujours fait un grand mal . . . un ennui complet succède. C'est ici le temps de ma vie où je me suis le plus horriblement ennuyée . . . . avec des nuits si douces" (*EP* 161).

By late February 1831, Hortense was determined to leave "cet amour inégal et encore plus terrible" (*EP* 162). Henry made his usual emotional scenes, but escorted her back to France. She later would philosophize on this latest rupture of two intelligent individuals who could not seem to let reason triumph over passion. "Nous avons ici l'exemple instructif de deux caractères immodérés. La raison, la mesure, la sagesse ne présidaient point à des passions, il est vrai, qui ne les comportent guère" (*EP* 162). Hortense knew only too well that the climate of England as well as the solitude of her life with Henry while he was involved in his work were too oppressive for her to endure. Nevertheless, whenever she and Henry spoke of separation, love overtook them.

Once back in France, Hortense kept fainting at the hotel in Abbeville. Henry was obliged to take a different room because the sound of his breathing made her faint again. The next day, the lure of Parliament was too much, and Henry left for the Channel, but the next day, he overtook her on the road. Hortense described this latest reunion as "un amour délicieux" (*EP* 163). At first, Henry could not bring himself to leave—"Il n'avait nul empire sur sa passion, excepté celui qui donnait son ambition" (*EP* 163)—but ambition eventually won out. In a few days, he left for England, while Hortense and Marcus regained Paris.

As usual, there were rewards to this latest separation, as it landed her back into the milieu where she could once again feel contented and productive. She always felt her talents and productivity were stifled during the intervals in England. "Je n'avais pas assez exercé mon intelligence en Angleterre, des sensations trop molles, des jours trop désœuvrés m'avaient troublée . . . Je retrouve avec enchantement mon pays et la conversation" (*EP* 163). She took an apartment at the Hôtel du Rhône, at 5, rue Saint-Nacaise, which would for a long time remain her Parisian *pied-à-terre.* There she received with pleasure visits from Didier ("Nous avions tant à nous dire sur l'Italie et sur tout!" [*EP* 163]), as well as Béranger, and then-undersecretary of state, Louis-Adolphe Thiers.

"J'étais ravie de retrouver le bruit, la politique, les talents de la France" (*EP* 164). The only blot on her newfound happiness was the fact that Chateaubriand, who was at that time still in exile in Switzerland, responded "froidement" to her letters. Pailleron observed that at this time it was a relief for Hortense to be away from Bulwer's intensity, and that she was beginning to feel nostalgic about the less frenetic times spent in the past with Chateaubriand.

> Il n'est plus question de larmes amères, de syncopes; elle a quitté l'Angelterre qu'elle détestait et ou elle étouffait, et il semble que l'absence de Bulwer la soulage, car Bulwer est un terrible tyran et sa passion est pesante. Bref, le souvenir de Chateuabriand si aimbale si courtois renaît.[6]

She began writing articles for *Le Temps,* and seeking a publisher for *Sextus.* In May 1831, Béranger introduced her to Sainte-Beuve whom she described as a "jeune et nouveau poète" (*EP* 164). Henry arrived "inquiet et jaloux" over this new acquaintance as well as the other male visitors (*EP* 165), and they spent several days together, before Parliament called him home once again. She accompanied him as far as Montlignon. She loved this spot, recalling that it was here that she had met Sampayo some six or seven years earlier. "Son souvenir remplissait ces compagnes solitaires" (*EP* 165).

Henry soon wrote that he was ill, and asked her to join him. The thought of leaving the pleasing nostalgia of Montlignon for yet another trip to England, was repulsive to her, but in July, she went, and stayed through October. "Je revois l'Angleterre avec horreur . . . . une idée horrible de me savoir en Angleterre" (*EP* 165). This time, she did not live with Henry, but procured for herself and Marcus an apartment on Renelagh Street not far from the Thames along whose banks she liked to walk. Henry complained that she lived too far away from him, but spent most of his nights at her place.   One evening, however, he left early for his own lodgings because he had business the next morning. "Ce départ me désola comme s'il partait pour toujours," (*EP* 166).   Hortense consoled herself by writing a long poem in couplet rhyme about this latest disappointment.   In the 66-line poem, she addresses Henry, as she later would do in her 1851 *Troisième Petit Livre*, as "Remi, " and suggests that since she had made a personal sacrifice for him by coming to a country she did not enjoy, he might at least render her time there more happy:

> Toutes les nuits, Remi, vous dormez dans ces lieux,
> Pourquoi ce soir, si tard, me faire des adieux,
> Et vous qui détestez ce cruel sacrifice,
> Me l'imposer ce soir d'un ton plein d'artifice?
> . . . .
> Climat de l'Angleterre, où j'ai suivi l'amour,
> Où je vis pour Remi, loin de l'astre du jour,
> Vous me deviez du moins des nuits toutes heureuses.
> (*EP*   166).

Sorely missing the sophisticated company and conversation of the Parisian salons to which she had been accustomed since her adolescence, Hortense sought a way to establish some kind of substitute in London. She thought first of the English mathematician, Babbage, whom she had first met in Rome four years earlier through Libri.   She wrote to him in July 1831, asking if he could visit her and bring along some of his better-known friends.   Her letter, however, was unsuccessful in stimulating any interest in a salon over which she could preside in London.   Babbage's response was to send her a copy of his two-volume work on sciences. Her next letter, dated Aug. 2, 1831, thanked him for the books, and again pressed him to visit. "J'espère vous y voir bientôt, j'y serai demain soir, amenez-y les savants échappés à votre vengeresse 'patrie.'"[7]

Babbage called on her, but came alone, and their visit served little purpose but to give Hortense the chance to bemoan her loneliness in London and her dearth of company.   Later in August, she wrote to Babbage again, pressing him for the address of a certain Lord Arthur

Dillon, whom she recalled was a relative of the Countess Bertrand.

She also mentioned the name Mr. Donblay, asking Babbage to bring him for a visit. She explained that women, unfortunately, needed a male representative to pave their way into the social scene. "Les femmes sont très à plaindre dans un pays étranger, où elles doivent attendre chez elles les connaissances au lieu d'aller les chercher. Elles sont à plaindre pour bien d'autres raisons, à vous seuls il est permis d'agir, de voir, de paraître et d'aimer" (quoted by Decreus 39).

Apparently, Babbage paid her more visits, but without bringing any other interesting people, because there is no indication in subsequent letters of her asking to meet any more scholars. Undoubtedly, states Decreus, this wise mathematician suggested reading as a remedy to her boredom and inactivity and promised to bring her a book on the Netherlands. In later letters, she commented on this work and also on a book about Wales that he had recommended to her (Decreus 40-41).

Hortense suggests in *Les Enchantements de Prudence* that Bulwer became jealous of her rapport with Babbage during this time. Decreus opines that this is unlikely, however, given the continuing friendship between the two men, and the probability that Babbage valued his liaison with the Parliamentarian more than he did the gratitude of Bulwer's French mistress. "Sans doute Babbage jugea-t-il, en homme du monde, plus convenable de ménager les susceptibilités de l'amant que de dissiper l'ennui de la maîtresse" (41).

Hortense's ennui remained so oppressive that she asked an Italian singer to visit, and even went so far as to pen for his voice some verses filled with clichés about the classic tragedy of sensuous nights that were inevitably followed by long, lonely days.

By October 1831, Hortense had given up on the possibility of establishing any kind of intellectual salon or of finding any other way of making herself content in England. "Devant l'impossibilité de se créer un tant soit peu de vie mondaine, toutes les bonnes résolutions d'Hortense pour endurer l'Angleterre s'écroulèrent" (Decreus 40). She spoke again of returning to France, and this time, Henry did little to dissuade her. She wrote to Babbage on Oct. 8, returning his book on the Netherlands, and bidding him farewell.

"Je ne pouvais supporter plus de trois mois l'Angleterre et son affreux climat; je devenais comme folle et désespérée" (*EP* 168). She and Henry left England in late October. He stayed briefly with her in Boulogne, then he returned to London and she to Paris. "Nous nous quittons le lendemain avec regret et tendresse" (*EP* 168). Henry soon wrote from England, again telling her he was ill. This time, although she still spoke of strong feelings for him, she did not run to join him, but rather lodged with her sister on the Rue de Rivoli, then took up residence at 19, Rue Bleue, where she settled in for what she described as a charming winter. Here, blessedly again on the other side of the Channel, she found the gregarious and stimulating atmosphere she craved. "Jamais je n'ai aimé Paris comme à ces retours d'Angleterre . . . . J'avais du monde tous les soirs." She speaks rapturously of "les visites affectueuses" from Sampayo, Libri, and Béranger. Sainte-Beuve called also, and she found him "très aimable avec une gracieuse et belle conversation" (*EP* 169).

From late 1831 to early 1832, she worked on her novel *L'Indienne.* *Sextus ou le Romain des Maremmes* ran in abridged form in the *Revue de Paris* in February 1832, then was published in book form in March 1832 in Paris by Heideloff et Campe under the name Mme. Hortense de Thérase Allart. The title page identifies her as "Auteur de *Gertrude, Jérôme,* etc." The volume also contains Allart's *Essaies sur Rome, sur Naples* and *sur la Toscane.*

The title hero of *Sextus* is a recreation of Gino Capponi, and the novel is an endearing story of the romance between a young Roman scholar and a Frenchwoman based, in part, upon her own persona.

> La blonde Thérèse de Longueville, au visage noble et animé, et qui a quelque chose d'élégant, de modeste et de naturel dans toute sa personne . . . de la grâce et de la cordialité, c'est évidement Hortense telle qu'elle se voyait et telle que nous-mêmes mettons quelque complaisance à l'imaginer, la chère femme (Billy 113).

Although Hortense's intimate relationship with Capponi had ended some months before she undertook the writing of the novel (one may recall how she sent back his gift of the cameo ring with very little compunction shortly before leaving Italy to follow Chateaubriand back to France), the story of *Sextus* indicates the ongoing respect and closeness she felt toward her suave, sensitive former lover, and her ideal of what might have been possible between the two of them.

She wrote to Capponi on Jan. 21, 1832, a few weeks before *Sextus* was published, and promised to send him a copy of the novel he had inspired. "Je vais vous envoyer bientôt ce roman où vous êtes . . . . C'est moi qui suis grande Dame ou plutôt c'est votre Thérèse, c'est vous qui m'avez donné l'inspiration et les noms." In this same letter she also shared with Capponi how she had missed Italy and how, although she loved Henry, she abhorred nearly everything about England. "Les souvenirs d'Italie me sont chers . . . . L'amour même se décolore, j'ai perdu mes espérences et mes grandeurs d'Italie."[8]

Sextus relates the trauma and eventual happy ending in the romance between a beautiful, 24-year-old widow, Thérèse de Longueville, who is French by birth, but residing in Florence, and Sextus, a 26-year-old Roman who writes emotionally of his sensitivity toward and adoration of his city's history and culture. Through other characters, the novel also touches on the question of certain options for ending unhappy marriages.

Sextus also is a sensitive tribute to the glories of ancient Rome and the contribution of the contemporary Roman culture to Romantic thought.   The novel also has its Staëlian component as it describes Sextus's intellectual struggle with how to reconcile his loyalty to Italian literature and culture with his newfound emotions as he travels through France, thinks back upon ancient Gaul, and realizes the power of northern, non-classical civilizations to inspire and to fascinate.

At the novel's beginning, Thérèse who loves living in Florence, is planning a trip to her native Paris with her five-year-old twins, Philippe and Anna. She confesses to her friend Côme Rucellai, that her marriage was imprudent and unhappy. "Enfin, le héros de son cœur n'est pas son mari," the narrator states.[9]   After the birth of her children, Thérèse met the man she truly loved, but they avoided each other because she was married. After M. de Longuement was killed in a hunting accident, she indulged her passion with her paramour, but he soon left her for an unknown reason. "Ainsi à présent, son cœur est libre" (*Sext.* 13).

There are hints in the first chapter that both Côme Rucellai and his brother, the abbé Guide Rucellai, love Thérèse. Her heart, though, now seems galvanized against men.   Côme tells the priest, "Une cruelle expérience semble l'avoir mise en défiance des hommes . . . . elle n'est pas coquette, elle est noble; elle éveille dans le cœur de l'homme des sentiments élevés qui font naître l'amour" (*Sext.* 14).

Thérèse still laments her ill-fated love affair, which now has been over for three years. "Richard! quel mal vous avez fait à vous et à moi! Qu'on se soumet lentement, même à une destiné irrevocable!" (*Sext.* 35).   Ennui is now beginning to replace her sorrow, and although many men pay her court, she has consistently resisted affections that are unworthy of her, and relationships that are superficial. "Son âme, facile à intéresser, restait maîtresse d'elle-même . . . . elle contint un cœur tendre par les principes d'un esprit élevé, et par les souvenirs d'une passion douloureuse" (*Sext.* 30-31).

Guide enjoys writing to Thérèse about details on Italy, (which she finds more charming than his conversation).   He offers to show her some letters he has received from Sextus, his friend from Rome, an orphan and protegé of a Catholic cardinal. Thérèse refuses, but Guide leaves three letters on the table. She reads, and recognizes that the most charming parts of Guide's letters to her actually were quotations from letters by this other man.   Some of the letters are quoted in the text as the readers learn more about young Sextus.

A native of Maremmes, near Rome, Sextus has been educated in Latin and history by Cardinal Salvati.   He now looks after the flocks of Maremmes, a spot he considers the "vrai séjour d'un romain moderne," (*Sext.* 41) but wishes to travel the world.   At age 18, he aided the Englishman Lord Mortimer with research on Italy, and fell in love with Mortimer's 16-year-old daughter, Lady Fanny, although the latter never really knew him.

His second letter tells of his love of Dona Marianna, the orphaned niece of the cardinal, who eventually left Sextus and married a wealthy cousin. In a series of intrigues, Sextus fell into a brain fever, arranged by messenger to meet Marianna, reproached her, threatened to kill himself, then recognized his own folly in forcing upon her the illusions he had build up about her. Embarrassed before the cardinal regarding his conduct, he wished to leave Maremmes. The cardinal persuaded him to stay, predicting he would become "un des premiers hommes d'Italie" (*Sext.* 71).

In the third letter, Sextus described his *mal de René.*   "Mes propres chagrins se perdirent au sien de cette mer de douleurs où je voyais l'homme plongé; mon chagrin se généralisant n'eut ni proportion, ni terme" (*Sext.* 73).

The cardinal introduced him into society where he met numerous women: "J'aimai, je fus aimé; mais je ne retrouvais plus les sentiments que j'avais payé trop cher" (*Sext.* 78).   After various adventures with unfaithful women, Sextus felt himself eclipsed by his country's noble past. "Nos souvenirs passés nous écrasent; nos héros, nos dieux, nos prêtres ont dominé le monde, et il ne nous restent pour distraction que nos femmes! . . . . et nous les entraînons dans notre chute!" (*Sext.* 80).

Thérèse is impressed with the letters. At the very moment she is leaving Italy, has she found a man who will make her turn around and stay?   Although the jealous Côme tries to persuade her to the contrary, she returns to Rome and arranges with the cardinal to meet Sextus.   She finds the young man now more sophisticated and charming even than his letters indicated. (The letters were written four years earlier. He is now 26.)

Sextus tells the cardinal at first that he finds Thérèse cold (like most *françaises*), but later admits he is enchanted with her. "Il s'était épris. Il aimait comme il aimait toutes les femmes."   He particularly admires her "air noble et doux" (*Sext.* 93).   Thérèse is less impressed with him, observing that Roman men in general do not regard women with sufficient respect and individuality. "Un romain traîte toutes les

femmes sur le même ton; le tort est au pays, pas à lui (*Sext.* 95)
.... Il ne lui sembla plus l'homme qu'elle avait cru deviner" (*Sext.* 96). As the couple's cautious friendship continues during trips to nearby sites, a boat ride on the Tiber, etc., Allart's description of Sextus's changing thoughts describes her idealized, much-wished-for metamorphosis of a stereotypically egotistical and snobbish Roman scholar into a newly sensitized man who can recognize the true value of a woman who is superior not only in intellect, but also in her expectations in love. "[Sextus] rencontrait une personne aussi complètement supérieure à la vie commune (*Sext.* 105) .... Il passait des jours dans la rêverie; il pensait que l'homme n'atteint pas tout par sa pensée, et il regrettait presque que la connaissance qu'il avait des femmes l'empêchât d'aimer" (*Sext.* 106).

He reads in Petrarch's and Dante's poetry descriptions of love, and becomes aware of a new sensuality that he had never known before in Rome. Thérèse feels the same kinds of exalted sentiments—"des impressions de grandeur et d'amour remplissaient son cœur" (*Sext.* 107).

The cardinal sees Thérèse's positive effect on his charge—"Je ne te reconnaîtrais pas; tu ne mériterais plus ta réputation" (*Sext.* 110), but urges him to return to Maremmes and reflect on the matter. Thérèse, hurt by his announced departure, says good-by coldly. Back in Maremmes, a bewildered Sextus, as did Thérèse, recalls his own unhappy love affair (with Marianna), and resists the temptation to return to Thérèse in Rome. "La voir encore est tout risquer!" (*Sext.* 113).

An English friend in Rome, Lord Norfolk, urges Thérèse to return to England with him. A jealous Sextus seeks Thérèse in Rome and learns that Norfolk once had an adulterous affair with Lady Fanny, now unhappily married, whom Sextus once loved. The chapter describes in detail the sad course of their liaison, which left Fanny back in the care of her husband, but still devastated. Sextus is scandalized that Norfolk did not protect Fanny more gallantly and spirit her away from an unsatisfactory marriage. "Les hommes faibles ne reviennent jamais sur ces résolutions-là. La crainte les retient (*Sext.* 142) .... Je trouve la société dans un état pitoyable; le plus souvent je la fuis" (*Sext.* 145).

The intrigue continues as Norfolk continues to pull Thérèse away from Sextus, and the young scholar responds by toying with the affections of a woman named Stella, and allowing the rumors about the two of them to fly about Rome. Thérèse longs for Sextus, but gives up hope. "Son amour naissant pour Sextus s'éteignit et se changea en douleur . . . " (*Sext.* 152). She still writes to him and dreams of "ce berger de Maremmes, cet homme que sa naissance, son pays et ses erreurs semblait proscrire" (153-54).   Back in Maremmes, her letters console Sextus.

A brief reunion in Rome reanimates Sextus and solidifies his love for Thérèse.   When Norfolk insults all Romans as cowards, Sextus challenges the Englishman to a duel, and wounds him; friends urge Sextus to take a trip to France.   Being in Thérèse's native country has a profound effect on him.   "En abordant son pays, il n'avait pensé qu'à elle; la France, c'était elle . . . . Il se plaisait à l'aimer dans son pays, à porter partout son image; quand il trouvait de la sensibilité sous le ciel de la France, il doutait si Thérèse n'en avait pas" (*Sext.* 186).

So begins Sextus's personal odyssey across France, his struggle with his loyalty to Italy's classical literary past, and his growing sensitivity towards the provocative mystery of rudimentary Gaulish territories.

> Avant d'entrer dans Paris, il chercha encore la solitude dans la forêt de Fontainebleau.   Il pensait que pour une contrée qui n'a pas l'éclat du jour, il faut des arbres et la richesses des bois: c'était la parure de la Gaule; il la cherchait dans les forêts, avec les inspirations druidiques.   Combien cette contrée, couverte d'arbres et remplie de l'humidité qu'ils donnent, avait dû paraître froide aux Romains ses pères, quand ils y avaient une première fois pénétré! (*Sext.* 187).

Sextus reflects on a series of comparisons between France and Italy.   First, French industriousness versus Italian idleness: "Il déplorait l'oisiveté de l'Italie . . . . Quand il vit la richesse de la [France] sa prospérité, un peuple probe et brave, faisant de bonnes armés, également fait pour l'industrie, la guerre et la liberté, il s'affligea que l'Italie fût si loin" (*Sext.* 206).

Then, the lack of passion in French history versus the lack of eminence in Italy's current position in the world:

> Jamais l'histoire [française] n'avait montré une raison si dégagée de passion . . . .   La France était la plus forte nation de l'Europe.   Non seulement son triomphe lui était glorieux; mais placée à la tête de la civilisation, son triomphe était celui de la civilisation même.   Sextus rêvait pour l'Italie des destinés rivales; elle aussi avait tenu une foi le sceptre du monde (*Sext.* 207).

The superficial nature of Parisian salons and human relationships versus the grander emotions of the Italians:

> Il ne vit que coteries, que salons; pas un homme ne quittait ces réunions pour chercher la solitude et retrouver la nature . . . . L'amitié régnait plus en apparence qu'en réalité; on avait des habitudes plus que des affections; un esprit aimable, mais qui dans le cours ordinaire de la vie ne nourissait rien d'élevé . . . . les grandes passions lui parurent oubliées pour les petites; il ne trouva pas d'énergie individuelle . . . . il trouvait que le pays n'était pas fait pour la poésie, la contemplation, ni pour les sentimens [sic] dont son âme s'était nourrie" (*Sext.* 208-209).

Although he still thinks tenderly of Thérèse ("Thérèse avait à tout jamais fermé son cœur [aux autres femmes]" [*Sext.* 198]), he longs to return to his own country. However, word is circulating that Thérèse and Norfolk are about to marry in Rome, so he travels on to England, where he meets his old friend Lord Mortimer, and his daughter Lady Fanny (who barely recognizes Sextus). When Fanny's husband is killed in a riding accident, Sextus wishes to send the news to Thérèse and Norfolk, thinking that perhaps Norfolk will wish to marry his now-widowed former lover.

He hurries back over France and Italy, only to find that Thérèse and Norfolk's marriage is imminent. Thérèse explains to him that Norfolk has a calming effect on her, but admits there is no passion between them. "Oui, [c'est] un mariage de raison . . . . Je n'ai dû à l'amour que des peines. Lord Norfolk est le plus estimable des hommes. Ce mariage me consolera" (*Sext.* 251). When Sextus declares how long he has loved her with a passion he cannot vanquish, she still protests, "Non, non, le ciel refuse à une femme d'être aimée deux fois comme je l'ai été" (*Sext.* 252).

She chides him for staying silent for so long about his feelings; he reproaches her for what he has perceived as her disdainful attitude. She asks him for time to reflect; he leaves with his hopes crushed. "Que la destinée de l'homme lui parut triste!" (*Sext.* 254). Adoring as she was of Italian culture and traditions, Hortense could not resist in *Sextus* this occasion to criticize through both characters what she saw as certain ridiculous aspects of Roman conduct—the shallowness of morals that had first spurred Sextus's cynicism, and the unwillingness to share true feelings even at the expense of one's own happiness. "L'auteur avait voulu représenter dans son héros ce qui en Italie subsistait des caractères antiques sous la frivolité des mœurs et de sentiments; sujet peu banal d'où, avec une âme sérieuse, on devait tirer de fortes leçons" (Billy 114).

The narrator wraps the story up quickly on the last half-page. "Comment Thérèse pouvait-elle rester insensible en apprenant qu'elle était aimée depuis long-temps [sic] d'un homme qui n'avait cessé de l'intéresser? Au moment de contracter un mariage où elle s'était décidée par raison, elle écouta avec enchantement les prières de la passion" (*Sext.* 255). With the lines of communication intact at last, Thérèse realizes that Sextus is the man whose mind, heart and imagination can make her the most happy. She breaks with Norfolk, and she and Sextus marry. Lady Fanny later sees Norfolk, but opts not to marry him, but rather to devote her life to her children.

Although it was Thérèse who was the most autobiographical character in the novel, the subplot involving Lady Fanny and her ultimate decision to pursue life on her own was more typical of Allart's own persona, and more indicative of personal choices she had made in her own life. Says Billy, "Le récit s'achève sur le portrait d'une femme qui refuse de se remarier par fidélité à sa vie passée et pour se consacrer à l'éducation de ses deux filles. Dénouement bien dans la manière d'Hortense, sinon dans sa nature" (112).

Billy also notes a certain Stendhalian tone in *Sextus,* due perhaps, in part, to this same, seemingly illogical, Julien Sorel-like choice that Lady Fanny makes—a choice true to the best within her, though unexpected and illogical from any traditional point of view. "L'allure du récit est parfois stendhalienne et il faut convenir que, dans son tableau de l'Etat romain et de sa décadence, l'auteur introduit des considérations pertinentes" (Billy 113).

The reaction in France to *Sextus,* which, more than any other Allart novel, demonstrates the personal sensibilities of her Italian connection, was mostly one of praise. The anonymous review in *Revue de Paris*, which had introduced the work in its abridged form, analyzed the novel after it appeared in book form. The reviewer compared the novel to *Corinne* because of its hero's sensitivity to the glories of Italian literary and historical tradition. "Action, intrigue, caractères, elle fait, j'en suis sûr, bon marché de tout cela; c'est la partie accessoire d'un livre qui est comme une pendant de *Corinne,* comme une peintre éloquente de l'Italie, de l'Italie telle qu'elle vivra toujours dans le rêve des poètes et des artistes." Superlative also was the reviewer's praise for Allart herself. "Sous ce rapport littéraire, de nos premiers écrivains; c'est un talent viril que la *Revue de Paris* se glorifie de compter parmi ses collaborateurs."[10]

Sainte-Beuve, whose anonymous review appeared in the *Revue des Deux Mondes* May 15, 1832, also applauded Allart's finely tuned intimacy with the Italian characters and Roman ambiance that envelopes the work. " . . . cette familiarité délicate, ingénieuse encore dans sa licence, où vivent pêle-mêle, en confidents ou en rivaux, cardinal, prince, abbé, intendant, favori: c'était là un fonds de roman tout à fait hors des données vulgaires, et duquel, avec une âme sérieuse et tournée à l'historie, on devait tirer de fortes leçons."[11] Sainte-Beuve particularly appreciates Allart's creation of a superior hero and heroine who could be destined only for one another.

> Un sentiment profond de dignité de femme une fois abusée respire dans Thérese. L'éternelle pensée de ce qu'il y a encore au fond du génie romain exalte et dévore Sextus. Ces deux êtres choisis sont destinés l'un à l'autre, et, après la lutte première venant de quelque malentendu, ils doivent tout vaincre pour s'unir (quoted by Uffenbeck 192).

Sainte-Beuve, however, was disappointed in what he considered Allart's insufficient development in her text of the rapport between the protagonists. The quick wrap-up of the happy ending seems to have left him wanting also, as he cites in her writing style a "brève négligeance, comme on fait à la fin d'une lettre, lorsque le jour baisse ou que le papier manque." In short, he counsels her simply to loosen up a bit and to let her sentiments flow more freely, or in other words, to be more the Romantic.

> . . . il lui faudrait se souvenir que si, dans le genre tendre et aventureux, il est permis, en composant, de laisser courir sa plume, qui va d'elle-même alors aux disgressions faciles, aux grâces variées et abondantes, il devient indispensable en abordant un order de sentiments plus contenu et plus réservé, de nourrir son expression et de marquer ses effets . . . . La négligence autrement environées de sévérité, n'a rien qui charme et ressemble trop à la sécheresse (quoted by Uffenbeck 192).

After all, Sainte-Beuve continues, even with the most serious of novels, a reader wishes to be swept into the pages, and to be able to escape and enjoy. "Et puis, dans toute espèce de roman, même le plus élevé, le plus sérieux, le plus digne, n'y a-t-il pas lieu, par instants aussi rares, qu'on voudra, mais quelquefois enfin, à s'assesoir, à s'oublier, à s'épanouir?" (quoted by Uffenbeck 192).

Sainte-Beuve concludes with a brief nod to the three essays on Rome, Naples and Tuscany that follow *Sextus* in the same tome, noting that Allart's research is done in the tradition of the best historians, "[avec] un coup d'œil moral et observateur" (quoted by Uffenbeck 193).

Hortense's personal correspondence with Sainte-Beuve began in March 1832. Their friendship, which would be mostly intellectual (with one notable exception), would go on through 1864.   Although Sainte-Beuve was not handsome, he was no doubt pleasing to Hortense for a variety of other reasons.

> "Il n'est pas douteux que, tout disgracié qu'il était physiquement, Sainte-Beuve plaisait à Hortense au moins par la piquante et onctueuse saveur de ses propos presque toujours orientés sur l'amour et les femmes, ses manières insinuantes de confesseur laïc, son sourire, son regard pénétrant" (Billy 111).

On March 25, 1832, she had written asking Sainte-Beuve to review *Sextus.* "Si l'article a votre nom, le succès de *Sextus* sera sûr."[12] By the time Sainte-Beuve's review appeared (without the benefit of his name, since it was unsigned), Hortense had already left France for England yet again, in response to Henry's illness.   In the March 25 letter, she also told Sainte-Beuve that because of the cholera that was in London, she had left five-year-old Marcus behind in Paris, and would return there soon to check on him.

She crossed at Boulogne, and soon settled in an apartment with Henry in London. This time they had "un amour chaste," since Henry was forbidden by his doctor to make love, "le seul et vrai secours qu'il lui fallût" (*EP* 171).   She begged him to leave England, but he was too devoted to Parliament, and insisted, ill as he was, on going to the Chamber as often as he was able. They still talked of marriage, and still put it off because of their opposing personal preferences.   "Si j'avais pu vivre en Angleterre, il m'aurait demandé de nous marier tout de suite" (*EP* 172).

She returned to Paris in June 1832. On July 2, Béranger wrote her about his reaction to *Sextus,*   noting that her writing style was improved, even masterful. "Il y a à la fois plus de flexibilité et plus de fermeté. Il est vraiment de main de maître." He also praised the sections in the novel about Italy, and urged her to continue writing more serious works. "Ne vous obstinez pas *au moins*, vous pouvez *le plus.*"[13]   After quoting from this letter in *Les Enchantements de Prudence*, she added, "Chateaubriand m'avait souvent dit la même chose, et que j'étais faite pour des études viriles" (*EP* 173).

At this point, Chateaubriand, had just returned from Switzerland to France. Coming to the political aid of his friend, the Duchess of Berry, he had run up against the government for a sum of money he had attempted to give to her on behalf of local cholera victims as well as for some subversive letters he had written. He had spent two weeks in prison during June (where the faithful Béranger—once in a similar situation— had visited him). As for Hortense, by August he was still turning her the cold shoulder. "Il refuse de me voir à moins que je ne veuille recommencer le passé." She, in turn, asked him to have dinner with her, providing he would *not* insist on resuming their former relationship. "Je voulais qu'il engageât son honneur et sa chevaliererie" (*EP* 174).

They fixed a rendezvous at their old, favorite spot, the Pont d'Austerlitz, and although he had made her no guarantees about his conduct, she decided to appeal to his sense of gallantry, and, thereby, to trust him. They walked together and had dinner at a favorite restaurant, L'Arc-en-Ciel. He behaved like a gentlemen, although his subsequent letters that week indicated his ongoing infatuation and frustration.

The next day Chateaubriand sent her a short letter:

> Ma cruauté est devenue folle de votre infidélité. Vous avez vu votre puissance; . . . . Que je suis bête et insensé! J'ai honte de ma faiblesse, mais j'y succombe de trop bonne grâce . . . . Je pars, sinon heureux, du moins portant plus légèrement la vie. Que sera l'avenir? Le mien doit être si court qu'il ne vaut guère la peine que j'y songe . . . . Adieu, magicienne, volage, trompeuse et toujours aimée.[14]

Three more letters followed in rapid succession before he left a second time for Switzerland. On Aug. 8, "Mais si vous jetiez un regard vers moi, vous me trouverez toujours. Adieu" (quoted by Pailleron 263), and in a separate letter later that same evening, "Mille tendresses, Aimez-moi, pensez à moi, reviens à moi . . . . vous pouvez toujours m'enchaîner . . . . Je vous reconnais pour la Muse de Rome et la Dame d'Étampes. Ne détruisez pas cette chimère . . . . Je veux aimer votre talent comme votre personne. Point d'adieu" (quoted by Pailleron 264).

This same month, Henry, jealous over word of her renewed correspondence with Chateaubriand, traveled to France. He wrote from Boulogne, asking Hortense to meet him in Abbeville. She declined, explaining that she was too engrossed in work on her fourth novel. Although she might not have stated it quite so plainly to Henry, her words in *Les Enchantements de Prudence* indicate that she was not in a humor to put aside her work yet another time for his sake. "[J'étais] en marché pour mon roman *L'Indienne*, lui ayant jusqu'alors sacrifié tout pour lui" (*EP* 176). She asked him to come meet her in Paris, then he persuaded her to meet him in Beauvais. He kept her waiting there for four days before they returned together to Paris.

They spent several weeks together in the capital. At one point Hortense left some of Chateaubriand's letters on a table while she went out, and returned to find Henry reading them.   Did she leave the letters out unthinkingly or by design?   "Tout séduisant qu'il était, Bulwer se montrait jaloux de Chateaubriand et Hortense se plaisait à exciter cette jalousie" (Pailleron 265).

Henry departed for England, perhaps out of anger over the letters, but most likely because he wished to resume his work. Somehow, Chateaubriand had heard in Geneva that Henry had been back in Paris with Hortense.   On Sept. 26, 1832, he wrote melodramatically, "Vous êtes jeune, soyez heureuse, et n'embarquez pas votre vie sur un vieux vaissaux naufragé. J'ai peu de temps à vivre, et je veux mourir seul . . . (quoted by Pailleron 269).

A little later, on Oct. 17, after Hortense had written about how autumn made her feel sad, Chateaubriand wrote, "Accoutumez-vous à voir disparaître tout ce que vous aurez aimé et cessé d'aimer. Profitez de vos jeunes jours mêlés aux vieilles heures de l'automne pour écrire quelque chose digne de vous. Faites mes adieux à la France et mettez-moi aux rang des morts" (quoted by Billy 122).

Not long after penning these words, however, Chateaubriand had grown bored with his second stay in Switzerland He would soon return to France and live another active and prolific 16 years.   Allart's correspondence, visits, and devotion would continue until his death on July 4, 1848.

It was during this same summer of 1832 that Hortense took an interest in the Saint-Simoniens,   one of the most prominent and controversial socialist groups of the day, whose central concern was the emancipation of women and sexual liberation in general, and whose "utopian" philosophy, she believed, was in harmony with her own cult of love.

At her urging, it was Sainte-Beuve who first tried to put Hortense in touch with some Saint-Simonian leaders so she could arrange to meet with them in person.   During winter 1832, he had written to Charles Duveyrier, author of *Exposition de la doctrine de Saint-Simon,* introducing Hortense with an eclectic list of praises—"C'est Mme Allart . . . l'auteur de *Gertrude.*   C'est une femme belle qui a depuis longemps fait bon marché des scruples de son sexe, elle est homme et homme fort loyal . . . . une femme très peu chrétienne, amie intime de Béranger . . . maîtresse de Chateaubriand" (quoted by Billy 115)—and asking Duveyrier to visit her.

He did not visit, but Hortense persisted, writing several times herself to the group's leader, Charles Enfantin, and asking to meet with him.   Although Enfantin finally wrote back inviting Hortense to attend the group's meetings, his letter was turgid, impersonal, and failed to satisfy her curiosity about his philosophy about women.   He claimed that he was waiting for women to take the first step and tell him what they expected for the future.   "Je dois attendre d'elles. Elle sauront mieux que moi ce qu'elles doivent entreprendre pour faire aimer les apôtres de leur afranchissement."[15]

Chateaubriand, writing from Lucerne on Aug. 21, did not approve of her interest in the Saint-Simonians, whom he believed were scoundrels. (Some of their meetings in Paris already had been broken up by the police, and they were under investigation by the government). "Vos saint-simoniens sont des débauchés qui veulent des femmes et de fripons qui cherchent de l'argent; quelques-uns sont venus me prêcher; ils ont bientôt vu que je n'étais ni un compère, ni une dupe" (quoted by Pailleron 266).   On Sept. 4, he added "Je méprise le saint-simonisme . . . . cela n'est que de la prostitution, du vol et du charlatanisme qui n'est plus en rapport avec le siècle." He claimed that Christianity ought to reinforce all philososphies of liberty and equality that she could desire, and advised, "Ne vous rendez pas ridicule et ne galvaudez pas votre vie" (quoted by Pailleron 267).

Hortense herself was disappointed in Enfantin's letter, suspecting that his cult was more concerned with abstract ideas than with action. Still, she persisted, writing one more letter to Michel Chevalier, director of the *Globe,* the newspaper that disseminated the philosophy Saint-Simonians.   She received no reply.   "Sans doute ni le Père Enfantin ni Michel Chevalier ne la prirent-ils au sérieux: on ne les devine pas très empressés à faire d'elle une adepte" (Billy 117).[16]

Two weeks later, on Aug. 2, 1832, Père Enfantin and two other male leaders went on trial for suspicion of corrupting public morality, were found guilty, and imprisoned for a year.   The Saint-Simonians were ordered to disband, and they would all but disappear by 1834.

The demise of the Saint-Simonians only marked the springboard of Hortense's interest in women's emancipation and sexual liberation, although it would not be until 1836 that her feminist spirit would really blossom beyond her fictional writings into eloquent journalistic and sociological urgings for reform, and when she would actually become involved in progressive groups.

The year 1832 continued to be eventful as well.   Snug in a rented apartment on Rue Mondovi, near the Rue de Rivoli and Place Louis XIV, she continued her correspondence with Chateaubriand, who complained about not being able to advise her on the creation of *L'Indienne.* "J'attends votre *L'Indienne,* écrivit-il, mais je regrette toujours de n'avoir point vu votre travail avant qu'il soit publié: J'ai foi dans mon expérience: les vieux soldats et les vieux laboureurs sont bons à consulter" (*EP* 178-79).   He also continued to urge her to give up Saint-Simonianism and to come visit him in the Jura.

Hortense continued through 1832 what would become her decades-long correspondence with Sainte-Beuve. On Nov. 11, she wrote asking Sainte-Beuve if he could procure some theater tickets for her and a group of friends to see Victor Hugo's play*Le Roi S'Amuse.* Sainte-Beuve wrote to Hugo on her behalf, and the latter graciously agreed to provide her with six seats in the loge that he had reserved from the Nov. 22 sold-out performances to give to special groups.[17]

Before the year was out, Hortense would make a new acquaintance and begin an even longer term of letter-writing. The nettlesome, sometimes adversarial, but mostly cordial friendship and correspondence would be with George Sand.

Notes

[1] Juliette Decreus. *Hortense Allart de Méritens et Henri Bulwer-Lytton.* (Paris: M.J. Minard, *Lettres Modernes,* 1961) 19.

[2] H. Bulwer. *Ode on the death of Napoleon; lines on the neapolitan Revolution and other poems.* (London: London, Gossling & Egley, 1822), quoted by Decreus 19.

[3] H. Bulwer. *Today and Yesterday, a satire.* (London: Chiswick, 1824), 161-162; 35-38, quoted by Decreus 21.

[4] H. Bulwer. *An Autumn in Greece.* London. John Ebers, 1826.

[5] "Il lui réclama ses lettres; elle les lui rendit après les avoir copiées, et il lui renvoya les siennes, mais non pas toutes, il garda les plus tendres," Billy 102.

[6] Marie-Louis Pailleron. "Hortense Allart et Chateaubriand I," *La Revue des Deux Mondes.* CX (Jan. 1, 1940): 83.

[7] Letter to Babbage, Aug. 2, 1931, quoted by Decreus 39. It is important to note here that Hortense Allart was fluent in English. Decreus states in her preface that all excerpts from letters from Allart to Babbage and to Bulwer that appear in her book have been translated by her from Allart's original English into French. Unfortunately, I did not have the opportunity to find these letters in their original form and quote them, as I would have preferred to do, in Hortense's exact English words.

[8] Hortense Allart. "Lettere di Hortense Allart de Méritens a Gino Capponi," *Studi Francesi* I (1957): 247-48.

[9] Mme. Hortense de Thérase Allart, *Sextus ou le Romain de Maremmes.* (Paris: Heideloff and Campe, 1832) 12. (Subsequent references to this work will appear in parentheses after the quotation, and will be indicated by the abbreviation *Sext.*)

[10]"E.," "Album.—Romans de dames. (*Les Blancs et les Bleus, Raoul, ou l'Enéide, Sextus, ou le Romain des Maremmes*)," *Revue de Paris* (Brussels edition), 4e année, I (April 1832) 299-302, quoted by Uffenbeck 190.

[11]Sainte-Beuve's review appeared anonymously in the *Revue des Deux Mondes*, VI (May 15, 1832), 491-92. It was reprinted in *Œuvres*. (Paris: Bibliothèque de la Pléiade [1949]), I, 441-43, quoted by Uffenbeck 191.

[12]Hortense Allart: *Nouvelles Lettres à Sainte-Beuve, (1832-1864)*. Lorin A. Uffenbeck, ed. (Geneva: Librairie Droz S.A., 1965) 2.

[13]Séché quotes this letter, 292, and Allart quotes parts of it herself in *Les Enchantements de Prudence*, 173. Italics are hers.

[14] Coll. Lovenjoul, F. 205. Quoted by Marie-Louise Pailleron. "Hortense Allart et Chateaubriand, II," *La Revue des Deux Mondes*, CX (Jan. 14, 1940), 263. Allart also quotes extensively from several of Chateaubriand's letters from this period in *Les Enchantements de Prudence*, 174-77.

[15] Enfantin's letter to Allart was published by Paul Bonnefon in *L'Amateur d'autographes* , XLI (1908), 327-28, quoted by Uffenbeck 198.

[16]Interestingly, although Père Enfantin did not appear to value an association with Allart, he did seek support later from George Sand. After the publication of *Lélia* in 1833, he approached Sand and asked that she formally become the "mother" of the Saint-Simonian "family." Although she agreed with the group's ideas on equality of the sexes, she politely declined the offer, indicating that she herself had no doctrine, but was simply a novelist. Speaking more candidly to her close friends, such as composer Franz Liszt, she condemned Enfantin, saying she disliked the cult status of his group and his doctrine on women and morality, which she considered too confusing.

"Sand was herself, of course, a *femme emancipée,* who did not mind shocking public opinion, but she wished to do it on her own and not under the aegis of Prosper Enfantin, whom she considered a charlatan," (Dorothy Zimmerman, "George Sand and the Feminists of the 1830's and 1840's in France," *Friends of George Sand Newsletter.* [Fall-Winter 1981]: 21).

[17]Excerpts of Sainte-Beuve's letter to Hugo and Hugo's response are in *Nouvelles Lettres à Sainte-Beuve*, 3, n. 1.

Chapter 5

L'Indienne: The Quest for both Love and Independence (1833-35)

Hortense describes her feelings during autumn 1832 as melancholy, although certain aspects of her life were progressing well. *Sextus* was receiving positive attention, she was writing and selling a number of articles on political topics, and she found contentment in furnishing her Rue Mondovi apartment. The 900 francs she received from *L'Indienne,* which was published by Vimont in December, allowed her to buy a new carpet. Vimont offered her 1,500 francs to publish a future novel, but she made no commitment. "Je ne voulais pas une telle obligation" (*EP* 179).

The melancholia and the uncertainty stemmed from the still tenuous relationship with Bulwer. Henry left for London in September—"Je lui disais adieu" (*EP* 178)—then returned. She heard from a friend that he had been courting an English lady in Dieppe, and was planning to marry her. Hortense angrily showed him the door, and he left "furieux" (*EP* 179). He returned three days later, thanking her for not calling him back, "afin qu'il put savoir combien je lui suis si chère" (*EP* 179).

At this point, Henry was trying to sympathize with Hortense's dislike of England, and attempting to work out some kind of compromise to accommodate his love for her while still boosting his career. "Il a compris qu'en dépit de son amour pour lui, la vie d'Hortense à Londres, sans société, sans les conversations d'un petit cercle était intenable" (Decreus 44). Hoping for a diplomatic post in Europe (which would come a few years later, but too late for Hortense), he vowed to her he would renounce the House of Commons, marry her, and settle in Paris.

With the elections near, and she weary and skeptical of Henry's promises, Hortense pressed him to choose at that moment between her and Parliament.   As he awaited word of the elections, Hortense recalled, "Ce temps fut terrible. Tiendrait-il sa parole? Pouvais-je croire? Est-ce possible?" (*EP* 179).   Henry protested that if he were not elected, Hortense would not love him any more. After all, he said, she loved Parliament, too.   She struggled with this concept, knowing there was truth there.   She always loved, admired and sought men of grandeur, just the sort who would be elected to a post of national prominence.   "Il me suppliait de le laisser partir, de le laisser s'aller dégager. Moi, je voulais finir ce supplice, et qu'il choisisse entre le Parlement et moi. Mais, avec mes goûts, l'homme qui devait me plaire n'était-il pas celui qui choisirait le Parlement?" (*EP* 179).

By November 1832, Henry was suddenly gone, leaving only a note to Hortense, to present himself before the Parliamentary elections. Hearing of his swift re-election to the House of Commons for Coventry, Hortense reacted in a more volatile way than she ever had before.

"Hortense, furieuse, rompt tout net et lui renvoie les lettres qu'il lui adresse," states Decreus (45), calling Hortense's behavior at this time "unreasonable."   Could this upstart Frenchwoman not see that poltical life in England quite simply was in Henry's blood?

> Voulait-elle le dominer au point de le faire renoncer à tout rôle dans la vie publique? . . . . Dès son enfance il a vécu dans un milieu de politiciens professionnels, seul élément substantiel du salon de sa grand-mère, et la Chambre des Communes était pour lui, comme pour son frère Edward, une étape aussi normale dans sa carrière que l'avaient été l'école et l'université.   Qu'auraient dit ses amis? (Decreus 45).

In fairness to Henry, then, the House of Commons was an understandable step in his career. He made mistakes during his liaison with Hortense,   but her efforts to understand and to tolerate his ambitions were limited, as well as clouded by devotion to projects of her own.   Also, she was growing increasingly incapable of putting aside her own agenda for the sake of his.   "Quels que fussent, qu'aient été et que seront les torts de Henry Bulwer envers sa maîtresse—et il en aura de nombreux et de graves—elle-même, surtout au début de leur liaison, semble avoir manqué de tact et de compréhension" (Decreus 47).

Hortense retired to the countryside for a time, where Sainte-Beuve visited and listened as she poured out her heart about the frustrations of the Bulwer affair.   At this same time, Henry made a rather ungallant entry in his personal journal in regard to Hortense's heady ego and his opinion as to the dubious quality and marketability of her books:

> J'ai l'habitude d'entendre de Mme Allart, car elle me l'a répété
> tant de fois, qu'aucune femme avant elle n'a réuni en sa personne
> ses talents et sa beauté, de sorte que, bien qu'elle ait dépassé la
> trentaine et que ses livres soient illisibles et invendables, je ne
> suis pas loin de l'en croire (quoted by Billy 125).

Although he sounds like a man who might have been trying to talk himself out of a further relationship with Hortense, by early 1833, Henry had already tired of their estrangement.   He returned to Paris, and took lodgings not far from her Rue de Mondovi residence.   He sought a reconciliation gingerly, first writing to Hortense's sister, Sophie Allart, then asking to see young Marcus.   In the meantime, he took advantage of his time in Paris by circulating in the French literary scene, where he made the acquaintance of Victor Hugo, Prosper Merimée and Alfred de Vigny.

Hortense stayed active in society herself, but with different friends, perhaps, says Decreus, in an effort to stave off the temptation to accept Henry back in her life.   "Hortense aussi voit du monde, et le plus possible, pour s'empêcher de courir vers son amant" (51).   She turned her attention to her correspondence with Chateaubriand, and his latest inflammatory pamphlet, for which he would be jailed as soon as he returned to France from Switzerland later that year.

Still nursing his bruised ego over her continued, though stymied liaison with Bulwer, Chateaubriand wrote from Switzerland, "Vous vieillirez, ô ma jeune maîtresse. Vous vieillirez et je ne serai plus. Voilà ce qui me vengera de votre trahison" (*EP* 181).   Hortense did not reply to this letter, much to his distress, and in his next missive, Chateaubriand addressed her as "Votre sublime Infidelité." He asked, "N'aurait-elle pu me donner un signe de vie pendant cette bagarre? A vos superbes pieds je m'incline" (*EP* 181).

Early 1833 saw her busy with a number of writing projects. Libri visited and told her of a translating opportunity. She translated into French a piece of fiction written in a Roman dialect about a 16th-century Roman hero, Cola de Rienzo, then later an early opera by Richard Wagner.   She received 500 francs (Billy 120).

Her article in the *Revue de Paris* on March 17, praising Béranger prompted a letter from the ever-modest poet urging her not to use too readily the words "grand homme," of which he felt unworthy. She published several articles in various publications that she had written while in England, including a work on the history of Italy.   She was paid for all of them.

Sampayo appeared to inform her that he had seen Henry at the opera with a young *Anglaise,* and added other uncomplimentary comments about Henry's appearance, calling him "laid, sans esprit, que c'était une femmelette, qu'il avait le visage d'une vieille femme."   The reason for Sampayo's unpleasant remarks was not lost on Hortense. "Il disait ce que dit un rival" (*EP*   183).   He also complained about her recent correspondence and visit with Chateaubriand.

Ignoring Sampayo's attitude, Hortense eventually agreed to a reunion with Henry, while he was still in Paris. Her feelings, if she had managed to keep them dormant during their separation, blossomed with the renewed contact. "J'avais livré mon cœur à l'homme le plus charmant de la terre! Comment m'en détacher désormais, et vaincre lui, moi-même, et ces nouvelles délices qui n'étaient plus qu'en lui, ni possible avec lui" (*EP*   184).

On another occasion, Henry and Sampayo inadvertently met at her house. Involuntarily, Hortense compared the two of them physically. Sampayo, for whom she would never lose her sentimental feelings of first love, came out ahead, although she was ashamed of herself for thinking so. "Ils avaient chacun le pied petit et la main belle; mais le pied d'Henry me parut trop petit. La beauté, la noblesse de Jérôme et de son air surpassaient tout. Je me trouvai injuste, car lequel savait seul les plus doux mystères, cette partie divine et adorable de la vie humaine?" (*EP,* quoted by Billy 122).

She could see Henry still struggling with the usual dilemma—love versus his ambition. "L'ambition l'emportait, mais comme il sentait que l'amour aussi eût pu l'emporter, son ambition s'effrayait tellement, qu'elle triomphait d'avance" (*EP* 184).   Therefore, his ambition, terrified that his love might vanquish it, won the round. Henry left Paris in February 1833, promising to write. For a long time, he did not. "Moi je lui envoie un adieu" (*EP*   184).

A new relationship was occupying Hortense's mind, this time a friendship with a woman, for she had met George Sand for the first time in December 1832.   They were in a similar position during this era, each an independent young mother and a rising and controversial novelist.   Sand, age 28, the mother of eight-year-old Maurice and three-year-old Solange, recently recently separated from husband Casimir Dudevant, left behind her old identity as Aurore Dupin Dudevant, and had produced her first two novels—*Indiana* and *Valentine* —that year under her new pseudonym.

Three years older than Sand, Allart, at 31, had a slightly larger number of published works to her credit—*La Conjuration D'Amboise, Lettres sur Madame de Staël, Gertrude, Jérôme, Sextus,* and *L'Indienne,* as well as her journalistic pieces.   Both women were as well known for their insouciantly unconventional personal lives as they were for their writings.

The two writers' early relationship was marked with an incident of jealousy and betrayal that might well have squelched another friendship in such an early and delicate stage.   Charles Didier, who had been Hortense's lover during her stay in Italy, and perhaps on and off since, eventually would become lover to Sand, after Allart introduced the two in early 1833.   "Rather foolishly, Hortense Allart had presented her tall, well-built, very attractive lover to George Sand on Feb. 2, 1833," writes Sand biographer Joseph Berry.[1]   Sand invited Didier to dinner several more times after that, sometimes with Hortense, sometimes alone.

There was a lapse of about three years from Didier's first meeting with Sand until the time they became lovers, apparently in spring 1836.   In the interim, Sand had a short affair with Merimée and a lengthier one with Alfred deMusset. During the first months of his budding relationship with Sand, Didier was still seeing Hortense. He wrote in his diary Aug. 20, 1833, that Hortense was "very jealous" of his increasing closeness to the other novelist. "Hortense, très jalouse, me fait ce soir de *Lélia* des critiques justes, critiquant quand je loue, louant quand je critique" (quoted by Billy 124). "Très jalouse"! Billy asks. "Hélas! Hortense n'était pas de force à lutter contre George Sand" (124).

Whatever hurt or frustration she may have been feeling at the time, Hortense gamely rose above it, ceding in her own mind to Sand's superior status as writer and seductress for the sake of their professional rapport. ". . . peut-être s'agit-il d'une retraite stratégique qui abandonne provisoirement le domaine affectif pour mieux conserver celui qui lui importe le plus: le domaine littéraire,"[2] states Mary Ann Garnett.

On Feb. 19, 1833, just after she must have noticed the growing attraction between Sand and Didier, Hortense wrote to Sainte-Beuve excitedly describing a project that she had proposed to Sand that they undertake together—a monthly publication of collected articles on a variety of literary topics. "Il s'agit de l'art et non du profit. Mme Dudevant ferait des nouvelles, moi ce que je pourrai[s]; on pense à vous pour la pensée, la hauteur, la sensibilité."[3]   (The publication never came about, but Billy notes that this was due more to Sainte-Beuve's indifference than to Sand's. "L'Editeur Gosselin en eût assuré la publication, à la condition que Sainte-Beuve promît sa collaboration.

C'est vraisemblablement son refus qui fit avorter le project" [Billy 129]).

Hortense added in the Feb. 19 letter, "Mme Dudevant . . . est charmante.   Si j'étais homme j'en serais fou, quel talent!   C'est admirable!" (*N.L. à S.-B.* 7).

She had written similar comments to Béranger about Sand, for he mentioned in a letter to Hortense in early 1833, how much he admired her high opinion of a rival writer. "Votre admiration pour Madame Sand est un nouveau trait de votre bon et noble caractère. Ce n'est pas vous qui jamais serez envieuse ou jalouse du mérite d'une autre femme. Je vous dirai à ma honte que je ne connais les romans de cette dame que par les journaux" (quoted by Séché 296-97).

As mentioned in the Preface, Sand's initial reaction to Allart was not so charitable.   In a March 10, 1833 letter to Sainte-Beuve,[4] she referred to Allart pejoratively as *une écriveuse*.   The invention of an unofficial feminine form of *écrivain* indicated that Sand did not wish to be grouped with other "women authors" of her time.   It was an age where "women's writing" connoted a certain fluffiness, or at least a lack of serious literary merit. A sense of sisterhood among female writers and the common struggle of women in creating a gynocentric language and purpose was still some 130 years away,[5] so Sand's reaction was not atypical.

Biographer Renée Winegarten notes that Sand, realizing that Allart's friendly attentions probably masked a fundamental jealousy about Sand's more rapidly rising fame in the literary scene, was wary of friendship for professional as well as personal reasons.

> Hortense Allart deeply admired and secretly envied the author of *Indiana,* ambivalent feelings of which the latter was well aware. George Sand remained wary of this handsome, intelligent, liberated, and as yet unmarried colleague who had something in common with herself but for whom she privately expressed distaste.   To her, Hortense Allart appeared as the person she herself did not want to be: "a scribbler" who talked politics . . . "a woman writer."   Any masculine opponent of women with literary ambitions could have said no worse. Indeed, these were the very words some were applying to *her.* [6]

Sand further criticized Allart and her writing style in a letter dated April 1, 1833, to her friend Laure Decerfz. "Je vois aussi Mme Allart, une femme de lettres qui a un style assez ronflant, et qui a fait des livres assez élevés mais ennuyeux et mal conduits. Elle ne vaut pas ses livres, elle est pédante . . . tranchante, politique, hommasse, femme auteur comme tous les diables." She also states, with some accuracy, that Allart was overstating her admiration to avoid the bad taste of seeming jealous of her. Sand continues, ". . . elle manque de simplicité, de grâce et je crois de cœur. Je ne l'aime guère" (*Corres. de G.S.* 2: 291).

This attitude is also evident in the thinly disguised irritation in Sand's letter to Allart in July 1833, which included a response to Allart's questions about *Indiana* and *Valentine*. Allart had had the temerity to suggest that Sand was "too feminine" in her writing and that her first two novels could have done more toward bettering the lot of French women. Allart had written earlier that summer:

> Bien que vos ouvrages aient de la vigueur et par moment une éloquence et une force qu'aucun des hommes du moment n'égale, je vous croyais femme par le caractère, la douleur . . . les femmes fléchissent sous les ennuis profonds dont leur vie est entourée . . . . j'avais compté sur vour pour améliorer un peu leur sort, car il dépend des femmes de le faire.[7]

In a tone rank with sarcasm, Sand tells her fellow novelist:

> Vous l'avez fort bien dit, je manque de précision et de suite . . . C'est l'infirmité d'une nature pauvre et boiteuse. Je n'ai rien étudié, je ne sais rien, pas même ma langue. . . . Vous voyez bien que je ne suis bonne à rien, mais vous êtes bonne à tout, et, par votre talent et par votre caractère vous n'avez pas besoin de mon aide. . . . Faites du bien aux femmes en général par votre zèle et votre chaleur de cœur, faites en à moi en particulier par votre douceur et votre tolérance (*Corres. de G.S.* 2:389-90).

Incredibly, Hortense never seemed to take offense at anything Sand ever wrote to her in these first tenuous years of their relationship. Over the next two years, she attempted to keep up with Sand's comings and goings (particularly the 1834 voyage to Venice with deMusset) through Sainte-Beuve. Allart's letters to and about Sand remained unfailingly cordial and enthusiastic from the outset up to their last documented correspondence in 1872, after the publication of *Les Enchantements de Prudence*. Their relationship would remain complex, but Sand's communication with Allart was to grow increasingly warmer over the years, and would burgeon into admiration by about 1854. Continuing excerpts from their correspondence will be discussed in subsequent chapters.

In spring of 1833, Didier hosted a soirée at which he introduced

Hortense to several literary figures. Although no doubt in her element
in such a setting, at that time she was at work on her history of
Florence and wished to retire to the countryside where she could have a
quieter place to write and calmer, more studious life.

She chose to settle in Herblay, an area on the outskirts of Paris
with a lovely countryside ambiance.   It had nostalgic value for
Hortense for it was here that she had first met Laure, then Sampayo. It
also was a place where she could enjoy a peaceful, bucolic setting,
while still being fairly close to the city.   A few years later, in a letter
to Chateaubriand from Herblay written Aug. 8, 1842, Hortense would
describe the area as an idyllic setting that reminded her of his writings
about the American wilderness in *Atala*. The Seine flowed by just a
few steps from her house, wild animals ran about, and the wind wafted
through the willow trees.

> Il y a ici, dans la Seine, une île assez grande, abandonnée à la
> nature, couverte de hautes herbes, d'arbres en liberté et d'animaux
> sauvages. C'est là que je vais penser à vous: on y entend le bruit
> des colibris, le frémissement des saules, les doux murmures de vos
> déserts d'Amérique: il y a une odeur de plantes marines, et les
> mauves bleues dont vous orniez le front d'*Atala* (quoted by Séché
> 134).

She would return to this favorite spot several more times until
1850. Hortense also chose Herblay because she wished to begin some
formal education there for seven-year-old Marcus. She placed him *en
pension* with the local priest, Father Bertrand, who was known for his
scholarly, liberal bent, and who already had attracted negative attention
from his bishop for a series of articles that he had published.   What
more likely candidate for the job of tutor to Hortense Allart's only son?
" . . . ce n'était pas sur un précepteur ordinaire que Marcus était tombé.
Nul doute qu'avec sa curiosité encyclopédique Hortense elle-même n'ait
apprécié en son curé un interlocuteur digne d'elle" (Billy 131).
Marcus' education would remain in the care of Father Bertrand until
1837, when his mother would take him for a three-year stay in Italy.

At Herblay, Libri and Didier visited, bringing along other friends
and spending pleasant summer days.   Bulwer arrived in the fall, and,
leaving Marcus behind, he and Hortense departed for Versailles, where
they spent a month. They settled in Paris in December, where they
would remain until February 1834.   Hortense continued to receive
friends at her apartment on rue Mondovi, although she lived with Henry
in a rez-de-chaussée lodging on the rue Basse-du-Rempart. Henry still
spoke of marriage and of finding a permanent diplomatic post in Paris.

"Il avait repris le language du plus grand amour," Hortense recalled. Though fraught with the usual discords, this brief time together was mostly happy. "Ces quatre mois furent heureux. Non sans orage, car nous étions l'orage même" (*EP* 187). Henry worked on his own two-volume writing project about France, and on *The Life of Byron*, which would be published as a preface to the Galignani's French edition of works by Byron. "Nos jours était parfaits, occupés, amoureux" (*EP* 188).

Henry made frequent forays into society, sometimes provoking Hortense's jealousy. ". . . aimable et élégant, il plaisait partout." Because Hortense did not like mustaches—"excepté aux hommes de guerre"—Henry humored her by shaving four times a day—upon arising, at two o'clock before going out, at six or seven o'clock before dinner, and finally, late evening before attending the theater or a ball. Hortense laughed at this indulgence towards her, and a Italian *valet de chambre* exclaimed, "Quattro volte la barba!" (*EP* 188).

They met with Madame Hamelin and the Countess Regnault de Saint-Angély (Hortense's "Countess of Vallon" or "Laure"). Henry suggested that he and Hortense host a soirée. A Russian ambassador who had once told Henry that he would never wish to attend a soirée with the learned Libri, was invited, and Hortense made sure that Libri was invited, too. The Italian scholar's attendance in the presence of the pompous ambassador amused both himself and his hostess. "[Libri] vint, très animé, très amusé, il resta fort tard." Henry himself was a congenial host. "Il fut aimable, distingué, montra beaucoup de gaité, d'esprit, des nuances exquises" (*EP* 188).

It was unsettling for Hortense, then, when Henry, only recently so buoyed with Parisian joviality, suddenly made an about-face, and announced he was returning to London. "Mais sa légèreté était inconcevable: dans le jours les plus tendres, tout à coup il changeait, formait de nouveaux projets" (*EP* 188).

A granddaughter of their friend Lord Arthur Dillon, who had spent time with them at Herblay, and who was well-acquainted with Hortense's *Gertrude*, observed to the author that Henry had rapidly deteriorated from the Romanticism and heroism of one of the novel's male characters to the shallowness and unreliability of another. "Gertrude a fini par Rodrigue; mais vous, madame, vous aimiez Rodrigue, et vous finissez par le comte [Alphonse] de Selmire" (*EP* 188).

Henry headed back to Parliament, pressing Hortense to return with him, and promising once again to marry her. She, however, was at a lull in her work, with her fifth novel, *Settimia,* barely begun, and she feared breaking her creative stride and losing her productivity, if she were to return to London.   She reasoned that it was useless to undergo the same torture she always had experienced in England, and to bore Henry all over again with the same complaints.   "Il fallait ne revoir l'Angleterre qu'avec une occupation forte qui me tint raisonnable. Je le laissai donc partir seul" (*EP* 189).

She moved back into the Mondovi apartment for the rest of the winter and spring of 1834, then spent the summer with Marcus in Herblay. She worked steadily on her *Histoire de la Republique de Florence,* and invited several historians over for frequent discussion, including some from the Bibliothèque Royale de Paris. Chateaubriand wrote, gently scolding her about having neglected him. She visited him again in Paris after his second return from Switzerland. "Elle revit l'Enchanteur à Paris. Il n'avait pas changé" (Billy 136).

Henry returned to France and asked her to meet him in Boulogne, but this time, she declined, so he made his way to Paris alone. Hortense soon arrived from Herblay, and they were reunited, but as soon as Henry heard that she had visited Chateaubriand again, he quit her apartment in a huff.   The same scene took place the next day. A hurtful letter from him followed.

Ruffled by the *contretemps* and wishing to avoid more unpleasant scenes from Henry, Hortense invited Libri to stay at her apartment. She described a stimulating intellectual conversation with him about nature, the universe, and eternity, and sighed privately that she and Henry did not share this kind of intellectual rapport. "Ah! pourquoi Henry n'avait pas avec elle de ces sublimes conversations?" (Billy 136).   Henry wrote again, wishing to see her. She agreed. The unflappable, philosophical Libri was not surprised, but only bid her good-by as she left to meet Henry in Versailles. Henry later followed her to Herblay. This short reconciliation was tender, then, suddenly, but not unexpectedly, he left France again—to present himself for re-election at Marylebone.

Hortense busied herself in Paris with soirées with a number of Italian friends—political refugees from Genoa, an exiled professor from Modena, and an outspoken former acquaintance, Niccolini Tommaséo, who thought Hortense had become "too anglicized" by Bulwer.   By February 1835, Henry persuaded her once again to come to England. From the beginning, this reunion went badly.   At first, they rented a home together in Putney, but he was often absent and she was unhappy.   Hortense reluctantly agreed to go to London.   She upbraided Henry for his infidelities; he hosted soirées and became jealous of the men she found interesting. Nevertheless, their violent scenes always ended in passionate *rapprochement.* "Son visage plein de sentiment, sa belle bouche, ses dents de perle me plaisaient plus que tout ce que je voyais de beau. Après ces soirées et ces jalousies, nous étions plus passionnés, plus tendres" (*EP*, quoted by Billy 137).

One evening, seated at a table with Henry's friends, Hortense felt she was seeing into the future and perceiving that the two of them could not long remain together.   She stayed with Henry another few months, working on her *Histoire de Florence* and her brochure *La femme et la démocratie de nos temps.*   He was too often absent, they disputed with one another, the climate depressed her, and by June 1835, in a greatly agitated emotional state, Hortense left England.   Once on French soil at Calais, she was calmer.

She stayed in Paris during July and read Sand's latest novel *André*, a tender story about a talented young woman whose life is ruined by marriage to a man she adores, who turns out to be indecisive and weak. The sad tale made Hortense feel grateful for the circumstances of her own life. "Ranimée par ce beau roman, j'aimais, je me disais que ma vie était heureuse" (*EP* 197).   Seated in the Tuileries on July 28, 1835, she read a newspaper article that virtually called for the murder of Louis-Philippe.   Though she was not a supporter of the July Monarchy, she was indignant.   At that moment, she saw Louis-Philippe pass by in his carriage.   An hour later, the news flew around that someone had shot at France's leader. (The would-be assassin was named Fieschi, and the attack took place on the Boulevard du Temple).   Hortense ran to Madame Hamelin's house seeking details. Paris was in an uproar, suddenly not the anchor of stability and joy that it usually was for her.

That very evening, she again headed for the coast, then took the boat to England, only to encounter the same difficult scenes in Putney with Henry as they had had so many times before.   During çalmer moments, they read together Sainte-Beuve's *Volupté*.   She wrote to the author from London on Sept. 10, 1835, praising the novel's sensuous and emotional tone, and explaining how she related to the heroine (who was about her age). "J'ai retrouvé à Londres un vol[ume] de *Volupté* . . . . j'y ai trouvé une quantité de belles choses. . . . Il y a dans vos souvenirs quelque chose de triste et de riche qui fait qu'on peut pleurer beaucoup . . . J'ai relu tout cela avec enchantement, car ce livre convient à mon âge" (*N.L. à S.-B.* 10).

After a three-month stay in England, which included a brief sojourn in London, Hortense could tolerate that country no more.   The reasons were the usual problems—the climate, her ennui, and her feelings of non-productivity while there.   In October, she crossed the English Channel for the fourteenth and final time.

Although the frantic voyages between France and England had ended for Hortense, the relationship with Bulwer had by no means yet played itself out.   Henry accompanied her back to Paris, where he made new declarations of his love, insisted he could not leave, and proposed a secret marriage, so he would not lose his mother's inheritance.   Hortense, though, knew that he was always the most devoted to her when he sensed that it was time for them to part, and she dared not hold too much confidence in his promises. "Je ne voulais pas abuser de sa faiblesse . . . . Il revient exalté, désolé, s'assit par terre, la tête sur mes genoux, et m'adore, et me supplie, et me jure . . . Mais moi je disais: —Tout va s'évanouir dès qu'il m'aura quittée!" (*EP* 197-98).

They spent a rapturous night together. "Il reste, passe la nuit avec moi: Quelle nuit! qui mériterait un souvenir immortel, par cet amour combattu porté au comble, par cet abandon irrésistible, par cette puissance esquise et sa vue du ciel" (*EP* 198).   Henry left the next day, accepting Hortense's challenge not to write to her for two weeks, until he had come to a decision about what to do.

Hortense struggled herself with the marriage question.   Should she accept a secret marriage, or exact a written promise from him that they would marry at a later time? "Mais quoi! Avec plus de douceur n'aurais-je donc pas pu raffermir un homme si bon, si estimable, si admirable même? N'aurais-je pas pu lui faire signer simplement l'engagement écrit de m'épouser plus tard et le lui faire jurer devant Dieu?" (*EP* 198).   She realized that a firm, official promise of marriage would require a love and two personalities that were much calmer than theirs, for any repetition of their former discords would undo the bond.   " . . . car cet engagement fût devenu nul à la première querelle, dès que je plaindrais de l'Angelterre, ou dès que je serais jalouse et que je lui rendrais cent fois sa liberté" (*EP* 198).   She was sure only a cold, calculating woman could make such a promise valid.

She considered that perhaps a secret marriage could succeed. "Mais mariés en secret, ce mariage pouvait-il réussir? Je le crois. Je m'en faisais alors le bonheur le plus grand et le plus charmant. Jamais mariage ne fut si passionnément désiré" (*EP* 198). If only, once such a marriage were sealed, she could bring herself to do what Henry wished, to be compliant, devoted, to avoid making scenes!   Knowing herself as she did, she doubted she could rise to (or condescend to?) the challenge.

Hortense, however, was looking at marriage at this point as a fairly young woman who had never experienced the ugly aspects that a legal union in 19th-century France could impose upon a trusting wife.   As she wrote of this 1835 moment in the 1872 *Les Enchantements de Prudence,* she was looking back from the point of view of one who had gone through a ghastly marital experience.

Avoir pour mari un si aimable amant, me semblait le plus
grand bonheur du monde. Je ne me figurais point le mariage
comme je l'ai connu depuis, comme il est, un joug insupportable,
avalissant, qui tient la femme esclave, mais je ne voyais que
l'amour rendu plus sacrée, plus chère, et immortel. . . . (*EP* 198-
99).

Inexperienced though she may have been at this moment, Hortense
thought lucidly about some of the sorrows that might well come after
marriage to Henry, not the least of which would be his probable
infidelities. He had already told her that if they married, he would fear
she would leave him after his next dalliance with another woman. He
had said to her, "Je veux la liberté mais je veux garder ma femme" (*EP*
199).

Given the rational self-analysis that Hortense was wrestling with at
the time, she hardly sounds like a Romantic heroine ready to sacrifice
everything if she can but have her man, but rather, like a more modern
woman concerned with the good of her own emotions and sanity as well
as the good of her own career.   What was slowly and painfully eroding
the romance between Hortense and Henry (although it would never
diminish the lifelong caring and concern that she would retain for him)
was the fact that love had slid into a secondary position for each of
them. For Henry, love was overshadowed by political ambition; for
Hortense, it was reluctantly undercut by her desire for independence,
literary output, and—perhaps most important of all—peace of mind.

She sadly, but realistically pondered what she would lose if she
definitively refused marriage to Henry.   After all, she had had to
renounce a similar passion years earlier with Sampayo. "Ma générosité
me servit bien: elle me dégagea, à vingt-quatre ans, d'un amour trop
tragique, et ici elle me rappela aux lettres sans entraver la course habile
d'un ambitieux; deux fois je rompis ainsi avec la passion, la lumière et
ici je perdis pour jamais, les délices qu'elle seule peut donner" (*EP*
199).

In a few weeks, Henry returned to England.   He was named
secretary the English legation at Brussels on Nov. 17, 1835, and wrote
telling Hortense he had changed his mind about marriage. She wrote
philosophically,   "Je n'en suis pas surprise, et je ne veux pas m'en trop
tourmenter" (*EP*   199).

Henry would write again. Nonetheless, from its beginning, 1836
became such a busy and rewarding year for Hortense, that his further
letters and supplications to join him no longer tormented or tempted
her beyond her own will to stay in France.

Decreus observes that despite the last proposal of a secret marriage in Paris, Henry had begun to think less and less of a marriage to Hortense as their relationship wore on. She speculates on possible reasons for the eventual winding down of their mutual devotion. Was it because he worried about escorting a wife who was a formerly unwed mother into his own milieu of British salons?   Although Hortense usually did not have a problem being accepted into French salons and other social settings, her own aunt, Sophie Gay, and cousin, Delphine Gay de Girardin, refused to receive her for some time after Marcus's birth. The British aristocracy and diplomatic corps might well have done the same.

Would it have made a difference if Hortense had given Henry a child? Always fond of children, Bulwer adored Marcus Allart when he was small, and later showed a fatherly concern in trying to help him establish a diplomatic career. He was also partial to his nephews, and a few years later, would adore Blandine and Cosima Liszt, the small daughters of Franz Liszt and Marie d'Agoult.   "Il avait la fibre paternelle, son affection pour Marcus Allart était réele, il le régale de cadeaux . . . . Il n'oublie pas les enfants de ses maîtresses ou amies" (Decreus 64).

Did Henry think that Hortense was to blame for the sterility of their union? Madame Hamelin was once heard to say that one of the reasons Hortense wanted her second son, Henri Allart (born in Florence March 21, 1839, from her union with Jacopo Mazzei), was to prove that it was Bulwer, not herself, who could not produce a child (Decreus 65). (More discussion of the birth of Henri Allart will be covered in Chapter 7).

The most evident reason for the rupture, aside from Hortense's preference for life in France and dedication to her own writing projects, was that life as a politician's or diplomat's wife simply would never have suited her, for she could not long tolerate being out of the limelight herself for the sake of playing a secondary role as wife.   "A Paris, de même qu'à Florence grâce à ses amis, elle jouissait d'une certaine réputation, à l'étranger elle n'était qu'une inconnue. Un mariage secret n'eût rien arrangé. Ils avaient beau s'aimer, ni l'un ni l'autre ne voulaient sacrifier leur position à leur amour" (Decreus 67).

Rabine adds, "Hortense and all her heroines can love only successful men of action, but they cannot live in their shadow. They can only love a man they cannot dominate but then they can love no one" (200).

L'Indienne, which had quickly sold out of its first printing in December 1832, continued to do well in late 1835. Although the novel appeared before Hortense had endured the last two difficult years with Henry, and before she finally had resolved herself to a life without

marriage to him, the story itself still contains a torturous rendering of a similar relationship. The protagonists are familiar—an ambitious English politician and a delicate half-Indian girl who loves him, but who cannot muster the wherewithal to relinquish the essence of self that a life with him would require of her.

   L'Indienne is Allart's most tragic love story. The novel's plot is, in fact, the worst possible scenario that the author might have imagined for herself as the wife of a English Parliamentarian. The heroine, Anna Berks, an unusual alter-ego for Hortense, is so-called by the novel's title because she has an English father and an Indian mother. The rich descriptions of the tropical "île de Bombau," which is so exhilarating to Anna, contrast starkly with those of the gloom and fog she will experience in London, where she dutifully travels to be near her lover, Julian Warwich. The ambitious Englishman (note the slight difference in the spelling of "Warwich" in *L'Indienne* and "Warwick," who represents Bulwer in *Les Enchantements de Prudence*) loves her sincerely, but is simply too devoted to his career to be able to accord her the caring she craves. "[Il] sentait l'amour et l'ambition avec une force égale."[8]

   In addition to the novel's parallels to her and Bulwer's true-life story, *L'Indienne* is also a vehicle for Hortense to protest the stifling situation that women of the time faced, particularly in England. The book castigates the institution of marriage in general, and how it inevitably brings injustice and sorrow to women's lives. It is by no means an anti-matrimonial novel, however. Allart, much like George Sand, was never against marriage, but rather an idealist and a reformist on the subject. In early 1832, when *L'Indienne* was still a work in progress, she had written in her first documented letter to Sainte-Beuve her ideas about the basic equality of women, particularly in matters of morality:

> Je crois qu'il y a une grande différence entre l'homme et la femme sous tous les rapports, d'intelligence comme de destinée et de délicatesse, mais je ne crois pas ces différence pousées au point où elles sont admises, ainsi je crois qu'une femme peut avoir de l'esprit sans être ridicule et un amant sans rougir. On suppose peut-être que j'ai arrangé mes idées pour ma position, je les avais avant (*N.L. à S-B* 1).

As for marriage, Allart retains a high ideal of what it should be, while opting for a different lifestyle for the time being for personal reasons—a lifestyle that, although it may not be in tune with society's expectations, does not preclude virtue. Her letter to Sainte-Beuve

continues:

> Mais j'aurais voulu tirer part de cette position pour donner
> l'exemple d'une femme, qui, tout en n'observant pas la loi prescrite
> aux femmes de son temps, avait pourtant de la vertu. J'entends par
> vertu combattre son cœur ou ses penchants quand il le faut,
> observer le devoir qu'on s'est prescrit. *Cette femme aurait une
> haute idée du mariage*, mais par des circonstance personnelles, elle
> n'aurait pas connu ce lien, du moins dans sa jeunesse (*N. L. à S-B*
> 1, my italics).

L'Indienne is Hortense's protest that men and society see marriage
(or even unmarried relationships) as situations in which women must
make every sacrifice. Through Anna Berkes, Hortense presents a
virtuous woman who is made unhappy through both a loveless
marriage and a frantic, increasingly untenable affair that suppresses her
natural capacity to love and her ability to attain fulfillment. In making
Anna a Eurasian woman, the author is able to step back, in the manner
of Voltaire and Montesquieu, and criticize her own (and English) society
through the eyes of a foreigner, suggesting that the exotic, more
primitive, and less "civilized" community of Bombay is untouched by
Western-style drive and ambition, thus more conducive to love and
happiness.

Also, in making her heroine a minority woman, Allart buys into a
racial stereotype, but uses it to her metaphoric advantage; that is, she
draws a parallel with European/British men's exploitation of women and
Europe's subjugation of its colonies. "Just as men destroy the very
feminine beauty they adore by confining it to complement them, so the
Europeans appropriate the wealth and beauty of Asia without letting
Asian culture and values contribute to Europe" (Rabine 202).

L'Indienne also comments on expedient political and social
situations in Great Britain at the time, particularly the proposed Bill of
Reform that advocated government aid and benefits to the lower
working class, and of which Hortense did not approve.   (After the
publication of *L'Indienne*, Béranger wrote to Hortense, telling her he
enjoyed the love story, but claiming that aside from that, the novel was
"une brochure sur le [British] bill de réforme" [*EP*   179]).   Woven
into the story as well are pictures of actual English political events
such as the revolt of farmers and manufacturers.

As the novel begins, Julien has fallen in love with Anna, who is
married to the indifferent Mr. Berks. Her much-older husband only
married her as a financial arrangement, and is mostly absent from her
life. Allart gives rich descriptions of the tropical Bombau colony:

" . . . mêlant la puissance de l'Angleterre à la richesse du climat."
Anna is Christian, but loves Indian traditions. Her house is adorned
with lovely things from India and Persia—gold, ivory, etc., "un luxe
asiatique" (*Ind.* 13). In the tradition of Staël's Corinne, Anna is multi-
talented in her own domain. She dances, plays the guitar, and sings
songs of India and of Ireland.

Allart describes Julien as "un homme d'un amabilité enjouée, dont
le rire charmant et les manières ajoutaient un nouvel attrait à la jeunesse
. . . délicat, noble, pâle, sans être beau" (*Ind.* 6).   Although he loves
the Indian culture also, his duties in Parliament are putting an end to
his stay, and he wishes for Anna to depart for England with him.
"Julien oublia la société près d'elle [Anna] . . . et il était prêt à lui
demander le sacrifice que les femmes passionées font à leur amant en
Angleterre" (*Ind.* 8).   Anna hestitates at first, not wishing to be an
adulterous lover among English ladies, and fearing unhappiness in a
country so different from her own. "Habituée à la riante chaleur des
Indes, elle redoutait un pays triste et froid" (*Ind.* 27). Julien offers to
stay in India for her sake, but speaks of the glory of England and of a
career in Parliament for a man of talent.   Anna arranges for a divorce,
and despite her tears of sorrow at leaving her country, Julien surrounds
her with servants and Indian birds and takes her on a boat to England.

Arriving in London (via Saint-Helena, where she visits Napoleon's
tomb), Anna is immediately stifled by the heat and the fog. "Les fruits
[étaient] sans sauveur et les fleurs sans parfum . . . . L'Angleterre est
morne . . . . " (*Ind.* 37). In the meantime, Julien throws himself
wholeheartedly into a campaign for election to Parliament.

Anna sympathizes with a new acquaintance, the unhappy wife of
another politician. Mrs. Bolton, "timide et soumise," suffers from
the demands of too many children and household duties. " . . . car on a
fait des occuptations publiques et des affections de famille une lourde
charge en Angleterre, où rien n'est compris d'un côté heureux" (*Ind.*
59). Seeing Anna's distress, Julien again half-heartedly offers to
abandon his career hopes for her sake. "Si ce départ vous afflige trop, si
mes affaires vous importunent, dites un mot, je reste, je vous sacrifie
mon ambition, je vivrai à vos pieds, je lirai, j'étudierai avec vous,
heureux de passion mes jours dans la retraite et l'innocence!" (*Ind.* 63).
Although Anna knows Julien's delicate health is not suited to public
life and that he really should leave Parliament for his own sake as well
as hers, she cannot accept his sacrifice.

Julien is easily elected as representative of a mostly aristocratic
providence, and takes his place in Parliament. He is gone most of the
time and constantly reads newspapers when he is home. Anna, who
takes little interest in his work, is distressed by his obsessive attitude.

"Ce n'est pas assez, dit Anna, de passer vos jours et vos soirées à la chambre, il faut encore que le matin vous lisiez ce que vous avez entendu la veille: c'est une fureur, une maladie" (*Ind.* 85). She threatens to return to India. Julien reacts violently, then apologizes on his knees. "La reconcilation fut passionée (*Ind.* 89).

Chapter 13 of *L'Indienne* introduces the circumstances leading up to and surrounding the proposed Bill of Reform in 1832 England. Newspapers report the plight of the poor in Marylebone, and subsequent violent uprisings, followed by executions of the poverty-ridden subversives. Allart contrasts the poverty of the workers and the prosperity of the upper class that both result from England's growing industrial efforts. Julien sympathizes with the workers, but finds the Bill of Reform, which would release national monies to improve factory conditions and ease poverty, to be too radical. The strain makes him ill, but when Anna hints that India would be a less stressful environment for him, he will not listen. "Il lui demanda avec ironie si on quittait la vie politique pour un doux climat? (*Ind.* 98).

The next chapter contains more political debates for and against the Bill of Reform. Julien's position is basically the one Allart soon would espouse in her upcoming *La femme et la démocratie de nos temps*—a plea for moderation and for government control to stay in the hands of a sophisticated, aristocratic elite. Julien's counsel for moderation loses out, and he considers voting against the Bill of Reform, then returning to India with Anna. He cannot commit himself to such abandon, though. In a speech that is reminiscent of Madame de Staël's comparison of mankind's attitudes in sombre northern countries with those in the sunnier, more exotic southern civilizations, Anna tells Julien of her longing to return to live closer to nature:

> L'homme du nord est né pour souffrir . . . vous préférez ces affaires à notre ciel bienfaisant et à l'amour. Vous me faites comprendre l'histoire des Indes: dans un beau pays on n'est pas subjugé par des intérêts si positifs. Nous laissons nos prêtres nous governer et nous instruire par des allégories . . . . [qui] nous enseignaient la pureté de l'âme; la fécondité de la terre, représentée par nos fleurs et notre cactus sacré, nous apprenait qu'il fallait être épouses et mères chastes, et nous ne craignions pas de boire à cette coupe d'ivresse que notre dieu, dans ses méditations, ne refusa pas des mains de sa suprême épouse" (*Ind.* 120-121).

The next chapter continues with speculation as to whether India may ever rise up in rebellion against England, which has no sensitivity to—or even acquaintance with—these simpler, yet more sensitive, philosophies of life. Anna thinks of the old Indian custom of burning widows alive, which is now forbidden by English rule. Ironically, she feels England condemns women to something equally heinous. "Anne se fit reconduire chez elle, saluant tristement Westminster et retournant *à l'isolement et à l'ennui où les Anglais, plus que tout autre peuple, ont condamné les femmes"* (*Ind.* 135, my italics.)

Anna's opinion is echoed by another Parliamentary wife, Lady Hampshire, who, although she is young, beautiful and aristocratic, agrees that England is the country where women are the most mistreated and the least valued. "L'amour seul et la faiblesse peuvent conduire une femme en Angleterre, le pays où les femmes sont le plus maltraitées et où elles ont mérité le moins d'admiration" (*Ind.* 143). Lady Hampshire notes that, with the exception of Queen Elisabeth I, England has produced no "superior women," whereas in Italy and France there are almost as many great women as great men. She continues:

> Notre sexe est inférieur à lui-même ici; je vous laisse à décider ce que cela doit nous faire penser des hommes. Faisant croire aux femmes qu'elles n'étaient créées que pour les servir eux et leurs enfans [sic], ils ont ignoré l'empire de la beauté, profitant de leur force comme les naturels sans barbe de l'Amérique (*Ind.* 144).

Even the lovely and sympathetic Lady Hampshire, though, cannot alleviate Anna's ennui by inviting her into society, because divorced women are not well-received in England. Anna soon abandons herself to despair. "Que ses pensées étaient tendres et tristes. Julien lui était aussi cher que jamais; mais elle ne croyait plus aux passions; le temps avait brisé sa foi, elle déplorait ce sort de femme aussi dur en Europe qu'en Asie" (*Ind.* 158). Anna knows she cannot live in England much longer without becoming ill. "Tôt ou tard, il faut rompre avec le pays" (*Ind.* 166).

Her behavior becomes erratic and desperate, and she is saved only by a timely trip with her Irish maid, Bess, to the servant's native country. Julien can only stay a short time with them in Ireland, before he must return to Parliament. Anna bitterly regrets her sacrifice that is so little appreciated by Julien:

> Il sacrifiait le bonheur de ce qu'il aimait à ses passions immodérées. Anna se reporta vers les Indes, qu'elle avait abandonées imprudent, ainsi que sa famille et ses amies, trop mal payés aujourd'hui de ces sacrifices que l'homme demande et apprécie dans un moment de délire, mais qu'il n'admire plus dès qu'il s'en voit gêné le moins du monde dans son ambition ou sa liberté (*Ind.* 168).

The narrator describes Anna's jaundiced view of marriage, as it is accepted in England. "La connaissance du cœur des hommes ramène au mariage tel que les nations l'ont compris, une institution avouée et sociale, où, dans les inégalités du cœur, l'homme et la femme trouvent les occupations du monde" (*Ind.* 168). In her difficult position as divorced mistress, Anna feels lost in a society that can assign women only to a narrow, preestablished niche. "L'Indienne portait seule le poids d'une position non encore établie. . . " (*Ind.* 168).

A passionate reunion with Julien in Ireland revives Anna for a time, but she senses a sadness in his love for her. Later, when they are back in England, she analyzes the difference in their expectations in love and passion. ". . . la femme aimant trop se vit reprocher une tendresse à laquelle l'homme eût préféré une affection plus froide et plus commode" (*Ind.* 192). Formerly, Julien had wished for Anna to take his whole life into her heart: "Voudrais-tu vivre avec moi, savoir que je t'aime et n'entendre rien que cela? Voudrais-tu te charger du poids de mon sort et sentir que ma vie entière est renfermée dans ton sein?" Now, however, his attitude is, "Il faut me laisser libre pour les affaires; je vous aime toujours, mais les affections calmes rendent seules heureux" (*Ind.* 192).

Through Bess, Anna meets Dolly, an English servant who was recently acquitted by a jury of having killed her illegitimate baby. Although repulsed by the crime, Anna sympathizes with Dolly and with other fallen women she knows and blames their misery on England. "Ce peuple n'entendait rien aux émotions de l'âme, aux vraies joies de la vie: il était fait pour le travail et l'argent; une politique savante, mais glacée; des interêts bien entenus, mais materiels." She longs for India. . . . "Terre de flamme et d'imagination, religion riante et magnifique, auguste plain ou s'est instruit le genre humain" (*Ind.* 211-12).

Lady Hampshire describes her daughter Juliette's bad marriage to an indifferent, preoccupied man. Juliette no longer cries, because she has learned to accept her lot—"Il faut vous soumettre" (*Ind.* 218). However, when Anna meets Juliette, she sees how the young wife has lost all joy in life. "Juliette semblait occupée de son mari en femme blessée qui se résigne à son sort et n'en jouit plus. . . . son mari, formé à l'ancienne école, voulait la tenir dans la soumission" (*Ind.* 219-20).

Hearing Julien is ill, Anna rushes back to London, but he refuses, even in his weakened physical state, to stay away from Parliament. "Si vous m'aimez, si vous voulez mon bonheur, si vous songez à mon devoir, soyez généreuse et pardonnez-moi. Croyez que je vous aime plus que jamais . . . mais ce soir je ne puis me dispenser de parler à la Chambre!' Anna is beside herself. "Rien ne pouvait vaincre cette passion terrible à laquelle Julien sacrifierait jusqu`a sa vie" (*Ind.* 225).

Julien speaks eloquently against the Bill of Reform, saying it would lead to too much violence.   The all-night debate and the subsequent rejection of the bill throws London into a state of agitation, and Julien into a more desperate state of illness.   Anna pleads to take him to India where the calm and the climate can restore him. Before they can leave, however, Anna herself falls ill.   The two cry in each others' arms, more in love than ever, but knowing they are dying. They hope for a happier life after death. "Julien lui parlait de la vie éternelle; retrouvant une tendresse extraordinaire, jamais durant sa longue passion il n'avait été plus amoureux que dans ce derniers jours" (*Ind.* 270).

Julien expires in Anna's arms, and she dies soon after.   She is not sent back to her native India, but is buried next to Julien, "au pays de ses maîtres, sous le ciel rigoureux de l'Angleterre" (*Ind.* 279).

Critics of *L'Indienne* were quick to complain that the author's preoccupation with English politics dampened the literary value of the work.   *La Revue de Paris* pointed this out, but also praised the author's talents, the accuracy of its descriptions of the current English political scene, and mentioned, as had other critics, that her talents went beyond those of typical female writers:

> C'est trop juger en femme un roman de femme, et oublier ce qu'il y a de talent de Mme H. Allart. J'ai lu, dans *L'Indienne,* des pages ravissantes, les unes comme description, d'autres comme analyse de sentiment. Mais ce livre a deux sortes d'intérêt. Est-ce un mal?   Dans quel journal, dans quelle revue, a-t-on mieux caractérisé les hommes politiques de l'Angleterre actuelle? Plaire et aimer suffit à la plupart des femmes. Celle-ci ne veut pas d'une devise si courte: plaire, aimer et *penser*, est la sienne."[9]

Béranger wrote to Hortense in December 1832, thanking her for the copy of *L'Indienne* that she had sent him, and gallantly praising it. "Ce n'est pas tout que bien écrire, faites-vous donc louer. Vous devez avoir un monde autour de vous?" (quoted by Séché 294).

There is no existing evidence at this time of any critic of *L'Indienne* mentioning the novel's bold stand against the abuses of the marriage institution and the general stifling atmosphere of male dominance in England as a whole.   Also, the novel has never been translated into English, and there is no written indication of how francophonic readers in England at the time (or since) may have reacted to its protests.   Nevertheless, the fact that *L'Indienne* quickly sold out of its first printing and continued to sell well in its second, indicates that this primary topic was not a point of contention among critics or readers. Although Allart's fourth novel did not address specific issues of sexuality from a woman's point of view, as did Sand's *Lélia,* published just a few months later, the feminist voice of *L'Indienne* was certainly as hardy and as clearly stated as any other woman's novel of the day, including Sand's.

Included after *L'Indienne* in the same 1833 volume is the short novella *Le Convict,* which seems to have remained one of the author's most obscure works. The story, more brutal and gristly than is typical of Allart, tells of Thomas, an English prisoner from Newgate, who is deported to New South Wales, Australia, for stealing. While working on a chain gang, he meets a beautiful, black, native girl.

Credited with "une imagination brillante et gaie,"[10] Thomas decides to commit one last crime that will set him up with enough money so that he will never again have to break the law. "J'ai eu des inconvéniens [sic] du crime, une mauvaise education, une jeunesse flétrie; je veux finir, mais en finissant je veux avoir les profits du crime: un dernier vol considérable me donnera les moyens de travailler, je rompra avec ma vie passée par un coup utile" (*Le Con.* 288).

Thomas escapes from prison, is reunited with his native lover, loses her to another Englishman, is turned in by an English guide he has hired, and sent to Moreton-Bay, the worst deportation spot. The odious prison chief, a criminal himself, has Thomas beaten and abused. Thomas manages to kill the chief with a chain. The other prisons, who also hated the chief, do not inform on him.

Thomas eventually is sent to a work for Mr. Burge, a planter in Sydney. He is well treated, but cannot resist the urge to steal from his employer. Just as he has embezzled enough to set himself up in his own business and marry the pretty daughter of a local merchant, Thomas is betrayed by a fellow servant, who finds his stash of ill-gotten money under his mattress.

Thomas saves his money and his future by suffocating the boy under the mattress. Although burdoned with guilt, Thomas proceeds with his plans—buys a business, marries, has children, and prospers. The guilt persists. "Il porta la peine du passé . . . . Plus il avait été ferme et forte, plus son crime lui resta grave, pesant" (*Le Con.* 318-19). He goes to his grave, carrying the weight of his *"education misérable;"* in other words, his plan to better his life through crime.

Critical commentary on *Le Convict* appears to be non-existent at this point. Perhaps this is not surprising since the story is overshadowed by the entirely different kind of fiction that proceeds it in *L'Indienne.* Why Allart would opt at this point in her career to write a rather didactic story about a male anti-hero and Christian retribution through guilt, if not through earthly justice, is a matter of speculation. In any case, this novella is an unexpected and radical deviation from the feminist, autobiographical thread that runs through her previous and future fictional works.

Her two main projects of the next year—*La femme et la démocratie de nos temps* and *Settimia* — were definitively back on her more typical track, and her personal involvement in the Parisian feminist movements would become more enthusiastic and productive than ever in 1836.

Notes

[1] Joseph Berry. *Infamous Woman or the Life of George Sand.* (Garden City, NY: Doubleday and Co., Inc., 1977) 206.

[2] Mary Anne Garnett. "La Reine noire et la reine blanche: George Sand et Hortense Allart," *George Sand Today: Proceedings of the Eighth International George Sand Conference,* (Tours 1989) 259.

[3] *Nouvelles Lettres à Sainte-Beuve (1832-1864),* Lorin Uffenbeck, ed., (Geneva: Librairie Droz, 1965) 7. (Subsequent references from this collection will appear in parenthesis after the quotation and will be indicated by the abbreviation *N.L. à S.-B* .).

[4] "Sauf à passer pour une écriveuse comme Madame A[llart], je veux vous faire l'injure d'un billet." Letter to Sainte-Beuve, March 10, 1833. *Correspondence de George Sand,* George Lubin, ed., (Paris; Classiques Garnier, 1967) 2:276. (Susequent references to this collection will appear in parentheses after the quotations, and will be indicated by the abbreviation *Corres. de G.S.*).

[5] The advent of a distinct school of feminist literary criticism is generally traced to 1968.

[6] Renée Weingarten. *The Double Life of George Sand: Woman and Writer.* (New York: Basic Books, Inc., 1978), 114, author's italics.

[7] "Lettere di Hortense Allart à George Sand," *Studi francesi*   6:3 (September-December 1958): 421- 22.

[8] Mme Hortense Allart de Thérase. *L'Indienne.* (Paris. Ch. Vimont, Libraire-Editeur, 1833) 7. (Subsequent references to this work will appear in parentheses after the quotation, and will be indicated by the abbreviation *Ind.*)

[9] "[*L'Indienne*] "Album," *Revue de Paris* [Brussels edition]. 4e année, IX (December 1832) 276, quoted by Uffenbeck 220, reviewer's italics.

[10]Madame Hortense Allart de Thérèse. *Le Convict* 286. This story appears directly after *L'Indienne*, and is marked with page numbers that continue from those in the first novel (283-319). (Subsequent references to the story will be marked with the abbreviation *Le Con.*).

Chapter 6

Settimia: Politics, Histories and Feminism (1836-1837)

Hortense calls the year 1836 "l'époque la plus forte de ma vie" (*EP* 202). Freed from the physical and emotional stress of the Channel crossings and the ongoing turmoil of her relationship with Bulwer, she became more energized and prolific than ever. During this year, she brought three major works to fruition, redoubled her journalistic output, and plunged with enthusiasm into the burgeoning feminist movement in Paris.

In January 1836 she published the work for which she would become the best known, the 124-page essay *La femme et la démocratie de nos temps.* In April, her fifth novel, the epistolary *Settimia,* was published by Arthus Bertrand, and in December she completed the first volume of her lengthy *L'Histoire de la République de Florence.* She published several articles for the short-lived (1836-37) Parisian publication *La Gazette des Femmes,* and towards the end of the year, she began attending feminist meetings in Paris, at one time associating with a group that wore a red ribbon at the neck as a show of solidarity:

> Quelques personnes s'occupaient de la question sur le sort des femmes, soulevée par le *Globe.* Je fais connaissance avec elles. Nous avions des soirées chez une de ces dames où l'on discutait les questions. Je porte un ruban rouge au cou; j'en voulais faire pour les femmes un signe de ralliement, et qu'il nous rappelât sans cesse notre oppression et notre devoir. Ces soirées durèrent tout l'hiver [1837] .... (*EP* 202).

She added that the dwindling remains of the Saint-Simonians as well as other feminist groups over the past few years had not achieved the emacipation that the Parisian women might have wished for. However, such efforts had laid some firm groundwork that now seemed to be getting results:

> Si les réclamations pour les femmes, commencées par les Saints-Simoniens, si des écrits, des journaux depuis, n'eurent pas un résultat apparent, toutes ces choses préparent en faveur des femmes, une opinion qui s'établit mieux chaque jour, finira par triompher, et adoucira enfin leur sort, leur éducation et les lois (*EP* 202).

Late in 1835, shorly after Henry had gone back to England, Hortense returned to Herblay, was reunited with Marcus, finished *La femme et la démocratie de nos temps,* and sent it off to Paris to be published. Henry wrote from London, but she was mostly untouched by his invitations for her to join him there, preferring to focus on the promotion of and the upcoming reactions to her essay, which she called "ma chère brochure" (*EP* 200).

La femme et la démocratie de nos temps testifies to Allart's expansive knowledge of history and governments past and present, which she gained entirely through self-directed study. In the essay, she claims that the basic equality of the sexes cannot be denied, asserts that society should create a new governmental hierachy that includes gifted, educated women as well as men, calls for better education for women, expounds on certain ideals for marriage and parenthood, and urges legalized divorce (at that time forbidden under the *Code Napoléon*). In Hortense's own words, the brochure's purpose was to "montrer que le monde doit être conduit par une aristocratie intellectuelle en hommes et *en femmes*" (*EP* 199), and the italicized emphasis on "women" is her own.

The pamphlet begins as a supplication to God and asks for a new sort of religion and hierarchy that would no longer allow women to be subjugated to men, but rather usher in a fresh echelon of gifted members of both sexes. "Souverain pouvoir . . . . [la société] regarde autour d'elle, remonte à sa source, et demande une nouvelle religion, un nouvel essor pour l'esprit, une nouvelle hiérachie; les femmes s'informent si la délicatesse des mœurs ne produira pas une morale plus belle . . . ."[1]

Chapter 2 steps away from Judeo-Christian traditions, and addresses Minerva, daughter of Zeus, pointing out that the ancient Greeks and Romans had both male and female deities; in fact, the goddesses were more durable than the gods. ". . . et quand de plus grossières idoles tombèrent, les déesses restèrent debout" (*FDNT* 7).

She next discusses the fact that women throughout history and in different societies always filled their traditional roles as wives and mothers, but still were forced to endure abuse from men. Allart despairs of the plight of women in other countries, especially India and other parts of Asia, where baby girls are killed. She defends the dignity of pregnancy and childbirth, and claims these roles, which women have been forced to bear with pain, have been associated unjustly with shame. Conversely, she says, these very roles entitle women to greater respect. ". . . Laissez-nous cherchez dans l'amélioration des mœurs s'il n'est rien de plus moral, de plus humain, de plus digne, de celui qui inventa la maternité et l'accouchement" (*FDNT* 9).

Women are partly reponsible for centuries of abuse they have endured, because they have not lived up to their potential, Allart states in Chapter 4. "La manière lâche et rusée dont la femme a secoué le joug en jouant son maître, le peu de force et de dignité qu'elle a montré pour s'emparer d'une vie meilleure lui seront justement reprochés." Nevertheless, she notes, some women in history rose above such abuse, and became successful political and military leaders. Therefore, why can there not be more women who are intellectural stand-outs as well? "Ceci est très remarquable: Leur faiblesse qui ne les empêche pas de porter l'épée, dompter les cheveaux, dominer un royaume, leur refuse-t-elle la médiation, le language, ces premières beautés qui ont placé les penseurs au-dessus de tous?" (*FDNT* 11).

The essayist answers her own question in the next chapter. Although the gist of her statement is familiar to late 20th-century feminists, it was a new and astute concept for Allart's day: For a woman to be thought of as man's equal, she must actually prove herself far *superior* to him. ". . . quand la femme a tout contre elle, il faudrait qu'elle fût supérieure à l'homme même, pour aller aussi loin que lui. . . ." (*FDNT* 11).

She continues to debunk the age-old idea of women's natural inferiority, asking, what man on earth can be really sure that he will never meet a woman who is superior to himself?

> . . . . et il y a cette observation à faire: les deux sexes avec des forces inégales à leur sommité, ont des formes assez balancées en général, de sorte que la sœur est supérieure au frère, la femme au mari, la mère au fils, et *qu'on ne saurait établir l'inférorité du sexe.* C'est un trait remarquable de la relation des deux sexes; que cette supériorité de l'homme effacée à tout moment (*FDNT* 12, my italics).

Therefore, since society has no right to contest women's ability to be in positions of leadership, should it not, then, provide them with a better education?   "Nous demanderons d'abord pour la femme une éducation plus forte, proportionée à l'intelligence qu'elles annoncent, et l'étude de la morale telle que la civilisation l'enseigne" (*FDNT* 12).

Allart champions marriage as an eternal law but recommends that it be regulated differently according to different peoples and cultures. "La famille, l'union de l'homme et la femme, le mariage seront des lois éternelles; mais la mode du mariage et sa duré varieront avec le caractère des peuples . . . . " (*FDNT* 14).   In an eerie prologue to what would be a brutal marriage of her own, she states that loyalty to husbands must be proceeded by a certain respect for wives as well as assurance of protection from physical harm. "La moralité des femmes sera au profit des hommes, mais pour être loyale, il faut être libre, ni forcée, ni battue. Quand le pouvoir morale succède au pouvoir matériel, la femme ne craint plus les coups" (*FDNT* 16).

She contradicts Rousseau's statement that women are always dependent upon men, and thereby defends the dignity of the wage-earning working woman. "Rousseau a dit que . . . les femmes dépendaient des hommes par leurs désirs et leurs besoins. Ceci est vrai jusqu'à un certain point; car si beaucoup de femmes vivent de leur travail, celles-là du moins sont indépendentes des hommes pour leurs besoins" (*FDNT* 19).

As she had nine years earlier in *Gertrude,* she also urges the legality of divorce, hailing it as a natural and vital outgrowth of changing and progessing times. "Le divorce suit les lumières et ce développement des intelligences cultivées . . . . " (*FDNT* 14).

At one point, she takes herself to task in one respect by discouraging unwed motherhood, citing the need for more reverence for marriage. However, her emphasis is less on righteous indignation over illegitimacy as it is on the possibility that a child may suffer if the single mother does not take sufficient parental responsibility.   "Le danger c'est que la fille soit mère, que, libre du préjugé, elle ne mette pas assez d'importance à la loi sacrée du mariage, et qu'elle ne livre imprudemment à la vie des enfans [sic] qu'elle ne peut pas soutenir." Society should caution young women about the impractical and difficult aspects of having children out of wedlock instead of simply lecturing them about the evils of lost virtue. "Ne comptant pas sur la raison des filles, on effraya leur pudeur au lieu d'effrayer leur prudence. La prudence appartint à l'homme" (*FDNT* 20).

Allart reminds her readers that religions do not support society's idea of a double standard of moral conduct for men and for women, yet where is the man who will live up to his own responsibility to be chaste? "Les religions ne mirent nulle différence entre les devoirs de chasteté pour l'homme et la femme, mais quel est l'homme qui voudrait souffrir et mourir pour observer la défense?" (*FDNT* 22). Such a double standard is not only illogical, she argues in Chapter 11, but it is also an insult to these enlightened times. "Quel est l'homme qui ne rirait pas, si on s'informat de sa chasteté? Ces préjugés ne vont plus avec nos lumières" (*FDNT* 24).

Chapters 11 through 13 address Allart's firm belief that a woman of superior intelligence is every iota equal to a man of the same intellectual status. Chapters 14 through 21 explain her anti-democracy and pro-oligarchic stance that nature has endowed only a small number of superior men and women with the right to sovereignty. "Un besoin également vif entraîne les talens [sic] au pouvoir et les nations à l'enthousiasme" (*FDNT* 29). She claims that the less gifted individual who is allowed power becomes quickly corrupted; also, he/she who is allowed riches soon becomes too materialistic. Therefore, those with talent, not riches, should be in positions of power. "La richesse compta par dessus tout, mais l'esprit le dirigea. Le principe était au rebours. Le talent doit dominer le monde matériel; alors le monde matériel domina le talent sans pouvoir s'en passer" (*FDNT* 37).

Allart analyzes the weaknesses of ancient Greek, Roman, Israeli and Asian governments—even innovative Greek democracy—where the majority of the people were slaves and not allowed a sense of their own moral worth. In the next chapter, however, she defends the feudalism and aristocracy born of the Middle Ages, maintaining that masses of people coming out an age of very little intellectual enlightenment could not be expected to take responsibility for political rights and responsibilities. "Ainsi . . . . les chefs se chargèrent des vertus et leur position, agrandissant leur âme et leur esprit, forma cette aristocratie chevaleresque à laquelle le monde moderne dut sa valeur, son élégance, et son éclat" (*FDNT* 55).

Later, she makes a more detailed plea for a well-organized, responsible aristocracy. She also supports the current tendency in France to replace the influence of the rich, landed gentry with that of a talented and morally and intellectually superior elite. ". . . il faut placer l'homme supérieur en sa présence, comme il est placé par la nature, graduer les forces matérielles sur les forces morales" (*FDNT* 103). She names Chateaubriand, Béranger, the poet/politician Alphonse de Lamartine and Hugo as natural artistocrats. "[Ils] ont naturellement le caractère d'une aristocratie hautaine, isolée et disciplinée" (*FDNT* 103).

Allart praises the English for sustaining a sophisticated aristocracy that has resulted in more political and economic success in their own country and in their colonies than continental European countries could claim. She expresses unabashedly her lack of respect for American government and society, which she sees as high on energy, but full of vulgarity and ignorance, and lacking in scholars and philosophers. "Ce peuple enfin, sans gloire et sans génie, est flatté par ses serviteurs avec plus de bassesse qu'on n'a jadis flatté les rois" (*FDNT* 73).

She claims that America is proof that absolute equality produces nothing to be admired. "Ce peuple nous montre comment l'égalité absolue ne produit rien de beau, comment une nation qui n'a été formée ni par la royauté, ni par l'aristocratie, est vulgaire, et comment, si le monde n'avait pas tout trouvé pour les Etats-Unis, ils n'auraient jamais fait faire un pas aux sciences, aux arts, ni à l'industrie" (*FDNT* 74).

Susbsequent chapters describe Allart's admiration of Bonaparte and the ongoing enchantement that his legacy has over the French people. Under Napoleon, youth were not slaves to a master, but rather, enthusiasts in whom a great leader awakened elements of virtue. She cites what she considers an unfortunate doctrine of "equality" in the current generation that leads youth into light-minded activities:

> Cette jeunesse qui suivait l'Empereur au combat, née maintenant sous d'autres influences . . . s'adonne aux métiers paisibles et subalternes. Le trait qui la caractérise est l'ignorance; de là, l'égarement de sa générosité, des convictions légères, proclamées et abandonnées . . . Leur tort est celui d'une démocratie sans direction et sans chefs (*FDNT* 80).

She even worries that France may be currently in danger of falling into the same kind of mediocrity as the kind infesting America. "Et voyons l'Amérique et sa médiocrité. Non, non, la France ne peut longtemps supporter cette bassesse" (*FDNT* 82).

Allart defends basic Judeo-Christian religious principles, but criticizes Catholicism for skewing certain doctrines. "L'Eglise catholique, ambitieuse et hautaine, a fait triompher la croix par les passions que la croix proscrivait" (*FDNT* 114). She also cites a certain arrogance among those who insist that Christianity is the embodiment of true religion, past, present and future. "Qui oserait dire que [Jesus Christ] est la dernière expression de la religion? Qui pourrait croire que Dieu ne se révèle pas selon les différens [sic] âges comme selon les différens [sic] peuples?" (*FDNT* 115).

She echoes from *Jérôme* her protest of convent life, and asks why priests and nuns cannot be married to one another, and still fufill their duties. Furthermore, why cannot women take on priestly duties in the service of other women? "Pourquoi ne pas marier à nos prêtres ces charmantes sœurs de la Charité . . . . Pourquoi la femme du prêtre ne serait-elle pas prêtre aussi, avec un habit religieux, des mœurs chartiables et la charge de confesser les filles?" (*FDNT* 116). In this so-called enlightened country of France, she adds, there are 20,000 unhappy girls shut up in convents, and their celibacy means nothing when it is forced upon them. "Rien de moins chaste qu'une chasteté forcée" (116).

She identifies the correlation between God's natural respect for women, the potential with which they are endowed, and women's role in the eventual rise of a natural artistocracy.   The chapter concludes, "La religion discipline le talent, enseigne à respécter à l'aristocratie naturelle, élève la femme, guide la civilisation, et trouvait ainsi sa place là où la femme et l'aristocratie sont défendues" (*FDNT* 118).

Included also is an ode to passion, which Allart believes is a special domain of certain women.

> . . . l'homme ne peut aborder la poésie, la tragédie, l'éloquence que par les femmes, comme par elles seules il obtient le bonheur domestique et la dignité privée . . . . quelques grands écrivains et quelques femmes supérieures l'ont bien décrite . . . . la passion sera la garde de ces personnes comme elle en sera le délice et l'effroi; elle trouvait sa place ici, moyen de vertu pour l'aristocratie naturelle et pour la femme (*FDNT* 120).

The conclusion of the essay states that if women are allowed freedom and respect, certain ones, hence, will rise to take their deserved honors alongside men in a natural artistocracy. Also, women will bless men's lives in moral and intellectual ways:

> La question ainsi se simplifie pour les femmes: si toutes seront libres et bien traitées, quelques-unes seulement parviendront, avec les hommes, à des postes ou à des honneurs mérités. Comme jadis la culture des femmes hâta la civilisation, adoucit les mœurs, ainsi ce nouvel âge de culture pour les femmes mènera loin la société de la justice et de l'égalité; comme autrefois l'homme rude et guerrier fut adouci par elles, ainsi l'homme libre sera moralisé par elles (*FDNT* 122-23).

The essay concludes with Allart's supplication for mankind to see nobility, happiness and basic aspects of marriage and family life as holy laws. "[Que l'homme] attendrisse son cœur dans un dernier regard jeté à l'amour, la maternité, le mariage, la fidélité, ces beautés morales que nous voulons rappeler à leur vrai caractère" (*FDNT* 124).

The *Bibliographie de la France* announced the publication of *La*

femme et la démocratie de nos temps on Jan. 16, 1836. Ironically, although the Saint-Simonians had snubbed Allart only a few years earlier in her attempts to learn more about the group, they subsequently included her essay in a volume called *Publications Saint-Simoniennes (1830-36). X: Publications faites par des femmes.* Enfantin's group was nearly defunct by this time, but copies of writings from the Saint-Simonians as well as a collection of several other previously published feminist essays were bound together in two volumes.[2]

At this point in her own life, Allart had been a living example for most of the ideals she advocated in her essay, as she vigorously achieved most of her own intellectual education on her own, and lived by her own pen, refusing marriage, and raising and supporting her son alone. Billy notes that she had represented in her time the most extreme limit of feminine emancipation. ". . . mère de deux enfants naturels, elle a courageusement rempli tous ses devoirs et bravé l'opinion sans éclat, en s'assurant l'estime et la sympathie de tous ceux et de toutes celles qui comptaient pour elle" (145).

Critical commentary on *La femme et la démocratie de nos temps* is in short supply. Most comes from the author's own and others' letters written just after its publication. Hortense sent copies of the essay to numerous friends and was quick to assure Capponi in a letter written Feb. 7, 1836, that it had been well-received by several prominent writers. "Ma brochure a du succès . . . . M. Thiers m'en a remercié, M. de Lamartine m'écrit qu'il en viendra causer."[3]

At this point, Sand was still reluctant to accord much enthusiasm to Allart's works. She wrote to Marie d'Agoult on Feb. 26, 1836, that she appreciated the ideas in *La femme et la démocratie de nos temps,* but not the writing style. "Mme Allart vient de faire une brochure où il y a réellement des choses fortes, belles et vraies. Mais elle est pédante et ne me plaît point" (*Corres. de G.S.* 3:290).

Despite Sand's dim view of her writings, Allart was still enthusiastically cultivating the friendship of her fellow novelist. That she might have tried a little too hard to gain acceptance is evident in Sand's May 15 letter to Liszt, in which she calls Allart "une bavarde méchante et à moitié folle" (*Corres. de G.S.* 3:373).

After three years of pursuing his relationship with Sand, Didier finally had become her lover during spring 1836. This apparently was another source of tension between Allart and Sand, for just 10 days after the letter to Liszt, Sand wrote to d'Agoult (May 25), saying she was breaking with Allart. She does not describe details, but it is evident she was offended by some remark or action by Allart relating to jealousies over Didier. "Je vous dirai de Mme Allart, que je n'ai jamais eu de sympathie pour elle. J'ai beaucoup d'estime pour son caractère,

mais un beau jour, elle m'a fait une méchanceté, la chose du monde que je comprends le moins et que je puis le moins excuser." Typically, Hortense had tried to make amends, but Sand was not mollified. "Depuis que je vous ai écrit, elle m'a fait amende honorable. Est-ce bonté? Est-ce légèreté de tête et de cœur? Je n'y ai plus guère confiance, et sans la maltraiter (car à vrai dire d'après cette conduite fantasque, je m'aperçois que je ne la connais pas du tout), je m'éloginerai d'elle avec soin" (*Corres. de G.S.* 3:401).

If Allart ever knew of Sand's intention to break off communications with her, she ignored it. Less than a year later—Feb. 12, 1837—she wrote to Sand congratulating her on the publication of the first *Lettre à Marcie,* which had appeared in *Le Monde.* Nevertheless, she still could not resist giving Sand a word of criticism about what she saw as overly prudish advice to young women about sexual conduct. (The first of the six *Lettres à Marcie,* each of which ran in separate editions of *Le Monde,* advocates traditional morality in the face of the free-love philosophies being touted by such groups as the Saint-Simonians). Allart wrote, "Mais prenez garde après avoir été Reine d'être bourgeoise, et de prêcher la morale des boutiques. L'austérité comme l'entend le vulgaire, c'est pour vous M. Dudevant et pour nous autres filles la chasteté; or nous ne voulons ni l'un ni l'autre . . . " (*Corres. de G.S.* 3:685).

This letter marked Allart's first reference to Sand as "la Reine," a nickname which she would use repeatedly not only to Sand herself but also in letters to mutual friends. Numerous examples of this moniker referring to Sand are found in Allart's *Lettres Inédites à Sainte-Beuve* and *Nouvelles Lettres à Sainte-Beuve (1832-1864).* (Béranger had been the first to refer to Sand this way in 1834, when, in a letter to Allart, he had called her "la reine de notre nouvelle génération littéraire" (quoted by Séché 135).

Sand's reaction to Hortense's latest criticism is not a matter of record, but she referred to the epithet "la Reine" some three years later after Hortense had returned from her second stay in Italy. In Dec. 28, 1840, Sand wrote in a much warmer tone than ever before. "Car si je suis reine selon vous, vous ne l'êtes pas moins selon moi . . . . J'aime à entendre parler de vous, à apprendre que vous êtes toujours jolie, toujours étincelante d'esprit . . . ." (*Corres. de G.S.* 5:190-91).

Billy speculates on just how much Sand's persona and philosophies as well as Allart's own may have figured into *Settimia,* which appeared in April 1836. The novel, published in two volumes, is Allart's most lengthy, most upbeat, and most assiduous appeal for respect and success for the superior woman who is determined to be her own person, yet still have the love of the man of her choice. The novel's preface describes a superior woman of the era. Allart does not mention a name, but Billy states that she is creating a portrait of Sand (Billy 142):

> Voici une femme qui a dépassé les écrivains de son âge, agrandissant et vivifiant tout ce qu'elle touche à la manière d'Homère. Sa beauté fière et délicate . . . son élégance et ses goûts poétiques . . . la feraient d'abord plus occupée de l'amour que des lettres. Les femmes s'informent curieusement des secrets de sa vie, sur lesquels s'égare follement la renomée; mais les hommes étudient ses livres, suivent les sources de sa puissance, et comprennent dans quelles travaux sérieux elle oublie sa jeunesse et ses charmes.[4]

Just how and where does current French society classify such an extraordinary woman, and will it ever offer her a rightful place of honor? The portrait continues, "Le monde l'y place; les plus anciens, les plus illustres dans cette assemblée fameuse, offrent de lui donner leurs voix; elle en rit ou n'en sait rien, *car l'usage n'a pas consacré la gloire des femmes*" (*Sett.* 1:xli, my italics).

A bold feminist bent characterizes the 61-page preface to *Settimia*, which Billy calls "un instrument de progrès social" (141).   In this preliminary essay, Allart reiterates several of the ideas in *La femme et la démocratie de nos temps*, most specifically, the need for a superior, intellectual artistocracy consisting of men and women alike to guide and ameliorate society. Again, she emphasizes women's natural rights and basic equality to men. She states that, in a period of political reconstruction, women have a key role in establishing moral reform and that women's work and women's novels will guide society toward better goals.   ". . . C'est aux femmes surtout qu'il appartient de reclamer la réforme morale, et leurs travaux et leurs romans seront des cris lancés vers ce but désiré" (*Sett.* 1:ii)

The author's goal is not only to characterize passion as an integral requirement in male and female felicity, but also to illustrate how it can and should be absolutely faithful and guaranteed for a lifetime. "[Une intention dans le roman] est de peindre la passion dans sa duré et sa fidélité; l'autre de la peindre comme elle est aujourd'hui chez l'homme et la femme" (*Sett.* 1:iii).

She claims that women are nearly always superior to men in the violence of their passions and cites as examples Queen Elizabeth I, Catherine the Great, Staël's Corinne, and Sappho. The passion associated with love, however, is not enough for every woman just as it is not enough for men. Whereas the ordinary maiden can be content with a life of domesticity, the superior female needs more in her life;

solitude is as torturous as exil. ". . . pour la femme héroïque comme pour l'empereur, la solitude absolue est Sainte-Hélène. La femme pas plus que l'homme n'est donc faite pour l'amour seul . . . la femme vulgaire a besoin de ménage et du soin des enfans [sic]; la femme supérieure a besoin de l'action ou des letters" (*Sett.* 1:iii).

Allart protests the rhetoric about the supposed inequality of the sexes that dates back to Biblical doctrine, and asks why God would create woman only to leave her out of any part in life in society. She takes on the role of all women who might question God:

> Qu'ai-je donc fait pour être frappée de cette malédiction? Pourquoi vous êtes-vous retiré de moi? . . . . moi qui suis une création de vos mains, moi que vous aviez douée d'une apparente richesse d'organisation, vous m'avez tout retiré . . . . Moi je sens ce que je suis, et je ne puis pas mordre le pied qui m'opprime, ni soulever la damnation qui pèse sur moi comme une montagne . . . . O vie, ô tourment! Tout aspirer et ne rien saisir, tout comprendre et ne rien posséder! (*Sett.* 1:v-vii).

Allart also adds that the laws of marriage and divorce are both eternal principles for the human race. ". . . La loi du mariage avec le divorce, et en permettant aux filles d'aimer et de choisir, est la loi vraie et éternelle du genre humain . . . " (*Sett.* 1:ix). She mentions how divorce was allowed for a short time during the Revolution, then taken away. Since then, its absence has been responsible for many crimes all over France:

> L'opposition, qui crie sans cesse, ne réclame pas cette loi, autrement importante aujourd'hui que . . . la liberté de la presse! Consultez les gens du barreau, les avocats; ils vous apprendront à combien de réclamations et de crimes l'absence du divorce donne lieu à Paris, en province et partout" (*Sett.* 1:xlv).

Interestingly, more than a century before women in the English-speaking world proposed the new word "Ms." as a more dignified and equitable way to address all adult women, regardless of their marital status, Allart suggested that the title "mademoiselle" was outmoded and degrading—at least to any woman over age 20. "Il faut quitter après vingt ans ce nom inférieur de mademoiselle, qui porte en lui le ridicule au-delà de l'âge charmant où il plaît" (*Sett.* 1:xii).

Allart calls upon the spirit of Mirabeau and Rousseau to urge men to adopt a more courageous and progressive attitude towards women. "Mirabeau! Rousseau! enseignez-leur à aimer! à s'oublier, à mépriser la foule, à avoir un cœur brave, à oser proclamer leur foi, à respecter le génie chez la femme, à vivre seuls avec leur maîtresse et avec Dieu!" (*Sett.* 1: xiii).

The epistolary *Settimia,* Allart's lengthiest and most complex novel, has a number of *raisons d'être.* Foremost, it is an eloquent case for freedom and tolerance for the superior woman who generally is condemned to solitude and denied love, if she chooses to pursue her scholarly or professional interests. The novel's main theme is that a few women simply are not meant to accept a life that is characterized only by domesticity. Even the most passionate love is not sufficient fulfillment in life for an intelligent woman any more than a lover is enough in and of herself to make a man happy in life. The novel also makes a plea for legalized divorce, while still sustaining the idea that marriage requires forbearance, dedication, and forgiveness from both partners. It also is a monument of admiration to any couple who can maintain the great passion of a lifetime *for* a lifetime.

The title heroine of *Settimia,* as Allart explains in the preface, is a poor, but gifted and scholarly Italian orphan, who loves the young Marcel Gerimé, also poor, but an ambitious and aspiring French businessman. Because of his tenuous financial circumstances and the disapproval of his family in France as well as numerous other obstacles that arise, Marcel cannot marry Settimia. The heroine, however, invokes at every turn the hope of marriage and the fulfillment of her passion. Allart is determined that her heroine will rise above the societal limits that were the ruin of Madame de Staël's heroines. "Madame de Staël a peint des femmes mourant pour les préjugés; notre époque plus avancée peint des femmes qui bravent les préjugés: Settimia veut le mariage pour son bonheur et pour la beauté, mais rien de mondain ni de petit ne l'occupe" (*Sett.* 1:ix).

Marcel is a happier and more sympathetic version of Bulwer than was depicted in *L'Indienne;* a hero who ultimately will be able to reconcile his ambition with his love for a woman. The letters between Settimia and Marcel are interwoven among other letters to and from their mutual friends, in particular, the unhappily married but devoted wife and mother Adélaïde Menerive. The correspondence describes the tribulations of the unfolding relationship between a young man struggling to arrange his life's priorities and a young woman who is trying to decide if it would be in her own best interests to love him unconditionally or—if it proves necessary to her well-being—to let him go.

Allart realizes that her heroine will be criticized for being a woman of the world. "Sans doute, Settimia sera blâmée; nous ne nous en effrayons pas; toute considération hardie est d'abord blâmée; les femmes seront charmées de dire: —Mais fi donc! Mais Settimia! Mais quelle horreur! une jeune fille qui s'en va courir le monde!" Nevertheless, the author charges her heroine to go forth as an example to women who are not so audacious or passionate as she and to make a show of faith that France ultimately will grant its countrywomen more respect and freedom:

> Allez, Settimia, sans crainte, vous présentez à ces femmes qui ne connaissent ni votre audace, ni vos douleurs, ni vos passions . . . . Née chez une nation ardente et qui fut austère, d'un peuple grand et pieux encore, vous n'avez rien à redouter de la France moqueuse mais légère et bientôt enchantée du courage (*Sett.* 1: xviii).

As the novel begins, Marcel and Settimia, both 20 years old, have been together for a year in Italy. He accompanied his family from Paris to Rome, where they came for his mother's health. The two young people met at the home of Adélaïde Menerive, a Frenchwoman who instructed Settimia about France and its literature. Settimia, who retains the lovely, dark-haired look of the ancient Italian race, also has had a rich education from her uncle, the abbé Vera, at his modest country home in Albano. Settimia has inspired Marcel not only with love but with the love of learning as well. "Notre sensibilité s'éveilla et s'enivra comme avaient fait nos esprits," he writes in the novel's first letter. "Tu me ramenais à l'étude; tu me diasais que l'amour ne fait pas toute l'existence d'un homme" (*Sett.* 1:5).

Each of them feels their union will be forever. "Nous sommes liés depuis un an; nous le sommes pour la vie" (*Sett.* 1:1). Because Marcel is young and poor and has not yet sought his fortune, the marriage they both desire must be delayed. His parents expect him to return to Paris and make his mark in the business world. Devastated at the thought of his departure just as she is experiencing passion for the first time, Settimia feels their separation is an inevitable part of a woman's lot. ". . . à mesure que vous aimez moins, j'aime plus. Mon préssentment me dit que c'est là le sort de la femme . . . Je ne connaissais pas les passions, je les éprouve pour la première fois" (*Sett.* 1: 8-9).

The level-headed Adélaïde, five years older than Settimia and married to a successful professional man, advises her friend to let Marcel go for awhile and to wait for the time when marriage would be more prudent and when they could both afford to leave the solitude of Albano. "Vous l'empêcherez de suivre sa famille; combien vous aurez tort! . . . . Marcel est à vous pour la vie. Il faut que la femme règle sa passion sur le caractère de l'homme. . . . Laissez Marcel chercher un emploi pour son ardeur et son activité . . . . vous avez autant besoin que lui d'une vie animée" (*Sett.* 1:19).

Marcel's domineering mother echoes even more strongly the idea that her son should return to Paris where family friends can offer him an honorable career, and that Settimia should not stand in the way of such a duty.   Settimia has observed that men are not meant to have love as the sole   concern in their lives.   How hard this is for a woman to accept!   "Je vois que l'amour n'est ni par la volonté de Dieu ni par   le penchant de l'homme, ce qui doit remplir seul notre vie . . . .   je m'afflige d'être femme, de ne pouvoir être l'émule de mon amant" (*Sett.* 1:26-27).   As for her own passion, she wants no other future for it except a lifelong commitment.   "Toute passion violente qui ne doit pas finir par un mariage, une famille, un lien pour la vie, est vaine et stupide" (*Sett.* 1:27).

Settimia's plight is that of all women of superior intellect and sensitivity.   "Le peuple dans sa simplicité aime tranquillement; mais croyez-moi, pour ceux dont l'éducation a développé la sensibilité, la passion n'a qu'elle pour but; Dieu en la créant eut ses vues, il y attacha les révélations de la beauté et de l'immortalité; c'est ainsi que je la sens" (*Sett.* 1:29).

The Romanticism is eloquent and touching in the next few letters as the two young people wrestle with the desire to fulfill their love and to please Marcel's family.   The practical appeal of France contrasts sharply to the artistic, literary,   and historical lure of Italy.   At one moment the young Frenchman considers the possibilities that his country can offer him—"Il pense à son pays, à la facilité d'y briller pour un homme de talent" (*Sett.* 1 :26)—then longs to settle in Italy with Settimia—"Eh bien! mourons dans ce pays de l'amour et de la volupté . . . . Fuyons au rivage de Naples la colère paternelle; éloignons nos faiblesses de ta Rome vénérée" (*Sett.* 1:43).

The pain of separation is too much for Marcel to consider. "Douleur extrême, consolation vaine! Settimia, tu souffres, et moi! et moi!   Je sens ce que tu sens, je languis comme toi, à ce moment je donnerais l'avenir pour une heure" (*Sett.* 1:48).   He fears   that if he leaves, she will become enamoured of some romantic and highly sensitized Italian.   "Les hommes de ce pays sont les plus sensibles de la terre, ceux qui aiment le mieux et souffrent le plus: tu seras rappelée vers ta race par ta nature même.   Marcel au loin, dans son monde prosaïque, dans ses occupations positives, perdra le charme qu'il recevait de toi seul" (*Sett.* 1: 48).

Similarly, Settimia is afraid that if Marcel leaves Italy, he will lose his poetic side.   "Il laisse en Italia la partie poétique de son existence; il faut que des idées élégantes et chères rappellent sa pensée au milieu de nos ruines" (*Sett.* 1:53). For a time, Marcel tells Settimia that talent and ambition do not matter to him, that he wants only love— "qu'il était né pour aimer et ne voulait rien de plus" (*Sett.* 1:71). Later, though, Marcel becomes restless and Settimia urges him to go to France to fulfill his destiny. He himself questions why Parisians and Londoners tend to be bored while languishing in the delights of Italy:

> D'où vient que je ne peux plus supporter le repos de l'Italie, et que j'ai besoin du movement de mon pays? C'est une existence factice que celle des hommes de Paris et de Londres; hors de ces deux villes on existe, on est heureux; pourquoi leurs habitans [sic] s'ennuient-ils ailleurs? . . . Est-ce un caractère malheureux que ce caractère ardent et actif qui m'enlève à chaque instant à moi-même? Je voudrais suivre la marche des choses en France, y aider, prendre part à ce movement de civilisation, vif partout, puissant chez nous (*Sett.* 1:78).

Suddenly, his scholarly efforts in Italy are not satifsying enough, and the offer of a family friend to set him up in a lucrative business position in Paris appeals to Marcel. "Il faut aller au siège des pensées et des découvertes. J'en saurai plus après trois mois passés à Paris que je n'en saurai ici en trois ans. Il faut partir. L'amour me retentait, mais l'amour ne saurait remplir la vie d'un homme" (*Sett.* 1:80). He says that even though Settimia has an intelligent *male mind*—"Avec des goûts pareils aux miens, avec un esprit actif et mâle" (*Sett.* 1:81)—she is troubling him with her fears and jealousies. "Je l'aime peut-être plus que dans nos beaux jours, mais je ne l'aime plus de la même façon: les femmes ne veulent pas comprendre cela" (*Sett.* 1:81).

Although he still hestitates to leave Italy, Settimia pushes him toward his duty. "Il souffre, je le vois; son ambition, son activité deviennent un supplice; il faut qu'il parte" (*Sett.* 1:83). He proposes that she come to France with him secretly, but she fears displeasing her uncle to whom she owes everything. They part sadly, agreeing to meet in the Alps in three months.

Settimia consoles herself by spending time in Rome with Adélaïde. She is also a comfort to her friend whose marriage is increasingly difficult. Interestingly, Adélaïde has named her small daughter after "a famous woman" who could be none other than Madame de Staël. "Nous avons appelé ma fille Germaine à cause d'une femme illustre qui avait ce nom" (*Sett.* 1:141).

After a series of intrigues, including being held up by bandits in an Italian carriage, then held hostage, Marcel arrives in Paris. The delays cause him to miss out on the position he had expected. He is sad and his letters to Settimia are discouraging. "C'est moi qui viens maudire la France, bénis l'Italie et l'amour" (*Sett.* 1:171). He also chides her for her jealousy of his career plans. "Tu te montrais trop jalouse de mon travail, tu n'étais pas assez calme, assez douce, mais tu étais énergique et passionnée" (*Sett.* 1:172). Nevertheless, he longs to be away from Paris and back in Italy with her. "Rends-moi l'amour et l'Italie; rends-moi ma maîtresse, que je la tienne dans mes bras loin de ce pays mensonger qui ne m'en laisse que l'image" (*Sett.* 1: 175).

Before Marcel's contradicting emotions can set him off on an odyssey of voyages back and forth across the Alps, reminicient of Hortense's and Bulwer's crossings of the English Channel, his employer in Paris. M. Herbé, sends him on a two-year assignment in India. He considers taking Settimia along, but Herbé insists the voyage and the setting are too dangerous for a woman. The stay will preclude their planned rendezvous in the Alps, but may render him financially secure enough to later settle permanently in Albano. "Je vous quitte, mais je vous quitte pour vous retrouver plus digne de vous," Marcel writes to Settimia (*Sett.* 1:180).

She tires to persuade him not to undertake a trip that may be deadly for someone of Marcel's tenuous physical and emotional health. He leaves anyway, swearing he will marry her when he returns. Furious at his decision, Settimia tries to forget him. She and her friend Margarita accept the attentions of other men. Margarita's mother, however, restricts their activities, and disapproves of all the men who come around. "Si je commence à m'amuser, il faut partir; je rencontre une sévérité pour les jeunes filles qui m'est insupportable; plus les femmes étaient sensibles et fortes chez nous, plus on les a assujéties" (*Sett.* 1:200). Weary of unending prejudice against bright, independent Roman women, Settimia decides she wishes never to marry. She tells Adélaïde (who first introduced her to French literature), " . . . en me faisant comprendre l'amour, tel que les femmes le sentent chez vous, vous m'avez rendu plus pénible l'assujétissement des jeunes filles romaines. Je n'ai de mon pays que les inconvéniens [sic]. Que faire? comment vivre ainsi? Je ne veux pas me marier" (*Sett.* 1:201).

Adélaïde offers her a home with her family, but Settimia would rather strike out on her own, even though this is not considered an appropriate option for young women. Again, Allart criticizes the fact that unmarried women have little acceptable alternatives in life except the convent. "Si dans d'autres pays que le nôtre de jeunes filles n'oseraient pas faire ce que je vais faire, combien l'oseraient-elles moins ici où leur donne le couvent pour retraite!" (*Sett.* 1:202).

She plans to take the money her late father left her, begin an independent life in Naples, and try to be an example of how a single women can live a respectable life of solitude and study.

> Vous savez que dès long-temps le sort des femmes m'a occupée. . . . Tant que je ne voulais qu'étudier, je n'en sentais pas tout l'ennui. Pour aimer, mon esprit m'a retenue encore plus que ma position; la pauvreté seule me séparait de Marcel; mais aujourd'hui le malheur de ma position est visible. Il faut donner l'example, et *commencer de loin à changer l'existence morale de la femme* (*Sett.* 1:202-3, my italics).

Settimia also attacks the double standard of morals for men and women. When virtue was made different for men and women, this was all right for the ignorant times, for a woman had to do nothing more than be chaste. However, when women act more independently, the situation becomes more complex and perceptions on morals must change. "On a tracé des devoirs plus éclairés aux hommes: il faut en tracer de plus éclairés aux femmes. Tandis que les hommes obtenaient une amélioration de *droit*, les femmes n'ont obtenu qu'une amélioration de *fait*, elles pensent et vivent selon le temps présent, et on les juge selon le temps passé . . . ." (*Sett.* 1:203, author's italics).

She identifies treatment of women as reprehensible in most other countries of the world, but concludes that no country has more need for reform than Italy. "Nul pays n'a plus besoin d'une réforme que le mien, et nulle femme ne doit mieux s'inspirer qu'une femme romaine. Nos couvens [sic] font l'horreur de ma vie (*Sett.* 1:204). Women's virtue should rest, as does men's, in the whole of her life, not in some meaningless definition of chastity. Basic Christian concepts of morality are good. Let us just make them more reasonable. "Partant d'où nous sommes, il faut améliorer et non renverser la loi ancienne . . . . La morale admise nous paraît vraie, éternelle; nous ne voulons changer que la sévérité de son application" (*Sett.* 1: 105).

Both men and women should be treated alike regarding pre-marital love and divorce. "Si les hommes sont estimés encore pour avoir aimé hors du mariage, pour avoir divorcé, les femmes qui auront fait comme eux ne seront pas jugées différémment qu'eux" (*Sett.* 1:206).

Settimia tells Adélaïde that achieving such independence and impartiality toward women will be her goal. "Je voudais servir d'exemple au petit nombre de femmes qui, souffrant trop, cherchent à sortir de la longue minorité où les hommes les ont tenues" (*Sett.* 1:209). While upgrading the role of women, society also would improve the lot of men by providing them with more capable and intelligent wives. "Jugez quelle différence pour eux de trouver, au lieu d'épouses frivoles et infidèles, des compagnes spirituelles et dûres qui les comprennent et les secondent" (*Sett.* 1:209).

She advocates a broader and more intensive schooling for women— in short, a *male* education, thereby bringing to the top the minority of women born to intellectuality and worldly activity. "Il ne faut pas seulement instruire les femmes dans les lettres, il faut les former au respect du courage, à l'amour de la patrie, à la connaissance des affaires, leur donner une *éducation mâle* et les principles de l'antiquité, faire sortir, de la foule, en un mot, celles qui sont nées pour la pensée et l'action" (*Sett.* 1:212, my italics). If only women would follow me, she concludes, I would find a new strength!

Adélaïde is horrified that someone as young and lovely as Settimia should start a life alone in such a large and intimidating city as Naples and begs her to stay with her in Rome. Settimia, however, is happy with her studies and her new milieu. She finds a fellow scholar, Don Andrea Colonna (apparently, a portrait of the real-life Libri), and the artist Guilio Reni, who teach her more about Neapolitan history and art. "Je suis heureuse, je vis, j'erre dans le plus doux pays du monde; j'aborde tout à la foi, l'histoire, la législation, la société; j'observe le sort des femmes; j'étudie mon pays et les causes de sa chute" (*Sett.* 1:222). As a timid girl and a submissive niece in Albano, she knew nothing, she tells Adélaïde. Now she has acquired a new kind of existence that, until now, men had kept only for themselves. "Les hommes s'étaient donc réservés pour eux seuls ces charmes de l'indépendance et de l'étude!" (*Sett.* 1:223).

Settimia tells Adélaïde about some of the love intrigues in which her Neapolitan friends are involved, including the tragic story of a beautiful countess who loved a much younger man. The 40-year-old countess made the 18-year-old artist her protegé, helped him develop his talent as a painter, then, despairing over his inevitable infidelities over the next few years, she stabbed herself.

In the meantime, Marcel has written to Settimia several times from Calcutta, but she has not answered. At first he loved the exoticism of India, but now he yearns to finish his work there as soon as possible and return to Settimia. "Pour moi je reviendrai humble comme un coupable, ne cherchant à m'excuser qu'en vous disant combien j'ai souffert" (*Sett.* 1:260). She, however, has not returned his letters, for she feels a renewal of their passion only would be her undoing. "O Dieu! vais-je le voir encore! O Dieu! me remettez-vous vaincue dans ses mains, dans les mêmes dangers, les angoisses, la démence que j'ai sentis . . . . Ah! tout l'enchantement de sa présence ne suffira pas pour me rassurer" (*Sett.* 1:262). The first volume of the novel ends with

Settimia's decision to somehow disappear.

The second tome and fourth book begins with Marcel's letter to his and Settimia's friend Manelli. He describes his harrowing experience in a shipwreck that occurred as he was sailing back to Europe via England. Although Settimia had not answered any of his letters, he had heard from others that her uncle had died, and that she was heading back to Rome. He planned to find her there. His ship, the Kent, was a few weeks away from its final destination to England when a storm came up. "... nous nous sommes trouvés subitement arrêtés par un coup de vent, dont la violence a augmenté de plus en plus" (*Sett.* 2:4). A separate incident set the ship on fire as well:

> Le vaisseau éprouve une violente secousse, l'officier laisse échapper sa lampe, et, dans son empressement à la remasser, il lâche la barrique qui s'ouvre; l'eau-de-vie entre en contact avec la mèche de la lampe, toute est bientôt en flammes, et notre vaisseau se trouve menacé à la fois par la tempête et l'incendie (Sett. 2:6).

He describes in detail the process of saving the survivors of the Kent on to the rescuing vessel, the Cambria. The only way to spare the passengers from a fiery death was to flood the ship with sea water. "Alors commence une scène d'horreur qui passe toute description: trouble, agitation, terreur . . . six à sept personnes . . . s'étaient forcées de s'enfuir . . . et couraient çà et là cherchant un père, un mari, des enfans [sic] . . . d'autres se livrent au désespoir" (*Sett.* 2:11).

Marcel was afraid many times that he would die, but memories of his passion for Settimia gave him strength to hang on. "Je ne sais où cette pensée m'aurait entraîné si je ne m'étais pas tout à coup rattaché à la passion qui me ramenait en Europe, le plus ferme garant pour moi d'une existence immortelle" (*Sett.* 2:34). He escapes in a daring crawl along the sinking and burning Kent and a slide on a rope down to the Cambria. The second ship takes the Kent passengers safely to Cornwall.

As the fifth book begins, a travel-weary Marcel has made his way from England back to Albano and is reunited with Settimia. "Il échappe ruiné à ces désasatres et accourt encore animé des dangers, se refugier à mes pieds," Settimia tells Adélaïde. "Pouvais-je refuser de le voir?" (*Sett.* 2:54). At the first sight of one another, the two lovers are overcome with passion and tenderness. "Je n'avais pas connu l'amour, j'en ignorai les douceurs. Depuis que [Marcel] est ici, une passion nouvelle m'enchaîne" (*Sett.* 2:54). Furthermore, Marcel seems a changed man; no longer a determined businessman who places his ambitions and projects in front of love.

They resume their former passion and intimacy in Albano.   All too soon, though, Marcel feels pressed to leave.   He goes to Rome, then to Florence on business without saying good-by.   Miffed and saddened by yet another separation, Settimia does not wish to be found, and disappears for a time from Albano.   A cat-and-mouse game of letters ensues as the two try to catch up to one another.   When Marcel finally returns to Albano to throw himself at her feet, she tells him, "Notre vie ici n'était pas si douce que vous disiez, ni votre ambition aussi morte qu'elle semble" (*Sett.* 2:91).   She fears their separation while he was in India was but a prelude for a permanent rupture.   He denies this, insisting he is sacrificing himself for her sake.   "A ces mots j'ai vu qu'il voulait toujours aller à Florence," Settimia writes. "Deux passion fortes le tenaient esclave et malheureux" (*Sett.* 2:92).

She reluctantly is persuaded to accompany Marcel back to Florence, where M. de Lesmède, an old friend of her late uncle, helps her understand how much Marcel truly loves his work.   Lesmède presses Marcel to return to Paris, saying a young businessman's future depends on it—"La puissance n'est plus en Italie, elle est ailleurs, elle est en France."   Again, Marcel's family will not allow Marcel to bring Settimia to France with him at this point.   She feels she must not hold him back.   "Je ne peux interdire à mon amant les goûts qui, à Rome, ne me rappelent qu'au passé.   Qu'il parte donc, c'est à moi d'être courageuse" (*Sett.* 2:98).   He leaves for Paris, still promising that some day they will marry.

Back in Paris, Marcel writes letters mostly about his sister Thérèse, and their mother's determination to see her married before she will consider letting Marcel think of a marriage of his own.   "C'est à votre sœur qu'il fallait songer. . . . je voudrais votre promesse de ne épouser [Settimia] que quand Thérèse sera mariée" (*Sett.* 2:127-28). Furthermore, Madame Gerimé insists on being in complete control of the choice of her son-in-law.   After considerable tribulation, Marcel and Thérèse manage to work around their peevish and manipulative mother finally to unite Thérèse with the man she truly loves.

In the meantime, Settimia is in Rome with Adélaïde, whose husband, Vincent, is increasingly moody and verbally harsh and unkind to her and to their three children.   The two women engage in a discussion about what qualities make a man worth marrying. Although Settimia says she would rather have an unfaithful husband than one with so many difficult moods, Adélaïde defends Vincent for his fidelity and responsibility.   "Vous vous trompez beaucoup, ma chère; un mari infidèle attaque le mariage à sa source, flétrit l'honneur et délie la femme. Celui-ci garde notre loyauté intacte. . . . ses défauts sont des nuages sur notre union, mais qui la laissent subsister dans sa beauté"

(*Sett.* 2:135). In short, Adélaïde focuses on the positive—a faithful husband, beautiful children, financial security. "Chacun a sa part de chagrin dans la vie; loin de me soulever contre la mienne"(*Sett.* 2:136). Settimia, though, is unconvinced that her friend's dedication to domesticity and forebearance in the face of difficulty is a sufficient foundation for a rewarding life.

The coming of spring only makes Settimia more depressed and agitated and Marcel's absence more difficult to endure. She leaves for Rési in the Alps, and writes asking Marcel to join her there. He arrives, but from the beginning their reunion is not a happy one, mostly because he is resentful that she pulled him away at an important point in his career. "Marcel a quitté Paris à regret et dans une passion d'ambition, égale a celle qui m'a fait l'appeler" (*Sett.* 2:178). Not only does he admit that Settimia has held back his career, but he also speculates on where he might be right now if he had married M. Herbé's daughter and become a provincial deputy. "Il y a deux choses au monde," he tells her, "et votre supériorité, votre beauté, la romaine et la déesse ne répareront pas le tort que me fait, par exemple près du minister, mon absence et mon séjour ici" (*Sett.* 2:180).

When she becomes irate, he continues, "Quoi! ne comprenez-vous rien aux affaires, au monde, aux villes? Je vous aime, mais l'amour nuit aux affaires" (*Sett.* 2:180). She accuses him of being a typically shallow and self-centered Frenchman, and, by the way, where is all the money he is supposed to be earning? "Vous êtes bien l'homme de votre pays, vain et frivole; vous attendiez jadis la fortune de vos talens [sic]; où sont-ils?" (*Sett.* 2:181).

Marcel insists that he has much more service to give to his country—goals that can go hand-in-hand with his pursuit of love: ". . . rendre à notre pays son éclat, preparer un pouvoir organisé et discipliné, la science politique et la vertu publique, c'est un but qui peut compter à côté de l'amour" (*Sett.* 2:183-84). Futhermore, he assures her that his efforts will involve the kind of moral reform and improvements in women's rights that she advocates. He complains again that she has pulled him away from work at a key moment. They argue further, he storms out, he returns and apologizes, they reconcile for the night, but the tension continues to the point that Settimia wishes to send him back to Paris and lose herself in the Alps. Steeping herself in *mal de siècle,* she embraces the sorrow that envelopes her, swearing it will serve a greater purpose. "Ma douleur a un charme de plénitude; je m'envire d'un mal qui me fait sentir ma force, qui me sépare des autres femmes . . . . j'ai une exaltation qui m'étonne et qui m'élève à mes propres yeux" (*Sett.* 2:189).

She decides to go back to Italy, work on behalf of women, and battle against the passion she feels.   "Je travaillerai pour les femmes; mais loin de vanter les passions, je les combattrai . . . . je parlerai des déceptions du cœur, des *illusions de la vie*" (*Sett.* 2:190, author's italics).   Later, she again mentions the dual passions that characterize Marcel's soul and sadly admits that one has vanquished the other. "Deux passions étaient dans son âme; une a vaincu l'autre, et ce n'est pas la mienne" (*Sett.* 2:204).   She cannot imagine being his wife without this passion that is the very essence of her being. "Moi être sa femme! vivre avec lui détrônée! manquer au passé, à lui, à moi, à cette religion de la passion que j'emporterai pieuse à la tombe!" (*Sett.* 2: 206).   Settimia leaves Rési without telling Marcel good-by.   She waits a few days at Milan, hoping he will follow her, but he returns to his work in Paris.

A sad and bitter Marcel writes to Manelli from Paris, insisting that love is an absurd and perpetual agitation, and that he does not need it. ". . . je me sens délivré d'un grand poids" (*Sett.* 2:215).   He works excessively hard, and decides to use the money he had saved for marriage to enjoy worldly pleasures.   Parisian gossip soon links him with three different young women, although he is not serious about any of them. He has become the kind of man that his society demands, but he secretly longs for his studious former life in Italy.   "Devenu homme et suivant la destiné où la société et le devoir nous appellent, je regarderai l'Italie comme la poésie fugitive que nous connaissons tous dans nos jeunes années et que nous perdons tous plus tard" (*Sett.* 2:226).

Back in Albano, Settimia struggles with the melancholia and regret as she watches her friend Margarita prepare excitedly for her wedding. In Paris, Marcel becomes the Platonic friend of Manelli's former mistress, Faustine, an Italian pianist and *chanteuse,* with whom he loves to talk about Italy.   He still loves Settimia, but realizes she must be content filling her chosen destiny with her independence and her studies:

> J'ai vu Settimia dans sa première jeunesse, désire beaucoup l'éclat; elle se voyait sur les jeunes filles et sur les femmes une supériorité qu'elle eût voulu établir fièrement; son caractère fort et ambitieux ne savait pas se renfermer dans la vie privée. . . . Settimia a reçu de son pays une majesté naturelle, indépendante des hommes et du sort (*Sett.* 2:243-44).

In the meantime, Manelli, believing Settimia is free of all commitment to Marcel, arrives in Albano and declares his love for her. She refuses to take him seriously, despite his tender attentions, and thinks only of Marcel, still ideally imagining a sweet reunion with him. She writes to Marcel, hinting that someone in Rome loves her. Manelli counters by telling her that Marcel loves Faustina. Fortunately, Settimia sees Marcel's letter to Manelli which verifies that, although he admires Faustina, he still loves Settimia. Marcel soon arrives in Albano to declare his love for Settimia in person.

Before the joyfully reunited lovers can make plans to stay together in Albano, Settimia is called away by her friend Guiditta to Genoa. Guiditta, whom Settimia met in Naples, is now married to the Neapolitan artist Guilio Reni. The faithless husband is now involved in an affair with a countess in Genoa, where he was called to complete her portrait. Marcel escorts Settimia to Genoa. He must travel on to Paris, though, to accept a promised appointment as undersecretary of state. At this point, though, Madame Gerimé has written Settimia a kind letter calling her a "daughter" and saying she is planning her marriage to Marcel.

Settimia finds a desperate situation in Genoa. The distraught Guiditta, crazed with jealousy, stabs her husband's lover. The countess survives and flees to Turin, fortunately not naming her assailant. Upon Settimia's urging, and the repentant Guilio promises fidelity hereafter to his wife, and she forgives him. Guiditta, though is confused. Had not Settimia always advocated the legal breakup of unhappy marriages? Settimia clarifies her stand. It is only hopelessly incompatible couples—such as those forced to marry by their parents at an early age—that she says should be allowed to dissolve their union. "Je n'ai jamais prétendu qu'il fallût briser les affections, mais briser les mariages mal assortis, où trop souvent les parens [sic] poussent leurs enfans [sic] sans expérience" (*Sett.* 2:305). As for couples who really love each other, they must sacrifice, pardon, and renew their bond. Settimia's work in Genoa is now done, and she wishes to join Marcel in Paris for their wedding.

The last book of the novel, however, is a long, near-tragic story of how this long-awaited marriage might not happen. In the position of undersecretary of state that was hurried upon him before he had sufficient time to train for it, Marcel has fallen victim to "une maladie nerveuse" (*Sett.* 2:312) His employer ordered him to the Midi to convalesce. Thérèse and her new husband take him to Genoa instead to reunite him with Settimia. Marcel, however, is so thin and ill that his fiancée hardly recognizes him. She berates herself for not having put aside her own desires, braved his family's prejudices and followed Marcel to Paris in the first place. "Fille folle, je ne rêvais que l'action, la guerre, une destinée mâle; vous me punissez par mes propers goûts" (*Sett.* 2:314). Marcel protests that Italy is where he belongs. Being in Genoa makes him feel better already.

During the next few weeks, the couple travels slowly from Genoa to Turin to Florence to Rome. About 15 pages of conversation between Marcel and Settimia show the fruits of Allart's extensive research on the history of Florence as the two of them speak of their favorite Florentine characters and events. They also rhapsodize about the beauties of nature along the way. Marcel wishes for Settimia to swear that if he dies, she will go on living without him.   "En présence de cette nature qui proclame la beauté des créations de Dieu, la supériorité de l'homme et son immortalité, dis-moi, Settimia, quel serait donc le malheur, pour une romaine intelligente et pieuse, de survivre à ce qu'elle aime?" (*Sett.* 2:344). She will make no such promise, preferring to die, if he dies. "Si Marcel meurt, je ne vivrai pas après lui; s'il vit, il m'épousera dans les jours heureux de sa guérison" (*Sett.* 2:352).

Arriving in Albana, they both fall gravely ill. Manelli and Adélaïde arrive to nurse tenderly each one, but the long deathbed vigil makes the reader fear that their fate may become that of Anna and Warwich in *L'Indienne.* After years of letting their separate preoccupations keep them apart, will the two of them be able finally to make their passion a sufficient bond to hold them together? It did not happen in *L'Indienne.* It did not happen in real life for Hortense and Henry.

In *Settimia,* however, idealism prevails. After a few days, Marcel miraculously rallies. His recovery brings Settimia back to life, and her revival further strengthens him. ". . . elle veut se reposer, se soigner, se calmer. Marcel respire, cette idée l'a sauvée" (*Sett.* 2:398).

Adélaïde writes to her husband to come to Albano and to bring their children. In one week will be the wedding of Settimia and Marcel.

Settimia stands apart from Allart's previous novels in its scope. "Son caractère romantique et grandiloquent distingue *Settimia* des autres romans d'Hortense, heureusement plus simples et plus modérés, parfois quaisi stendhaliens" (Billy 143).   Allart has progressed to a bolder, more convoluted linear plot progression in *Settimia* while leaving behind the Stendhalian undertones that are perceptible in her earlier novels such as *Gertrude* and *Sextus.* In *Settimia,* the author still presents a heroine plagued by sense of isolation in a world of callous orthodoxy that functions at the expense of women. The difference is that she allows her protagonist to triumph in her own dual desires—love and self-fulfillment—without first paying the same kind of painful or tragic price as did the heroines in *Gertrude,   Jérôme, Sextus,* and *L'Indienne.*

If Settimia must wait for frustratingly long periods of time before she finally can be reunited with Marcel, she retains enough control of her life's choices to protect her tender psyche from insensitive or unscrupulous men. She is never bandied about by an unwise or naïve choice in a lover or husband. Also, the times when she is without Marcel are usually neither lonely nor completely isolated, but filled with friends and intellectual productivity. Though she does not always chart her own course entirely without sorrow and regret, she charts it with a healthy lack of self-sacrifice and self-flagellation.

At the novel's end, the happy lovers are together, but one might, nonetheless, criticize the *dénouement* for its vagueness. The narration implies that after the happy wedding of Marcel and Settimia, the young husband will forgo his Parisian career, which nearly killed him, and live a life of grateful solitude in Albano. Is he now truly void of all his former ambitions? Will life in Italy be satisfying for someone who was once so determined to excel in business in France? Also, Settimia was ready to follow him to Paris, perhaps at the expense of her own studies and personal preference. Will she be pleased enough with her own self-development to be willing again to do this, should Marcel take another turn for the ambitious?   The resolution of these basic conflicts still is not precise.

Rabine notes that in *Settimia*, that Allart does not subscribe to the stereotype that women have nothing but the ideal to aspire to and dream about, for they are not inherently weak. "Like Daniel Stern [the *nom de plume* of Marie d'Agoult], Hortense Allart's social propaganda consists in proving that women do grow and develop as the years of their life proceed. . . . Allart concentrates on the details between the stages" (183). Since Settimia, as did Allart, wants a man worthy of her, she must allow him to go off to Paris to seek his potential. She cannot marry him, however, without seeking the same kind of self-actualization for herself.

The reaction to the newly published novel was largely favorable. Gustave Planche wrote in the *Revue des Deux Mondes* in September 1836:

> Il y a passion vraie, il y a élévation toujours. Il y a enfin peinture . . . En somme, *Settimia,* par la gravité du ton, par l'élégance de certains pages et la science combinée de l'ambition et de l'amour, n'est pas indigne de ce grand nom de Rome qui sans cesse y revient et dont l'adoration y domine. . . . (quoted by Billy 144).

Chateaubriand, who had read the manuscript for the novel, also praised it to Hortense. However, a note from Allart to her publisher Arthus Bertrand in March 1837, indicated that *Settimia* was only

mildly received by the public. She had only one copy of the book in
her possession, and wanted some others to distribute to friends,
including her sister. The publisher apparently thought money was too
tight to give her any free copies:

> Vous êtes un homme inflexible, monsieur, mais j'espère
> que le roman continuera à se vendre un peu et qu'enfin vous serez
> mon débiteur, ce que vous souhaitez autant qui moi.
>   Puisque vous me refusez tout, ayez l'obligeance de
> m'envoyer encore trois or quatre exemplaires de *Settimia*. Je
> voudrais l'envoyer à ma sœur, à Rome, où elle ne pourra l'acheter.
> Vous me ferez plaisir, car je n'en ai qu'un seul exemplaire à moi.[5]

As he anayzes *Settimia* and mentions the merits of her earlier
novels as well, Billy concludes that Allart's fiction in general is worthy
of a closer look by 20th-century readers and critics.   "Romancière,
Hortense sait écrire et composer et elle a des passages d'une écriture
agréable, qui, parfois, vont assez loin."   If, at this point, she has not
gained a reputation as a literary heavyweight, this should not preclude a
better, overall acquaintance with her works. "Sa légèreté, sa facilité ont
empêché trop longtemps qu'on y regard d'un peu près" (144).
Settimia, then, is the culmination of five estimable Allart novels that
deserve to be drawn out of a century of obscurity into the modern light
of awareness and analysis of feminist literary efforts of the mid-1800's.

After the publication of *Settimia,* Hortense finished out most of
the year 1836 calmly and happily at Herblay, working on *L'Histoire de
Florence,* which would be completed in January 1837.   She returned to
Paris on Dec. 10, where Didier met her at the door of her apartment in
the Rue Mondavi, where he had gone to inquire if she had arrived.
Thus began a winter of pleasant visits with old and new acquaintances
in Paris.   Dider, Sampayo and Chateaubriand called on her, and letters
continued to arrive from Bulwer, who had been named *chargé d'affaires*
in Belgium.

She also began to frequent George Sand's salon in the Hôtel de
France, No 23, Rue Lafitte. Liszt and d'Agoult, recently returned from
a stay in Switzerland where they temporarily had left behind their small
daughter Blandine (born in Geneva Dec. 18, 1835), had moved to the
hotel first in October.[6] They invited Sand to take an apartment that had
the same living room as theirs so they all could host soirées, sharing
the space and the company of mutual friends. Hortense does not drop
any names in *Les Enchantements de Prudence* of those she may have
met at these salons over a period of several weeks.   Some of the
writers, composers, intellectuals and other luminaries circulating

there with whom she might have spoken include Chopin, Berlioz, Meyerbeer, Rossini, Balzac, Hugo, the Abbé Lamennais, editor of *Le Monde*, and Pierre Leroux, a former Saint-Simonian who was then trying to develop his own radical philosophy.

With her literary, historical and journalistic efforts all in full swing at this time, and her successes finally catapulting her into such eminent circles as this one, it is somewhat surprising that Hortense opted in spring 1837 to leave for another extended stay in Italy. However, Sand's salons had ended early that year when she left Paris for her country home, Nohant, and d'Agoult, Liszt and later, Chopin, followed there within a few weeks.

On Feb. 10, 1836, Sophie Allart had married Pierre Gabriac in Rome. No doubt wishing to see her sister and meet her new brother-in-law as well as renew acquaintances with her myriad of Italian friends, Hortense announced to her Parisian friends her plans to spend April at Herblay (where, for reasons she does not explain, she passed the time reading about Asia and studying Chinese), then departed for Florence the next month.

Among the many Parisian friends who came to say good-bye was Chateaubriand, who offered, as always, friendly professional advice. "Il voyait avec bonté mes ouvrages, et me donnait des avis" (*EP* 203). Henry wrote that he was expecting to be named to a post in Turkey, and that he would visit her in Italy on the way there.

Hortense took Marcus, now age 11, off for new adventures in the country of his and her birth in May 1837. They arrived in Florence on June 14.

Notes

[1] Hortense Allart. *La femme et la démocratie de nos temps,* (Paris: Chez Delaunay, Librarie, Palais-Royal et A. Pinard Libraire, 1836) 1. (Subsequent references to this work will appear in parentheses after the quotation and will be indicated by the abbreviation *FDNT*).

[2] Uffenbeck cites the existing record of this publication in the Bibliothèque National as *Publications Saint-Simoniennes (1830-1836). X: Publications faites par des femmes.*   Allart's essay is in Tome I1: No. 11. Uffenbeck 259.

[3] *Nouvelles Lettres à Sainte-Beuve,*   13, n. 2.

[4] Madame Hortense Allart. *Préface, Settimia.* 2 vols. (Paris : Arthus Bertrand, Libraire-Éditeur, 1836) 1:xli. (Quoted by Billy 142). (Subsequent references to *Settimia* will appear in parentheses after the quotation, and will be indicated by the abbreviation   *Sett.*).

[5]Hortense Allart to Monsieur Arthus Bertrand, rue Haute-feuille, 23, "Ce mardi [mars 1837]" in Paul Bonnefon, "Prudence et ses enchantements. II1: Hortense Allart et les saint-simoniens," *L'Amateur d'autographes, revue rétrospective et contemporaine,* XLI (November 1908) 330-331, quoted by Uffenbeck 268.

[6]Biographer Dominque Desanti, author of *Daniel ou le visage secret d'une comtesse romantique: Marie d'Agout.* (Paris: Stock, 1980), states that Hortense first met Marie d'Agoult through Hortense's cousin Delphine Gay de Girardin (38). Hortense herself does not indicate exactly when the two met, but their acquaintance probably dates to 1836-37.

Chapter 7

Les Petits Livres: A Failed Marriage, a Literature of Protest (1837-1846)

After the whirlwind that was 1836 and early 1837, Hortense was ready for a slow, calm voyage through the Alps and a more tranquil lifestyle among her friends in Florence and other towns in central Italy. "On aurait cru Hortense plus éprise de solitude," says Billy (150). She had made her last trip to Italy in 1825 filled with high hopes and *joie de vivre*, but at that time she was 24 years old, pregnant, uncertain of her future projects, and had only one successful publication to her credit (*Lettres sur les Ouvrages de Madame de Staël*). This time she was a well-known 36-year-old writer with five novels, a scholarly history of Florence, and several other various kinds of writings to her name. She was traveling towards a group of prominent and sophisticated friends in Italy and had left behind an equally impressive crowd of Parisian well-wishers.

When she and Marcus arrived in Florence, she was invited to a soirée at the stately home of Libri's mother. She also renewed her friendship with Capponi, whom she found thinner, but more handsome, than he had been a decade earlier. Letters from Capponi to their mutual friend Niccolini Tommaséo indicate that the former thought Hortense more lovely, vivacious and spontaneous than ever (Billy 150).

From summer to autumn she stayed at Arricia, then at Arezzo, where she was elected to the local literary academy and read to its members from some of her own writings about women. During a visit to Sienna, M. de l'Espine, an old acquaintance, and some of his friends said she looked "Venetian" because her fair hair had darkened to ash blond. From mid-December to March 1838, she resided at Via

Melaranccio in Florence.

Young Marcus, educated by Father Bertrand, the liberal priest in Herblay, had always believed he was Catholic.   As they settled into the very cradle of Catholicism, his mother informed him he was Protestant and launched him on a crash course on the Reformation, describing how Martin Luther had "avenged Christianity." They took trips to Rome, where Hortense visited her sister, Sophie, and M. Gabriac, "son beau et excellent mari" (*EP*   206).

She worked on the second volume of her *Histoire de Florence,* studied theology, and often went to the theater. She began to think of settling permanently in Italy and of eventually finding a man there whom she could marry, who would make her happy, and be a good father for Marcus.   Looking back upon this time, she wrote rather wistfully that she never had been able to make a lifelong commitment to a man, and that perhaps the time had come to do so.   "Je ne pouvais ni rappler ni retenir un homme envolé pour jamais. Ne saurais-je au contraire trouver entre mes amis ici, une affection pour la vie, un mariage dans l'avenir qui fît mon bonheur et convînt à mon fils?" (*EP*   208).

She received visits from d'Espine and Capponi, who had her named to the Academy of the Colombaria, of which he was then president.   However, Capponi, who had found Hortense charming at her return, soon thought her insufferable.   Six months after the two had become reacquainted, he judged her vain and frivolous, supposedly because of her "unfeminine" social and political ideas. "[Capponi] déclarera alors, ne plus rien voir de la femme en elle tant ses sophismes l'égarent, elle défend toutes sortes d'infamies avec une véritable noblesse d'âme et de sentiments et les monte en système social" (Decreus 70). There may have been another reason that Hortense's conduct galled Capponi.   Details are scarce, but she may have had other lovers over the next few months among her small circle of scholarly Italian friends. "Lequel, lesquels d'entre eux avait eu auprès d'elle un accès plus intime?" (Billy 152).

The man who would become her most constant companion for the next three years and the father of her second son was Jacopo Mazzéi, although Hortense mentions him only perfunctorily in *Les Enchantements de Prudence,* and there is little written elsewhere about what kind of man he was, personally and professionally.   Their son, Henri-Marcus-Diodatei Allart, was born in Florence on March 21, 1839.

In January 1838, a few months before Hortense met Mazzéi, Bulwer wrote, still unsure of his travel plans. She tried to chase Henry from her mind by dedicating herself to her studies. She spent the spring and summer at the Villa Belvédère near Sienna where a large library was available for her use.   While she was in the midst of her research, Bulwer made good on his promise to visit her on his way to Constantinople, where he was to serve in the British Embassy for a few months, then move on to Russia to fill the same position at the embassy in St. Petersburg.   He surprised her at the Belvédère, and again declared himself ready to rekindle their love.   For the moment, he seemed sincere—"un Bulwer bien différent de l'amant bien désolé qu'elle avait quitté naguère, un Bulwer dégagé, désinvolte, mais se disant prêt à sacrifier à Hortense un nouvel amour" (Billy 152).   He wished for Hortense to accompany him to Rome, then to Naples, where they would await the ship that would take Henry to Constantinople. (He wanted Hortense to accompany him there as well, but if she did, she would have to take a different ship than the one commissioned by the British government.)

They passed *"deux jours et une douce nuit"* together at Belvédère, but Hortense again worried that her love for him might endanger the new life she had carved for herself as well as her current intellectual project.   "J'avais peur de lui, je pensais à mon *Histoire de Florence,* à des amitiés sages et sûres. Devais-je tout oublier pour cet astre charmant et errant?" (*EP* 209).   How could she leave on another adventure at this point and go where she would have no Italian library, none of the needed books at her disposal?   Also, she would have to take Marcus along and interrupt the tutoring she had arranged for him.

She proposed that Henry make a sacrifice, and pass up his latest diplomatic assignment to stay in Florence, where they could research together her *Histoire de Florence.*   He was not impressed.   Decreus states that Henry was no longer considering marriage to Hortense at this point; in fact, he was not even in love with her in the same way as he had been before.   "Henry le lui a dit: il lui voue une affection, un dévouement auxquels il sacrifierait éventuellement toute passion que l'avenir pourrait mettre sur son chemin, mais il n'est plus épris" (69).

Hortense no doubt sensed some of these feelings in Henry.   She accompanied him part of the way to Rome, bade him farewell on the Appian Way, then wrote to his Rome address on April 9, 1838, telling him that it was his attitude about leaving her rather than his actual conduct that hurt her.

> Sacrifiez une femme à votre ambition, la délicatesse de ses anciennes mœurs, et tout ce qu'elle espérait de durable et de saint avec vous, mais ne l'insultez pas, gardez un souvenir plus honorable de votre jeunesse et du commencement de votre vie politique où l'amour et le plus noble du monde, fut beaucoup mêlé![1]

Henry became ill in Rome, but this time Hortense so engrossed in her work that she declined to go to him. A few days later she again wrote to him, saying she was displeased not only that his visit was so short but also that he had not changed his *idée fixe* that his projects were more important than hers and that she should abandon hers in favor of following him. She had proposed that they make a new commitment to each other based on their common intellectual interests, whereas he had expected her to be content in the role of his wife or "girl." She would never stoop to that level! Her letter to Rome on April 19 reads, "Moi, j'ai souffert depuis votre départ autant que je peux souffrir et vos lettres y ont contribué. Je vous avais parlé d'un lien intellectual au-dessus du mariage, vous me parlez d'une vie de fille où je ne m'abaisserai jamais" (quoted by Billy 153, and Decreus 72).

More letters crossed between them as Henry waited in Rome, then Naples. At one point, Hortense asked him to return to Sienna and work on an English translation of *L'Histoire de Florence*. This idea did not seem to tempt him either. Within a few weeks, he traveled on to Turkey, then wrote telling her how much he loved that country.

Hortense's June 21 letter to Bulwer in Constantinople indicates that she had little regret about not having accompanied him there. She realized that if she were with him at that moment, she would be obscure, and therefore, unhappy. How much better to be respected in her position as a woman writer, even one of a lesser rank. "Il y a une partie de la vie qui est exaltée et déchirante, mais il y a une partie positive, brillante et forte. Obscure près de vous, je n'eusse été jamais calme. Femme écrivain (même au dernier rang) j'aimerai votre ambition qui respectera la mienne." Still, this letter ended with a tender note. "Soignez votre santé, prenez des notes, écrivez-moi ce que vous voyez . . . Adieu, Adieu, je vous rappelle aux lettres puisque c'est mon seul moyen de vous plaire" (quoted by Decreus 74).

In July, she sent Henry a piece of the red ribbon that she had worn around her neck at the 1836 Parisian feminist meetings so that it would serve as an inspiration for Turkish women also to seek emancipation. In another letter, she wrote that she had turned to God, as did David of the Old Testament, asking for guidance on the right paths. Her prayers helped her realize that men who flout their society's morals and go against nature are guilty enough, but still worse is the woman who loves such a man and suffers because of him. "Mon cher Henry, s'il y a quelque chose de coupable, c'est un homme qui flétrit son cœur, perd sa santé et ses mœurs et se joue de la nature. Mais s'il y a quelque chose de honteux et de méprisable, c'est une femme qui aime cet homme" (quoted by Billy 153).

Despite a few lingering regrets at letting Henry go, Hortense resumed her life in Florence with her usual industry and optimistic point of view. Her relationship with Mazzéi began this same summer, and she was buoyed by her upbeat philosophy about the joy of constant, self-disciplined study on a variety of topics. "Dans l'étude il faut deux choses pour le plaisir et le bonheur. C'est que l'action soit *forcée et variée.* Sans la contrainte on ne fait rien, le premier moment d'application coûte, et sans la variée on se lasse" (*EP* 211, author's italics).

In October 1838, Hortense, now pregnant with her second son, renewed her acquaintance with Liszt and d'Agoult, who had continued their Bohemian existence from Sand's Nohant in the Berry region of central France to Milan to Venice to Florence. The purpose of Liszt and d'Agoult's travels at this time was partly to accommodate the composer's piano concertizing, but mostly to humor Marie's desire to stay away from Paris, where their illicit relationship and illegitimate parenthood were subject to more scrutiny and prejudice. (D'Agoult had left her husband, the Count Charles d'Agoult, and their young daughter, Claire, early in 1835 to live with Liszt). This latest trip had reunited Liszt and d'Agoult with their three-year-old daughter, Blandine, whom they had left with a Swiss family near Geneva. Their second daughter, Cosima, was born in Como, Italy, on Dec. 25, 1837.

Hortense especially was pleased to become friends with d'Agoult, whom she esteemed for having left behind an unhappy marriage to be with the man she loved. "Elle admirait en Marie la femme qui avait eu le courage de mettre sa conduite en accord avec ses principes d'émancipation féminine et de liberté amoureuse" (Billy 154). The two writers would become closer in the ensuing years. (Marie's writing career under the name Daniel Stern would begin in late 1841 after she and Liszt had had their third child—a son, Daniel, born May 9, 1839 in Rome—and were beginning to drift apart). The two women's friendship was not an easy one, though. Over the next decade they would become competitors for the affections of Bulwer, Didier and Sainte-Beuve, all of whom would at one time pursue Marie, much to Hortense's barely concealed dismay. It was only Hortense's forgiving attitude and refusal to be jealous or bitter about any of this rivalry that kept their friendship intact until Marie's death in 1876, three years before Hortense died.

Because of d'Agoult's tendency to be self-centered, petulant, and most of all, insouciant about the consequences of pursing men that other women loved, her faithful female friends such as Hortense were few. Desanti's biography of d'Agoult contains a photograph of a medallion of Allart in profile with the caption "La seule amie fidèle: Hortense Allart de Méritens, romancière."[2] Jacques Vier concurs,

"Hortense Allart de Méritens pourrait revendiquer entre tous les amis, hommes ou femmes, de la Comtesse d'Agoult, le privilège de la plus grande constance dans la plus fidèle affection. La mort seule interrompit leur correspondence."[3]

When the two women became better acquainted during the fall of 1838, Marie's impressions of Hortense and her books were not complimentary. In her journal entry in October, just a day after meeting with this studious woman, Marie wrote, "Je la crois très sincère: je respecte cette vie pauvre et occupée. Elle a des convictions, bien que, dans l'expression, elle soit assez proche du ridicule. Ses livres m'ennuient" (quoted by Billy 154). In another entry a short while later, she wrote of Hortense: ". . . esprit brillant, style diffus, point de bonté." Billy takes issue with d'Agoult's idea that this new friend was lacking in natural kindness. After all, Marie was typically the disagreeable one, not Hortense. "Point de bonté, Hortense? Il ne nous semble pas que la méchanceté, si elle en avait, ait été un de ses défauts. Marie aurait pu prendre des leçons d'elle à cet égard" (155).

Another opinion from Marie in 1838 compared Hortense unfavorably to Sand, maintaining that Hortense was not an artist, but rather an inexorable political thinker who was overly eager to talk in a stubborn and jumbled manner:

[Hortense] est tout l'opposé de George avec qui elle a été liée et s'est brouillée par suite d'une entraînement de sincérité qui n'a pas plus à notre amie. Elle n'est ni artiste, ni poète, s'occupe presque exclusivement de politique et discute avec une persistance, un acharnement, un désordre et un absolutisme qui vous divertiraient beaucoup.[4]

In this same entry, though, Marie admitted to Hortense's basic goodness and again admired the serene way she lived a life of simplicity and poverty. "Au fond, bonne personne, franche, intelligente et portant fièrement et simplement sa pauvreté" (Billy, *Sainte-Beuve: Sa Vie et Son Temps* 348).

Hortense was particularly delighted with the common thread of free maternity that she and Marie shared. On April 4, 1839, just two weeks after the birth of Henri Allart, Hortense wrote inviting her friend to come see the baby and urging Marie, who had tried to keep her illegitimate children as secret as possible, to speak out for women's liberty to give birth under whatever circumstances they wished. "Venez donc faire ici un petit Dante   . . . . [j'ai] accouchée il y a quinze jours d'un second fils que je nourris . . . . quittez Albano pour venir donner un bon exemple, car il est temps qu'on puisse accoucher quand on voudra." Hortense gently reproached Marie for not having used her own three pregnancies by Liszt as a chance to speak out for the cause of feminine emancipation.   "Il serait temps, qu'après avoir obtenu la liberté de la presse, la liberté individuelle, on nous accordât la liberté de l'accouchement et que la maternité, comme la charte, fût une vérité" (quoted by Billy 155).

Marie could not have taken this advice less to heart.   About a month after receiving this letter from Allart, she gave birth to her son Daniel and left him in the care of a wet-nurse in Palestrina. Neither she nor Liszt would see the child again until autumn 1841, when he would be two and a half years old.

George Sand observed the differences in the maternal attitudes of Hortense and Marie in her *Journal Intime* written in January 1840. After noting that each woman recently had given birth to a son, she wrote:

> Il y a pourtant cette différence que Madame (Allart) emporte ses enfants, les nourrit, les élève et leur donne son nom, son temps et sa vie, tandis que l'autre les abandonne, les oublie, les fait élever dans un taudis, tout en vivant dans le velours et l'hermine, ni plus ni moins qu'une femme entretenue, et ne s'occupe de sa progéniture non plus que d'une portée de chats.[5]

Based on a letter that she had received from Hortense at about this time, Sand also noted that Hortense was an exceptional mother who could balance her duties to her child with the intellectual goals she had set for herself.   Typically, Hortense could speak intelligently on a variety of esoteric topics, then excuse herself to go nurse her baby. "Elle a rempli ses devoirs de mère, comme bien peu de femmes eussent été capable de le faire . . . . Et puis elle parle d'histoire, philosophie, religion, politique, avec une abondance froide et une érudition frivole, et tout d'un coup, elle vous quitte pour aller donner à téter à son enfant" (*Journal Intime* 101. Quoted by Uffenbeck 299).

This is not to say that Hortense did not have to deal with prejudices and haughty attitudes from others when she became an unwed mother for the second time. Back in France, Chateaubriand had written rather tactlessly, "Un second enfant! Cette fois vous auriez dû mourir!" (*EP* 241).   Madame Hamelin, hearing of Henri's birth, expressed the opinion that, although she would always love her amorous, impetuous friend, this latest affair with its resulting child was a foolish act on Hortense's part.   "Mme Hamelin, informée de sa vie, l'appelait 'une noble folle qui fait la forte,' mais disait ne pouvoir s'empêcher de l'aimer, car elle avait 'de l'honneur et de la bonté'" (quoted by Billy 151).

Madame Hamelin also hoped that Hortense would marry Mazzéi. After Henri's birth, however, Hortense refused a proposal of marriage from her child's father, believing it to be offered out of a gallant sense of duty rather than inspired by true passion.   Also, she confessed that she had never really loved Mazzéi with the fire and ardor for which she would wish in a marriage.   She did esteem him, though.   In a letter to Sainte-Beuve in October 1842, she spoke fondly of Mazzéi,   calling him "le plus honnête homme du monde." She continued, " . . . après la naissance de l'enfant, [il] est venu m'offrir de m'épouser, ce que j'ai refusé, parce qu'ayant voulu l'aimer je ne l'ai pas pu, et que jamais mon ancienne amitié ne s'est changée pour lui en amour."   She made this choice a matter of prayer, but felt that God never gave her spiritual confirmation that she should marry Mazzéi. With Bulwer, however, it was different. Although the marriage question never would be resolved between the two, their love was still more spiritual in nature.   "Entre Bulwer et moi, [Dieu] est sans cesse présent."[6]

The only melancholy aspect of Henri's birth was that the man for whom he was named was not his father.   At this point in *Les Enchantements de Prudence,* Hortense inserts into her autobiography her formerly published novella *Marpé* in its entirety. The story is narrated by a woman, Marpé, who longs for her former lover, Remi, and later bears a child by another man. The story did not appear originally until 1851 with the publication of Allart's *Etudes Diverses: Troisième Petit Livre.*   However, at the time she wrote the story, she was thinking of her separation from Bulwer in 1838-39, and how she wished this second son could have been his.

On Dec. 1, 1846, when Henri was 7, and still several years before the publication of *Marpé,*   she wrote in this same spirit to Sainte-Beuve.   "Mon enfant m'amuse et il annonce beaucoup d'esprit. Entre Marcus et lui j'ai connu la volupté, et j'ai eu pour ce deuxième enfant une autre sorte d'amour que pour le premier. *Je l'ai cru fils de l'homme qui, sans me faire mère, m'a fait mère"* (*L.I. à S.-B.* 230, my italics).

A few weeks after Henri Allart was born, the elder Henry became ill in Turkey and was unable to travel directly to St. Petersburg for his next diplomatic assignment, as planned.   At one point he wrote to Hortense, promising to spend the winter with her in Florence or Rome. This was not to be, for he returned directly to London in June 1839. Hortense did not write to Henry from the latter part of her pregnancy until she returned to France when the baby was 14 months old. Therefore, Bulwer must have become *au courant* about the birth of small Henri through Parisian gossip, for he was back in the French capital by July.   At that time, it was he who renewed their correspondence, advising, if not demanding, that she return to France.

(Of all her friends, he was the one who knew the best how important it was to her not to be absent from Paris for too long).

By early 1840, d'Agoult had begun the long, painful processes of breaking up with Liszt (their relationship would not end permanently until 1844).   By January—while Hortense was still in Florence—she had left Liszt and gone back to Paris, where she opened up a brilliant literary salon.   The usual notables gathered—Hugo, Lamartine, Balzac, Lamennais, Didier, Eugène Sue, Sainte-Beuve, Delphine Gay—as well as prominent foreigners and diplomats. One of these was Henry Bulwer-Lytton, who had just replaced British Ambassador Lord Grandville, and was currently negotiating a treaty between England and France regarding each country's involvment on different sides of a dispute in the Middle East.   (Bulwer's recent service in Turkey was invaluable in these negotiations that involved French support of Egypt and British support of Turkey).

Bulwer probably had met d'Agoult in Italy during his brief visit there to see Hortense in 1838.   Now a distinguished member of her Parisian salon, he offered Marie the use of his diplomatic position and paid her court. He avoided talking with her about Hortense. "Peu flatté sans doute d'être l'amant d'Hortense, il évitait de parler d'elle" (Billy 157).   On Jan. 20, 1840, Bulwer told Marie that he loved children and wished that he could adopt one. She laughingly told him that he ought to adopt *"le petit Allart II,"* but it was a girl he wanted. Marie invited him to dinner that night, where he insisted on seeing young Blandine.   Despite Marie's casual attitude about motherhood (her three children by Liszt eventually would be raised mostly by their paternal grandmother, Anna Liszt, in Paris), she did not take him seriously. It was such strange moods as this in Bulwer that would end their relationship within a few months. "[Bulwer] était, nous le savons, d'humeur instable. Ses relations avec Maris se relâchèrent peu à peu pour cesser au bout de quelques mois" (Billy 158).

For the moment, though, Hortense had heard rumors about Henry and Marie, even as far away as Florence.   The harsh 1840 winter kept her from leaving Italy right away. Also, she wondered about the wisdom of going back to Paris for the sake of her friendship with Henry. She did not know how seriously he might be involved with Marie. What might she find when she returned?

Allart finished out her stay in Italy with her usual productivity. She completed the second volume of *L'Histoire de la République de Florence,* and handed it over to the minister of France, who agreed to deliver it to Paris for publication.   She also began outlining a new project, which, after eight more years of work would become her *Essai sur l'histoire-politique,* and began planning her lengthy treatise on

religion, *Novum Organum,* which would be published in 1857.

Her domestic life was enjoyable as well. She cared for Marcus and baby Henri in a pleasant Florentine setting surrounded not only by numerous books, but also by pet birds and a lamb. In summer and autumn 1839, she stayed in Scaperia, then returned to Florence. Back in Paris, Henry was still courting d'Agoult, who made sure that Liszt, then in Vienna, knew all about it. "Bulwer et Clear sont mes seules joies," Marie wrote to Liszt on Feb. 14, 1840. "Je n'ai pas plus de prévisions que vous quant au premier. Il s'attache à moi plus qu'il ne faudrait et l'idée de durée indéfinie se glisse dans son cœur. Il n'entend plus prononcer votre nom sans tomber dans la tristesse" (quoted by Decreus 83).

Whether Marie ever truly loved Henry, or whether she was just trying to make Liszt jealous, is unclear. On Feb. 28, 1840, she again wrote Liszt, "J'ai la plus haute opinion de Bulwer. Il est fier, point vantieux et je suis convaincu [sic] qu'il m'aime avec tout le désintéressement possible. . . . Il est très préoccupé de ma dignité, de ma réputation, et m'a toujours donné les meilleurs conseils, par rapport à ma famille, au monde. . . . " (quoted by Decreus 84). Liszt replied on March 3, "Vous m'avez bien peu écrit depuis longtemps. Je ne puis croire que ce soit à cause de votre vie agitée, ce doit être à cause de Bulwer?" (quoted by Decreus 84).

After Liszt returned to Paris in April, Henry did not see Marie as often, although he still frequented her salon. He kept up this casual friendship lest Hortense think he was the cause of friction between Liszt and d'Agoult (at this point, he was not). In late May 1840, Hortense and her sons left Florence for Paris. Anticipating her arrival, Bulwer rented a Parisian apartment, planning to live there once again with her. Displeased with the knowledge of his relationship with d'Agoult and now accustomed to solitude, Hortense refused his offer once she arrived in Paris, and took her children to Herblay for the summer and fall.

If Hortense was not torn enough between wishing to keep her friendship with d'Agoult and resenting her friend for toying with the affections of Bulwer, she soon was to encounter a similar problem with Bulwer and another friend—George Sand.

Sand and Allart had resumed their correspondence in 1840 while Hortense was still in Florence. Sand's portrait of Allart in her *Journal Intime* in January 1840—the same entry in which she praised Hortense's maternal qualities—is not altogether flattering. Among other negative comments, she reveals that Chopin once referred to Allart as "a schoolboy in skirts." However, Sand does have some kind words for her fellow writer, and also provides the best physical description available about Allart at this time–from her hair, grown

darker with time, to her petite figure, to her charming dimples and engaging smile:

> Madame [Allart] m'a été longtemps anti-pathique, mais j'ai toujours estimé en elle de grands côtes de caractère. Elle m'a blessée par des petitesses et les a grandement réparées. Elle est petite, maigre, mal mise et mal faite, jolie pourtant. Elle n'a de grâce que dans les fossettes des joues, et son sourire rachète toute sa personne. . . . Chopin dit que c'est un écolier en jupons. Elle avait de superbes cheveux blonds cendrés il y a six ans. En Italie ils sont devenus bruns, ce qui ne lui va pas plus mal. Elle ne les teint pas, car elle n'a pas l'apparence de coquetterie.[7]

Sand was apparently under the impression that, with the exception of Bulwer, Allart could not attract men, and therefore, ought to be more the *coquette*. She did, however, admit that Bulwer loved Hortense, and that her complete naturalness might well be pleasing to other men.

> Elle n'en a même pas assez, car elle manque absoluement de charme et sauf Bulwer, qui l'a aimée mal et longtemps, je n'ai jamais vu une homme à qui elle plût. Il me semble que si j'étais homme, elle me plairait pourtant, car j'adore les femmes sans affectation et elle est admirablement naturelle. C'est un être très singulier, doué de grandes vertus à coup sûr et rempli de contrastes et d'inconséquence (*Journal Intime* 101. Quoted by Uffenbeck 298).

As stated in Chapter 6, Sand wrote to Hortense Dec. 28, 1840, with a warmer tone than in her earlier letters, indicating that Allart was every bit as much a "queen" as she was herself. "Chère cousine (car si je suis reine selon vous, vous ne l'êtes pas moins selon moi) . . . . J'aime à entendre parler de vous, à apprendre que vous êtes toujours jolie, toujours étincelante d'esprit . . . . Je suis bien tranquille chez moi et j'y songe souvent à vous, désirant que vous trouviez en ce monde tout le bonheur que vous méritez" (*Corres. de G.S.* 5:190-91).

On Jan. 19, 1841, Sand asked Allart to dinner, and also invited Sainte-Beuve, whom she knew would be glad to see the "prodigal child" returned from Italy. "Venez dîner avec nous . . . causer au coin de mon feu avec madame Allart, qui est revenue à moi comme l'enfant prodigue, et qui est toujours prodige d'esprit, d'érudition, de vie" (*Corres. de G.S.* 5:216). The letter reached Sainte-Beuve too late for him to accept the invitation, but he later wrote to Sand affirming that he would be happy to see Allart again.

During this same month, however, there arose some jealousy

between the two women regarding some questions Sand had asked about Bulwer. Although Allart actually was older than Sand by three years, Sand tried to make the jealousy sound foolish by referring to herself as "an old hare," and to Allart as the much speedier "frog," (a reference to the fable by Jean de La Fontaine).

> Savez les nouvelles de M. Bulwer? J'ai tellement peur de vous que je n'ose pas m'informer de lui. Faites-vous l'intermédiaire de la politesse que je lui dois et de l'intérêt que je lui porte. De cette façon-là, j'espère que vous n'aurez pas d'inquiétude. Je me fais l'effet du lièvre effrayant les grenouilles. Comment chère reine, pourriez-vous être assez grenouille pour avoir peur d'un vieux et triste lièvre comme moi? (*Corres. de G.S.* 5:221-22).

The ongoing antipathy that underrode their friendship at this point is evident in the polarity in their characters that Sand suggested in the above January 1841 letter when she referred to Allart as "the white queen" and herself as "the black queen": "Est-ce que ma reine blanche est malade qu'elle n'est pas venue ce soir? La reine noire est plus noire que l'encre" (*Corres. de G.S.* 5:221).

Allart, who had moved back to Paris in November 1840, and taken an apartment at 4, rue Trudaine, eventually did agree to see Henry from time to time. On Nov. 10, she ran into Marie in Paris and could not help but gloat a little about the fact that Henry was spending more time with her (Hortense) at that moment than he was with Marie. "Ah ça!" Hortense told Marie. "On dit que Liszt fait une fortune énorme et que vous avez pris un autre amant! J'ai cru un moment que vous étiez en coquetterie avec B..., mais il m'a proposé de venir avec lui à Fontainebleau. Alors, j'ai bien vu que non" (quoted by Billy 159).

Hortense smoothed out the rumpled feelings between her and Sand after the January 1841 jealousies and ensuing correspondence. She attended salons hosted by both Sand and d'Agoult that winter, although there remained some tension between the three women over Bulwer, who also was a frequent guest at Sand's and d'Agoult's soirées. "[Allart] revoit Bulwer parfois dans ces deux salons, mais comme leur situation ambiguë n'est un mystère pour personne on hésite à les mettre en présence l'un de l'autre" (Decreus 88). Sometime during this year, Sand wrote another letter to Allart stating how uncomfortable she felt about inviting them both to the same social gathering. She thought it better to let Hortense invite Henry to her (Sand's) salons, provided Hortense was comfortable being in the same place with him:

> Voulez-vous que j'invite M. Bulwer à venir nous voir le soir?
> Il est si riche et si magnifique que je n'oserais l'inviter à dîner. Et
> puis je ne sais pas si vous vous voyez avec peine ou plaisir. Si
> cela vous agrée, voulez-vous vous charger de lui faire savoir que ce
> soir-là il vous trouvera au coin de mon feu? Moi, je suis si
> ennuyeuse pour lui que je n'ose rien. Et puis si vous me faites
> l'honneur d'être jalouse de moi? Je voudrais vous être agréable et je
> crains de vous être désagréable.[8]

The often catty Madame Hamelin always was quick to apprise
Hortense of Bulwer's pecadillos with other women. At about this same
time, Hortense wrote to Henry, telling him that Madame Hamelin had
labeled him a Don Juan:

> Je ne pourrai point voir de femmes sans entendre parler de vos
> galanteries   . . . . Mme Hamelin qui revient de la forêt . . . dit que
> vous êtes un nouveau Don Juan, qu'elle sait des choses charmantes
> de vos bonnes fortunes, que vous avez reculé les   bornes du
> Dandysme, que c'est un Dandysme nouveau, infini, inconnu . . . .
> Quelle femme bien informée![9]

From this, Hortense gleaned that Henry was becoming more
French than English in his attitude and conduct. "Je vous trouve aussi
bien français pour un vainqueur du cabinet français; vous avez pris la
mise, la tournure, le language de nos hommes; il n'y a plus d'anglais
chez vous" (quoted by Decreus 90). The reference to Don Juan
seemed to bring forth a kind of epiphany for Hortense—a realization
once and for all that she never would be able to retrieve Henry as hers
alone. She claimed in this letter to have no more designs on him.
"Pour moi, je m'enchante de vos succès de Don Juan puisque je n'ai
plus prétention sur vous" (quoted by Decreus 90). In addition to his
apparent success with women at this time, Bulwer was also riding a
crest of success in his diplomatic career. He had just successfully
negotiated an important French-Anglo commercial treaty, and thereby
avoided what might have become at the time a bloody conflict between
the two countries, or at best, what would be termed in modern times as
a cold war (Decreus 90-91).

This same letter mentions that fact that Hortense recently had
visited Sampayo. (A short time later, on April 7, 1841, the father of
her first son died. The next autumn, she met with her former lover's
brother, Osborne de Sampayo, and discussed the matters of
inheritance and future education for Marcus). During 1841, Hortense
also was in touch with Lamennais, Chateaubriand, Béranger and Didier.

It was, though, a time when none of these men seemed to appeal to her from a more personal point of view. "Il n'était homme lui plaire d'aucune façon" (Billy 159).

It was in summer 1841, with Bulwer slowly fading from the picture, that Sainte-Beuve, who had known Hortense for 10 years, and had been corresponding with her on and off for nine, saw the opportunity to take their relationship to a more intimate level.   To Hortense, though,   it would be more than a mere physical consummation. Her overall relationship with France's most prominent and respected literary critic of the 19th century would be, for her, the most cherished emotional tie of her life. This rapport was, says Billy, "dans la vie sentimentale d'Hortense l'élément majeur, le plus profond, le plus émouvant, et qui lui fait le plus d'honneur" (177). (She opted not to discuss in *Les Enchantements de Prudence* any details about this brief affair with Sainte-Beuve, although she does sporadically mention their ongoing friendship and correspondence both before and after it occurred).

Not long after she met Sainte-Beuve, Hortense wrote that he was one of a very few male friends, along with Sampayo and Libri, with whom she really could discuss scholarly topics. As for Chateaubriand, he only chatted.   "J'ai connu peu d'hommes qui savaient causer. Sampayo, Libri, Passy, Sainte-Beuve. Quand à Chateaubriand, il ne discutait pas, il plaisantait doucement, il était fin, agréable, mais il ne traitait pas une question. Je n'ai vraiment causé qu'avec Sampayo, Libri et Sainte-Beuve."[10]

At this time, her letters to Sainte-Beuve usually were full of literary commentaries, philosophy, and politics as well as evidences of fond friendship that was growing stronger all the time.   She was spellbound, as were so many others, by Sainte-Beuve's charming writing style. However, she was one of very few among his many readers and correspondents who really could respond to him with intelligence and share with him viable and varied materials for literary critics. "Car si elle fut ensorcelée commes les autres par sa parole dorée . . . Hortense fut peut- être la seule capable de lui tenir tête, de discuter sur toutes choses avec lui, de le redresser à l'occasion et de lui donner, sur les auteurs anciens et modernes de belles et bonnes références" (Séché 183).

It was Hortense's habit while she was living at Herblay in 1841, to travel to Paris every Wednesday, study for a few hours at the Bibliothèque Nationale, then receive friends at her Parisian residence. One Wednesday in August, she did not see one of her most frequent visitors, Sainte-Beuve, because he was sick in bed. Knowing that he had promised to write some verses for and about her, she wrote to him on Aug. 24, "Votre maladie, c'est le talent, permettez-moi de ne point m'en inquiéter. J'espère vous donner à dîner, Hôtel du Rhône, à la fin de la semaine . . . . Vous m'avez fait des vers! J'en suis curieuse, envoyez-les-moi donc tout de suite par la poste" (*L.I. à S.-B.* 6).

She came to Paris on Aug. 26, and received Sainte-Beuve for dinner on Aug. 27. He gave her a copy of his poem in which he described his now-famous philosophy about the *clou d'or*. In other words, he proposed that since the "golden peg" of friendship had been well-established between them, it was now time for them to solidify the peg by making love, even if for one time only—"posséder vers l'âge de trente-cinq à quarante ans, et ne fût-ce qu'une seule fois, une femme qu'on connaît depuis longtemps et qu'on a aimée, c'est ce que j'appelle planter ensemble le clou d'or de l'amitié" (quoted by Billy 179).

The poem, dedicated thusly— "A Hortense, avec un Marc-Aurèle qu'elle m'avait demandé"—figures as part of Sainte-Beuve's *Joseph Delorme*. Consisting of six stanzas, each with five or six lines, the poem starts out describing Hortense, as had other writers before him, as having "male wisdom":

> Voici donc le stoïque et *sa mâle sagesse*
> En retour d'un présent plus doux:
> Il faut être Aspasie ou vous,
> Pour songer à tels noms le soir d'une caresse
> Ou le matin d'un rendez-vous.

The poem continues in praise of her knowledge of history and literature and the joy the poet finds in discussing these topics with her. The last stanza contains the proposition:

> On écoute, on s'enflamme. A vous sur toute chose
> La politique plaît, et pour vous plaire on ose;
> Sur un fond de désire je m'y sens animer;
> Pitt ou Thiers, peu m'importe, et ma verve est rapide.
> Tout d'un coup, un regard humide
> Avertit tendrement qu'il est temps de s'aimer. [11]

Most Allart scholars concur that Allart and Sainte-Beuve made love that night, and perhaps again for a few nights after. But the passion was short-lived on Sainte-Beuve's side. At age 40, Hortense was three years older than he, and probably was of the same opinion about the "clou d'or." The difference was that she wished this could be more than a brief affair, and that the physical love could continue to complement and embellish what already long had been a meeting of two particularly sophisticated minds.   Immediately following their physical consummation, and for years afterward,   Allart discreetly and unsuccessfully tried numerous times to persuade Sainte-Beuve to visit her at Herblay, hinting that she wished to resume their intimacy.

On Sept. 5, 1841, just days after their sexual encounter, she wrote of her pleasure at drawing closer to a poet and assured him that she aspired to attain the kind of "great mind" that she knew he already admired in Marie d'Agoult:

> Rien de si commode, pour ne pas dire de si doux, que de plaire un instant à un poète . . . . Allez, inventez, créez, je vous regarde faire, je sais que les poètes ont de pareilles fêtes, je m'y prête avec complaisance, et pour finir par railler j'ai toujours en vue, pour garder une éternelle modestie, le grand esprit que vous trouvez à Marie [d'Agoult] (*L.I. à S.-B.* 18-19).

She received no more letters of a tender nature from Sainte-Beuve over the next few weeks.   Her letters to him focused on literary discussion, plus some information about her family—her sister Sophie gave birth to a girl in Rome (she and Gabriac eventually would have three children) and Sampayo's brother was asking to be involved in providing an education for Marcus (she soon would agree to send her elder son to Paris to study with a professor whom the boy's uncle had recommended).

By early fall, though, Hortense could maintain the small talk no more.   She wrote in an urgent tone asking Sainte-Beuve to visit at Herblay.   The passionate ache in her request to see him is palpable, as she suggests that he ought to follow through with a venture that he began, and not fade into the background, treating her as though she were somehow guilty:

> Si vous ne venez pas demain soir mardi, je croirai que vous me trouvez coupable, venez, car je ne le suis point.   C'est vous qui avez tout fait, c'est vous qui avez jeté au vent une parole sérieuse qu'on a écoutée trop facilement et se flattant . . . . En vous avouant la vérité sur ce qui s'est passé cet été, j'en suis plus à mon aise pour vous dire des choses tendres et le charme qu'on aurait trouvé près de vous (*L.I. à S.-B.* 31).

She asserts that their relationship had put down roots, which could not be pulled up by any act of fate. "Mais si l'homme hésite, la vie nous presse et se hâte, et les anciens sentiments seuls ont poussé des racines qu'on ne peut arracher en dépit du sort" (*L.I. à S.-B.* 31).

Sometime during the early fall, she saw Bulwer again. Her letter admits that Sainte-Beuve's love was helping her to forget her still-ardent Englishman, but that his continued neglect would only send her back toward the arms of her former lover.

> Vous m'avez rendue plus hardie pour avoir un homme que j'ai trop aimé et que je craignais beaucoup; vous avez enchanté des jours qu'il ne charmait plus, mais on était bien aise aussi de l'appeler contre vous, et de renaître à lui quand vous montriez qu'il n'y avait pas d'avenir avec vous (*L.I. à S.-B.* 31).

She does not hestitate to speak her mind about wishing to be a permanent and intimate part of Sainte-Beuve's life. "Il n'y avait rien parfois qui m'eût paru si doux que de vivre pour vous; de soigner une santé dont vous vous plaignez souvent, et descendre (ou monter) dans cet intérieur où vous vivez solitaire avec vos rêveries et votre sensibilité" (*L.I. à S.-B.* 31).

Again, she blames him for starting something he did not wish to finish. How happy she would be, if only there were still some tender feelings on his part!

> Que veux-je en vous disant tout ceci? Simplement vous montrer que tout fut votre ouvrage et que j'ai eu un penchant très tendre vers vous. Si vous blâmez ma conduite, blâmez aussi les complications de la vie, vos hésitations à vous-même, ce qui vous éloignait le premier. Mes plus beaux jours de cet été ont été dus [sic] à vous seul (*L.I. à S.-B.* 32).

The letter concludes with a veritable supplication. "Venez ce soir, ou je vous croirai fâché. Venez, donc, venez" (*L.I. à S.-B.* 32).

Sainte-Beuve ignored her invitations, made excuses, avoided her. She brushed aside her hurt, and proposed in early October that they meet in Paris at the Hôtel du Rhône, while she was in town meeting with Marcus's uncle. She promised to act "virtuously and wisely" and to talk about Marie, if Sainte-Beuve so wished. "Nous serons sages et vertueux, amis dévoués, nous parlerons d'elle [Marie]" (quoted by Billy 181). On Oct. 4, she again invited him to the Hôtel Rhône, claiming that henceforth, she would be content with their "golden peg"—if that was all they could have upon which to hang their relationship. "Venez demain, je serai très fâchée si vous ne venez pas . . . . On se contentera des 'clous d'or,' cependant, si on n'a que cela pour se pendre" (quoted by Billy 182).

Despite these attempts to put up a brave façade, her candor about

wishing to share a solitary life with Sainte-Beuve continues in a letter
written Dec. 21 from Herblay.   "Il me semble que j'aurais bien aimé
de vous faire partager ces douceurs de la retraite et des champs. Nous
eussions goûté ensemble les sciences et la solitude . . . . Que l'étude est
une aimable chose! qu'on vit bien seule avec ses livres!" (*L.I. à S.-B.*
34).

Finally, she admits that their encounter fell short of true love—but
she paints an eloquent picture of the ambiance of sweetness and liberty
in which she would have wished to love him:

> Nous sommes-nous aimés? Non, ce n'est point aimer. Je sais ce
> que c'est qu'aimer, je vous aurais montré comment je le sais.
> Aujourd'hui, peut-être, nous pourrions commencer. C'est lent,
> c'est saint, c'est douloureux, c'est tour à tour triste et délicieux.
> Jamais vous n'aurez été aimé dans la pleine douceur, dans la pleine
> liberté où j'aurais pu le faire (*L.I. à S.-B.* 34).

Hortense's last letter to Sainte-Beuve during 1841 contains a tone
of resolution and a promise not to be angry or jealous of him—"Ne
craignez rien de moi, ni fureur, ni jalousie" (*L.I. à S.-B.* 36)—even
though she knows he has become the lover of Marie d'Agoult. "Ceci
pourrait devenir ennuyeux pour l'homme du monde amant de M[arie]"
(*L.I. à S.-B.* 38).

Why did Sainte-Beuve back away so quickly and thoroughly from
such continued and tender devotion from a beautiful, intelligent woman?
It most likely had nothing to do with Hortense's age or appearance, for
she still was youthful and as attractive as ever at 40—slender, dimpled,
and beautifully coiffed.   Perhaps his unwillingness to maintain a
personal relationship had to do with his perception of her intelligence
and critical spirit as too manly.   "Hortense avait une qualité qui pour
un homme comme Sainte-Beuve était un vice incorrigible: elle avait
trop de savoir et trop de critique, et elle était trop raisonneuse, trop bon
garçon, pas assez femme" (Séché 190).   Sainte-Beuve preferred his
women languid and mysterious.   Women *à la Staël* interested him
only from a mental point of view. As for Marie d'Agoult, she always
maintained a more coquettish demeanor that tended to belie rather than
display her intellectual prowess.

Sainte-Beuve biographer M.J. Bonnerot believes that the critic
sincerely was attracted to Hortense because of her uncommonly fine
mind and her boldly non-conformist lifestyle, and that his friendship
with her really did evolve into love:

> [Il était] attiré par cette femme charmante, d'une intelligence merveilleusement douée, qui a appris le latin et le grec, discute histoire et philosophie et raisonne avec bon sens. Sa vie aventureuse et indifférente à la morale courante lui permet une indépendance de paroles et d'allures fort rares. Dix ans de causeries et de correspondance—très espacées—mais sincères, ont insensiblement transformé l'amitié en amour. [12]

Contrary to this view, certain other biographers have speculated that Sainte-Beuve might have taken advantage of Hortense in the way he did because of his interest in obtaining the private details of her affair with Chateaubriand, which he wished to use in a study he was preparing on the Enchanter.   Hortense was open enough about this affair (and most of her others) that she would not have kept the information from Sainte-Beuve, had he but asked her about it.   "On a beaucoup dit qu'il n'en avait fait sa maîtresse de quelques jours que pour approcher de plus près les secrets de René. Il eût put les connaître sans tant de façons, Hortense ne demandant qu'à parler." [13] However, vicarious knowledge of the details of this earlier and infamous affair apparently would not have been enough for Sainte-Beuve. He wanted to know the source of Chateaubriand's passion, to have the same experience as this man whom he was striving so hard to research.

Therefore, as Hortense herself sadly recognized in a matter of weeks, the step the two of them took after the establishment of the *clou d'or* probably did not involve true love on Sainte-Beuve's part Séché and Billy both agree with the theory that Sainte-Beuve persuaded her to take this step to satisfy his *curiosity* about Hortense rather than to indulge a true passion for her.   Says Séché, ". . . je crois qu'il était entré dans l'alcôve d'Hortense plutôt pour satisfaire sa curiosité que sa passion.   Comme il le suivait déjà la trace, il tenait à passer par le petit chemin couvert où avait passé Chateaubriand, pour pouvoir en parler en connaissance de cause" (190). Therefore, having appeased this brief desire, Sainte-Beuve drew away from Hortense for fear of ruining any future chances he might have with d'Agoult, with whom he had become smitten.

D'Agoult's success with Hortense's former paramours took another turn in January 1842, when Marie became the lover of Charles Didier. In his unpublished journal, Didier hinted that Marie submitted to him on the night of Jan. 30, 1842 after an evening at the opera. [14]

At this point, it surely must be said that Hortense was cut from the most philosophical and forgiving kind of cloth that is found in the fabric of human life.   Although she struggled with the emotional pain therefrom, Sainte-Beuve's rebuffs and his subsequent interest in d'Agoult did not diminish her feelings of friendship for either one. As mentioned earlier, she would correspond with Marie for the rest of the Marie's life, and with Sainte-Beuve until a different breach of trust on his part in 1861 would begin to sour their friendship and would scotch their correspondence by 1864 (see Chapter 8). Hortense's only other show of irritation with Sainte-Beuve would be eventually to destroy most of his letters to her. Only a few survive. Bonnerot's collection includes the following from March 1842, in which Sainte-Beuve insists that he was avoiding Hortense because she tempted him too much. Most likely, she was not fooled by his true reasons for wanting to keep a certain "barrier" between the two of them:

> J'ai besoin de faire appel à votre amitié, à votre générosité. Que rien ne soit changé entre nous, rien excepté un point. Quand je vous vois, je suis faible, je désire; cela est suivi de longs troubles. Je veux trouver en vous un appui contre vous, contre moi-même. Vous me verrez toujours ami, toujours touché, mais *qu'il y ait entre nous une barrière* et que je reste en deçà du serment! (quoted by Beaunier 278-79, my italics).

Hortense still hated the idea of this "barrier," but during the balance of 1842, her correspondence with Sainte-Beuve remained warm and focused mainly on their mutual exchange of critical literary commentaries. She also corresponded and visited occasionally with Didier, but there is no evidence that she ever reproached him for his involvement with Marie. She was in touch with Châteaubriand as well, although he was in failing health and she did not see him any more this year after the spring.

In October, she met through mutual friends at Herblay a man with the formidable name of Napoléon-Louis-Frédéric-Corneille de Méritens de Malvézie de Marcignac l'Asclaves de Saman et l'Esbatx. A former army officer who had served in the Lyon area in the cavalry for 16 years, he was the seventh son of a gentleman from Languedoc in southern France. He had no fortune, but Hortense was impressed with his genealogy, which could be traced back to Charlemagne and the Crusades. At age 35, some six years younger than Hortense, he was beguiled with this confident and well-known writer and scholar, still lovely at 41, who spoke English, Italian, Latin and Greek, and who was a friend and correspondent of several famous writers, and the former lover of Chateaubriand, Sainte-Beuve, and a prominent English diplomat. As for Hortense, she admired Méritens's fine singing voice and was flattered by the fact that he began asking her—over and over again—to marry him.

She was not in love with Méritens, but marriage ever had been a fond ideal, which always seemed to have eluded her until now. (After all, her novels *Gertrude, Sextus* and *Settimia* all ended with happy marriages, and all were idealized accounts of relationships she had had in real life). After the recent fading of her hope for marriage and a loving and secure future with either Bulwer or Sainte-Beuve, she began to think hard about the advantages of marrying a man who was willing to overlook her unorthodox lifestyle and the fact that she had two illegitimate children, and offer her his home and his name.   She hesitated, though, fearing she never would be able to forget her preference for Bulwer, or, for her second choice, Sainte-Beuve.

She remained realistic, however.   In November, she wrote to Sainte-Beuve telling him she knew that d'Agoult would always be a disruptive presence in any personal relationship the two of them could have.   She also was still concerned about what might be going on between d'Agoult and Bulwer. "N'a-t-elle donc pas d'amant?   C'est ce qui m'étonne. Si elle en a un, elle l'aime bien peu, puisque c'est vers vous qu'elle jette ses cris et dirige sa douleur et ses reproches. *Je n'aurais jamais été heureuse avec vous à cause de cette femme"* (*L.I. à S.-B.* 54-55, my italics). The most important purpose of this letter, though, was to tell Sainte-Beuve about the man who was asking for her hand. ". . . Dieu m'a donné de nouvelles espérances et a appuyé un homme qui demande sans cesse à m'épouser tout de suite" (*L.I. à S.-B.* 54).   She admitted she was hesitant to make a commitment, and that, if only Sainte-Beuve had loved her better, how much easier it would have been to accept him than this other man.   "Je crains sa jeunesse, je crains tout.   Si vous m'aviez aimée l'autre anneé, j'aurais voulu vivre pour vous, moins violente que vous ne pensez" (*L.I. à S.-B.* 54).

Sainte-Beuve had no comment about her wedding plans, although numerous other friends—Béranger in particular—tried to dissaude her. A woman of her non-conforming, independent nature simply did not seem cut out to be a wife, especially under traditional French circumstances. " . . . Hortense n'avait aucun goût pour le mariage, et tous ceux qui la connaissaient se demandaient si elle devenait folle" (Séché 56). "Elle se maria! Aucune femme n'était moins destinée à ce dénouement" (Beauvais 295).   She herself admitted to Sainte-Beuve in a December 1842 letter that a couple should experience at least two years of intimacy before deciding upon marriage. "Pour moi, je me fierais aux femmes qui ont ces craintes; quelle légèreté de se marier! Il faut au moins deux ans d'intimité avant cela" (*L.I. à S.-B.* 67). Later that month, after Méritens had become angry with her for not agreeing right away to a February wedding date, she wrote again to Sainte-Beuve, asking for his opinion. "Vous ne me dites pas un mot de mon mariage, vous ne me dites pas en ami: Achevez donc! ou comme Béranger: Arrêtez! . . . . Enfin vous ne m'écrivez ni avec liberté ni avec abandon" (*L.I. à S.-B.* 68-69).

Sainte-Beuve did not respond, and despite her own reservations, Allart decided to ignore the naysayers.   There were, after all, some positive aspects to consider about this marriage. In *Les Enchantements de Prudence,* she recalls how she was impressed during their early acquaintance with Méritens's handsome, sophisticated mien as well as his talents:

> Il chantait comme le rossignol . . . . avec un goût et une légèreté incomparables. Sa taille était moyenne, sa tournure militaire, sa main et son pied petits, sa main jolie, jolie, mais rude et faite aux armes.   Son visage dans sa résolution et sa fierté, était celui d'un chevalier . . . . (*EP*   240).

She and Méritens took long walks in the countryside, which he filled with the sound of his splendid singing. He was proud, haughty, and bore the aristocratic aura of his impressive lineage. Yet, with Hortense, he was humble, courting her as a man who dared not hope she ever would accept him.   "Le plaisir que me causait son chant lui était très doux et sans rien oser espérer il m'adresse une cour timide, vive, enjouée" (*EP* 240). Furthermore, her years of experience with Bulwer and his ambition had given her a taste for a man who seemed content to while away his days at her side. "Ma longue fidelité à Henry rendit très vif ce penchant vers un homme jeune et plein d'ivresse" (*EP* 240).

Hortense almost had made up her mind to try marriage. Nevertheless, her last letter to Sainte-Beuve in mid-December 1842 has a rather melancholy tone of resignation as she describes the regrets at leaving behind the lovers she would rather have married in favor of the man she had decided to wed.

> J'ose même vous dire ces choses, homme réservé, seulement parce que mon brûlant fiancé sort de chez moi, je vous assure.   Je l'épouserai   peut-être . . . . *Dien m'a destinée à vous autres avec une volonté divine, mais cruelle.* Celui-ci est bon, dévoué, jeune, il me laissera tous mes amis, vous tous. Mais vous, mes amants, il faudra vous dire adieu! (*L.I. à S.-B.* 72, my italics).

She arranged for the wedding to take place in in the quaint, medieval church at Herblay, and on March 20, 1843, she plunged into marriage with her characteristic enthusiasm. The next month, the newlyweds traveled to southwestern France and settled in Méritens's ancestral home in Montauban, just north of Toulouse. With the help of her friends Hippolyte and Antoine Passy, Hortense soon was able to procure for her husband a position as an architect in the local government (*EP* 240).

At first, the marriage seemed to go well, though not perfectly. She wrote Sainte-Beuve on May 28, 1843:

> Je trouve le mariage excellent au fond, mauvais dans quelques parties qu'on peut corriger, l'homme en disant parfois *"je veux"* le gâte; former un mari seul est plus difficile que si la loi était changée pour le genre humain. Mon mari est aussi bon que brave et généreux. Je le souhaite un jour de vos amis . . . . (*L.I. à S.-B.* 80, author's italics).

The honeymoon quickly was over, and the remainder of Allart's marriage was short and unhappy. *Les Enchantements de Prudence* contains virtually no kind words about her husband, but describes several occurences that indicate that soon after the marriage was solemnized, M. de Méritens showed himself to be a hot-tempered and tyrannical man. She began referring to her husband as "Ajax" after the warrior in Greek mythology who was known for his ill-mannered and violent behavior. In short, Méritens's strong, traditional ideas about how a husband should be absolute master over his wife clashed to the fullest extent with the liberated and unconventional persona that Hortense had been shaping for herself for more than 20 years. The new wife knew she would either have to give in to him completely or get out of the marriage. There could be no compromise.

Hortense wrote to Sainte-Beuve on Oct. 10, 1843, when she had been married for about seven months, about her unhappiness. Her complaints, though, were more about the institution of marriage itself than about her husband as an individual. She had thought mistakenly that love could conquer all the oppressive tactics that men were legally allowed to use against their wives. ". . . j'ai cru que ce que la loi du mariage avait d'oppressif et de mauvais n'était rien avec l'amour et les promesses d'un homme . . . Or, je sais bien pardonner à l'amour, juger avec indulgence, mais je déteste la loi . . . . j'aime assez le mari, je déteste le mariage" (quoted by Decreus 102).

She told Sainte-Beuve that she was grateful she had not married at a young age. If she had, this institution with its insidious indulgence of male power would have taken away forever her strength and her capacity for happiness. Women must no longer be deluded into believing that living the single life—even as unwed mothers—cannot be a happy and fulfilling experience. "Les filles seules (surtout les filles-mères) ont su exister, respirer, vivre fières et heureuses. Et voilà ce que les hommes craignent que nous ne sachions." All women—even the most ignorant and the most timid—must know this truth—that they need not be oppressed! "Il faut connaître la vérité. Vous allez dire: Vérité pour vous: Non, la pauvre femme bête ne doit pas non plus être opprimée, ni la femme timide, ni la femme dévouée" (quoted by Decreus 102).

As for the current situation with her husband, how could she describe how terrible it was becoming? "Comment peindre cette union et l'idée qu'elle me donna du mariage?" she asked years later in her memoirs. "J'avais trouvé un maître, un caractère aussi décidé que le mien. Il fallait plier ou il fallait fuir, c'était une volonté irrésistible, l'emportement furieux de ces guerriers troubadours, les plus redoutable de tous" (*EP* 242).

Hortense admits that she was not the easiest person to live with. Nevertheless, could her husband's efforts to subdue and control her through fear be considered justifiable? "Mettons que j'ai eu des torts de froideur, de hauteur, mais l'homme doit-il les venger par l'épouvante? Je vivais renfermée chez moi avec mon mari, je n'allais dans le monde qu'une ou deux fois par semaine" (*EP* 242).

As if being confined to her home most of the time would not be awful enough for someone of Hortense's gregarious nature, she also had to endure her spouse's increasingly ill tempers and jealousies. He even was jealous of Sainte-Beuve, who was miles away in Paris, and at one point angrily tore up one of the critic's letters to Hortense. Méritens was unfaithful, too. He unabashedly carried on with a pretty neighbor in Montauban. This was not Hortense's main complaint, though. In fact, she was grateful for anything that might distract his bad moods away from her. ". . . mon mari s'en occupa sans cesse de me tourmenter; c'était bien ici le Turc, épris de plusieurs femmes et tyran pour toutes. Loin d'être jalouse de mon mari, je souhaitais ses infidélités pour être moins opprimée, mais elles ne le rendaient pas moins intraitable" (*EP* 243).

Before long, she took a separate bedroom. She did not lock the door for fear he would break it down, but she did bar it with a chair so she could hear him coming in. One night, he forced the door open. "Il se moqua de ma précaution" (*EP* 244). She did not dare show anger, but did not mind letting him know she did not admire him. ". . . mais il voyait ma froideur" (*EP* 244). One day while they were out walking together, Méritens threatened to shoot himself. Hortense managed to talk him out of it. The next day, he had a fit of anger because she had hidden his pistols.

She could tell that her husband wished to punish her for igniting a passion in him, then resenting him so that he could not fully relish it. "Singulière passion! Passion féroce! Il me menaçait d'une persecution éternelle, il disait que je ne pourrais jamais l'échapper" (*EP* 244). He even talked of killing her, but even this gave her no recourse for a legal separation under French law. The *Code Napoléon* stipulated this would be possible only if a woman could show physical proof on her body that she was being battered.

> J'étais livrée sans défense, sans protection, sans appel, puisque pour une séparation, il faut des coups, des marques, des signes barbares! Il me parlait sans cesse de cette loi oppressive qui me mettait en son pouvoir. . . . Quoi donc! L'homme sera tyrannique, odieux, haï, et la femme sera punie par lui pour les défauts qu'il montre! Mais c'est un arrangement épouvantable (*EP* 244).

Fortunately, the intimate aspects of their marriage were not violent. However, if they had been, she still would not have had any protection from the law in that respect. "Dans nos rapports du mariage, il était fier et délicat, mais s'il ne l'eût point été, la loi ne lui laissait-elle pas le droit d'exigeance?   . . . . il avait reçu de son père de hautes manières, mais s'il eût été vil, n'étais-je pas de même en sa puissance?" (*EP* 245).   At one point, Méritens told Hortense in front of his father to go to her room.   She refused to be treated like a child bride.   "Il me prenait pour une mariée de vingt ans. Je n'obéis point" (*EP* 245).

The situation deteriorated to the point that her heart would habitually pound whenever she heard her husband come in.   Her servants also would tremble.   Nevertheless, even at this point, Hortense had one positive thing to say about Méritens—he was a good stepfather to little Henri. "Mais il était très bon pour mon enfant" (*EP* 246). (Marcus was again *en pension* at this time).

In a letter to Sainte-Beuve dated March 2, 1844, Hortense confided that she was plotting her escape for the next month, using five-year-old Henri as a pretext.   Before his mother's marriage, Henri had had an accident while at play at Herblay and injured his hip.   The doctors in Toulouse had told Hortense that it was time for medical procedures to make sure he would not become permanently lame.   Hortense planned to take him to a doctor in Paris in a few weeks when he would be better able to travel.   She told Sainte-Beuve that her husband was good for Henri, but very bad for her:

> Mon mari est . . . bon pour le petit et il voudrait être bon pour moi, car il m'aime, mais il est dur, despote, jaloux, emporté; je

déteste nos liens, aucune femme fière n'en supportera de pareils et je les aurais brisés si ce n'eût été mon enfant que je ne peux transporter que dans un mois. . . J'ai parlé du mariage et je ne le connaissais pas (*L.I. à S.-B.* 86).

During this last month with her husband, it was only the fond memories of happier relationships with other men that sustained her. In the same letter to Sainte-Beuve, she wrote, "O mes amants, mes aimables amants, amants d'un jour, de dix ans, amants d'imagination, amants de cœur, combien tout cela revient avec charme à la mémoire quand on vit seule et opprimée!" (*L.I. à S.-B.* 86).

In April 1844, just over a year after the wedding day, Hortense was able to escape from her husband, never to return.   She could do this only by lying and telling him as she left for Paris that she would be back soon.   Still, she was afraid up until the last moment before she stepped into the carriage with Henri that M. de Méritens would try to restrain them both by force.

What a feeling of liberation it must have been for Hortense to toss her wedding ring from the window of the vehicle onto the road as she sped away from that terrible union forever!   She realized that by making her escape, she was among of the luckiest of many abused and desperately unhappy wives. How many others like her were forced to stay in such situations, and even die as a result of them!

> Je jetai bientôt sur la grande route mon anneau de mariage comme un monument de mon opprobre. M. Saman gardait les plus grandes qualités, mais je m'imaginais sur quel joug pire, tant de femmes avait souffert, avait péri! Un nouveau jour se leva à mes yeux sur le sort affreux des femmes. Il faut avoir en quelque échantillion des maux pour les bien comprendre. Mon mari, par des scènes furieuses, m'initia à l'horreur d'un loi qui soumet la faiblesse à la force (*EP*   246).

From this point on,   Allart   said little more about her own spouse, but turned her ensuing fury upon brutal husbands in general, and upon the inequities toward women that were part of the institution of marriage in France.   In a straightforward, sociological manner, she also describes tragic cases of young wives who were beaten and murdered by their husbands because they had no legal path toward freedom or protection. Specifically, she describes the sad case of a 22-year-old bride of whom she had read, who died of a gunshot at the hands of her husband. The wife had been too afraid ever to complain about his violent conduct. "Elle mourut en silence" (*EP* 246).   Allart also pinpoints male alcoholism as a demon in marriages that often makes a bad situation even worse for many wives. "Et pour ces femmes du peuple, il y a de plus un breuvage qui rend l'homme plus entreprenant à la foi et plus redoutable, qui égare sa raison!" (*EP* 247).

Her next paragraph boldy asserts that no woman should ever have to submit to violence nor to suffer the burden of proof that she was being abused.

> Elle veut au premier mauvais traitement être libre de partir ou de pardonner. Elle veut sa vie, son corps garanti de la mort, des coups, des mertrissures, de la fureur, de la folie, du vin; des indécences et de la profanation. Elle ne veut point être forcée à montrer des membres brisés ou à présenter des témoins, puisque les forfaits sont commis dans l'ombre, dans les tortures, à l'heure des délices (*EP* 247).

Finally, she calls for financial responsibility on the part of an estranged husband toward the family he has wronged, and legal rights for the wife, including full custody of the children. "L'homme brutal sera contraint de nourrir encore la famille qu'il a profanée. La femme gardera les enfants tant qu'ils ne seront pas en métier, et les filles jusqu'à leur établissement" (*EP* 247).

When Hortense and Henri arrived in the capital, Sainte-Beuve and Marcus met them as they stepped from the carriage. The critic found her thinner and her attitude more resigned. She herself felt trodden down by the drawn-out spell of oppression. "Elle se sentait elle-même comme flétrie par cette longue année d'humiliation" (Billy 198). She had little contact with her husband after her escape, and she mentions him only rarely in the rest of her memoirs. It was not characteristic of her to remain resentful, however. Another sign of her effort not to be bitter about her marriage is her choice to use portions of her married name professionally. *L'Histoire de la République de Florence* was the last work that she published under her maiden name. Henceforth, she would be known as Hortense Allart de Méritens or Madame de Méritens, and occasionally as Madame de Saman. It is interesting also that she used another part of her husband's circumlocutory name as a pseudonym for her autobiography: *Les Enchantements de Prudence de Saman et l'Esbatx.* Also, she would use others parts of her married name for various characters in the short fictional works in *Les Nouveaux Enchantements.* Nevertheless, the trauma of her marriage had taken its toll. In spring of 1844, a few months before she turned 43, Hortense was through with physical passion forever. Her husband was her last lover. As soon as she fled Méritens' home, she and Henri

settled into to the Hôtel de Rhône in Paris. In June, she, Henri and
Marcus returned to their home in Herblay. Her attitude about her
reclaimed freedom was near-euphoric. Passion was in the past, but
she felt a new, brillant existence. She arrived:

> . . . dans la joie et la délivrance: Le plus heureux des êtres est
> l'esclave affranchi. Je me sentai flétrie pour ces mois d'esclavage
> où j'avais supporté une oppression que le courage venge avec éclat
> . . . mon sentiment de joie et de délivrance se soutint tout l'été
> . . . . Je venais d'éprouver la tyrannie et la violence. Je jouissais
> passionément de les avoir fuies (*EP*   247-48).

It was evident that she never would risk another bout with such
debilitating tyranny again. Eight years later, the principal story in her
Etudes Diverses: Second Petit Livre , entitled *Germaine de Saman,*
would focus on a middle-aged woman's reasons for refusing marriage
with a loving younger man in favor of a life of solitude and personal
study in the countryside.

There were money problems, however. She was out of cash,
Henri needed medical care, and Marcus, who for the past year had been
suppored by his uncle, Osborne de Sampayo, a well-to-do wine
merchant, was now back in her charge.[15]   Though angry with his
wife for deserting him, Méritens was gallant enough to offer her
financial help. She refused to take any money from him. The Passy
brothers offered to help her apply for government subsidies, but in the
meantime, she needed funds to tide her over. Hortense had been in
touch occasionally with Bulwer during her marriage, and now she did
not hesitate to write to him and ask for a loan of 1000 francs.
Before he could reply, Chateaubriand, whom she did not ask, sent her
500 francs. Hortense returned Chateaubriand's gift, fearing he was too
generous. He insisted that she keep it, so she wrote Henry again asking
that he reduce his loan to only 500 francs to be sent to Marcus.

Henry complied, but her letter to him on May 27, 1844, indicates
that she still was afraid that her husband might accost her as she went
to the bank. "Si Ajax par hasard savait cela, je serais brisée comme
Cassandre . . . . Croyez-vous que la femme d'un gentihomme s'en aille
chez votre banquier? Je ne peux ainsi risquer ma vie. Ajax n'a rien
moins que des armes; c'est un diable" (quoted by Decreus 103). By
February 1845, Hortense had applied for and was accorded a yearly
literary indemnity by the Ministère de l'Instruction publique, which
would help sustain her for the rest of her life.

Hortense's many friends with whom she reestablished bonds and
correspondence during 1844 were all glad to see her free of her husband.

In a letter to Bulwer on May 18, she noted that Sand had told her she would have left such a spouse even under less traumatic circumstances. "Tout le monde s'amuse de mon histoire. Mme Sand dit qu'elle serait partie pour moins" (quoted by Decreus 103). She dined with Sand, renewed her acquaintance with d'Agoult (and was happy to hear the latter was not in close touch with Sainte-Beuve for the moment), and reveled in again being a part of the Parisian literary social scene. She told Henry, "J'ai repris ma place à la cour, je suis redevenue dame du Palais" (quoted by Decreus 103).

In a letter on July 15, she confessed to Bulwer that she had decided to remain chaste for the rest of her life. "Je vous disais que si j'avais pu vivre chaste je ne me serais jamais mariée. Eh bien! j'ai perdu mes sens dans la bagarre du mariage. Je vis seule et chaste, amazone qui a déposé ses armes" (quoted by Decreus 105). Although her marriage never cured her of her lifelong passion for Bulwer, it finally put this impossible relationship in perspective. From this moment on, Hortense had no more delusions about being reunited with Henry, but only vague dreams and fantasies about him. "Désormais il sera pour elle surtout un prétexte à rêveries. Rêveries de ce qui fut, de ce qui aurait pu être, de ce qui pourrait être encore. Elle caresse un vague projet de le retrouver quelque jour, quelque part, et qu'ils finiront leur vie ensemble, lorsque l'âge l'aura forcé à renoncer à ses frivoles conquêtes" (Decreus 106). Henry left France that summer for a new diplomatic post in Spain, but he and Hortense would continue to keep in touch.

Shortly before Bulwer's departure, the two met in Paris. His attitude during their conversation made Hortense realize that if she had married Bulwer, a legal union with him only would have been unhappy as well. He remarked that, had she been his wife in England, he never would have allowed her to leave him. "But you always let me leave London when I wished," she told him. "I was not your husband then," he said. "Si j'eusse été votre mari, vous n'eussiez point quitté Londres." Hortense continues their dialogue in *Les Enchantements de Prudence:*

"Quoi?"she exclaims. "C'est ainsi que vous entendiez le mariage? "Sans doute," is Henry's reply. *"Il vous eût bien fallu obéir."*

"Quoi!" cries Prudence (Hortense) again. *"Le mariage m'eût faite esclave, même avec lui!* Il fallait donc mieux rester libre" (*EP* 250, my italics).

Her decision to hold men at arm's length no doubt contributed to the peace and happiness that characterized the next four years of relative solitude at Herblay. Her goal now was spiritual as well as literary: " . . . de vivre avec moi-même en cherchant Dieu . . . La jeunesse et son trouble insupportable étaient passés. On n'avait plus qu'à jouir des lettres et son indépendance" (*EP* 248).   She compared her natural calling as a writer to the innate industry of a bee or an ant.

> J'étais ambitieuse autant que jamais . . . . je lisais beaucoup, j'étudiais, j'étais très attentive. J'ai remarqué que les gens de lettres travaillaient, même avec des talents médiocres, comme les abeilles et les fourmis, sans pouvoir s'empêcher. L'abeille ni la fourmi n'ont pas de vanité; elles vont, elles vont par une loi d'en haut. Les gens de lettres, bons ou mauvais, vont de même. Il travaillent, ils travaillent, ils impriment, ils impriment, c'est une loi d'en haut (*EP* 249).

She realized that marriage never would have been a good option for her because intellectual goals and passionate love did not mix.   "Je n'aurais pas su cultiver des lettres ni jouir de mon esprit . . . dans l'agitation d'une passion toujours à l'aventure. Je n'aurais été utile à rien" (*EP* 249). Not only was marriage a bad choice for her, but she had noticed that it was not a particularly rewarding for many of her acquaintances as well.   She was only too happy to embrace solitude again:

> . . . je m'étais mariée: j'avais connu le mariage dans son injustice, son despotisme, pour le dénoncer et demander qu'on le rendit plus doux . . . . J'avais rencontrré des gens mariés qui racontaient qu'ils s'étaient beaucoup aimés, mais on ne voyait nul charme entre eux, il ne se plaisaient plus de tout, il voyaient surtout les défauts l'un de l'autre. C'est le sort ordinaire du mariage. Je préfère beaucoup à cela la solitude (*EP* 249).

Although she was happy to be living without any man in her life for the moment, she still was not pleased with a comment made by Sainte-Beuve in early 1845 that a person should take a maximum of three lovers in a lifetime.   "Vous avez dit insolemment que trois amants c'était assez, et que plus menait à je ne sais quoi," she wrote to him on March 31, 1845.   She protested that young women, most of whom are married off at a young age by someone of their parents' choosing, should not be judged on the number of lovers they may have. In Italy no one judges women in such a way.   "Et si un français est là qui demande 'A-t-elle des amants?' Ils rient et disent: —Et comment doutez-vous qu'une femme en ait? —Et combien? —Et qu'importe?" (*L.I. à S.-B.* 94).

This letters continues with her thoughts on her own current celebate life.   For now, it was a lifestyle she had chosen, but if a desirable man were to appear in her future, who could say what might change?   "Depuis que j'ai quitté mon mari, je suis restée seule dans cette campagne et sans amant, car il n'y en a pas, mais s'il y était venu en exilé d'Espagne, ou de Pologne, logé près de moi, triste, aimable, quel mal eussé-je fait de le consoler, et, en causant, en se promenant, de l'aimer?" (*L.I. à S.-B.*   93).

She added that since she was still married, she would never do anything that would be odious to her husband.   However, she did not believe that she owed Méritens any fidelity at this point.   (He probably was not, she noted, maintaining any fidelity to her).   It was mostly her age that was keeping her from seeking out further relationships with men.   However, she said, age should not be necessarily a factor in choosing to take or not to take a lover.   "Mon âge serait la plus vraie raison pour me retenir.   Aussi, est-ce encore plus mon âge qui m'a retenue que tout autre chose, si l'occasion d'un exilé trop jeune s'est présentée.   Eh bien, serais-je blâmable pour être moins prudente ou plus jeune? *Pourquoi une femme ne pourrait-elle pas aimer comme vous autres?* (*L.I. à S.-B.* 93, my italics).

She reiterates that Sainte-Beuve should not place limits on how many lovers one can have, for there are virtues in love that are far more important than numbers.   "Ne dites donc pas qu'il ne faut pas dépasser trois dans toute sa vie.   Ne mettez pas des nombres.   Dites seulement qu'il faut garder l'honnêteté, l'estime, ne faire que ces choses qui ne sont pas toujours la passion, mais que Dieu voit et accepte, car c'est sa loi entraînante et invisible qu'il impose" (*L.I. à S.-B.*   93).

Hortense's own productivity continued at a steady rate during these years at Herblay.   The second volume of *Historie de la République de Florence,* which was published the month before she married, continued to sell well.   In March 1847, she published her *Lettre à Abdel-Kader*, a brochure on the government of France, and her work continued on *Novum Organum*, and on what would become the three volumes of her *Etudes Diverses*.

Her friendship with Marie continued to grow as her correspondence with Sainte-Beuve, which always had centered primarily on intellectual exchanges, focused less and less on their personal relationship.   On Oct. 4, 1845, she wrote to him in a wistful tone, indicating that since they could no longer cultivate their love for each other, she still imagined a different kind of special bond based on their cerebral rapport. "Ah! si nous pouvions de ce moment former, je ne dis pas un amour . . . mais *une habitude éternelle, un lien cher* à tous deux au-dessus de la rapidité du temps et des inégalités du cœur, tout affermi par les muses et par cette délicatesse de vos sentiments et cette richesse de vos idées! (*L.I. à S.-B.*   119-20, my italics).   On Oct. 6, she ended her letter,

"Adieu, mon poète et mon amour, mon dernier amour, *mon mourant amour* . . ." (*L.I. à S.-B.* 122, my italics), and by Oct. 9, she closed with "Adieu, mon frère" (*L.I. à S.-B.* 128).

Only a few times during this year did Hortense's letters to Sainte-Beuve lapse into a confession of the strong feelings that she still retained for him. On Oct. 10, she wrote in a melancholy tone of her regrets about losing Bulwer (whom, she knew, was now living with a Spanish woman in Madrid), and confessed her sentiments for Sainte-Beuve and her resignation to the fact that they would never be entirely assuaged. "Et moi, durant ce temps-là, je vous aime, je vous aime comme une femme prudente et d'un âge qui la retient, mais je vous aime enfin, et tout est mal engagé, car vous aussi, vos souvenirs, vos sujets de roman, vos regrets sont ailleurs" (*L.I. à S.-B.* 130).

Séché quotes a later part of this same letter, indicating that Hortense had particular difficulty letting go of her hopes for a long-term relationship with Sainte-Beuve because her feelings for him were something she had rarely felt before. ". . . elle en conçut un vrai chagrin, car, ainsi qu'elle l'avoue plus haut, elle avait pour Sainte-Beuve un sentiment qu'elle avait rarement éprouvé" (Séché 191). Furthermore, he had so many qualities that charmed her (she found his thoughts even more admirable that those of André Chenier!) and she appreciated the many characteristics that the two of them had in common. From the Oct. 10, 1845 letter:

> Nous avons pour nous consoler notre *esprit,* notre *connaissance;* c'est une belle chose, nous sommes des sages stoïciens, ce sont les meilleurs, les plus désintéressés. Vous aviez tout ce qui peut au monde me charmer le plus; votre talent est de ceux que je préfère, vous avez la profondeur et quelque chose de si élevé, de si doux, que je vous ai trouvé tout ce que vous dites de votre André Chenier que vous surpassez bien du côté de la pensée et des autres écrits (*L.I. à S.-B.* 130, Allart's italics).

She did not expect much from Sainte-Beuve, and did not count on ever being a woman who would especially please him. She knew she inspired friendship, but she knew that as part of the *"race de René,"* he was looking for a truly great love, and that this was not she.

> Je n'attends pas beaucoup de vous pour moi, je vous admire avec un certain désintéressement, je ne crois pas être des femmes qui vous plaisent le mieux, il faut autre chose, je ne sais quoi, que je n'ai pas, je vous inspire plutôt l'amitié. Je ne crois pas non non plus que votre vie sera désormais, comme vous dites, froide et

sans amour. Non, vous aimerez encore. Bah! cette race de René ne
cesse jamais . . . . Vous aimerez encore, mais je ne serai pas cette
heureuse femme qui sera aimée de vous" (*L.I. à S.-B.* 131).

Despite the intensity of these lingering feelings, it was mostly
literary criticism and pleasant small talk about family matters that
continued to Sainte-Beuve in her letters from Herblay.   She mentioned
in Dec. 2, 1845 that Marcus, then age 19, was becoming quite the
ladies' man.   " . . . les femmes lui courent après" (*L.I. à S.-B.*
164), and noted on May 25, 1846, that her elder son had moved to
Paris (where, since he did not receive any inheritance from Osborne de
Sampayo, the Passy brothers had helped him procure a job with the
Ministère de l'Intérieur). Later that year, Marcus and his young
mistress made Hortense a grandmother, and it would be she who would
take most of the responsibility for raising her grandson, Anthony
Allart. (Marcus would not get married until 1863, to a different
woman).
   Hortense's correspondence with Sand at this time still contained
much of the same prickly tone as before, since Hortense continued to
comment with unabashed candor on Sand's works, and Sand continued
to bristle to the defensive.   In a letter to Sainte-Beuve on April 18,
1844, Allart mentions a recent letter from Sand that responded to her
comment that Sand must not have been sufficiently hurt by marriage to
warn about it in her novels.   She had advised Sand not to end her
novels with a happy marriage, which she felt was unrealistic.

> Je lui porte une accusation grave, celle de n'avoir pas été assez
> blessée du mariage et de n'avertir pas assez dans ses livres le genre
> humain. Elle finit ses romans souvent par un mariage. Il ne faut
> plus rien finir par là. Vous autres hommes, vous ne comprendrez
> jamais cela, vous ignorez la force du poing et du joug, vous ne
> devez répondre que par l'épée (*N. L. à S.-B.* 8).

One might well guess that such an accusation did not sit well with
Sand, whose own marriage had been adequately miserable and who had
been labeled during the first decade of her career as an "anti-
matrimonial" novelist because her critics didn't think she revered
marriage enough.   Furthermore, Sand was always a champion of
exalted love and respect between husbands and wives.   Allart's
emotion came obviously from the too-recent memories of her own
nightmarish experience in matrimony from which she had escaped just a
month earlier.
   In the fall of 1844, Hortense, now completely mellow about

d'Agoult's past involvements with Bulwer, Sainte-Beuve, and Didier, invited her friend to come spend the season with her in Herblay. Marie, less trusting of Hortense's motives, waited a year before she accepted. When she arrived in summer 1845, Hortense gave Marie the house in which she had been living and took a smaller one nearby. Hortense later wrote to Sainte-Beuve several times urging him to come visit the two of them at Herblay, and promising him there would be no jealousies. She kept her word, and the three of them spent a short, but pleasant visit together early that fall.

The two women settled in for an autumn of writing and critiquing one another's works. Marie later departed, but returned for another season in Herblay in 1846. Hortense read her friend's manuscript that would become *Nélida* by Daniel Stern. The novel, whose title is an anagram for Daniel (the name of Marie's son by Liszt as well as the first part of her own pseudonym), is closely based on her failed relationship with the composer.

Hortense told Marie she found the novel beautifully written, but hestitated to praise it because she felt it slandered Liszt. (The male protagonist of *Nélida* is a tempermental artist who violates his lover). She wrote candidly to Sainte-Beuve on May 11, 1846 of her mixed feelings about a novel that she considered imaginative, but too frivolous. "Ce livre est frivole à périr tour à tour ou sublime. Et c'est ce qu'elle est très femme, très futile, mais d'une imagination élevée" (*L.I. à S.-B.* 200).

Similarly, Hortense found Sand's *Lucrezia Floriani* offensive because she felt the character Prince Karol was based too obviously on Chopin. In a letter written June 22, 1847, Sand defended her novel, but her words indicate how much value she was beginning to place in Hortense's opinion. She especially valued Allart's criticism, for she saw it as more sincere than her praise. Sand wrote, "Je suis plus sensible à vos reproches qu'à vos louanges. . . . j'ai hâte de vous dire que votre lettre m'afflige beaucoup . . . . " Protesting that the comparison of Karol to Chopin was absurd, and that Hortense was naive to see the hero that way, Sand continues:

> Apparemment, nous nous connaissons moins bien l'un l'autre que le public ne nous connaît. . . . Je m'étonne que vous, qui êtes artiste aussi, vous ayez la naïveté du public vulgaire qui veut toujours voir, dans un roman, l'histoire véritable et le portrait d'après nature de quelqu'un de sa connaissance (*Corres. de G.S.* 7:757).

If they had wished to do so, both d'Agoult and Sand might well

have pointed out that Hortense had created heroes in her own novels that were fairly obvious retoolings of *her* former paramours as well—for example, the title characters in *Jérôme* (Sampayo), and *Sextus* (Capponi), and Warwich in *L'Indienne,* Marcel in *Settimia* and Remi in *Marpé* (all Bulwer).

Hortense had nothing but superlatives, however, for Sand's 1845 novel *Isidora,* the story of a former courtesane, who leaves behind her quest for love, learns to relish solitude and domestic arts, and lives out her life happy in her role as a single woman and adoptive mother to a 16-year-old orphan girl.   In a December 1846 letter to Sainte-Beuve, Hortense says of Sand's book, "[C'est un] ouvrage si profond, si gracieux si vif et sur lequel le critique pourrait s'exercer" (*L.I. à S.-B.* 240).

Billy (167-68) observes that Sand's preliminary *Notice* in *Isidora* describes a woman who sounds a lot like she might have been Hortense, particularly in the description of the solicitous way Hortense tended to treat Sand. The peaceful resolution of *Isidora* consisting of the heroine's retirement to the countryside and a life devoid of further romance indeed is parallel to the life Hortense had chosen for herself at this time.

> C'était une très belle personne, extraordinairement intelligente et qui vint plusieurs fois "verser son cœur à mes pieds," disait-elle. Je vis parfaitement qu'elle posait devant moi et ne pensait pas un mot de ce qu'elle disait la plupart du temps. Elle eût pu être ce qu'elle n'était pas. Aussi n'est-ce pas elle que j'ai dépeinte dans *Isidora.* [16]

Although Hortense did not publish her *Etudes Diverses: Premier, Second* and *Troisième Petits Livres* until the early 1850's, the potpourri of essays, short fiction, poetry, and prayers consists mostly of a sentimental focus on memories of a decade earlier in her life. The studies are also a monument to the value of study and writing in a peaceful, bucolic setting, as illustrated in *Germaine de Saman* in the *Second Petit Livre.*   The best-known work in the trilogy is the novella *Marpé,* which appears in the *Troisème Petit Livre* and is a yet another thinly veiled description of her relationship with Bulwer.

The *Premier Petit Livre,* published by Renault in 1850, contains a preface addressed to "Ma chère Louise," that defines the purpose of these three small books—to emphasize the basic worth of a quiet life in the countryside that is filled with simple pleasures and appreciation of literature. "La préoccupation du public le rendra peut-être indulgent pour ce qui viennent encore, quoique si imparfaitement, lui rappeler, dans le loisir de la campagne et de l'été, la rêverie, l'étude, l'amour, la littérature enfin. C'est dans cet espoir que nous publions les petits livres."[17]

In a short section called "Rêverie," Allart praises the value of a busy life followed by a peaceful, solitary retirement, for this sequence assures happiness instead of restless *ennui* in one's later years. "Une personne qui n'aurait rien senti, rien vu, ne pourrait que revenir sans cesse sur ses propers émotions étouffées, sur la contrainte et le tourment de son cœur, sur le poids et l'ennui de son existence" (*1er P.L.* 17).

A brief essay entitled "De la Justice" lists in vertical columns qualities that she identifies as both human and divine—goodness, charity, mercy, truth, wisdom, prudence, patience, justice and munificence. In another column are those she considers simply human—generosity, sincerity, fidelty, humility, austerity, modesty, temperance, sobriety, etc. (*1er P.L.* 40-41). Another section, "Poésie de la Nature," speaks of the dignity and the poetic nature of peasants at work on daily chores. "Voici des événements bas, des personnages bas; ainsi pense-t-on dans la jeunesse. Mais il n'y a ici rien de bas; c'est l'innocence, des impressions, la gaieté des aperçus, une parfaite bonté de part et d'autre" (*1er P.L.* 47-48).

"Lenteur Champêtre" continues to laud the simple life. "Plus l'être est faible et petit, plus la douceur du contentement est senti. Les enfants, les petits animaux, se prêtent à tout avec le plus grand plaisir. . . . Nul souhaite par delà leur heureuse existence. Ils abadonnent à la douceur, à la lenteur, une vie sans ennui, sans trouble, sans épines" (*1er P.L.* 63). Allart compares this happy attitude of rural dwellers to the frantic pace of the disconcerted folk who live in the city. "Et aussi peuvent-ils sourire en entendant les gens des villes, si hâtés, si soucieux, si tourmentés pour si peu, les plaindre et leur souhaiter des biens par delà cette douceur même, par delà cette lenteur qui font de leur vie un traînant et continuel contentement" (*1er P.L.* 63).

The first book ends with some simple, Christian prayers, similar to those that later would be printed at the end of *Les Enchantements de Prudence.*

The *Second Livre* contains only two sections. The first is another essay entitled "Rêverie," but unlike the piece of the same name in the previous book, it contains a sanguine feminist tone reminicent of *La femme et la démocratic de nos temps.* Allart recommends that French women engage in meditation and contemplation, and while so doing, to realize the futility of their country's long history of forbidding women's involvement in the more glorious and active parts of life " . . . et dans cette contemplation, nous, femmes, et privées de toute action chez cette nation légère, où les hommes qui agissent ont souvent des caractères moins sérieux que les nôtres; nous femmes qu'on a bannies de ces luttes . . . . " She finishes this clause with the idea that France's suppressed women can glean some satisfaction from the fact that no man in the past two decades has united successfully the country's goals of glory and liberty: ". . . nous femmes nous nous amuserons à constater une chose depuis 20 ans, c'est l'absence . . . d'un homme, d'un homme d'action, d'un homme de taille aux circonstances qui ait su réunir ces deux questions de la gloire et de la liberté."[18] This section launches in to a political and historical essay on France.

Germaine de Saman, the longer section of the *Second Petit Livre,* is a novella with a distinctly autobiographical bent. The heroine (whose last name comes from a part of Hortense's married name), is a middle-aged, never-married scholar, who has come to the countryside outside of Paris for study and repose. Germaine also is somewhat similar to Sand's Isidora in that she has led a full life, traveled widely, is now in tenuous health, and wishes only to be left alone with her adopted daughter, a young half-Indian girl.

The narrator of the story is Germaine's neighbor, a retired military officer, to whom she relates the day-to-day difficulties of her current situation. She is being wooed by an ardent young Italian admirer named Celse, who desperately wants her to marry him. Germaine, however, wants only *amitié* from him. "Je ne veux plus rien ici-bas," she tells Celse. "Ce que je demande à Dieu, c'est la paix du cœur, une vie forte, douce et solitaire ou sa grandeur et sa bonté remplacent la grandeur et la bonté de l'homme, qui m'ont manqué" (*S.P.L.* 83).

With Germaine, it is evident that Allart has created a wiser, more idealized version of herself; a heroine with better foresight than she had when it comes to the question of whether or not to marry. Germaine never hestitates to say no to marriage because she is perceptive enough to know that it only would bring her unhappiness. "J'ai craint toujours le mariage. Oh! Quel homme appuyé d'une loi tyrannique, n'en abuserait pas!" (*S.P.L.* 97).

The narrator asks if she ever considerered marrying when she was younger. Even at that time, though, Germaine knew that her country's law was inadquate to protect her personal rights and liberties. "Non, la loi me paraît trop imparfaite. Un lien légale avec l'homme serait sans doute respectable, mais il est encore à faire" (*S.P.L.* 98).

She explains how some of her women friends, who had characters just as independent as her own, became wives and trusted their husbands to treat them kindly. However, they soon found marriage to be a dreadful prison that engulfed the very essence of themselves as individuals. " . . . mais bientôt le mariage est retombé sur elles de tout son poids; elles l'ont fui. . . .   Elles m'ont dit qu'elles s'y sont senties esclaves et que toute leur âme avait été, pour un moment, avalie" (*S.P.L.* 99).

When Celse protests that he would be nothing like these husbands, Germaine explains succinctly that power accorded to husbands under the law sooner or later will corrupt every one of them. "L'homme quand on lui donne un droit tyrannique, s'en servira tôt ou tard. Il s'en servira s'il est jaloux, s'il est blessé, s'il est homme, en un mot" (*S.P.L.* 99). She tries to persuade Celse to forget about love. As for herself, she would rather spend the rest of her life urging other women to tap into the strength that lies within themselves and to create rewarding lives on their own. "Du   moins . . . eusse-je voulu apprendre aux femmes qui ont du caractère et des passions, que la force est en elles, qu'elles la retrouveront si elles la cherchent. . . . " (*S.P.L.* 103).

Celse departs, but the narrator perceives that his letters and the friendship between him and Germaine will comfort them both until death. "Elle m'en parla souvent avec charme, mais jamais je ne lui vis ni faiblesse, ni regret" (*S.P.L.* 106).

As *Germaine de Saman* mirrors Allart's actual situation at the time she wrote the story, her next novella, the epistolary *Marpé*, the longest piece in the *Troisième Petit Livre,* reaches a few years into her past before her relationship with Bulwer had wound down to only written correpondence. The tone of the novella also responds to the trauma Hortense felt at the news of Bulwer's marriage, which occurred in 1848 (see Chapter 8).

Marpé, the heroine, was raised by a heroic father who defended the liberty of the mountains of Romania. When her father was killed, her Italian lover, Remi, took her to his country. Now separated from him, she worries for his safety since he has gone back to war.   Mostly, though, she instinctively fears she eventually will lose him to another woman.

> J'ai vécu près de toi, hors de moi, enivrée, transportée . . . . j'ai vécu, j'ai pensé, j'ai dormi avec toi; prends une épouse puisque tu t'abandonnes au courant du monde, connais pour elle les ennuies, les froidures d'un telle mariage, mais quand tu penseras à Marpé, un éclair de tes yeux peut-être, un soupir de ton âme, diront que là était ta jeunesse et ton ravissement."[19]

After more exchanges of letters, the two set a rendezvous. Remi confesses he needs to confide to her a "terrible secret." Marpé thinks she has guessed it already. "Vous êtes marié . . . je le craignais toujours . . . tout esdonc fini! Cruel jour!"(*3em P.L.* 30-32).

Although Remi never affirms her suspicion that he is married, she tries to forget him. She cannot. The passionate prose over the subsequent letters describes the heroine's longing for Remi and sighing over his preference for ambition. Amid sumptuous descriptions of the scenes of nature and history around Rome, which are, again, reminiscent of Madame de Staël's *Corinne*, Allart's Marpé addresses such questions to her lover as, "Combien votre language est amoureux, suis-je destinée à en subir toujours l'enchantement?" (*3^{em} P.L.* 15).

A few years later, the two are still separated, but have remained in touch by letters. Remi has lost a child from his marriage. Marpé now has a child, which she despairs is not Remi's. "Le mien! qui' n'est pas à lui, qu'il ne connâit pas." She insists that it was not for vengeance that, while traveling back to Romania, she became a mother "loin de Remi," then married (*3^{em} P.L.* 37). In a lengthy passage, Marpé compares herself to the tragic Julie d'Etanges of Rousseau's *La Nouvelle Héloïse,* who was forced by her family to leave behind the man she adored, marry someone she did not love, and bear his children. Addressing Rousseau's heroine, she exclaims, "O Julie! Quand vous fûtes mère, loin de Saint-Preux, crûtes-vous trouver Sainte-Preux dans cette maternité? La mienne, réparatrice a donné à mon enfant la volupté de mon unique amour" (*3^{em} P.L.* 38).

Ironically, Remi is now free, since his "légère épouse" left him to return to her family. Marpé agrees to meet with him in Paris. She waits at a designated spot with her son who was named for him, but he does not keep the appointment. When they finally do meet, Remi's reaction is cooler than that of Rousseau's Saint-Preux—he does not throw himself into her arms. Later, she refuses his invitation to come to his Paris apartment for "cette nuit de délices" (*3^{em} P.L.* 56).

Nevertheless, she defends Remi's light-minded behavior to her woman friends. She may not be able to give in to his requests, but she is enough in tune with him to *understand* why he makes them. "Mais sa félicité, sa bonté; son affection ôtaient à sa conduite le caractère que des motifs moins aimables lui essuent donné. Je pouvais le comprendre sans pourtant lui céder" (*3^{em} P.L.* 59).

Marpé continues to act sanely and bravely, though somewhat sadly, out of self-interest and self-protection instead of responding to her passions. When she hears that Remi has become the lover of *une portugaise,* she refuses further rendezvous with him, and decides to devote herself to study, reading, her garden, her child, and to preparing a written work. Marpé discovers (as had Hortense during her 1826 stay in Milan, and her 1843 return to Herblay) that the studious life is rewarding enough to dispel at least some of the melancholia and regret over lost love. "Quand je reviens à ces études quand je me vois dans mon jardin, avec mes livres, mon enfant, je me trouve la femme la plus heureuse du monde" (*3em P.L.*   64-65).

With difficulty, Marpé resists the temptation to return to Remi and try to establish with him what she knows would be an "insane passion."   "[Je] pense à laisser Remi, à ne pas lui livrer une vie si heureuse et si facile. J'échappe à un retour de passion insensée; eh! cet enchantement qu'il me cause, c'est la folie de mon cœur, c'est ma faiblesse éternelle!" (65).

Time passes, and she accepts an invitation to dine with Remi. Temptations to return to him remain, but the friends she has made help her to resist. "Quelques amitiés, quelques femmes distinguées m'aident à oublier l'amour!" (*3em P.L.*   73). She continues to meet with Remi briefly from time, knowing that, although they live separate lives, she will never be able to deny that they somehow will be linked for eternity. "Mais je ne le quitte plus avec la vaine idée que c'est pour toujours, un adieu éternel, je ne le lui ferai pas même en mourant, je ne le lui ferai jamais" (*3em P.L.*   96).

Allart's *Marpé* is an interesting short work in that it contains simultaneously a sentimental and often excessivly Romantic tribute to her feelings for Bulwer and a calm, analytical feminist solution as to how she should handle them. Decreus sees the novella as Hortense's attempt to explain through Marpé how she wishes she and Bulwer could redefine, then recommence their relationship slowly, based on intellectual bonds. He, however, was never on her wavelength in that respect. "Elle se sentait incertaine de l'estime de Henry, elle voulait, avant de lui céder, le convaincre qu'elle se donnait par amour et non par veulerie ou par sensualité. Remi ne le comprit pas plus dans *Marpé* que Bulwer dans la vie" (Decreus 87).

If the plot of *Marpé* tends to grind Allart's personal ax a little too loudly, it nevertheless represents some of her best writing in terms of Romantic musings: "Il vit. Avec quelle langueur et quelle mélancolie je reviens sur ses idées, il vit, je le sais, qu'importe si je ne le vois plus, la terre est son habitation, il existe, qu'il soit heureux, et moi je me plairai encore sur la terre qu'il habite" (*EP* 212).

 The novella also stands, perhaps even more so than does *Jérôme,* as a fluent echo of Madame de Staël in terms of imagery, particularly in its descriptions of the beauties and grandeur of Italy and of nature. As only one example: "Le soleil d'Italie se couche, et quel coucher! Quel roi en a un plus magnifique! Le bas du ciel à l'horizon est un infini de teinte rosée, où la vue perce et se perd dans l'immensité" (*3em P.L.*   15; *EP* 216).

Most important, *Marpé* builds upon Allart's goal of creating heroines who do not fall into the trap of Staël's protagonists. That is,

Marpé, like Gertrude, Elisabeth, Thérèse, Germaine, and Settimia, is not foiled by society's cruel limitations on and punishments of superior women, but rather, successfully charts a happy and independent course for her future. Furthermore, the Bulwer experience created a new pheonmenon in Allart's two heroines in the *Petits Livres.* Instead of funneling the story's hero on to a course that will lead to happy marriage (as in *Gertrude, Sextus* and *Settimia*), Allart allows Germaine and Marpé the strength to find peace of mind *in choosing to live without a man,* and with a minimum of regrets about their choice.

The *Troisième Petit Livre* also contains essays and poetry on Old Testament stories (most notably, commentaries on David and Saul) and poetry on Greek legends as well as Romantic verses dedicated to Remi and others. The volume concludes with more sentimental Christian prayers.

As France moved toward another radical and briefly violent change in government in 1848, Allart sustained and strengthened her friendships, old and new, and prepared to say good-bye to the ill and aging, but still passionate Chateaubriand. One friendship would become more solid and dear to her than ever as she and George Sand drew closer on both a personal and professional level. Another friendship slowly would come to an end as Sainte-Beuve finally betrayed her beyond the limits at which she could overlook and completely forgive.

Notes

[1] Several letters written by Allart to Bulwer in Italy and Constantinople during this period survive in the Heydon collection. Decreus quotes here in French translation, 72.

[2] Desanti, iconography at beginning of text. (Photo Hachette).

[3] Jacques Vier. "La Comtesse d'Agoult et Allart sous le Seconde Empire, d'après une correspondence inédite," *Archives des Lettres Modernes* 33 (1960): Paris: Minard 3.

[4] André Billy. *Sainte-Beuve: Sa Vie et Son Temps.* (Paris: Flammarion, 1953) 348.

[5] George Sand. *Journal Intime.*, ed. Mme Aurore Sand. (Paris, 1926), Jan. 7, 1840, 101-2. (Quoted by Uffenbeck 299-300).

This quotation is also cited by Billy (156) as coming from "Le Journal de Piffoël," *Revue de Paris*, 33em année, III (1926): 20-60.

This passage also was quoted by Charles Dupêchez. *Marie d'Agoult.* (Paris: Libraire Académique Perrin 1938) 147-48, n. 58. Dupêchez gives the reference: George Sand, "Entretiens Journalières" (7 janvier 1840), *Œuvres Autobiographiques*. (Paris: Gallimard, Bibilothèque de la Pléïade, 1971) 2:1013.

[6]Hortense Allart to Sainte-Beuve. *Lettres inédites à Sainte-Beuve (1841-1848).* (Paris: Société Du Mercure de France, 1908) 53. (Subsequent references to letters in the collection will appear in parentheses after the quotation, and will be indicated by the abbreviation *L.I. à S.-B* .).

[7]George Sand. *Journal Intime.* Jan. 7, 1840, 100, quoted by Uffenbeck 298.

[8]George Sand to Hortense Allart. Heydon Ms., no date, probably 1841, quoted by Decreus, 88-89, n 5..

[9]Hortense Allart to Henry Bulwer-Lytton. Heydon Ms., no date, probably 1841, quoted by Decreus 90.

[10]Hortense Allart. *Notes inédites,* quoted by Séché, 179, n. 2.

[11]Sainte-Beuve's poem to Hortense is quoted in its entirety by Séché 185, and Uffenbeck 312-13, my italics.

[12]J. Bonnerot. *Correspondance Générale de Sainte-Beuve.* (Paris: Stock 1942) 4:130.

[13]Marie-Louise Pailleron. "Hortense Allart et Sainte-Beuve," *La Revue des Deux Mondes,* CX (Jun 1, 1940): 460.

[14]Alan Walker. *Franz Liszt: The Virtuoso Years,* 2 vols. (New York: Alfred A. Knopt, 1983) 1:385-86, n. 10.

[15]Osborne de Sampayo, who had been overseeing Marcus's education in Paris, later would enroll him in a school at Versailles in preparation for futher education at the military school, Saint-Cyr. At Hortense's return from Montauban, however, Marcus took some time off from school to stay with his mother (Billy 197). (Marcus later attended Saint-Cyr in 1844).

[16]"Notice," *Isidora.* Originally in (Paris: Michel Lévy Frères, Editeurs, no date). Reprinted in *Œuvres Complètes de George Sand.* (Geneva: Slatkine Reprints, 1980) 18:5.

[17]Hortense Allart de Méritens. *Etudes Diverses, Premier Petit Livre.* (Paris: Chez M. Renault, Libraire, 1850, 1851) xii-xiii. (Subsequent references to this work will appear in parentheses after the quotation, and will be indicated by the abbreviation *1er P. L.*)

[18]Mme Hortense Allart de Méritens, *Etudes Diverses, Second Petite Livre.* (Paris: Chez Renault, Libraire, 1850) 6. (Subsequent references to this work will appear in parentheses after the quotation, and will be indicated by the abbreviation *S.P.L.*)

[19]Madame Hortense Allart de Méritens. *Etudes Diverses, Trosième Petit Livre* (Paris: Chez Renault, Libraire, 1851) 14-15. (Subsequent references to this work will appear in parentheses after the quotation, and will be indicated by the abbreviation *3^{em} P.L.*)

Chapter 8

Clémence: Sainte-Beuve and George Sand: Friendship Betrayed; Friendship Solidified (1847-1865)

In February 1847, Hortense heard that Madame de Chateaubriand had died (Feb. 9) and sent her condolences to the ailing widower. A short time later, a visitor was announced at her Parisian apartment. She descended to the street and found Chateaubriand wrapped in an elegant coat, proposing that they take a ride together. Hortense sat next to him in his carriage, and they rode about Paris, recalling their long past days together in Rome, their rendezvous at Étampes, their dinners at the Arc-en-Ciel in Paris. René was 79 years old and had grown too weak to walk, but Hortense found him still handsome, charming, and as gallant to her as ever. "L'âge, au lieu de changer la beauté de son visage, le rend plus remarquable . . . Il est aimable et tendre" (*EP* 252).

They went on several more rides together, and she visited for the first time in his home, where she had never before felt it proper to enter. From Herblay, she wrote to Sainte-Beuve on April 5, "Chateaubriand est dans une belle langueur. On est charmé en le revoyant de sa manière si distinguée, si fine, si douce, si différente, et si au-dessus de tout." She spoke of watching René as he sat beside his window, looking at the sun, complaining only slightly of his infirmity. She compared him to the great eagle that she used to see in the aviary of the *Jardin des plantes*—a proud bird, eyes fixed on the sun, beating its large wings that could not be contained within the cage. "Il est touchant, il est aimable, on peut encore l'intéresser à tout, aux écrivains, aux ministres" (*N.L. à S.-B.* 55).

Gossip began to fly about Paris suggesting that Chateaubriand, finally free to pursue his much-younger former mistress openly, was planning to run off with her to Italy.   An indignant and ever-loyal Béranger dispelled the rumor in an April 4, 1847 letter to Louise Colet, rightly pointing out that Hortense hardly had the financial means for such a project and that she would not permit Chateaubriand to spend money on her in that way. ". . . je ne puis croire   à ce voyage qu'Hortense n'a pas le moyen de faire et qu'elle ne ferait aux dépens de personne, à moins qu'elle n'ait beaucoup changé."[1]

Interestingly, Hortense admitted just days after Chateaubriand's death the next year that if he had been in better health, she would indeed have liked to go off to Italy with him at that time.   To Sainte-Beuve on July 17, 1848, she wrote, "Si encore, il y a un an, il eût été mieux portant, j'aurais été avec lui en Italie, mais le trouvant fatigué, enlacé de mille chaînes, j'ai estimé plus sage de faire ce que j'avais toujours fait, de suivre avec lui le courant" (*N.L. à S.-B.* 61).

After a few more visits in spring 1847, Chateaubriand asked her to come lodge near him in Paris.   She did not change her residence at that time, but still kept in close touch.   Another rumor soon circulated that Chateaubriand was about to marry Madame Récamier.   Greatly distressed, Hortense wrote to him to ask if this were true.   He put her fears to rest in a letter   dated April 15, 1847.   "Je vous réponds un mot en courant. Vous devez savoir que je ne me marie à personne, que je reste et que je resterai toujours garçon. Je n'ai pas fait une si longue épreuve du mariage pour être tenté de recommencer" (quoted by Decreus 119).   In August, Hortense called on Chateaubriand again, and indulged him in a way she had done many years before—by reading aloud to him from his own works.   This time they shared parts of his *Mémoires de l'Outre Tombe* about the July Monarchy.   As this was still a work in progress, she also helped make corrections in the text.

In a July 1847 letter, part of which was later printed in his 1860 *Chateaubriand et son groupe littéraire,* Sainte-Beuve praised Hortense for doing for the Enchanter something that no other woman in his life—even Madame de Récamier—could have done, especially during his last year.   She had renewed his sense of himself as the young, emotive, and visionary René whom he created, then personified in a generation of new Romantics:

> C'est vous, Hortense, qui aurez donné à M. de Chateaubriand ses
> dernières joies, ses derniers ressouvenirs de René; car Mme
> Récamier le prend avec lui sur un ton plus bas; ce n'est plus notre
> Chateaubriand, elle en fait un *autre;* mais pour vous il retrouve des
> restes de souffle et des bruits loin de Germanie et de Gaule sauvage.[2]

In this same correspondence, Sainte-Beuve charges Hortense to keep all of Chateaubriand's letters to her so that she someday would be able to use them to honor his memory. ". . . ce seront des choses vraies de la part d'un génie illustre, mais qui a eu trop peu de ces éclaires de vérité. Vous lui ferez honneur un jour avec ces gages imprévus" (*Ch. et S.G.L* 320). Of course, as will be discussed later in this chapter, Sainte-Beuve had selfish ulterior motives for urging Hortense to retain as many details as possible from her relationship with Chateaubriand.

As for her professional projects this winter, Hortense temporarily had put aside her interest in novel writing and was working with her usual fecundity on political and historical projects. In March, she published her brochure on French government, *Lettre à Abdel-Kader,* and was working on her *Essai sur l'histoire politique* and *Novum Organum,* both of which would appear in 1857.

At this time, Marcus, age 22, was still a womanizer and also had become a rather shallow dandy, who showed no interest in study. How could this be, his mother wondered, considering the fact that both his parents were serious intellectuals? She worried about Marcus's frivolous ways, but deemed it best to let him sow his wild oats for the moment. She wrote to Sainte-Beuve from Herblay on June 13, 1847:

> Mon fils . . . ne connaît que deux choses: la beauté et la toilette. Mais comment est-il né de deux philosophes? Je n'y comprends rien. Il vient me voir ici dans les costumes les plus élégants du monde, suivi je crois de loin par une belle qui l'attend dans les environs. Il ne fait de la philosophie que si je le prends au collet, il a beaucoup d'esprit, mais à quoi cela lui sert-il? Une si profonde frivolité me confond, j'espère que cela passera, et je le laisse s'amuser comme il l'entend (*N.L. à S.-B.* 57).

As for her younger son, who was still at home with her, Hortense showered Henri with all the love she could, still wishing—as she soon would illustrate in *Marpé*—that he had been Bulwer's son. Decreus asserts that Bulwer himself did not discourage such fantasies:

> A Herblay, Hortense vit du souvenir de l'homme qui mène toutes ces affaires et reporte sur son fils, le petit toscan, la tendresse qu'elle ne peut plus dispenser à son lointain amant et elle se plaît à le croire un peu le fils de l'Ambassadeur. Bulwer ne décourage pas cette innocente fantaisie. Elle s'imagine découvrir dans l'enfant de Jacopo Mazzéi des similitudes de goût et de caractère avec Bulwer et les lui signale (Decreus 117).

As Hortense compared young Henri with Bulwer, she noted that each was in delicate health (the boy, unfortunately, also was still lame), and credited her son with the ardent nature and studiousness that she admired in her former lover. Several years later, in letters sent to Bulwer, she would maintain that—as in the "system of the Mormons"—Henri was so much like him that it was hard to say whose son he really was.[3] She wrote from Montlhéry on Jan. 7, 1858:

> Henri a tant de rapports avec vous pour les cheveux, la santé, la fierté . . . que je me [demande] s'il n'est pas votre fils. Il y a un nouveau système à ce sujet chez les Mormons, je crois, ainsi soyez content d'avoir donc une fois . . . Mais ceci est encore d'un ton qui ne convient plus dans les lettres (Heydon M., quoted by Decreus 117).

In the same vein, she wrote from Bourg-la-Reine to Bulwer, who was again in Constantinople, on Nov. 7, 1859:

> Mais souvenez-vous que d'Henri vous m'avez dit que le père n'avait fait que le gros de l'ouvrage, et qu'ainsi le système des Mormons est fait vrai. Henri est consommé d'une vague ardeur, il travaille dans une étude, et s'y plaît, il est agréable mais boiteux. Il a de beaux cheveux, un air éveillé; il préfère le grec à tout ce qu'il apprend (Heydon Ms., quoted by Decreus 117).

As 1847 drew to a close, she was still in touch with Sainte-Beuve and with Bulwer, whose activities in Spain she did not fully understand. "Et Bulwer?" she wrote to Sainte-Beuve from Herblay on Oct. 11, "J'appelle ces affaires d'Espagne singulières sans rien m'en expliquer" (*L.I. à S.-B.* 268). (This was not surprising, since the situation was complex. The intrigue, which involved the marital problems of the queen of Spain, and the resulting diplomatic headaches this caused for England, would come to a head in March 1848).

In October, Hortense temporarily left her home in Herblay and took an apartment in the Passy area of Paris, near the Place Trocadero and the future site of the Eiffel Tower, where she would spend most of the winter 1847-48. She chose this area for its closer proximity to the *Bibliothèque Royale,* where she would have access to the books she needed to complete her *Essai sur l'histoire politique.* Little did she know that this move soon would put her uncomfortably close to the turmoil of the impending revolution, which began to swirl about Paris in early 1848.

The past 18 years of constitutional monarchy under Louis-Philippe and his conservative prime minister, François Guizot, ironically had geared post-Revolutionary France into a plutocracy wherein the years of growing industry and prosperity had favored the rise of a small elite of rich while the masses had grown increasingly poorer. In the meantime, the Romantic movement had helped to create a backlash of young idealistic protesters who now began crying for a new chance for republicanism and reform.

Despite his taste for pretty women and fine clothes, Marcus did not shirk his military duty. He served in the unit of the *Garde Nationale* based at Herblay. He was not on duty Feb. 22, 1848, but was at his mother's side as they witnessed a brief, but violent and sobering, slice of French history—the fall of the July Monarchy. Marcus met his mother at her Passy residence that day, and they walked together to the Champs-Elysées, not expecting to see mobs of people, mostly young university students, collected in groups on the streets crying *"A bas Guizot! Vive la reforme!"* The demonstrators ripped up paving stones from the streets, chopped down trees and erected barriers. Some threw stones at the national guard troops that were dispatched to restore order. In turn, many of the guardsmen joined the protestors, calling for Guizot's resignation.

The prime minister resigned that day, and 74-year-old Louis-Philippe, besieged by more mobs outside the Tuileries Palace, abdicated on Feb. 24. Within two days, the poet and political reformer Lamartine was placed in power by a revolutionary contingent with whom he began forming a provisional republican government. The Second Republic was proclaimed Feb. 26. Marcus, back on duty with the national guard, was among the troops who patrolled the streets of Paris that night.

Hortense, ever the Bonapartist who favored government by an intellectual elite, was devastated by the upheaval. Years later, she recalled the events of the day: "La République est proclamée . . . le peuple stupide a envahi la Chambre. . . . Il semble alors qu'il n'y avait plus en France que de rude et grossières affaires, que la science était brisée. C'était comme si la pensée avait disparu du monde" (*EP* 255-56). She was even more incensed for the sake of the feeble Chateaubriand, who was still faithful to the concept of a constitutional monarchy and to his memories of his loyal diplomatic service under Charles X. "Un touchant objet pour moi durant ce grand bruit fut M. de Chateaubriand. Il en était frappé et comme tué" (*EP* 258). (Neither of them could have foreseen the short life of the Second Republic, and the rise of Louis-Napoleon Bonaparte, who would be elected president later in 1848, seize more power illegally in 1851, and head the Second

Empire as Napoleon III by 1852).

Sand's letters to Allart during the tumultuous 1848 show a tenderness heretofore unseen in their correspondence. On Feb. 16, Sand chided her friend good-naturedly for letters that hid information about her personal life "derrière la vie générale." She concluded by thanking Hortense for her years of constant and honest friendship, "Si vous sentez la confiance et la joie, écrivez, ma chère Impératrice, cela nous fera du bien et à vous aussi . . . . vous m'avez montré depuis longtemps une sympathie franche et fidèle que je vous rends bien, n'en doutez jamais. A vous de cœur, George S." (*Corres. de G.S.* 8:293).

The 1848 revolution left Sand disillusioned as well, but for reasons different than those of her fellow novelist. Unlike Hortense, the sentimental Bonapartist, Sand was a socialist republican and supporter of Lamartine. She was disappointed to witness Lamartine's popularity and the public enthusiasm for a progressive government diminishing that spring. She was, therefore, horrified to see Louis-Napoleon Bonaparte looming ever larger as a possible leader of France and a probable enemy of the ideals of the Second Republic.

On June 12, Sand wrote to Hortense, observing that their different political views forever would mark some fundamental gaps in their mutual understanding. "Ainsi, ma chère Hortense, vous avez peur de la république comme je la voudrais, et moi, je me résigne tristement à la république que vous voulez . . . ." However, Sand also indicated how she loved her friend despite their differences. "Et quant à vous, ma belle doctrinaire, je ne vois et ne pense comme vous sur rien de ce qui se passe. Mais je vous sais bonne, courageuse, franche et désintéressée. C'est pourquoi je vous aime en dépit de tout. A vous, George" (*Corres. de G.S.* 8:508).

During this time of agitation, Hortense made a trip to Burgundy in search of calmer lodgings far from the chaos of Paris for herself, her small grandson, Anthony, and nine-year-old Henri, who was still in fragile health. (She would move to Burgundy and live in two different spots there between 1851 and 1853). Meanwhile, she returned to Herblay. Sometime during March or April 1848, Hortense and Chateaubriand met in person for the last time. She kept in touch with the aging writer during the next few months, but he grew increasingly weaker and less coherent. He died on July 4, 1848 at age 80. Hortense, who was convinced that the 1848 revolution hastened René's death, wrote to Sainte-Beuve on July 16, "Il est mort brisé par cette révolution, il souhaitait que la mort le dérobât à la violence de ces affaires. Il est allé vivre ailleurs, avec son génie et ses amours" (*N.L. S.-B.* 60).

The next day she wrote Sainte-Beuve again, this time a lengthy and moving tribute to the deceased master. She mused on the tender nature her relationship with a man that began when he was 60 years old and she only 28. It was a friendship that they kept alive for two decades, and their last moments together were as loving as the first. She also praised Chateaubriand's intense capacity for love and tenderness. She admitted that if it were not for the difference in their ages, she would have asked for a "sacrifice"—specifically, she would have made him leave his wife. " . . . si nos âges s'étaient rapprochés, je lui aurais demandé des sacrifices, il aurait fallu quitter Mme de Ch[ateaubriand], je le lui ai dit . . . Je pense qu'il eut pu quitter sa femme" (*N.L. à S.-B.* 61).

Finally, in this same letter, Hortense imagined Chateaubriand, who had been frustrated with the limitations of old age, now enjoying an eternal youth. "D'abord, il désirait mourir; dans sa fierté, il était blessé d'être vieux, assis, brisé. Laissons-le donc retrouver peut-être une forme jeune ou s'enchanter peut-être dans l'éternelle lumière" (*N.L. à S.-B.* 61).

Earlier that spring in Spain, Bulwer was dealing with a political situation that was becoming increasingly difficult and disadvantageous for England. Ironically, the trouble followed on the heels of Henry's acceptance of one of the greatest honors to which an Englishman could aspire. On April 27, he was knighted by Queen Victoria, and was now addressed as "Sir Henry Bulwer." In May, the young Spanish monarch, Queen Isabella II, whose marriage to Francisco de Asis had been arranged by Anglo-French agreements, took a lover, thereby unraveling Bulwer's plans to gain the prince-consort as a British ally. As other British attachés suggested the very un-Spanish solution of divorce, Henry tried to safeguard English interests in the peninsula by offering asylum in the British Embassy to Spanish liberals. After the insurrection by Maréchal Navaez in Madrid in May, Bulwer protested formally in the name of England and tried to restore civil liberties for the sake of the young queen. Navaez was so furious that he gave Bulwer 48 hours to leave the country. Henry returned to England the same day that the Spanish ambassador to England left that country in a huff.

Queen Victoria was displeased with the turn of events in Spain, and castigated Bulwer in an official statement that spoke of his "extreme vanity" (Decreus 121). The disgraced diplomat, who felt he was just following orders, was bewildered by the brouhaha. He soon was exonerated by Prime Minister Lord John Russell, who stated that the cabinet approved of his conduct.

Hortense wrote on May 22, congratulating Henry on his

knighthood and expressing agreement with the cabinet's support of his
service in Spain.   On Sept. 9, she wrote Henry with a jaundiced, but
philosophical view on the political changes that she was now
grudgingly tolerating in her own country's new Second Republic.
"Venez ce qui se passe à Paris vous fera rire . . . . Le monde ne finit pas
à cause de cette ignoble république qui n'aura qu'un jour. . . . . Paris
reste le même . . . . Notre pays est toujours gai dans ce moment le plus
ridicule du monde" (Heydon Ms., quoted by Decreus 132).

On Dec. 9, 1848, Henry Bulwer-Lytton married Georgina-
Charlotte-Mary Wellesley, daughter of Baron Cowley, British
ambassador in Paris.   Much younger than her husband, Georgina was
an elegant, decorative bauble, who, with her sisters, would be part of an
elite, if vapid, entourage of young ladies who would flit about the
Empress Eugénie, wife of Napoleon III, at the advent of the Second
Empire. (Such women would become known as "cocodettes").
Hortense heard about the marriage just days later, and passed on the
news to Sainte-Beuve on Dec. 13, claiming that the bride was "old and
ugly" and that Henry had agreed to the union simply to advance his
career.   "On dit que Bulwer épouse le vieille laide Miss Cowley, je ne
sais si c'est vrai, il ne m'en parle pas, ce serait par ambition, c'est la
bataille de Waterloo" (*N.L. à S.-B.* 65).

Once the news of Bulwer's marriage became a little more real to
her, Hortense's reaction was one of outrage and heartbreak.   Only
weeks before his wedding, Henry had written to Hortense and suggested
that they meet in Paris. In a letter to Sainte-Beuve on Feb. 9, 1849,
she refers to Henry as "the world's worst scoundrel."   She was sure that
he could not possibly love his wife, and she predicted that his marriage
would probably end up as meaningless as her own. Nevertheless, her
sorrow was oppressive. The only way she thought she could cope was
to make sure she did not see him:

> Bulwer a été jusqu'au bout le plus grand scélérat du monde; il
> annonçait son arrivée sans cesse, il disait: "Je vous retrouverai"
> . . . . Vrai je l'excuse, car il se sera laissé marier, comme il se
> laisse tout faire. Enfin il ne veut rien expliquer et date ses lettres
> de notre Paris. N'est-ce pas le comble de la perfidie? Ce mariage
> dans quelque temps peut-être ne sera rien du tout, comme le mien.
> Mais le mieux est de ne pas le voir et de garder mes pleurs . . . pour
> vous et votre absence (*N.L. à S.-B.* 73).

Soon after his marriage, Bulwer was named a British minister to
Washington, D.C., where he would stay for three years and become a
key negotiator in an accord to protect both English and American

interests in Central America. The British Navy was protecting Indians whom Nicaragua had attacked. The United States feared this aggression and alliance threatened its influence in Panama and its future canal. (France, in negotiation with Columbia, of which Panama was then a part, was the first country to begin work on the canal in 1881, but, daunted by diseases and the rough terrain, gave up the project in 1887). Bulwer's eloquence stood up well before American austerity. It took a few months to smooth out the compromise of the Bulwer-Clayton Treaty, which was signed April 19, 1850, and safeguarded each country's claims in Panama, but this agreement solidified Bulwer's reputation as one of the foremost diplomats of his time. It also assured a place for him and his new wife in the most prestigious society in Washington (Decreus 126).

His personal life was not quite as sterling as it appeared. Hortense was correct in guessing that Bulwer did not love his spouse. Sadly, young Lady Georgina Bulwer-Lytton was enthralled with her handsome husband, and had entered the union in good faith that it was a love match on both sides. Her letter to Henry just a few years after the ceremony indicates how she had become ruefully aware that their marriage was—as Hortense had predicted it would become—a sham.

> On m'avait faire croire que vous m'aimiez, que vous désirez m'épouser depuis longtemps . . . Je me suis rendu compte de mon erreur fort peu de temps après notre mariage, mais j'espérais que mes soins auraient raison de votre indifférence. Je voyais bien que j'échouais, mais j'espérais toujours et me flattais qu'en Amérique, loin de nos amis, je vous serais nécessaire . . . ."[4]

Referring to the many times she and Henry already had been separated during his various travels, Georgina offered in this letter no longer to live with him so she would not be tormented further with the task of trying to make him love her. " . . . je préférerais être fixée tout de suite sur mon sort que de subir le supplice de me demander quand vous viendrez, espérant toujours, lorsque vous viendrez que vous m'aimerez davantage" (quoted by Decreus 125).

While Henry was in America, Hortense continued to invite Sainte-Beuve numerous times to Herblay, then later to Bezons (Seine-et-Oise), where she had moved to a home in May 1850, claiming that the country air would benefit his always-touchy health. Sainte-Beuve already had moved to Belgium, where he had accepted a position as a professor of literature at the University of Liège. In spring 1850, he returned to France for a short time, and visited Hortense at Bezons.

This was the last time they would see each other. He soon returned to Belgium and stayed for several more years. Hortense still invited him to return and visit, but he never did. She recalled, "Il ne vint pas, et resta pour moi toujours le Sainte-Beuve frêle, maigre et un peu malade que j'ai connu, mais il garda plus réellement, et à jamais, ces deux traits de son haut caractère: le désintéressement et la sincérité" (*EP* 260).

Marcus completed his military obligations, resigned from his job with the minister of the interior in Paris, and took an extended trip to Rome, where he often saw his Aunt Sophie, his uncle, and his cousins, who included twins. He was fascinated with the Roman revolution that was going on. (Beginning in April 1848, Guiseppe Garibaldi led troops in Italy's fight for independence. His exploits included battles against the French forces supporting Rome and the Papal States). However, Marcus was more interested in the many Roman ladies of his acquaintance, although he was even more fond of fair-skinned English women. "Il était ravi des Romaines, mais il leur préférait les Anglaises à cause de l'angélique pureté de leur teint" (Billy 227). His mother would insist that he return to France within a few months in 1849.

Hortense kept up her visits with Didier, and in March 1848 she did her best to help her old friend, Libri, who was accused by civil officials in Grenoble and Carpentras of having mismanaged some precious books and manuscripts that had been entrusted to him in those cities. He was able to flee to England, but several of his cases of books were held in Le Havre. At Libri's urging, she appeared to the officials in Paris, testified to his admirable character, maintained his innocence and accused clergymen and Jesuits of slandering him. Thanks in part to Hortense, Libri was able to retain at least some of his good name. He settled in London and soon married Mélanie Double, a widow whom he had loved before he fled France.

Hortense worked on her *Petits Livres* "avec le plus grand plaisir" (*EP* 260). The *Premier Petit Livre* was published August 1850. The *Second Petit Livre* appeared in November, two months after Hortense had taken Henri and Anthony and moved to a different country home at Coulanges-la Vineuse (Yonne). The *Troisième Petite Livre* came out in April 1851. At this point, she began a rather vagabond existence, always in search of a place that would be best for Henri's health. In October of that year, she left Coulanges-la-Vineuse for Ville-neuve-le-Roi, near Sens in Burgundy, where she would stay until September 1853. During these years, she went only rarely to Paris and no longer attended salons, but kept in touch with numerous friends including Sand, Sainte-Beuve, d'Agoult, Madame Hamelin, Béranger, Capponi, Mazzéi, and, occasionally, her husband. Madame Hamelin died in April 1851. From this point on, with no more chatty, gossiping letters from this ever well-informed correspondent, Hortense was not nearly as *au courant* about the latest Parisian scandals, the current issues in diplomacy, or every detail in Bulwer's life and career.

Contrary to what she had hoped, the damp Burgundian climate proved bad for Henri's heath, so they moved back to the outskirts of Paris in September 1853, staying in Thiais and Mazarin until October 1854, then Chilly-Mazarine (Seine-et-Oise) until October 1855, in Montlhéry until May 1859, in Bourg-la-Reine until October 1860, then back to Montlhéry, where she would remain for the next 10 years.

During this time, her friendship with Marie d'Agoult continued to grow in trust and intimacy through their candid correspondence. With the jealousies over their common interests in several different men finally behind them by the mid-1840's, they concentrated on sharing views on philosophical and literary matters as well as personal concerns. Vier emphasizes that any kind of warm rapport with a woman was unique for Marie, who did not maintain good relationships with members of her own sex. She opened up to Hortense as she would to no one else. "Il y a chez ces deux amies, de part et d'autre, un abandon et, pour reprendre un mot affreux mais cher à la Comtesse, une *'communicativité'* justifiée par des relations anciennes encore qu'exceptionnelles du côté de Marie, surtout à l'égard d'une autre femme" (Vier 6).

By virtue of her openess and affection, Hortense was able to be a sounding board for Marie's often painful memories about love and about Liszt. "De son côté, Hortense Allart, par la franchise de son dévouement et la simplicité de son affection, a acquis le droit de toucher aux plaies secrètes: Marie souffre qu'elle lui parle du passé qu'elle évoque en différentes circonstances, le souvenir de Liszt" (Vier 6).

During this period, there appears to be only one incident between the two in which Hortense became annoyed with the countess and it was a matter of intellectual piracy rather than personal jealousies. In their exchange of letters in 1849, Hortense shared frequent thoughts on a philosopher who had become her recent passion: Cicero. Marie, in turn, relayed to Lamartine, with whom she had a Platonic friendship, everything she had learned from Hortense about the ancient Roman statesman. The poet-politician was so impressed with such depth of knowledge coming from a woman that in his novel *Raphaël,* he created a heroine, based on Marie, who spoke eloquently and constantly about Cicero. When Hortense read the novel, she was quick to realize exactly where these speeches on Cicero had originated. This occurrence, however, ended up amusing Hortense more than it aggravated her (Decreus 127).

The two women did not agree on certain basic philosophies such as politics and religion. By 1851, Marie's formerly Catholic beliefs had evolved into a stoic atheism. Hortense's Protestant views of God were tempered with her natural optimism. After recognizing the traditional characteristics attributed to God and Jesus—goodness, charity, indulgence—Hortense also concluded that God surely must be a *"penseur profond,"* as she would write to d'Agoult in 1863. Marie only smiled with indulgence (Vier 8). They were in accord, however, on the idea of women's rights, and each was able to avoid the ridicule that was heaped on other feminists of the day, mostly because they were careful not to align themselves too closely with specific women's groups. Marie was especially skeptical, although she tried to discipline herself not to say too much against women's clubs, which she knew meant well. "Avez-vous conservé des relations avec les femmes saint-simoniennes ou socialites de ce temps-ce?" she wrote Hortense on May 16, 1851. "Je désapprove les clubs, les candidatures, les banquets. . . . Mais je ne dirai rien de dur; du moins, je tâcherai car ma plume tourne quelquefois malgré moi à un sévérité qui est dans ma façon de dire bien plus que dans ma façon de penser" (quoted by Vier 12). Years later, in 1869, Hortense would write to Marie on the question of women's suffrage, saying she did not object to giving voting rights to women, but that she would first like to remove that right from "a lot of men" (quoted by Vier 27, n. 41).

Their friendship also persevered because Marie and Hortense respected one another's literary works. Vier credits the "excellent character" of Hortense for the cordial rapport they maintained on this subject. Although Hortense's works generally were not widely read, and she herself was excessively intellectual and in danger of being considered an "insufferable blue stocking," she was down-to-earth and generous in her support of the novels of Daniel Stern and completely devoid of malice and sarcasm. "Hortense est dénuée de fiel et d'ironie, sans avoir, le moins du monde, l'esprit courtisan," says Vier. In this spirit, she wrote to Marie in praise of her novels, "Vous avez l'avantage, avec du talent, d'être lu, de plaire; vos livres, vos articles sont connus d'un bout de la France à autre" (quoted by Vier 13).

Although Hortense initially was critical of *Nélida* (1846) for its unflattering portrayal of Liszt (see Chapter 7), she ended up with nothing but praise for this book as well as for Marie's 1849 novel, *Esquisses.* Upon rereading *Nélida* during the summer of 1869, she wrote to Marie that she found the opening scene as beautiful as anything written by Sand. "Les premières scènes, le modèle, c'est aussi beau que la Reine et la suite est plus sérieuse et d'un autre genre. Ce roman devrait être réimprimé sans cesse, mais c'est trop bien écrit, ou peut-être vous n'avez pas voulu le donner encore, mais il ira malgré vous" (quoted Vier 13).

Hortense also praised Marie's principal work, *L'Histoire de la révolution de 1848,*   even though the two disagreed on their interpretations of the events of that year. (Hortense loathed the outcome of the revolution while Marie took a more detached and holistic view of the happenings).   In any case, Marie valued Hortense's opinion, and kept her apprised of the progress of the work as she went along.   Hortense, in turn, lauded Marie's research and presentation. "On est entraîné . . . on sait tout, on voit tout, on suit chaque action. Le caractère, l'impétuosité de la nation sont bien rendus, et le style toujours élevé, élégant," she wrote to the author after the third volume appeared in 1853.   This was no small praise coming from a research historian as sophisticated as the author of *L'Histoire sur la République de Florence.*   Allart esteemed her friend's ability to present a portion of history as emotional and controversial as the 1848 revolution with fairness and impartiality. She concluded her letter, "Vous êtes enfin la première voix libre et hardie, élevée à Paris sous régime. Honneur à vous!" (quoted by Vier, 27-28, n. 52).

When Marie, who still was not on good terms with Sand during the 1850's, criticized the latter's *Historie de Ma Vie,* Hortense laughed indulgently, never losing her own admiration for Sand.   She wrote to Marie on Dec. 6, 1855, good-naturedly defending Sand, and comparing her persona to Sand's earlier heroine, Consuelo (from the 1842 novel of that name). "J'aime la Reine qui garde ses beaux yeux, son front, ses cheveux. Elle est belle encore. C'est chez elle, ce ton doux, bon, des *Mémoires.* C'est *Consuelo*" (quoted by Vier 23).

As for the correspondence between Allart and Sand, it was growing warmer still, especially from the late 1840's as the two became grandmothers. On June 22, 1847, Sand concluded her missive with some small talk about her own children, and asked about Hortense's sons. "Mon fils fait toujours de la peinture avec rage. Et le vôtre, où est-il? et l'autre comment va-t-il? Parlez-moi d'eux et voyez à mon empressement à vous répondre, moi qui n'ai le temps de rien, que vous n'avez pas *perdu mes faveurs* et que c'est moi qui tiens à conserver les vôtres" (*Corres. de G.S.*   7:759, Sand's italics).

The calm that settled in with middle age helped form a bond between the two writers. "La Reine m'a dit qu'il n'y a rien de si doux et de si calmant que de vieillir," Allart related to Sainte-Beuve March 4, 1849 (*N.L. à S.-B.*   77).   Two months earlier, Sand had written calling Allart "bonne reine," and ending, "Et pourtant je ne vous quitterai pas sans vous dire que je vous aime, et vous embrasse de tout mon cœur" (*Corres. de G.S.* 9:25-26).

Amid this flourishing friendship, Allart still showed herself confident enough to venture a few opinions on Sand's novels, although she did not always share them with *la Reine* herself. Writing to Sainte-Beuve on Feb. 13, 1850, Allart flatly stated that she did not care for the "plebian philosophies" that she felt Sand espoused in her pastoral novels *La Mare au Diable* and *François le Champi.* However, she praised *Jeanne* and *Consuelo,* and called *André, Horace* , and *Isidore* "les chefs d'œuvre de morale et de sentiment" (*N.L. à S.-B.* 90-91). In 1852, completely enthralled over the French translation of Harriet Beecher Stowe's *Uncle Tom's Cabin (La Case de l'Oncle Tom),* Allart opined to Sainte-Beuve that Stowe's writing was superior to Sand's. "Cette dame américaine surpasse Mme. Sand, elle est plus sensible, jamais dévergondée, moins haute et élégante, peut-être, mais quel grand sujet et bien prise! . . . . Il me semble que c'est un des plus beaux livres que j'aie jamais lus; quel peintre!" (*N.L. à S.-B.* 109).

Therefore, as their personal rivalry wound down, the friendship between Sand and Allart still seemed to struggle with professional differences due largely to their different opinions on how to approach the novel. This lingering tension eased off, however, toward the end of the 1840's and particularly during the 1850's after Allart's principal writing projects and successes began to turn away from fiction. Although she published her novella *Clémence* as late as 1865, during the previous decade, Allart's main focus was on her extensive *L'Histoire de la République de Florence* and *L'Histoire de la République d'Athènes,* as well as on her numerous essays on politics and religion.

The correspondence between the two shows that each tended more and more to mark her own territory and respect that of the other in both the personal and the professional domain. "En effet, la reconnaissance de la souveraineté de chacune dans son domaine leur permettra de dresser un traité d'aimité qui assurera, faute d'une véritable sympathie d'âmes, des rapports amicaux" (Garnett 256).

Before this moment, the friendship between the two writers had been growing ever warmer, and by April 1854, Allart was bold enough to suggest in a letter that her friend might write a preface for a second printing of *Gertrude,* or for any of her other novels that might be published in a new edition. Sand apparently was generous enough to speak kindly of Allart's first novel and suggest that it ought to be reprinted. Allart wrote to her, "Mais, puisque vous m'avez parlé de *Gertrude,* si vous le jugiez digne d'être réimprimé, faites y donc une préface . . . . Si j'offre l'ouvrage on n'en voudra pas. Vous seule lui donneriez une valeur pour le classer dans les romans qu'on réimprime . . . . "[5] This never came about, but Allart did receive from Sand a

more than satisfying review of another one of her works, *Novum Organum ou Sainteté Philosophique,* some three years later.

In Sand's *L'Histoire de Ma Vie,* which she wrote between 1848 and 1854, she draws a superlative portrait of her colleague. First she describes her as "une femmes très supérieure dont je parlerai plus tard." (A footnote in Sand's text identifies this "superior woman" as "Madame Hortense Allart".)[6] Gone is the unflattering word *écriveuse,* as, a few chapters later, Sand describes Allart as a writer who is able to combine the best of feminine sensitivity and masculine viability into her work. "[Mme Allart est] un écrivain d'un sentiment très élevé et d'une forme très poétique . . . esprit courageux, indépendante; femme brillante et sérieuse, vivante à l'ombre avec autant de recueillement et de sérénité qu'elle saurait porter de grâce et d'éclate dans le monde; mère tendre et forte, *entrailles de femme, fermeté d'homme."* [7]

In 1857, Allart published her 300-page religious essay *Novum Organum ou Sainteté Philosophique.* The treatise reflects Hortense's religious philosophies at the time that centered around meditation, spirituality, and sensuality based on stoic Epicurianism combined with the mysticism of Rousseau and elements of both the Enlightenment and early Romanticism. "Telle est Hortense; une femme savante qui connaît la Bible à travers Voltaire, l'*Encyclopédie* et Bernardin de Saint-Pierre" (Billy 241). One chapter was dedicated to Madame de Staël, whom Allart praised for depicting a morality drawn from both religion and philosophy. This chapter states, "Mme de Staël a peu écrit sur la religion, mais ce peu rappelle à la vie spirituelle et, en unissant cette vie spirituelle à la philosophie, elle a atteint le nouvel Organum que nous signalons" (quoted by Billy 241). The essay also contains meditations, exhortations, and invocations much like those that later would comprise the concluding pages of *Les Enchantements de Prudence.* (The intensity of Hortense's religious faith and mystic prayers would continue to grow as she became older).

Sand was so impressed with *Novum Organum* that she asked *La Presse* editor Charles-Edmond to print her article praising the essay and honoring Allart as a writer who, heretofore, had received far too little recognition for her works. She wrote to Edmond on Dec. 5, 1857, "Il s'agit de Mme Hortense Allart qui est un esprit de premier ordre, trop peu connu malgré d'utiles travaux." (*Corres. de G.S.* 14:543). Her review, which originally appeared in *Le Courrier de Paris* on Dec. 23, 1857, later became part of Sand's *Souvenirs de 1848.*

The review not only is a tribute to *Novum Organum* but also becomes a kind of "lifetime achievement award" as Sand speaks glowingly of Allart's decades of literary output and of her entire

persona. " . . . c'est le résumé concis des études et des réflexions de toute une vie savante et lettrée. L'auteur est une femme charmante qui a étudié les langues mortes et les philosophies abstraites, sans que sa figure blanche et rose trahît par un pli les veilles et les méditations."[8]

One may well speculate that Sand found it easier to praise a non-fictional work of Allart's than it would have been to speak kindly of her as a rival novelist. Nonetheless, for the first time, she was broad-minded enough to testify to Allart's value as a novelist and a historian—"Elle écrivait quelquefois des romans, des romans agités de passion et traversés de grandes plaintes éloquentes. Et puis elle a écrit de forts bons livres d'histoire" (*S. de 1848* 356).

By this time, Sand also had warmed completely to Allart's particular style. Whereas she had once accused Allart of being pedantic and lacking in simplicity, she made a point in this review of praising *Novum Organum* for being, despite its formidable title, a work with a pleasing, flowing style. "[C'est] un de ces livres clairs et brillants . . . qui peut se lire aussi facilement qu'un ouvrage frivole." She added that, after reading the work, "on se sent plus fort, plus instruit, plus sage, plus honnête, plus heureux" (*S. de 1848* 355). Later in the review, Sand stated, "La manière de l'auteur est originale. Ses défauts sont presque toujours des qualités. Son style court toujours et vole souvent" (*S. de 1848* 362).

Furthermore, Sand, who had formerly described Allart as *hommasse,* defended her friend's feminine demeanor, stating that this femininity may have erroneously led some would-be readers to doubt her validity as a writer. "A la voir si animée, si active, si dévouée aux nobles fardaux de la famille et avec cela si brillante causeuse, nous avons eu besoin de la connaître longtemps pour croire qu'il y eût tant de sagesse, d'érudition et de tranquillité dans cette jolie tête blonde qu'elle portait comme si elle ne l'eût pas soupçonnée sur ses épaules" (*S. de 1848* 356).

Finally, at this point, Sand not only had come to terms with what she described as Allart's *male* genius, but she also now wished that her friend would reveal more of the admirable woman behind it. "On ne voit pas assez dans son œuvre *la femme excellente que ses amis adoraient en dépit de son mâle génie* " (*S. de 1848* 357, my italics). Finally, Sand credited Allart for the value *Novum Organum* held for women readers. "Nous conseillons aux femmes intelligentes la lecture de ce livre . . . . Madame Hortense Allart est, par ses travaux sérieux, ses vertus privés, la noblesse de son caractère, l'élévation de son talent, et la haute direction de son esprit, une des gloires de son sexe" (*S. de 1848* 362-63).

Sand also maintained that Allart had not received the praise and fame she merited for reasons that were particularly dear to Sand's own heart—because she lived on her own terms alone, and refused to pander to public taste. "Elle a vécu simplement et par un grand esprit d'ordre, de prudence ou de stoïcisme. . . . elle a écrit pour écrire ne demandant appui et courage qu'à elle-même. Elle ne s'est peut-être pas assez soucié des choses littéraires . . . parce qu'elle n'a pas suivi attentivement le goût du public" (*S. de 1848* 356-57).

Correspondence between Sand and Allart seems sparse during the 1860's, although Hortense wrote several letters to Sainte-Beuve through 1864 that mention "la Reine." George Lubin, editor of Sand's many volumes of correspondence, notes that several letters from Sand to Allart are verified, but missing. Garnett also observes that, perhaps out of respect for her own and others' privacy, Hortense burned a good many of her papers and letters she had received over the years. "Quant à Hortense Allart, elle brûla beaucoup de papiers (par discrétion?) vers la fin de sa vie" (Garnett 259). The two friends would be back in touch, however, by 1872 (see Chapter 9).

In 1857, in addition to publishing *Novum Organum* and her *Essai Sur l'histoire politique,* Hortense began her *Histoire d'Athènes,* and settled in Montlhéry. She also continued her correspondence with Bulwer during the 1850s, as he made more strides in his diplomatic career (and maintained his less-than-ideal marriage). During these years he served as a British minister in Italy. He and Georgina moved to Florence in 1851, but he traveled frequently across Europe and made several trips through Paris without seeing Hortense.

In September 1858, Bulwer passed through the capital again on his way to a second assignment in Constantinople. Decreus states that Sand wrote a letter to Hortense at this time urging her to see her former lover. (Decreus does not quote from the letter, which is not included in the volumes of Sand's correspondence). Hortense declined, telling Sand she wished only to keep up her written correspondence with Henry— "nous nous écrirons toujours" (Heydon Ms., quoted by Decreus 123)— because she feared that even the shortest meeting with him would affect her too much. She wrote to Henry a few years later (in an undated letter, probably 1861):

> J'aurais fort aimé de vous retrouver q[uel]q[ue] jour et j'aurais fort à causer avec vous de mille choses, mais la vie entraîne les gens de divers côtés, et l'on ne revoit plus ceux que l'on eût voulu revoir. Mais pour un jour en passant, non, vous savez, cela est plutôt triste, et je ne l'ai pas cherché (Heydon Ms., quoted by Decreus 123).

In a letter to Bulwer in Constantinople dated April 26, 1860, Hortense told him she would like to help him with his latest writing project, but she feared her English had grown too rusty. "J'aurais fort voulu vous être utile pour votre ouvrage et corriger les épreuves, mais cela passe l'anglais qui me reste." She also repeated how she preferred written correspondence to face-to-face contact with him, knowing he was still flighty and fickle. Furthermore, she would not care to be part of his "harem" in Constantinople. " . . . je vous préfère dans les lettres et l'amitié, car vous serez toujours volage, toujours en l'air. Je ne voudrais pas présider à Constantinople à votre harem, et ce serait mon sort aujourd'hui" (Heydon Ms., quoted by Billy 207).

Finally, she shared with Henry her opinion that God had worked everything out for the best between the two of them, and that she henceforth would remember him as the one who could express the deepest feelings the best. "Dieu a tout arrangé pour le mieux. Vous pouvez plaire encore, vous serez souvent séduit. Mais je vous conserve dans mon souvenir comme celui qui savait le mieux parfois représenter les sentiments divins" (Heydon Ms., quoted by Billy 207).

Correspondence continued during these years between Hortense and Sainte-Beuve with letters that consistently testify of her extensive intellectuality and of her vast knowledge of ancient *belles letters* as well as of literature and philosophy of modern France and other countries. In late 1848—after the publication of Chateaubriand's *Mémoires de l'Outre Tombe* and the subsequent death of the author— Hortense and Sainte-Beuve began an ongoing disagreement as to whether she had been unfairly neglected by the Romantic master. Hortense herself had helped critique parts of Chateaubriand's last work, and had never expressed any disappointment or irritation over the fact that he did not include anything more than a brief mention of her name in the entire manuscript.

The only time her name occurs is in a list of other women writers whom Chateaubriand knew and with whom he had collaborated. "Mme Tastu marche au milieu du chœur moderne des femmes-poètes, en prose ou en vers: les Allart, les Waldor, les Valmore, les Ségalas, les Revoil, les Mercœur. etc., etc."[9]

Hortense claimed that she did not mind such a paltry mention in René's memoirs. He had placed her name in good literary company, which was reward enough. Also, she would not really wish for him to discuss their personal relationship. Besides, it was she, not he, who decided to end their affair when she became involved with Bulwer. Perhaps this did not break Chateaubriand's heart, but it hurt him emotionally and definitely bruised his ego. Thus, she figured that the lack of further mention of herself in his last book was somewhat of a

just dessert that she was willing to digest.
Sainte-Beuve did not comprehend her attitude. Just days after
Chateaubriand's death, he wrote, claiming he was incensed that René
had left her out of his memoirs. "Ce silence qu'on fait partout, cette
omission absolue de vous m'indigne; lui-même a eut tort . . . . C'est à
mes yeux un de ses crimes de ne vous avoir nulle part nommée" (quoted
by Billy 221).

She sprang to Chateaubriand's defense in her already-mentioned
July 17, 1848 letter, telling Sainte-Beuve that one should not be too
quick to judge René's attitude about a relationship he had at age 60 with
a much-younger woman whom he always treated with respect and
discretion. "Il ne faut pas juger des affections d'un homme par une
liaison formée à soixante ans avec une jeune femme . . . . Si j'ai cru un
homme capable d'une affection ferme et haute, c'est lui . . . . Mais il
n'aurait rien fait jamais par aucune influence contre l'honneur et la
délicatesse" (*N.L. à S.-B.* 61).

In May 1850 she again wrote Sainte-Beuve telling him she never
wanted to be mentioned in *Mémoires d'Outre-Tombe* because she had
been too little a part of Chateaubriand's life and that their paths had
ended up being too diverse (Billy 224). Finally, in 1860, she wrote
from Bourg-la-Reine with a response to yet another of Sainte-Beuve's
complaints about her absence from the book. She reminded him what
had happened in England and how this had put a damper on her
relationship with Chateaubriand for years afterward. René himself had
told her that she had ruined her chance of being "the lady of his
Mémoires."

> Votre billet est bien d'un homme de lettres. Vous êtes très
> sévère pour René (comme toujours). Et puis vous oubliez ce qui
> s'est passé en Angleterre; quel homme pardonne qu'on le quitte?
> Votre billet me rappelle (ce que vous avez oublié) qu'il me
> demandait si je voulais être la dame de ses *Mémoires* (pure phrase).
> Plus tard il me dit que je n'y serai point, que le voyage d'Angleterre
> avait tout gâté.[10]

Hortense's good sportsmanship, though was of no consolation to
Sainte-Beuve, and he would not be appeased. His agitation was rooted
in a plot that was hatching in his mind and whose motives were mostly
selfish. Even before Chateaubriand died, Sainte-Beuve had recognized
the value of the collection of the letters from the Enchanter that
Hortense still had in her possession. He wrote to Hortense, advising
her to keep the letters and to use them one day as a way to honor

Chateaubriand's genius:

> Gardez bien ces derniers billets; ce seront des choses vraies de
> la part d'un génie illustre, mais qui a eu trop peu de ces éclairs de
> vérité. Vous lui ferez honneur un jour avec ces gages imprévus. Sa
> mémoire aura fort à faire, car il est de ceux qui ont trop longtemps
> vécu . . . . C'est ainsi que moi-même je voudrais être traité (*Ch. et
> S.G.L.* 320).

The idea of one day publishing something about her relationship
with Chateaubriand already had crossed Hortense's mind. By 1860, her
writing of *Les Enchantements de Prudence* was under way, but the
passage about her relationship with Chateaubriand, which included
quoted excerpts from his letters, was material she hesitated to put in
print.

It was with her usual faith in Sainte-Beuve's discretion, and with
no feelings of bitterness, vanity, or desire for revenge upon
Chateaubriand that she turned this section of her writing over to the
literary critic for his perusal. "On ne soupçonne pas Hortense d'avoir
obéi à un movement de rancune ou de vanité en comminquant à Sainte-
Beuve des passages de ses *Enchantements* . . . . (Billy 221).

Sainte-Beuve was delighted with the autobiographical piece with its
revelatory material about Chateaubriand. He specifically urged Hortense
to publish these pages for the sake of bringing to light a side of René
that few people knew. He also advised her not to bother disguising any
identities with false names.

> Rendez à sa mémoire le service de publier un jour et sans l'altérer,
> sans le masquer de faux noms (ce qui déroute et désintéresse le
> lecteur), le chapitre que vous me faites lire en ce moment . . . .
> Vous avez un Chateaubriand à vous et que bien peu connaissent. Je
> ne l'ai pas vu tel, mais je le comprends tel en vous lisant (quoted
> by Billy 222).

Sainte-Beuve, however, did not have sufficient patience to wait
until such a time as Hortense would decide to publish her Chateaubriand
story herself. Emile Henriot suggests that Sainte-Beuve may have
desired so fervently the publication of this portion of Hortense's life for
egotistical reasons. He was miffed that Chateaubriand had not made
more mention of Allart in his *Mémoires,* for if he had written of their
affair, it would have made Sainte-Beuve look better in the role of her
subsequent lover.

Car, en somme, lui aussi . . . [Sainte-Beuve] avait obtenu les
faveurs d'Hortense Allart, et ce pouvait, étant donnée sa nature
assez compliquée, lui être un titre assez flatteur, aux yeux de la
postérité, d'avoir été le successeur de René dans le cœur d'une de ses
sylphides officiellement reconnues.[11]

In any case, the critic took the matter of publication into his own
hands. Séché calls Sainte-Beuve the godfather of Allart's autobiography
since he gleefully and without her permission inserted under the title
"Extraits des mémoires inédits" all the material about Chateaubriand
that Hortense had given him, including some quotations from the
letters, at the end of the second volume of his 1861 *Châteaubriand et
son group littéraire.* "On sait avec quelle malice et quelle joie le grand
critique y inséra le morceau des *Enchantements* qui se rapporte aux
relations de René avec Prudence" (Séché 21).   Although he did not
name Hortense as the author, he hinted about her identity in a footnote,
pegging her as an intelligent woman who was interested in politics and
who had grown up under the star of Madame de Staël.   "La femme
distinguée qui a écrit ces pages était, on le devine, une de ces femmes
dont l'intelligence s'intéressait fort à la politique et qui étaient nées et
avaient grandi sous l'astre de Mme de Staël" (*Ch. et S.G.L.* 2:360,
n. *.)

If Sainte-Beuve can receive credit for any gallantry at all in this
affair, it is for his honesty with his editors in establishing that it was
he and not the author herself who chose to publish the Chateaubriand
material. He wrote to Saulnier, "Quant aux pages de la fin, elles sont
vraies; l'auteur, *Mme Allart, n'est point coupable de les avoir publiées,
c'est moi seul qui l'ai pris sur moi.*   Ce sont des choses très vraies"
(quoted by Billy 251, my italics).   When Sainte-Beuve's book was
published, he was accused by many of quoting apocryphal tales about
Chateaubriand, or inventing stories on his own.   However, as sneaky
and dishonest as he was in his use of Allart's manuscript, Sainte-Beuve
was not a liar. "Sainte-Beuve était ce qu'il était: méchante langue et
jaloux," says Séché. "On lui portait facilement ombrage, mais il était
incapable d'inventer une histoire, de fabriquer une pièce, ou seulement
de l'altérer, pour écraser un rival ou un ennemi, et, depuis que je
l'étudie, je n'ai jamais pu lui prendre la main dans le sac aux
mensonges" (17).

Partly in response to those who disbelieved this portion of Sainte-
Beuve's book, Hortense eventually would decide to publish the material
about herself and Chateaubriand on her own as verification that her 20-
year relationship with France's great Romantic writer indeed was real

and was particularly precious to her.

For the moment, though, Allart felt betrayed by Sainte-Beuve's publication, and her relationship with him cooled to the point that their correspondence faltered, then ceased.   This probably is also the reason that she eventually destroyed most of Sainte-Beuve's letters to her. "Mais il en rejaillit sur elle un discrédit dont il est probable qu'elle lui garda rancune et qui explique peut-être qu'elle ait détruit ses lettres . . . . Entre temps, leur amitié s'était quelque peu gâtée. Leurs lettres étaient devenues rares . . . . "[12]   It is not sure whether she even attended Sainte-Beuve's funeral in 1869.

In 1857, Hortense wrote of the different characteristics and personalities of her two sons and her grandson. Marcus was bright, and much like his mother, gifted with languages.   A credit to the education that both Hortense and his uncle, Osborn de Sampayo, had arranged for him, he knew Portuguese, Spanish, Italian, German and English. However, since his return to France from Italy in 1849, he had worked unenthusiastically as a notary.   Henri (sometimes Hortense spelled his name the English way, Henry) was more shy and introspective, but also intelligent, creative, and interested in law. Grandson Anthony, 13 years old, was handsome and lively:

> Marcus, qui paraît grave sans l'être, entraîné, emporté, ne sachant trop ce qu'il veut; Henry, dévoré par un ardeur inquiète qui le fait errer d'étude en étude, occupé de la loi, plein de nouveautés, timide avec les femmes, mais vrai poète au fond et dédaignant la poésie pour la loi. . . . Le fils de Marcus a déjà treize ans. . . . . il est très beau et très spirituel (quoted by Billy 243).

In 1858, Hortense wrote to Père Enfantin and to writer-politician Louis-Adolphe Thiers, asking their help in procuring a job for Marcus with the railroad in Lyon. When neither of them were of much service to her (they merely suggested that Marcus make application), Hortense wrote to Bulwer, who was passing through Paris on assignment from his post in Constantinople, asking if he could help Marcus find a diplomatic position. Bulwer had been fond of Marcus ever since he was a child, and had at one time wanted the young man to join him in Spain and to take a position there. Hortense had refused to let her son go at that time.   This time, when Bulwer secured a position for Marcus in Constantinople, the son was eager to go, but the mother again vetoed his departure.   Always the diplomat and compromiser, Henry arranged a job that was agreeable to both Marcus and Hortense—a position in Vienna with the railroad of the Lombards and Venetians.

Unfortunately, Marcus had to cut his career in Vienna short after one year because of the outbreak of a war in which French troops were fighting against Austria for the liberation and unification of Italy. He returned to France in May 1859. (Although Hortense supported Napoleon III's efforts to help Italy, she wished neither for Marcus to fight in the army nor for him to work in Vienna, which was now a hostile city towards France.) Before long, Bulwer's influence again helped him find a railroad position in Marseilles. In 1860, Hortense again asked both Bulwer and Enfantin for help in placing her son Henri, who was now 21, in a position with the railroad as well. Bulwer secured a job interview for Henri, but Hortense soon informed her former lover that Henri was tired and ill and would have to put off his search for work for a few months. Eventually, Henri was able to take a railroad post for a year before he became too ill to continue.

On July 19, 1862, a wave of sadness swept through Hortense's life. Henri, who always had been sickly, died at age 23. Details are scarce as to the cause of his death, and Hortense seems to have written little about her ensuing grief. Religion had become an increasing comfort to her over the years, and now she used both her writing and her spirituality as therapy as she turned to the production of essays on religion.

Séché writes that Henri's death was a cruel trial for his mother that she was able to bear only because of her strong spirit and her religious faith. "Cette dispositon d'esprit, toute nouvelle chez Mme de Méritens, ne lui fut pas inutile dans l'epreuve cruelle qui lui était résevée: la mort de sons fils Henri, en 1862, la trouva résignée à la volonté de Dieu!" (72).

In December 1862, a few months after Henri's death, Allart published *Nouvelle concorde des quatre évangilistes,* the story of the life of Jesus, culled from Matthew, Mark, Luke and John in the New Testament. She published her *Essai sur la religion intérieure* in March 1864.

Marcus married Berthe Vernier Aug. 22, 1863—a union that would bring Hortense two more grandchildren within the next two years. She wrote to Bulwer in Constantinople on Sept. 27, 1864, "Je suis revenue ici, avant un second accouchement de ma belle-fille, après moins de deux ans de mariage" (Heydon Ms., quoted by Decreus 114, n. 4).

In the meantime, she had raised Marcus' eldest child, Anthony, who, in 1864, turned 18, and wished to join the army. She wrote to Bulwer this year about wishing to keep Anthony with her, because she feared losing him in one of the wars in which France was involved in foreign countries. (In addition to the war in Austria, Napoleon III had committed French troops to occupations and disputes in Mexico, Russia, and Poland). She was distressed that Marcus had taken the boy back, and that they disagreed about how to treat him (Hortense was gentle and indulgent. Marcus, in her opinion, was too harsh).

> Mon petit fils Anthony est venu me voir ici: il a 18 ans, il est bel homme et très fort. Je l'ai élevé, mais son père l'a repris et le traite très durement: Marcus est sensible, faible et dur, c'est un singulier mélange . . . . Anthony voudrait entrer dans l'armée, mais je ne veux pas, nous avons des guerres trop meurtrières et trop loin (Heydon Ms., quoted by Decreus 114).

It is not clear who came out ahead in the power struggle for who would gain the greatest influence over Anthony, but there is no indication that he ever went off to war. Hortense most likely was successful in exerting her influence in keeping him out of the army, as she had done with both Marcus and Henri.

Béranger, Hortense's oldest and probably her dearest friend, died July 16, 1857. Since they had met at the château of Madame de Surpré in Val when she was a tutor for the Bertrand children, they had exchanged letters of warm encouragement to one another for more than 30 years. In 1864, Hortense published *Lettres choisies de Béranger* picking out his missives that she considered the most touching and beautiful. (The first letter in the collection was addressed to her on March 20, 1825, the last on Jan. 27, 1855). The bookstores with which she consulted did not want to publish the letters unless they could make money without sharing any profit with Hortense. She was not interested in personal gain and wished for the letters to be affordable to the public. Therefore, she decided to publish the collection at her own expense and to offer them free or for only two sous per copy so more people could buy and enjoy them.

The last letter in the Béranger collection, written when he was 75 years old, urges Hortense to keep up with the changing times. "Votre histoire est-elle enfin terminée? dépêchez-vous. L'ancien monde s'en va. Il en naît un tout nouveau qui rira bien de celui qui l'a précédé. Voyez quel chemin il a fait depuis [17]89." [13]

Allart's last major work of fiction, her novella, *Clémence,* was published in 1865. Though it was a short work (31 pages) with a traditionally gratifying ending, it nevertheless exhibits some continuing examples of the author's determined urgings for betterment of the lot of French women, and for a more determined attitude on the part of women themselves to pursue the kind of love to which they should be entitled. This time, Allart made the autobiographical voice in the novella two-fold. The title heroine is a young, intelligent, and beautiful orphan, alive with troubling passions, and, once again, recognized by a friend as having *un esprit mâle.* The story takes place in 1830, at the same time that Hortense herself was in the prime of her youth and beauty.

In this work, however, Allart also sidesteps genially and gracefully into another autobiographical role—that of the older, wiser mentor, Madame de Saman, who stands back and watches Clémence's personal tribulations with a sage, perceptive eye, then comforts and advises the more tempestuous younger woman.

Before the characters and plot are introduced in *Clémence,* the work begins in the form of a short, philosophical essay. The author asserts that God has given women unique characteristics, but also that He sometimes wishes that they exhibit a male mind and fill traditionally male roles, particularly in government. She notes that Plato supports this idea as well. "Dieu, qui a marqué la femme de caractères si propres à elle seule, a voulu qu'elle eût parfois un esprit d'homme. De là de nouvelles vues. Dieu destina-t-il quelques femmes au Governement, comme il y a destiné quelques hommes? Platon le croit. "[14]

Continuing in first person, the narrator states that her heroine will be depicted in the bloom of her beauty and youthful passions, yet with a mind that is *virile* (an adjective that nearly always refers to *male* prowess of one kind or another). "Occupé toujours du sort de la femme, je voudrais la peindre dans sa beauté, ses passions, sa jeunesse et sa liberté. J'en voudrais peindre avec l'esprit *viril.* Je vais montrer *une femme avec l'esprit, l'ambition d'un homme,* agité par la politique" (*Clém.* 1, my italics).

Protesting against a society that allows a woman to approach the world only through a husband—"une jeune fille ne peut aborder le monde que par un mari . . . "(*Clém.* 2)—Allart introduces Clémence, the heiress of a noble family, who possesses both "un cœur trop tendre and a noble ambition" (*Clém.* 2). The first half of the story poses the intriguing questions: Is it possible for a man and a woman to form a purely *intellectual* friendship? If so, must this friendship necessarily preclude love and passion between them? On the other side of the spectrum, is passion alone sufficient for a couple in love, or will one or the other of them regret the lack of intellectual stimulation that generally is absent from an ardent union?

The heroine's ensuing cerebral, though emotionally charged, relationship with Adrien Arlington, a married Scotsman, treats this dilemma in the first 17 pages. The focus then turns to more sentimental relationships that Clémence forms with two other men. Although she will end up marrying a young man who "sees into her soul" rather than the one who "sees into her mind," the establishment of her character as independent and insistent upon sincere love and quality treatment in marriage carves a bold niche in women's literature of its time.

Allart describes Clémence's dark, delicate Persian-type beauty and charming demeanor—"[Elle] était brune et belle, d'une taille élégante et d'un air distingué. Son front et ses yeux étaient très beaux et son sourire très fin et très doux; ses minces sourcils noirs étaient dignes de la Perse, mais son visage avait tant de charme et d'expression qu'on la trouvait jolie avant de la trouver belle" (*Clém.* 2)—and her turbulent Romantic soul. Since Clémence stands to inherit a fortune of her own and does not need a husband to provide her with financial security, she gives vent to her fairy tale-like dreams of a heady romance and eventual marriage to a man of her choosing whom she will love deliriously. She shares such thoughts with her friend Madame d'Etiny, wife of her former tutor. Although the friend has seven children and seems a bit jaded with marriage and motherhood, she still encourages and draws vicarious pleasure from Clémence's chivalric fantasies:

> Mais loin de modérer les vagues rêves et les espérances encore plus vagues de Clémence, elle s'en amusait, et au lieu d'opposer à cette jeune fille les principes ordinaires d'une vie heureuse et réglée, elle se laissait elle-même entraîner au séduisant pays des chimères . . . elle aimait d'entendre Clémence s'égarer aux palais des Rois, aux amours ambitieux des cours, à des folies parfois coupables, à des guerres et des conquêtes injustes (*Clém.* 2).

Clémence and the d'Etiny family winter in Paris, but spend spring and summer at an ancient abbey eight miles from the city. Allart indulges in Staelian-style descriptions of the area—a recreation of the abbey of Val where Hortense spent her young adult years near the Countess Regnault de Saint-Angély, the widow of her late father's friend and the "Laure" of *Les Enchantements de Prudence.*

> La contrée était boisée dans une grande étendue, et aux alentours on voyait d'autres châteaux et de grandes fermes. La fraîcheur de ces grands bois produisait une multitude de sources, le pays était charmant l'été et embaumé du sauvage parfum des forêts. Madame d'Etiny et Clémence aiment vivement cette campagne des Gaules, ombragée, humide et silencieuse (*Clem.* 2-3).

Clémence, however, is as seriously intellectual as she is passionately romantic. Madame d'Etiny introduces her to Arlington, who has left his wife and daughters behind in Scotland and brought his eight-year-old son to France to try to cure the boy of an ailment. Clémence's first conversation with the visitor focuses on the historical and the political as she speaks enthusiastically about Catherine II, whose reign as founder of Russia's greatest period, proves that certain women are naturally born to leadership. A startled Arlington realizes that Clémence is more occupied with action and glory than with the beauties of the country spring. "Mais, dit-il, en pressant amicalement le bras de Clémence qu'il tenait sous le sien, vous n'êtes pas si faible, vous ne pensez qu'à l'action, à la gloire, ce n'est pas vous que le printemps occupe" (*Clém.* 5). As their intellectual exchanges continue, the visitor realizes he is developing a friendship with an extraordinary kind of woman. "C'est ici *un esprit mâle,* dit-il en riant, qui modère vos enchantement de jeune fille." In all modesty, she agrees—"Clémence pensait qu'en plaisantant il disait vrai" (*Clem.* 5, my italics)—while she credits his eloquence and intelligence for helping her comprehend more about current politics, including the recently established July Monarchy.

Arlington contrasts Clémence with his Scottish wife, who is religious, timid, deferential, and never joins in conversations with her husband and his friends. Clémence asks why he did not try to cultivate his wife's mind. He says that he tried to do so, but she wished only to discuss the Bible. Convinced that Arlington does not love his spouse, Clémence begins to wish he were free—"S'il était libre!" However, she suspects that his erudite mind would not compensate for his lack of tender sensibility. "Hé bien! il ne me convenait pas du tout. Son esprit m'éclaire, me ravit, mais il n'a nulle sensibilité, nulle intelligence même des choses de la sensibilité. C'est un homme extraordinaire, d'une élévation de tête prodigieuse et d'une pauvreté de cœur inouïe. S'il avait autant d'âme qu'il a d'esprit! (*Clém.* 7).

Nevertheless, the two still enjoy their political conversations, and she admires his progressive attitude towards humanity and his perception of future social development. "Je l'espère, l'avenir verra des choses dont nous n'avons encore que le rêve" (*Clém.* 9). She even begins to believe that this kind of relationship is more rewarding than love would be. "Clémence pensa que l'amour serait peu de chose auprès de ces spéculations." Adrien promises to return to France after a brief stay back in Scotland, and continue their intellectual friendship. "Et puis je reviendrai pour vous, ne voulez-vous pas contracter avec moi une de ces amitiés intellectuelles, fondées sur des études pareilles et telles que les stoïciens les estimaient?. . . . Pourquoi pas? Croyez-vous qu'une amitié sacrée ne puisse exister entre homme et femmes?" (*Clém.* 9).

Clémence, however, is skeptical as to whether love and friendship between men and women really can coexist. She vaguely remembers a quote from the 17th-century philosopher LaBruyère, who said, "Celui qui a eu l'expérience d'un grand amour néglige l'amitié; et celui qui est épuisé sur l'amitié n'a encore rien fait pour l'amour" (*Clém.* 10). Predictably, the two become more and more attracted to one another, but fight against the passion, fearing it will ruin their intellectual rapport. Clémence wishes passion could take a backseat to the typical physical pull that arises between men and women, and that they could establish more *equality* between them. "Pour un jour, il faut que l'homme et la femme aussi soient rendus à des impressions moins exaltées, plus égales, qui font la solidité, la durée de la famille et du monde" (*Clém.* 12).

She departs for a week to spend time with her friend, the energetic 50-year-old Madame de Saman. In her description of the middle-aged woman, one sees Allart's conflicting views about her own status as an aging scholar who, on the one had, is grateful to have youth and passion behind her, and on the other hand, regrets the ever speedier passage of time:

> Madame de Saman connaissait ce chagrin, ce poids de la jeunesse. Elle se félicitait tous les jours d'avoir cinquante ans, d'être libre de ces brûlants soucis; elle eût voulu seulement pouvoir aujourd'hui arrêter le temps, mais le temps volait toujours, et ce bel âge de cinquante ans passerait aussi (*Clém.* 13).

The older woman assures her young friend that Adrien is wrong for her, not only because he is married, but also because he is too austere. Besides, she is hoping to interest Clémence in her nephew, Jacques. The matchmaking fails, but Clémence does become interested in Jacques' cousin, whose name Allart has used before—Remi. "Mais Remi avait reçu du ciel ce charme inconcevable qui domine partout où il paraît. Et tel était le seul rival qui pût paraître après Adrien" (*Clém.* 17). Remi awakens in her the tender and sensitive impressions that were missing with Adrien. "Oh! que Remi était doux! qu'il était aimable! comme il s'abandonnait! comme il riait! comme il semblait heureux! Heureux de la revoir . . . Quelle noble et sainte tristesse." Still, she misses the Scotsman's power of thought. "Pourquoi pensa-t-elle à Adrien? Remi éveilla dans son cœur mille impressions sensibles et tendres. Adrien ne l'avait pas fait ainsi, mais Adrien revit dans sa mémoire ceint d'un diadème, celui de la pensée" (*Clém.* 17).

Clémence begins to see how she and Remi are traveling on the same kind of path, and that he and Clémence can support one another in their goals to be active rather than passive members of the upper class. "Je veux prendre part aux affaires de mon temps, " Remi telles her. "Je veux être de la noblesse qui se rallie, non de celle qui retire." In a bold statement that illustrates Allart's beliefs that men and women should stand side-by-side in the achievement of professional as well as personal goals, the author says through Remi:

> Une jeune fille seule m'a dévoilé un monde de délices, d'espérances, de noble ambitions. Ses goûts, ses idées m'ont paru pareils aux miens; elle a la grâce et l'agrément et montre que l'esprit et l'ambition peuvent se joindre à l'amabilité. Je l'aimerais si elle voulait, comme l'ambition même, comme mon avenir, et j'ai l'énergie et la passion pour la mériter (*Clém.* 20).

The two of them feel the love and rapport between them, although they do not yet speak of it. This time, there is no nagging doubt as to the compatibility of their intellectual rapport and their ability to sustain sentimental love for one another. "La passion était autour d'eux sous ces ombrages, sa magie enchantait leurs regards, leurs discours, mais ils n'auraient osé encore s'expliquer mieux" (*Clém.* 20). Madame de Saman continues to push Clémence towards a relationship with her other nephew, Jacques, and Remi's father tries to arrange a marriage between his son and another woman, Aurélie. However, the situation seems to be resolving itself neatly as Jacques and Aurélie turn towards each other, leaving Clémence and Remi free to pursue their relationship. "Ils s'aimaient déjà passionnément; ils étaient liés pour la vie avant de s'être rien promis" (*Clém.* 24).

While Madame de Saman tries to pave the way for the two to marry, her brother-in-law, Remi's father, becomes furious with his son for scorning his planned match between Remi and Aurélie. The father decides he will ask Clémence to marry *him,* thereby getting revenge on Remi, whom he hopes will then depart for America, and perhaps the birth of a second son who will become his heir.

More intrigues follow as the father and son both vie for the heroine's affections, but the action culminates in a secret night of passion between Clémence and Remi. The elder M. de Saman realizes that a young woman of Clémence's independent nature really would not be right for him at all. "J'irais retrouver une épouse, non pas de mon âge et timide et soumise comment était la mienne, mais une jeune fille charmante, dont l'esprit indépendant ferait mon tourment" (*Clém.* 25).

Eventually, he vows to be only her *vieux chevalier* (*Clém.* 29), and asks Madame de Saman for Clémence's hand for his son in marriage. He, also, has come to realize that Clémence and Remi have a natural compatibility and will sustain each in other in fulfilling their noble goals.   "Mon fils est ambitieux. Cette femme sent le rôle qui reste à la noblesse; elle est noble par sa naissance. Elle saura à la fois guider et retenir Remi, le présever des périls des affaires publiques et de Paris" (*Clém.* 31).

The wedding date is set, and Madame de Saman, concluding the narration in first person, credits Clémence not only for being the ideal wife for Remi, but also for her influence in softening the hard heart of an old man.

Rabine observes accurately that with the creation of Remi, Allart has turned the tables on traditional Romanticism, and fashioned a male character who is "simply the charming extension and complement of her charming heroine" (204).   The character of Remi does seem a little too perfect and too timely.   His presence, from the moment he is introduced, is so entirely good and right for the heroine that he eclipses almost immediately Clémence's former love interest, Adrien, who would have been an impossible partner anyway, and who completely disappears only halfway through the novella. The addition of the love triangle between Clémence, Remi, and his father is almost a perfunctory device that conveniently kills time and gives a little requisite resistance to the two young lovers' process of leading up to the consummation of their love and the sealing of a lifelong commitment.

As was her technique in her earlier novels, especially *Gertrude, Sextus,* and *Settmia,* Allart has constructed a heroine and a scenario that virtually are bereft of guilt, bitterness, or other kinds of distressed attitudes about the crippling nature of the society in which they live. Clémence holds nicely at bay all of society's prejudices and limitations on women—even the gifted, aristocratic ones—as she and Madame de Saman smooth out the rough spots in the road toward successful young love.   The unique aspect of *Clémence* is the development of the character of the older woman "whose tolerant serenity spreads some sunshine over the young heroine's intense growing pains," and who "acts as a mediator between the young heroine and the stern representatives of Law, Custom and Society" (Rabine 204-205).

Clémence, Rabine continues, was Allart's "last attempt to solve the insoluble problems of love in fantasy before accepting the contradictions and transforming them into the charm of the *Enchantements*" (204).   A few years after the novella's publication,

Allart had completed the lengthy project of her own memoirs. The persona of Madame de Saman would recur not only as the pseudonym of the author of *Les Enchantements de Prudence,* but also would function as narrator and as benevolent overseer of and commentator on her own life—a life of calm and matter-of-fact defiance of society's restrictions on a true-life heroine's quest for personal fulfillment and romantic love.

Notes

[1]Marie-Jeanne Durry. *La Vieillesse de Chateaubriand, 1839-1848.* 2 vols. (Paris: Le Divan, 1933) 2:378 (n.1 from 1:507).

[2]Charles-Augustin Sainte-Beuve. *Chateaubriand et son Groupe Littéraire sous L'Empire,* Edition annotée par Maurice Allem, 2 vols. (Paris: Editions Garnier Frères, 1948) I: 320, author's italics. (Subsequent references to this work will appear in parentheses after the quotation and will be indicated by the abbreviation *Ch. et S.G.L.*)

[3]Apparently, Hortense was envisioning a twist on the American Mormons' practice at that time of polygyny—plural wives—and imagining for herself a scenario of polyandry—plural husbands. In such a case, had the timing been right (which it was not), it might have been impossible to tell whether Henri was fathered by Mazzéi or Bulwer.

[4]Although Decreus (125) quotes this letter from the Heydon Ms. in French, the original text, which was not available to me, was most likely written in English.

[5]"Lettere di Hortense Allart a George Sand," *Studi Francesi,* 6:3 (September-December 1958): 425.

[6]George Sand. *Histoire de Ma Vie* (Part 5, Chapter 7). *Œuvres Complètes de George Sand.* (Geneva: Slatkine Reprints, 1980) 14:302.

7George Sand. *Histoire de Ma Vie* (Part 5, Chapter 18). *Œuvres Complètes de George Sand.* (Geneva: Slatkine Reprints, 1980) 14:460, my italics.

[8]George Sand. *Souvenirs de 1848.* (Paris: Calmann Levy, no date). Reprinted in: [Genève: Slatkine Reprints, 1980 (same pagination as original)] 356. (Subsequent references to this work will appear in parentheses after the citation and will be indicated by the abbreviation *S. de 1848*).

[9]René de Chateaubriand. *Mémoires de l'outre-tombe,* quoted by Billy 222.

[10]Letter from the Collection Lovenjoul, D. 538, folio 174, quoted by Billy 224-25.

[11]Emile Henriot. *Portraits de Femmes.* (Paris: Editions Albin Michel, 1951) 238.

[12] Billy, "La Femme Qui A Aimé Sainte-Beuve," *La Revue de Paris.* 68 (janvier 1961): 28-29.

[13]These letters also are reprined in: Mme. P. De Saman. *Derniers Enchantements.* (Paris: Calmann Lévy, Editeur. Michel Lévy Frères, Editeurs, 1874) 349-423. This last letter appears on page 423. This letter is also quoted by Séché 315 and Billy 246-47.

[14]Madame Hortense de Méritens. *Clémence.* (Paris: Sceaux, 1865) 1. (Subsequent references to this work will appear in parentheses after the quotation and will be indicated by the abbreviation *Clém.*).

Chapter 9

Les Enchantements de Prudence and *Les Nouveaux Enchantements:* Looking Back with Delight (1865-1872)

With the publication of *Clémence,* Allart's fiction-writing career almost had come to an end. Only small samplings of short fictional works would appear for the first time in her subsequent *Les Nouveaux Enchantements* and *Derniers Enchantements.* These last two works mostly contain truncated and revised versions of her former novels, plus some polemical and philosophical writings, letters, poetry and prayers.

Allart's correspondence with her surviving friends would continue throughout the last 15 years of her life. Although she did not see Bulwer-Lytton during this time, their exchange of letters remained steady. In a personal letter to Henry dated Sept. 27, either 1864 or 1865, she chided her former lover 32 years in retrospect for what she still considered his overly avid devotion to Parliament and to his so-called duty as an Englishman that caused such a strain on their personal lives. "Je revois encore vos yeux, toujours errants, jamais fixés sur rien une minute, c'est le regard de l'anglais, de l'homme agité, qui fait la loi du blé, s'empare des Lords et du marché de Paris, et ne peut rester en repos; race de tourment et de dominations" (Heyton Ms., quoted by Decreus 47).

In her *Notes inédites* on Sept. 26, 1868, Hortense looked back on the influence of Sampayo and Bulwer as the great loves of her life and on how she had wished to recreate each of them in her novels. Her goal was to immortalize Sampayo in *Jérôme* as a hero of sentimentality and Henry in *L'Indienne* as a light-hearted, sweet and sensuous lover.

Ce que j'aurais voulu . . . c'est établir les deux caractères de Jérôme

et d'Henry, de façon qu'on les connût dans les lettres: l'un sublime, l'autre délicieux . . . . Quand on aurait dit *Jérôme,* on aurait dit un grand amour, un héros de la pensée et du sentiment. Quand on aurait dit Henry, on aurait nommé ce qu'il y a de plus aimable, de plus léger, de plus doux, de plus voluptueux (quoted by Séché 53, n. 1).

On his way back from a trip to Egypt in early 1865, Bulwer-Lytton fell ill in Athens. By August he had recovered, but he retired temporarily from diplomatic service and returned to England. His continuing ill health and the fact that he had become, in the words of his brother Edward, "thinner than a phantom," did not dampen his irrepressible ambition and youthful and energetic lust for life. Edward wrote to his son July 3, 1866, "Sir Henry est en Angleterre, plus mince qu'un fantôme, mais si débordant de vie, d'énergie et si tourmenté d'ambition qu'il est la plus belle incarnation de la jeunesse que j'ai vue depuis que j'ai quitté les bancs de l'école" (Heydon Ms., quoted in French translation by Decreus 147).

Henry's health rallied enough to permit him to run again for election in November 1868. He returned to a seat in Parliament as a liberal for Tamworth. (What a shame, says Decreus, that the letters that Hortense surely must have written him on this occasion no longer exist). He made one of his most famous speeches in the House of Commons on the situation of the Church of Ireland. In 1870, he published the first two volumes of his *The Life of Lord Palmeston* (the third would be published posthumously). On March 21, 1871, he received the title of the Baron of Wood and of Dalling. Still concerned with political questions regarding England and the Middle East, he made his last trip to Egypt later in 1871. On the way back, he became ill in Naples and died suddenly on May 23, 1872. *Les Enchantements de Prudence* was published in August of that year, but Bulwer never had the chance to read what would become Hortense's best-known and most enduring work, and to know the extensive role that he played in it.

In the same vein as Chateaubriand, Bulwer did not make much mention of Hortense in his written works. Her name appears only perfunctorily in his 1834 *France: Social, Literary and Political.* However, in *The Monarchy of the Middle Classes,* which was published in London two years later, he did pay a tribute to her writing talents—albeit under a pseudonym—placing her among the contemporary authors whom he thought best represented the Rousseau school. Although Bulwer gives Allart the moniker Madame de Thérèse (taken from a portion of her full name, Hortense-Thérèse-Sigismonde-Sophie-Alexandrine Allart), he names her second and third novels accurately, thus making her identity clear:

Mme de Staël et M. de Chateaubriand sont les seuls disciples populaires de l'école de Rousseau, bien que Mme de Thérèse ait donné dans *Jérôme* et *L'Indienne*, deux histoires touchantes et éloquentes qui méritent l'attention, ne serait-ce que pour la correction élégante de leur style, la fréquente profondeur de la pensée et l'absence de toute affectation de mauvais goût.[1]

The decades-long, often frenetic, mostly tender, and always sincere and caring friendship between Henry Bulwer-Lytton and Hortense Allart thus ended only with his death seven years before her own. Although each one of them at one time or another had projects and goals they allowed to take precedence over their relationship, their genuine concern for one another never wavered. The paths that their individual lives followed indicate, however, that neither the friendship nor the passion was ever meant to evolve into a legal and binding union. Hortense, with her dedication to her research and writing, and Henry with his career ambitions were not disposed to set aside their individual aims for the sake of commitment to one another. Even if she had not already had Marcus when she met Henry, Hortense never would have met with the approval of Henry's haughty and powerful mother nor fit into the artistocratic British milieu that was essential to the development of his chosen career.

Also, if the pair had tried a secret marriage, as they considered doing in 1835, each one most likely would have branched off into areas of interest that did not involve the other. They would have devastated one another with various infidelities, as they did even while they were the most enmeshed in each other's lives. "Mais le mariage n'eût pas eu raison de l'instabilité ni de l'inquiétude de ce grand nerveux," says Decreus of Henry. "Il eût trompé sa femme et elle lui eût rendu la pareille comme elle le fit étant sa maîtresse" (150).

The tenacious attempts, particularly on Hortense's part, to make their relationship lasting and tenable were doomed to incompatibility inevitable between two such dogged individualists. The frustrating discords, rifts, and reconciliations that were followed consistently only by more estrangements and resentments proved ultimately to be too stressful. Hortense finally let go of her physical hold on Henry, though never her emotional tenderness for him, simply because she could take the strain no longer. "Ses [Henry's] hésitations, ses tergiversations, ses retours sans cesse retardés, ses brusques départs, ses scènes de jealousie, ses infidélités la maintenaient dans un état de tension insoutenable," says Decreus. Hortense eventually reined in her remaining hopes for a permanent relationship, then, not only to

preserve her sense of self, but to protect her own peace of mind. "...
C'est-à-dire, parce qu'elle n'en pouvait plus" (Decreus 150).

In 1872, then, Henry was gone forever from her life, but the
palpable energy of his presence nevertheless surged through the work
that Allart finally published just months after his death. *Les
Enchantements de Prudence* was the result of a 15-year effort that she
had created with her usual dedication, enthusiasm, and sincerity. As
mentioned in Chapter 8, she had vacillated about ever publishing the
work partly because she feared that the material—particularly that about
Chateaubriand—might be considered too personal and indiscreet. The
breach of trust on the part of Sainte-Beuve in 1861, his subsequent
publishing of her Chateaubriand passages, and the skepticism that
resulted from them helped give Allart a certain impetus to publish her
memoirs herself to offer proof of their authenticity.

Most of the salient portions of *Les Enchantements de Prudence,*
including Allart's own comments on her life's events, portions from
Marpé, and her sociological outbursts about the dangers hidden within
the institution of marriage and inadequate government protection of
wives and families, already have been quoted or paraphrased in the
previous chapters of this book. Allart's autobiography is eclectic and
multi-faceted and, in many ways, a microcosm of her lifelong *œuvre*
in its straightforward and sensitive illustration of a 19th-century
Frenchwoman's dual search for ideal love and for self-actualization,
fulfillment, and a meaningful voice in her society.

The title itself testifies to her transcendent attitude about the
various loves of her life in that she can look back on each one during
her last decade and refer to them as "enchantments." It was Allart's
astonishing lack of rancor about any of the difficult moments of her life
or the less-than-ideal outcome of many of her adventures with romance
that would lead to the laudatory preface by George Sand in the book's
second printing.

Just as he calls Sainte-Beuve the godfather of *Les Enchantements
de Prudence,* Séché notes that Sand surely must be the godmother of
the work (21). Her praise of the book marked the culmination of a
friendship that had been developing for decades. Allart had sent a copy
of the first edition of *Les Enchantements* to Sand at Nohant. Upon
reading it, Sand wrote, at first chiding Hortense for being out of touch
for "centuries." "Où êtes-vous, astre errant? Vous sembliez fixée à
Montlhéry, mais votre livre annonce une fois de plus un tel amour de la
promenade que vous n'y êtes peut-être plus, et il y a des siècles que
vous ne m'avez écrit" (*Corres. de G. S.* 23:236).

Sand then focused on *Les Enchantements.* and the talent she
recognized in the writer. "Vous êtes une très grande femme. Voilà le

resumé de mon opinion" (*Corres. de G. S.* 23:236). She volunteered to review the book in *Le Temps,* the journal to which she already was a regular contributor, and asked if Hortense would prefer to be named in the review or to remain anonymous (under the name "Madame Prudence de Saman l'Esbatx"). Apparently, Hortense declined to be identified, for in Sand's enthusiastic review, which appeared in *Le Temps,* on Oct. 16, 1872, she states in the first paragraph, "Je devine bien pourquoi, mais je n'ai à juger que le livre, dont j'accepte et ne trahis point le pseudonyme."[2]

Sand agreed to let Hortense use this article as a preface to *Les Enchantements* in its second printing in 1873. In her review/preface, Sand, who was not known to have stayed on good terms with many of *her* former lovers, focuses largely on the book's testimony of Allart's lack of bitterness toward all the past men in her life and her uncommon gift of maintaining close ties and generous feelings toward each one. To paraphrase Sand's metaphor, Hortense never wished to extinguish any of the hearths she lighted.

> Elle ne veut pas éteindre les foyers qu'elle a allumés, elle les respecte et elle les entretient comme des autels, avec une coquetterie pieuse et charmante. Qu'on ne se scandalise pas! elle se défend et se réserve pour l'homme dont elle partage la passion, elle confie ce nouvel amour à ceux qui lui redemandent le passé, elle échappe aux périls des ces entrevues, tout en avouant qu'elle en a senti le charme et l'émotion (quoted by Séché 51).

Even those men whom she opted to leave for one reason or another retain her lifelong caring and respect. "Elle a pour principe de cœur qu'on ne cesse pas d'aimer ce qu'on a aimé, que ceux qu'elle a quittés par lassitude ou par crainte du joug étaient dignes de son éternelle tendresse, et elle laisse volontiers à ces amitiés le nom d'amour qui sied encore à leur délicatesse" (quoted by Séché 51). With this philosophy, Allart was able to preserve in her own life a portion of each one of her former lover's successes, as well as an ongoing sense of love and esteem that she felt for them and that they felt for her:

> Elle suit les travaux de ces esprits éminents, elle s'intéresse à leurs succès dans les lettres, dans la politique ou dans le monde, elle garde leur confiance intime qu'elle provoque par la sienne. Elle s'est emparée de leur estime, elle la conserve et un peu de leur amour lui revient encore, par chaudes bouffées, bien qu'elle n'y prétende plus (quoted by Séché 51).

Sand sees in such a singular attitude a recreation of the more esoteric love relationships of the 18th century without the libertine influence of the 19th century. "Il y a dans tout cela une facilité de relations qui rappelle les amours philosophiques du siècle dernier, moins ce qui les gâtait, la galanterie libertine" (quoted by Séché 51.) She also praises Allart's unusual spiritual sentiments that include dimensions beyond the bounds of Christianity. "J'ai beaucoup de sympathie pour cette âme fervente, qui n'est point exclusivement chrétienne, et qui entre tranquillement dans les temples de son temps et de son pays, sans renoncer à sa personalité, à ses sentiments et à ses idées" (quoted by Séché 24).

She concludes by defending Allart's courageous and individualist lifestyle that was depicted honestly and unapologetically in the book, and by dressing down the religious and monarchist press that were treating *Les Enchantements de Prudence* as a scandal.

> Quant au grand combat de la vie livré par elle et terminé si bravement, choque-t-il la raison, le droit personnel, qui est de se sacrifier à une croyance ferme et raisonnée? Non, assurément. Choque-t-il la morale? Dans cette situation particulière et avec ce fonds de grande loyauté et de parfaite tolérance qui caractérise madame de Saman, nul n'est autorisé à lui jeter la pierre . . . (quoted by Séché 24).

As for herself, Sand felt like wreathing Hortense with a crown of roses and oak leaf clusters. ". . . et pour mon compte, tout en faisant, en théorie, certaines réserves que je n'ai point à dire ici, je lui jette une couronne de roses à feuilles de chêne" (quoted by Séché 24).

Not all the responses to *Les Enchantements de Prudence,* however, were so positive.   The description of Hortense's relationship with Chateaubriand ignited wrathful reactions from critics who were scandalized at the idea of a woman describing a literary master in what they considered a vulger and disrespectful manner.   As Sainte-Beuve had remarked to Allart years earlier, her writings showed an entirely different side of Chateaubriand—a Chateaubriand who was hers alone and a Chateaubriand who ought to be revealed to others (See Chapter 8). Her descriptions of the Enchanter presented a dimension of him that departed somewhat from the long-accepted portrait of him as distinguished author and defender of the Christian faith.   Two critics in particular, Barbey d'Aurevilly and Armand de Pontmartin, seethed at the appearance of a book that added new splashes of color to that image.

D'Aurevilly's 1878 *Les Bas-Bleus* contains 26 chapters on various women writers of the day, including Allart, Madame de Staël, George

Sand, Daniel Stern, Louise Colet and Sophie Gay. The term "blue stocking," which tends to be pejorative under any circumstances, becomes a veritable vilification under the pen of d'Aurevilly. In Chapter 16, entitled "M** de Saman" (the entire section refers to Allart only by this *nom de plume,* although d'Aurevilly mentions several of her works by their proper titles), he launches a venemous, two-fold attack, first of all, on women who, as he sees it, posture as intellectuals, and secondly, on this specific woman who indiscreetly flaunts her past with an eminent male author.

With an audacious misogyny that would seem almost inconceivable from a late 20th-century point of view, d'Aurevilly makes a barrage of statements meant to slap women intellectuals back down into what he believes should be their place: Women may do what they like, but ought to have the decency to keep quiet about it. If they must speak, they would be better off acting like hypocrites and paying homage to a virtue that they do not possess. These "Rousseau women" have no shame about revealing their secrets to the public at the expense of their husbands and children. Such women fancy themselves as men, and are envious of men. They put on, as one would put on a bonnet, their vices with their knowledge.[3] D'Aurevilly questions whether he can review *Les Enchantements de Prudence* decently because of Allart's "revolting sincerity" in divulging the bold details of her private life:

> Quelle plus flagrante violation du respect que l'on doit à la vie privée qu'elle vient d'accomplir sur la sienne et avec quels détails plus hardis!—Et si hardis même que la Critique, obligée d'être plus pudique que la femme qui s'est faite, sans peur et sans honte *l'historienne* de tous les amours de sa vie, ne sait comment s'y prendre pour décemment y toucher (*Les B.-B.* 203, author's italics).

He never denies that what Allart wrote about Chateaubriand is true, but he is insensed that she would ever bring these events to light, suggesting that Madame de Saman ought to have died in the "nobility of silence" rather than to have revealed such information. "Elle pouvait mourir du moins dans la noblesse du silence, sans remuer ce fumier de fleurs. Elle ne l'a pas voulu, C'est triste . . . . Le voici donc, ce livre . . . Selon moi, il est épouvantable." The book is horrible, he continues, because it shows the frightening direction that modern women are taking in a world of changing morals. ". . . ce que les femmes de l'ancienne société française sont en train de devenir dans la transformation actuelle de nos mœurs, et, ma parole d'honneur, c'est à faire trembler!" (*Les B.-B.* 204).

He is equally unimpressed with Sand's preface to *Les Enchantements de Prudence,* calling her "la reine indiscutée du bas-bleuisme contemporain [qui] a voulu faire le bonheur d'un de ses sujettes" (*Les B.-B.* 207).   He also does not think much of Sainte-Beuve for having been the first to publish the material about Allart and Chateaubriand.   "Sainte-Beuve, qui aimait à conduire ces eaux corrompues dans les détours sinueux des coteaux modérés de sa littérature, en avait filtré quelques gouttes dans son livre sur Chateaubriand" (*Les B.-B.* 209).

D'Aurevilly's ire is the most vehemently kindled against Allart herself.   He insults her at every turn, from denouncing the liberal, Voltairian education that her father gave her to disparaging her avowed affair with a young prelate priest (which Sampayo, in reality, was not), to sniffing at her involvement with an English parliamentarian.   He is the most outraged, though, over her termerity at "soiling" the memory of the author of *Le Génie du christianisme*   by writing of him as though her were an ordinary notch on her belt of male *gallants.*

> N'est-ce pas là quelque chose d'ignoble et d'affreux dont la mémoire du grand poète religieux en prose restera éternellement souillée, et que tous les efforts futurs de la critique et de l'histoire, qui l'essuieront, ne pourront effacer? Ceci restera, et c'est le crime du livre d'aujourd'hui . . . . Hélas! il est évident qu'une femme ne peut pas avoir beaucoup de respect pour un homme quand elle l'a vu dans de certaines attitudes (*Les. B.B.* 209-10).

He refers specifically to Hortense's descriptions of Chateaubriand's "lovely teeth" and pleasant, amusing demeanor, which she should have kept to herself instead of publicizing at the expense of his dignity. "Elle aurait gardé sans le donner à risée ou à mépris sérieux, le souvenir touchant de ce fou à elle et fait par elle" (*Les B.-B.*   210).   He accuses Allart of exploiting Chateubriand for the sake of bragging that she was once his:

> . . . la question n'est ni l'honneur de Chateaubriand, ni leur propre honneur de cœur. La question est l'exploitation d'un nom illustre, dans l'intérêt d'un dernier scandale, avant de mourir tout à fait . . . . Mais Chateaubriand!   Chataubriand ayant pour table d'amphithéâtre le lit encore chaud d'une maîtresse qui l'y dissèque par volupté de ressouvenir et d'orgueil d'avoir été à lui! . . . . Mais que je plains sincèrement, mon Dieu, les maris, les fils ou les filles de femmes (si elles en ont) qui écrivent de ces livres-là! (*Les. B.B.* 210-11).

Not content merely to trounce the parts of Allart's autobiography that deal with Chateaubriand and her other lovers, D'Aurevilly also belittles the religious poems and prayers found at the end of the book, which he calls "la négation de Dieu,—l'insulte à Jésus-Christ,—des prières hystériques au Dieu-Nature,—et par dessus-tout: le Saint Sacrement de l'amour!" (*Les B.-B.* 210-11).

D'Aurevilly's reaction to the so-called scandal of *Les Enchantement de Prudence* soon caused another brouhaha in and of itself as Marcus Allart rose indignantly and violently to the defense of his mother's work. At this point, Marcus was a 52-year-old opinionated journalist who had written a number of pro-Bonapartist articles for various publications. D'Aurevilly's diatribe had hurt both Hortense and Marcus deeply.

The son (it is not known whether he acted under his mother's sanction or not) fired off an insulting and threatening letter to the author of *Les Bas-Bleus* and challenged him to bring witnesses and participate in a pistol duel. To refuse such a dangerous (and illegal) provocation, d'Aurevilly easily could have fallen back on the excuse of his age (he was 64) or his orthodox religious beliefs, but he chose to write back, claiming he had done nothing to insult Marcus. A letter from the critic to Marcus through the Vicount Saint-Sauveur is preserved in the Barbey d'Aurevilly Museum and quoted by Billy. "M. Barbey d'Aurevilly n'a point à recevoir les trois témoins (pourquoi pas douze?) de M. Allart, qui n'ont pas donné leurs noms. Il n'a nulle réparation à faire à M. Allart, ni par les armes, ni autrement. Il n'a jamais vu M. Allart. . . . Il n'a jamais provoqué M. Allart . . . . " (Billy 257-58).

Marcus was not mollified. Perhaps d'Aurevilly had not insulted him personally, but he had insulted his mother. Rather than appearing at the door of the critic's home, he stormed into the office of the *Constitutionnel,* which originally published the article on Hortense's book, and began to hit the first editor he saw, a man named Matagrin. The editor did not challenge Marcus to a duel, but he did press charges. For his chivalrous, if precipitous and obstreperous attack on Matagrin, Marcus was sentenced to a month in prison and ordered to pay 100 francs in damages.

As unpleasant as this incident was, it did have the effect of attracting some positive responses to *Les Enchantements de Prudence* from people who found the book more worthy of praise than disgust. Jules Troubat, a former secretary of Sainte-Beuve, wrote that the book did honor to Chateaubriand rather than harm. After all, what detriment was there in showing the great author involved with a pretty woman who loved and admired him?   Troubat believed that the worst scenario wrought by Allart's book was that it showed a Chateaubriand whose halo had slipped a little from his head:

> Ce qu'elle a dit de Chateaubriand, et même ce qu'elle rencontait sous le manteau fait le plus grand honneur à l'auteur du *Génie du christianisme*. Elle le dépeint en familier, dans l'intimité, tel que doit être tout grand homme en tête-à-tête avec une aimable et jolie femme qui le comprend, qui l'aime, qui l'admire, mais auprès de laquelle il ne garde pas son auréole sur la tête.   Ce serait gênant pour la causerie (quoted by Billy 258-59).

The insults continued as well.   In a review published a few months after d'Aurevilly's *Les Bas Bleus,* Armand de Pontmartin castigated Allart, refusing to accept her portrait of Chateaubriand as an addition to the preconceived image he had of an infallible, unsullied Romantic poet. Like d'Aurevilly, however, Pontmartin did not dispute that what she wrote was true.   Also as did d'Aurevilly, he accused Hortense of being an audacious hoyden who published this work only because wished to brag about her relationship with a famous writer. "Songez donc! Chateaubriand! Quelle aubaine pour une fille d'Eve, blindée d'une libre-penseuse . . . . Il n'est pas impossible qu'un femme-auteur, belle, féconde en romans . . . hostile au catholicisme, au clergé et aux jésuites, se soit vantée des faveurs de Chateaubriand. . . " (quoted by Billy 259).

Séché questions why such respected critics as d'Aurevilly and Pontmartin did not have a broader appreciation of the complexity of Chateaubriand's artistic nature.   He suggests that, as scandalized as the two were about René's relationship with Hortense, they were even more disgruntled about her description of how Chateaubriand wooed a poet (Béranger) to write about him (see Chapter 3). Because the friendship between the two men was set in motion by Hortense, the critics blamed her all the more for her role in a relationship of which they did not approve.   "Et comme cette alliance de l'écrivian royaliste et catholique avec le chansonnier républicain et voltairien avait été cimentée par l'amour d'une femme, il est tout naturel que cette femme ait en sa large part de leurs réprobations" (Séché 15).

The negative reactions to *Les Enchantements de Prudence,* however, pale in the face of its popular success.   The book was still selling well in its third edition, which appeared in 1873.   One of the first of Hortense's friends to come to her defense after the d'Aurevilly and Pontmartin criticisms was her former lover Gino Capponi, who had been a member of the constitutional assembly of Tuscany, and a senator of the kingdom of Italy.   He was by now elderly and blind, but this did not prevent him from continued reading and writing (presumably, through oral readers and scribes).   He published his own version of the history of Florence in 1875, one year before his death.

From Florence, Capponi wrote to Hortense that he had put aside Marcus Allart's book, *Nos frontières, morales et politique, Dieu et Patrie*[4] to read the copy of *Les Enchantements de Prudence* that she had sent him.   He witnessed to the truthfulness of the material, and praised the book as a testament to the author's ongoing talent.

> Pour vous, on doit vous estimer plus hautement après ce livre qui pourtant est vrai, très vrai, comme un livre doit l'être. Il est très bien composé, le style en est soigné, enfin c'est vous entière. Saint Augustin commence son livre par une prière, vous avez fini le vôtre par des prières qui sont très belles; cela aussi a son mérite (quoted by Séché 30).

Hippolyte Passy, a friend since the days when they both frequented the adored "Laure" at Vallon, wrote to Hortense, admitting how he reveled in the nostalgia of the Romanticism that he read in *Les Enchantements de Prudence,* and how it reminded him of a world that was now fading away.

> Vous m'avez ramené à des temps bien éloignés de nous maintenant; de nombreux souvenirs, parmi lesquels il en est de tristes, se sont réveillées en moi, et j'ai vu revivre une société dont il ne reste aujourd'hui que de rare débris dispersés dans un monde qui n'est plus celui au milieu duquel nous avons passé notre jeunesse au temps d'aimer (quoted by Séché 30).

Passy also praised the very candor of the author that d'Aurevilly and Pontmartin had attacked.

> . . . Vous êtes, je crois, la première femme, qui se soit confessée aussi franchement au public; ce que vous aviez éprouvé, pensé et fait, vous le racontez dans un style alerte et ferme qui en dit plus qu'il ne semble vouloir en dire, et qui vous montre de la tête aux pieds. Vous prêtez à une étude psychologique à la foi curieuse et instructive, et c'est un mérite réel (quoted by Séché 30).

He also recognized her uniqueness among other woman writers. "Vous êtes femme, cependant vous n'êtes pas *la femme,* car il y a en

vous une originalité qui vous est propre et qui vous sépare de la multitude des filles d'Eve, notre grand-mère à tous" (quoted by Séché 30, my italics).

Hippolyte's elder brother, Antoine, also admired the *Les Enchantements de Prudence* for its indication of how Allart always sought the kind of love that was a combination of sentimentality and an intellectual meeting of two minds. He noted how her marriage was an inexplicable deviation from this consistent desire.

> Vous avez peint très librement et d'une façon touchante cette disposition à vouloir être séduite par une forte intelligence, pour finir par la satisfaction des sens, qui n'ont été pour vous que l'accessoire de la passion, est-ce vrai? . . . . Vous êtes arriveé à l'amour par le contact des deux intelligences. Le mariage a été une désertion de votre vie antérieure (quoted by Séché 31).

Antoine also was amused by the pages about Chateaubriand. He found the description of a literary, religious and political icon kissing her young feet to be nothing short of delightful. "Vos révélations sur Chateaubriand m'ont amusé; cette grande figure littéraire, religieuse et politique baisant vos pieds, est un tableau ravissant" (quoted by Séché 31).

There still was no greater tribute paid to *Les Enchantements de Prudence,* however, than Sand's hearty and heart-felt preface, which marked not only the zenith of their friendship but also their professional rapport as modern, free-thinking intellectuals with a sense of history, philosophy and the Romantic spirit.   Sand's preface should be read and reread, says Billy, as a key document in understanding Allart and her strengths and gifts as an author. Sand recognized her friend's 18th-century ties; that is, her tendency to associate intelligence with sentiment. She also noted that the kind of love Hortense practiced in her life was the embodiment of the Romantic spirit of 1830.   She credits Allart with recognizing and expressing the spirit of Romanticism before its more systemized onslaught in 1830.   "Mme de Saman en est un spécimen et y jette une vive lumière. On était romantique sans le dire, sans le savoir, sans cesser d'être classique par beaucoup d'endroits" (quoted by Billy 260).

Les Enchantements de Prudence indicates from its first few pages the combination of 18th- and 19th-century sensibilities in the earliest stirrings of self-awareness in Allart's alter-ego. Prudence possesses this sentient combination of intellectual strivings with deep-seated personal feelings as she begins her life's quest under the emotional tutelage of the lovely and emotive Laure. "Le monde commençait à

m'apparaître et à me séduire, pourtant, dans son [Laure's] agrément d'esprit," Prudence relates in the early pages of the book. ". . . . J'étais dès lors ambiteuse, aventureuse, agréable, et ainsi en danger. *Je n'aurais pas voulu une vie obscure.* J'aimais les lettres et j'y mettais mes espérances. La vie, le monde, loin de m'inquitéter m'attiraient vivement. Je m'élançais avec transport vers l'avenir" (*EP* 12, my italics).

More than any other sampling from her autobiography, this lovely passage embodies the complex and extraordinary philosophy upon which Hortense seized at age 20 and developed to fruition over the next 50 years. In her determination not to have, as she stated, an obscure life, she indeed placed her fondest hopes in *belles lettres.* She combined her goals of ambition, adventure, and optimism with awareness, but no fear of the possible dangers that such desires might throw into the path of a 19th-century Frenchwoman.

Les Enchantements de Prudence concludes with Allart's personal prayers (277-87) that include odes to the seasons, the woods, and supplications for the betterment of mankind. The final prayer reflects her lifelong and eternal vision for a fraternal and moral *rapprochement* between the sexes. She addresses God, "Vous voulez que la femme et l'homme s'unissent dans un mutuel ravissement. Plus tard, dégagés de ces chaînes, nous venons à vous, nous vous trouvons dans nous-mêmes, dans ce cœur tranquille et rassuré qui ne conçoit plus d'affection ni d'études en dehors de vous" (*EP* 287).

Even Hortense's profoundly mystic Christianity, which bordered on the pantheistic, never would diminish her concern for the earthly human condition and her belief in men and women's equality, which she saw as a spiritual as well as a sociological given. "Inspirez encore à notre recueillement, des prières non pas dignes d'être portées à vos pieds, mais capable du moins d'entretenir nos âmes dans les saintes pensées réservées pour la fin!" (*EP* 287).

A few months after the third edition of *Les Enchantements de Prudence* appeared, Allart published *Les Nouveaux Enchantements* (1873) under the name Madame P. de Saman. The collection contains a number of reprinted and retooled works—excerpts from *Jérôme ou le jeune prélat, Sextus ou le Romain des Maremmes,* and *L'Indienne,* and earlier essays that she had written on the political scene in England during her months there. Other pieces include her opinions on Pitt and Burke, and essays entitled "Aperçus sur la Chine," "Les Indes," "Harmonies de la nature, de Bernardin de Saint-Pierre," and "Diogène," and others, all of which indicate her ongoing awareness of inequalities in the human condition and her pleas for greater liberties for mankind. Other essays pay tribute to her friend Madame Hamelin and to the poetry of Chateaubriand.

The short fictional works that appear for the first time in *Les Nouveaux Enchantements* include *Le Duc Antonio des Algarves, La baronne de Marcoussis, Sébastien de Gama,* and *Myrtéa.*

The first of these is little more than a political essay in the form of a dialogue between a young couple in 1847 France, who, before they decide if they are compatible enough to marry, engage in a long discussion of the political climate of the day.   The heroine's name is taken from another of Allart's recent characters as well as from her current place of residence. Thus, the heroine becomes the Duchess Clémence de Montlhéry.   When the story opens, the Duchess Monthléry and the Duke Antonio des Algarves have loved one another for two years, but the widowed duchess hestitates to accept the duke's proposal of marriage.

On a recent trip to Italy together, she is disillusioned with Antonio's jealous and tyrannical conduct toward her. She fears that, as a husband, he would be too much like her late spouse, a kind, but possessive older man who kept her cloistered in his château while he talked about the dignity of his life.   She now seeks a life of more lively involvement.   "Vous êtes tout jeune, mais vous n'en êtes que plus jaloux," she tells the duke.   "J'aime le monde et la politique. Souvenez-vous de votre tyrannie en Italie."[5]

Clémence admires a Protestant politician named Lindor, whom the duke insists in on a losing course.   Nevertheless, she stays firm in her loyalties to the idea of an oligarchic government, her aversion to orthodox Catholicism and her hatred of democracy. When the Republic is proclaimed in 1848, Clémence agrees to marry the duke, suggesting that they stay aloof from politics, and, in Voltairian tradition, cultivate their own gardens. "Célébrons ce mariage que vous m'avez proposé depuis si longtemps, cultivons nos champs, jouissons de la vie domestique" (*NE* 126).

They marry, the Second Empire is proclaimed, and years of happy union ensue for the spouses, enlivened by their continued correspondence and comments on the events of the day—Napoleon III's incursion into Mexico, the Franco-Prussian war, and opinions on the naiveté and ignorance of the United States of America.   "Chez les moderns on cite les États-Unis, mais c'est un État qui commence, composé de marchands et de sauvages déjà divisés, et qui ne peuvent servir en rien de modèles, puisqu'ils ignorent tout" (*NE* 135). (It is tempting for Allart scholars on the other side of the Atlantic to wish that Hortense had paid at least a short visit to the United States, and to speculate on whether such a trip might have tempered her prejudice against our country's government.   As it was, her opinions never were mitigated, even in her advanced years).

Clémence and Antonio thus pass their years in spirited discourse on the political climates that characterized their lifetimes. "Ils passèrent leur vie à discourir ainsi" (*NE* 137).

La Baronne de Marcoussis, the next short fictional work in *Les Nouveaux Enchantements,* is an even shorter essay that pays tribute to happy family life in the countryside. The story introduces another young, widowed noblewoman, the Baroness Louise de Marcoussis, and her paramour, the County Amable de Montlhéry, both of whom believe that government should be in the hands of an intellectual elite. The loving, though imperious, count hestitates to propose marriage to the baroness, fearing he may produce children with blood less blue than his own. He would prefer a life of solitude, seeking a way to improve the flagging sophistication of French society.

> J'ai en horreur de notre société du moment. Je pense, comme vous, madame, qu'une aristocratie naturelle pourrait seule conduire la société, mais quand cette idée se réalisera-t-elle? Jamais peut-être. Je veux vivre seul avec quelques amis. Je ne veux jamais me marier. Jamais je ne veux donner l'existence à une famille . . . . J'étudierai les moyens de servir la société, de la sauver, je donnerai mes idées dans des écrits si j'en ai le talent (*NE* 177).

The baroness chides him for his intention to sacrifice himself so radically for his political scruples. "La politique n'est pas une chimère, mais elle n'est pas toute, et vous vous sacrifiez en tout" (*NE* 179). He leaves in a huff, but, after a short time away from the baroness, realizes that his future children could serve society just as honorably as governmental ministers and deputies as they could as artistocrats. The two marry and have four sons and four daughters whom they raise as Protestants in the Bourbon countryside.

The count helps people who have been financially ruined in Parisian economic affairs by renting them portions of his own lands. His happiness and service to others inspires many of his other friends in Paris to leave the city and seek felicity near his own bucolic setting.

Sébastien de Gama, the story of a young Portuguese scholar who woos the daughter of French baron, contains slightly more Romantic intrigue. In this piece, Allart takes a sentimental backward look at what kind of a fulfilling relationship she might have enjoyed in her own life, had she been granted an extended and committed liaison with a man with a literary mind like unto her own.

More than any of her other stories, *Sébastien de Gama* is a

Romanticized view of her relationship with Sainte-Beuve, who as Billy speculates, was more the soulmate of her life even than was Bulwer-Lytton. With Sainte-Beuve, she enjoyed the closest rapport of two intellectual minds, even though the feelings of tenderness were much greater on her side. "On serait tenté de penser que l'homme de sa vie a été Bulwer. A la réflexion, on se demande si, en dépit des apparences, son préféré n'a pas été Sainte-Beuve . . . . [leur] liaison prend peu à peu un caractère tout intellectuel, elle devient pure amitié, une véritable communion de deux esprits de portée pourtant très inégale" (Billy 272-73).

Sébastien loves and wishes to marry his young protégée, Denise de l'Esbatx, but he is committed to an arranged marriage in Portugal. He knows little about the land of his heritage (because, like Sampayo, he spent most of his life in England), and secretly wishes to settle in Paris. Sadly, even if he were free to ask for her hand, he feels he would have no chance with the lovely and sought-after Denise. He keeps his feelings to himself, but urges her to accept his offer of friendship, claiming she is worthy of a higher liaison, that is, the meeting of their scholarly minds. She even agrees to eschew marriage to any other man so she will never bring any jealousies or tensions into her mental rapport with Sébastien. He calls her "une femme haute par l'esprit qui sait dominer son cœur, une femme faite pour ce lien extraordinaire" (*NE* 190).

Denise is equally pleased with their intellectual *rapprochement.* "Elle voyait en lui la pensée. Elle croyait cet homme supérieur à tout par la hauteur aussi de ses sentiments, et elle le voulait à elle. En trouverait-elle jamais un autre qui eût tant ses goûts de discussion, et la dépassât tant, et l'élevât si bien au-dessus d'elle-même?" (*NE* 191).

This seemingly ideal Platonic harmony is placed in clearer perspective when Denise's aunt intimates that her niece ought not to settle for such a dispassionate and impersonal relationship with a young man. "Cet homme exalté et fantasque s'amuse à rêver un héroïsme impossible," the aunt observes. "Il vous immole aux intérîts de son père et à sa propre faiblesse." You would not be a true Estatx if you accepted such an arrangement, she tells her niece (*NE* 196).

Madame de l'Esbatx urges Denise to put Sébastien's true feelings to the test by pretending to abandon him. ". . . envoyez-lui son congé, qu'il parte demain pour le Portugal" (*NE* 196). The aunt dictates a letter which Denise sends to Sébastien, telling him they are taking off for the Pyrénées. "De quoi se mêlait cette tante impudente qui lui ôtait son héroïsme!" an indignant Sébastien thinks to himself (*NE* 197). He receives the letter too late to urge them to stay, but realizes that the Pyrénées are on the way to Portugal. However, even if they were headed for Russia, he would go after them. "Mais fussent-elles allées en Russie, il trouverait la route!" (*NE* 197).

The women arrive at their family estate in the Pyrénées, and Sébastien is not far behind. Denise's heart beats frantically at the sight of the man she had thought would be only an intellectual companion. The aunt allows them some time alone together, at which point Sébastien asks for Denise's hand. He reluctantly admits that her "dangerous aunt" had a good plan. "Je suis vancu," he admits. "mais c'est une défaite qui dépasse tous les triomphes" (*NE* 199).

Sébastien writes to his father in Portugal asking to be released from his promise to marry the other woman. Monsieur de Gama, surprised, but pleased, arrives at the Pyrénées estate in time to see his son married to Denise.

The *dénouement* of *Sébastien de Gama* appears to be a self-flattering twist on Hortense's own longing—particularly during the 1840's and 1850's—for a relationship that was at the same time a celebration of intellectual closeness and romantic and sexual gratification. This was the very phenomenon—*le clou d'or*—of which Sainte-Beuve had given her a sweet taste before blithely and callously denying her any futher enjoyment or fulfillment therefrom. Through Denise, a recreation of her younger self, the author reverses the roles, creating a heroine who becomes insulted at the idea that a man should suggest that the lofty nature of their *amitié* be downgraded by *amour*. "Vous pouvez m'aimer malgré moi, et moi je n'aurai jamais d'amour pour vous," Denise tells Sébastien toward the end of the story. "Votre caractère ne me convient pas, mais votre esprit, oui" (*NE* 194). She further chides him, "D'ailleurs je suis refroidie, je vous ai cru maître de vos sentiments, vous parliez d'une belle amitié, où en êtes-vous donc?" (*NE* 194).

At this point, as she had done in *Clémence,* Allart inserts a second alter-ego into the narrative in the form of an aunt, Madame de L'Esbatx. While allowing Denise to keep her reserve and her supposed aversion to passion, the older, wiser woman can gently help her niece understand that *amitié* with a intellectual young man simply is not enough, and to help her achieve the entire gamut of male-female intellectual and sentimental consummation.

Myrtéa is one of Allart's most unusual novellas involving a number of romantic and would-be romantic relationships that finally lead to an ending that would seem the most unlikely of all—the happy resolution of a long-standing marital union that had seemed throughout the story to be loveless and hopeless. Perhaps it is speculation on the part of the aging author on the possibility that a scholarly, faithful and ever-virtuous wife eventually will be rewarded with contentment and peace in marriage that will comfort her on through middle age.

Myrtéa takes place in the bosom of misty Normandy, a setting Allart will exploit unabashedly for the last vestiges of traditional Romanticism that she can extract from it.   The title heroine's story is narrated by her close friend, Claude, who has known Myrtéa ever since the two were educated in a convent. Myrtéa marries M. de l'Asclares (the author does not give him a first name) and has a son. Although she loved her husband in the beginning, he quickly proves unfaithful and their union becomes—in one of Allart's most typical phrases to describe marriage—a "cruel yoke" to her. ". . . sa vertu et son mariage, la tenaient sous un joug cruel" (*NE* 202).

Two years later, Claude marries a friend of Myrtéa's husband and they have a son and a daughter.   This spouse soon proves faithless as well.   When both husbands leave for military duty, Myrtéa, who is intelligent, philosophical and a lover of poetry, finds solace with Claude at the home of Claude's parents. There, she meets their family friend, Count Rodrigue de Bragance, and they soon recognize the special rapport between them and fall in love.

Claude realizes that Rodrigue is the man that Myrtéa should have married. "Voilà le mari qu'il eût fallu à mon amie. Et comme il serait bon et dévoué! Comme il s'informe de sa santé, de son bonheur!" (*NE* 203-204).   Myrtéa adores Rodrigue, but, much to his dismay, she insists on remaining faithful to her absent husband. Claude's husband is later killed in a revolt in Africa. Mytrtéa's husband is involved in the same battle, and, although he is unharmed, he stays away, leaving his long-suffering wife still alone. Rodrique resigns himself to her virtuous conduct and leaves, promising to keep in touch. The memory of Rodrigue has all but effaced Myrtéa's memory of her husband. "Deux impressions la retenaient; l'offense que lui avait faite son mari, elle trouvait l'amour insulté; et l'impression qu'elle avait reçue de M. de Bragance, dont la beauté et l'émotion avaient effacé l'empire premier de son mari" (*NE* 209-10).

Myrtéa and Claude spend two calm years together with their children, during which Rodrigue writes, but Myrtéa does not reply. Through Claude's parents, Myrtéa meets a married, aspiring poet, Valère de Malvezie, who tries to persuade her to run away with him. Although she has not seen her husband in several years, Myrtéa remains faithful to their marriage vows, and resists the flowery language with which Valère attempts to seduce her.   She imagines the day when l'Asclares will return and he and Valère may become friends.   Claude accuses her friend of throwing away potential happiness— "Vous repoussez les délices"—but Myrtéa insists that honor is more important—"Fi donc! Et mon honneur?" (*NE* 213).

Valère schemes to trick Myrtéa into running off to Italy with him while he leaves his wife behind in Paris. Claude is even persuaded to help him deceive Myrtéa into believing they are going on only a short, innocent outing. Myrtéa, however, becomes wise to his plan, and indignantly refuses to continue on with him, insisting that they turn back. Later, she tells Claude why she took the moral high road. "Mais vous ne voulez donc pas comprendre qu'une femme peut préférer la délicatesse de sa vie à sa vie? Vous n'aimez donc pas ma gloire de femme? Vous n'avez pas voulu prendre les choses sur ce haut ton, mais souffrez-le pour moi et pour mon fils. Les devoirs d'une épouse et d'un mari sont-ils pareils?" She asks how Claude could conspire to help a man in a plan to deceive his own wife. "Enfin, madame de Malvézie, la comptez-vous pour rien? Ferai-je son malheur? Ne savez-vous pas que je ne voudrais pas acheter à ce prix un seul jour de bonheur?" (*NE* 227-28).

Later, she urges Valère to go off to Italy and not to write to her while he is there. "Seule je suis forte, car je suis avec Dieu, mais vous m'enlevez à Dieu même. Si des ordres ne suffisent plus, je vous prie, je vous supplie. . . " (*NE* 231). He leaves under protest, and Myrtéa is proud of the way she handled the situation. He soul is calmed, but her health is not restored. "Myrtéa pleura beaucoup, mais s'applaudit de tout et trouva dans ses prières, dans sa haute dévotion, un appui qui calma son âme sans remettre sa santé" (*NE* 323).

Myrtéa's fever continues for a year, as, miles away in Italy, Valère suffers from the same symptoms. Rodrigue, hearing of Myrtéa's illness, returns from Portugal, vowing to stay in Normandy for the rest of his life. Claude's mother wishes for her widowed daughter to marry Rodrigue. Claude and Rodrigue both recognize that Myrtéa now feels only friendship for the Portuguese nobleman. Myrtéa wishes Claude and Rodrigue well, and they marry. The next year they have a son, and Rodrigue works on a history of Portugal. In the meantime, Myrtéa corresponds with her husband, tries to suppress her lingering feelings for Valère, and slips deeper and deeper, René-like, into Romantic melancholia.

Although by this time—1873—the purest essences of Romanticism largely had played themselves out in French literature, Allart revels in this last opportunity to seize on the traditions of Chateaubriand and to hone her descriptions of a quintessential Romantic heroine. She compares Myrtéa to ancient Druidic women of this area who were inspired by nature's most terrible displays of power. "Parfois pourtant Myrtéa retrouvait une mélancolie sans bornes . . . . Comme autrefois les Druidesses qui habitaient ces rivages, elle semblait s'inspirer de l'orage, du vent et ne s'éloignait juste qu'au moment où éclatait la foudre" (*NE* 235). A wild instinct draws her toward the ocean, where she recites poetry aloud before the wind, rain and waves. She steeps herself in the love of Medieval traditions, and adores sadness in the same way that others love joy. For her, suffering becomes synonymous with existence. "Parfois elle aimait la tristesse comme d'autres aiment la joie, et vivant dans des passions combattues, elle apprenait à souffrir et elle appelait cela exister" (*NE* 235).

Myrtéa's husband returns and attempts to bolster her spirits. At about the same time, Valère returns from Italy with his wife. Myrtéa gamely resigns herself to accepting the love that still exists in her marriage, although it is half-good, half-disillusioning. ". . . elle voulait se résigner à cet amour combattu, moitié content, moité désolé" (*NE* 236). Claude is still puzzled at her friend's acceptance of a mediocre marital passion, especially in the presence of the still-ardent Valère. "N'est-ce pas ce que vous vouliez. . . un sentiment idéal qui ne s'informe pas des instincts de la vie! Valère vous aime comme une divinité, c'est ce que vous vouliez" (*NE* 236).

Valère, however, fades from the story at this point, and Myrtéa turns her attentions simultaneously to her husband and to Rodrigue. She recalls Rousseau's *La Nouvelle Héloïse,* and how, toward the end of the story, Julie d'Etanges retained her original love for Saint-Preux and still loved her spouse, Wolmar. At the same time, Saint-Preux still loved Julie while also becoming attracted to her friend, Claire.

A bizarre reenactment of the last pages of Rousseau's novel seems to take place in the last few paragraphs of Allart's story. Rodrigue's old passion for Myrtéa resurfaces and Myrtea's husband begins to fall in love with Claude. However, when M. de l'Asclares becomes jealous of his wife, the old passion between the spouses is ignited again. Claude describes the reconciliation of the two couples. "Les nuages s'amoncelaient sur nos amours: une tempête devait éclater . . . M. de l'Asclares perdit la tête de joie et montra à sa femme le premier feu de leurs amours. Myrtéa, poussée aussi par mes regards qui lui redemandaient Rodrigue, accueillit son mari; la soirée se passa en chuchoteries des deux ménages réconciliées" (*NE* 240-41).

The next year, Myrtéa has twin girls. Her health comes back, and later she has a second son, which solidifies the renascent happiness of the marriage. " . . plus tard un fils encore consacra cet heureux mariage, retourné à ses plus brillants jours" (*NE* 241). Years pass, and the two couples agree to establish a sane and wise happiness through their children. "Nous pensons dans l'avenir à compter beaucoup l'amour dans l'existence de nos enfants," Claude concludes. "Rodrigue dit qu'en cela consiste la sagesse" (*NE* 241). At the story's conclusion, more time has passed, and Claude's eldest daughter and Myrtéa's eldest son plan to marry. The four parents look forward to a joyous wedding ball.

Thus, the theme to *Myrtéa* must be that even the most profoundly Romantic ideal must necessarily pale in the face of the rewards that can come to a long-suffering wife if she but endures to the end, braves years of infidelities and despair, and resists her own temptation toward sexual sin. The happy twist on *La Nouvelle Héloïse* undoubtedly is overly idealistic and illogical, even for an author who managed such unlikely gratifying endings as those in *Gertrude* and *Settimia*. Allart, though, in the mellowing sentimentality of her old age, seems determined not to allow her last heroine to go the way of the despondency and eventual suicide of Rousseau's Julie. Rather, she stubbornly insists that love can be resurrected in a loveless marriage and that long-dead briars can blossom and bear fruit that is brighter and sweeter than ever before. Whatever fulfillment still may have been lacking in the resolution of two happy marriages is provided vicariously later on as the children of each couple fall in love, and presumably, live happily ever after.

Myrtéa was Allart's last fictional work to deal intimately with the sentiments and the point of view of a woman. Nevertheless, in late 1873, at age 72, she was still far from retirement as a literary writer. She would produce two more original novellas that would appear in the eclectic *Derniers Enchantements* published in 1874 by Michel Lévy.

In her *Notes inédites* in 1873, Allart wrote about how George Sand recently had complimented her on her still-youthful persona, telling her, "You will die still full of life." Hortense quotes Sand, "Elle dit que je n'ai rien de la vieillesse et je mourrrai toute vive. Sa lettre est très aimable. Elle est découragée et ennuyée de notre temps singulier. Mais c'est qu'elle espérait beaucoup plus que moi . . . " (quoted by Séché 23, n. 1).

In 1873, neither Sand nor Allart was ready for retirement. The years ahead would be limited for each, but rich in productivity and fellowship in their respective bucolic neighborhoods.

Notes

[1] Henry Bulwer-Lytton. *The Monarchy of the Middle Classes,* 2 vols. (London: Richard Bentley, 1836), quoted in French translation by Decreus 151.

[2] George Sand. *Préface, Les Enchantements de Prudence,* 2nd ed., quoted by Séché 24.

[3] J. Barbey-d'Aurevilly. *Les Bas-Bleus*. (Paris: Société Générale de Librairie Catholique, 1878) 204-5. (Subsequent references to this work will appear in parentheses after the quotation and will be indicated by the abbreviation *Les B.-B.*).

[4] Marcus's book, which reflected his nationalist and pro-Bonapartist views, was published in Paris by the Librairie générale in 1872. It had as its epigraph patriotic verses penned by both Béranger and André Chenier.

[5] Mme P. de Saman. *Les Nouveaux Enchantements*. (Paris: Calmann Lévy, Éditeur, 1882) 110. (Subsequent references to this work will appear in parentheses after the quotation and will be indicated by the abbreviation *NE*).

Chapter 10

Derniers Enchantements:
Conclusion (1873-1878)

Allart stepped lightly into the role of septuagenarian with all of the generosity and enthusiasm that always had characterized her life. From her modest home in Montlhéry, she welcomed the company of the simple, peasant people of the area. Much in the same vein of George Sand, who would die at Nohant in 1876 at age 72, Allart grew fond of the local folk and sought to help them out. With the small writer's pension of about 1000 francs per year, which she had been receiving since 1845, she busied herself with as much local charitable work as she could manage. Soon, the Montlhéry population nicknamed her "la bonne dame" (Séché 73).

Séché, who was in touch with Allart's grandchildren during the research of his 1908 book, quotes from a written source to which one of Marcus's daughters had referred him. The letter tells of how the Montlhéry area, with its charming medieval aura, agreed with Hortense's health and intellectual disposition:

> Dans sa retraite de Montlhéry, Mme Hortense Allart de Méritens vivait au milieu des paysans de l'endroit. L'air de Montlhéry convenait à sa santé. La vieille tour féodale, encore solidement debout, s'harmonisait avec ses méditations sur la politique et l'histoire. Du haut de ses créneaux, elle revoyait dans une immense et ravissante étendue circulaire, des châteaux et des domaines familiers aux jours de sa jeunesse.[1]

During the warm seasons, she would sit for hours writing letters in the shade of the nearby pine forests that reminded her of Italy. She had replaced the simple, but elegant, dresses she had worn in her younger years with clothing more typical of women her age, made with the cotton fabric worn by the local people. A bonnet protected her face from the wind, and on her many walks through the rain, she carried a blue cotton umbrella. She draped herself in a warm shawl and her dress fell to her ankles, leaving a view of her small, wooden clogs.

A sack, which she always carried on walks for the materials she was reading or writing, dangled from her tiny, but strong wrist. "Un sac, où elle emportait toujours de quoi lire et écrire lorsqu'elle partait en promenade, pendait à son fin poignet dont la délicatesse cachait une force d'acier" (quoted by Séché 74).

As a grandmother, she was full of effervescent love of life. Her attitude was jovial, her laughter loud and strong. Sometimes she cried, but tears only made her seem youthful and lovely. ". . . on retrouvait . . . cette grand-mère si étincelante de vie, d'intérêt et de gaieté, dont le rire olympien sonne encore aux oreilles de ceux qui l'ont entendu. Elle pleurait cependant presque aussi facilement, mais, par un don singulier, les larmes l'avaient toujours embellie et rejeunie. . . " (quoted by Séché 75).

Her literary productivity paralleled the ongoing energy of her personal life. *Derniers Enchantements,* published by Michel Lévy in 1874, includes a reprint of *Gertrude,* plus two new novellas entitled *Harold* and *Le Jeune Comte Henri,* and some previously published letters from Béranger. The heretofore unpublished fictional pieces will be the focus of analysis from this publication.

Harold offers an interesting twist on Allart's third novel *L'Indienne.* The story involves a young English parliamentarian, Harold Colywall, who marries Sacountala Melriver, a lovely, young and naive woman from the West Indies. (As was Anna Berkes of *L'Indienne,* the girl is half-English, half-Indian). This time, however, the story is told entirely from the husband's point of view, and focuses uniquely on his uncertainties about their marriage and their compatibility rather than on any feelings of hers. Over the course of a few years, Harold observes his ingenuous, but inscrutable wife with a bewildered eye, and ends up frustrated in his inability to truly feel confident about her love for him.

Harold, who has traveled extensively in his diplomatic career and loved, in turn, a Chinese musician and a sophisticated French woman of letters, reluctantly allows his father to arrange a marriage for him to the 16-year-old Sacountala. He is immediately entranced with her dark-haired beauty and languid, passive personality. "C'est peu de me donner la vie," he tells his father, "mais vous m'avez donné la femme la plus passionnée et la plus ravissante qui fût jamais."[2] The marriage takes place, and Harold finds himself so taken with his new wife that he is missing sessions of Parliament to spend more time with her. Sacountala, who is not concerned with world affairs, encourages him to do so. "Mon Dieu! Modérez, je vous prie, cet amour qui me fait manquer les séances du Parlement et toute étude. Sacountala n'est contente que quand je lui abandonne une longue journée désœuvrée" (*DE* 249).

One may recall that during Hortense's sojourns in England with Henry Bulwer-Lytton when she felt her productivity was stifled, the idea of a "journée désœuvrée" was abhorrent to her. ("Je n'avais pas assez exercé mon intelligence en Angleterre, des sensations trop molles, des *jours trop désœuvrés* m'avaient troublée . . . Je retrouve avec enchantement mon pays et la conversation" [*EP* 163, my italics]). In *Harold,* then, Hortense seems to be taking some retrospective satisfaction in imagining another fictionalized Bulwer, who now is mired in the same kind of role into which he once placed her. The slavishly devoted husband continues to lose ground in his professional life in order to make sacrifices for his wife's happiness.

Harold is both flattered and troubled by his wife's possessiveness and absolute devotion to him. "Mais elle a les principes de l'Angelterre: son mari est son Dieu. Je suis très flatté, je suis apprécié au delà de ce que je mérite; mais je m'y soumets doucement . . . " (*DE* 251). In a year's time, the birth of their son does accord Harold more time for his own interests, since Sacountala now is occupied with the baby, and later, with three more children.

Harold is aware that there are two kinds of women whom he finds charming—those like his wife and those who are more intelligent and who possess a *male mind.* It is to the latter kind of woman that he can best relate. "Il y a pour moi deux sortes de femmes charmantes, celle qui est comme Lady Colywall, et celle plus intelligente qui a l'esprit mâle et peut nous entendre" (*DE* 253). He recalls that his old flame, the Frenchwoman Louise, was just such a superior woman. However, she was capricious and vain and he never felt he could count on her. He believes that he is better off with Sacountala and all of her naive preoccupation with domesticity.

Nevertheless, Harold continues to praise the influence of France as an energetic influence on the rest of the world, and recognized in particular, the positive power of that country's intelligent and productive women:

> C'est en Europe qu'on a l'activité, l'ambition, et la France,
> entre toutes les nations, est agitée et lancée toujours avec

fracas dans quelque nouveau mouvement. Les femmes de ce pays-là aussi sont hardies, excitent les hommes aux révoutions, aux chimères, et montrent autant de résolution qu'eux et autant d'intrépidité. On est surpris de voir tant de femmes douées tout à coup de courage le plus héroïque. Elles sont bien les mères de tels soldats. (*DE* 256).

At one point, the reader wonders if Harold will rekindle his former relationship with Louise, who is spending some time in London. Although he visits the Frenchwoman several times and finds her as lovely and vivacious as ever, the two agree that there is nothing left between them but friendship. In the meantime, Harold is troubled by Sacountala's attentions to a young Frenchman, the Count of Leuville, who visits her constantly. One day, when Sacountala and Leuville are away together for an entire day, Harold is beside himself with worry for his wife's safety and fear over a scandal. Sacountala returns and explains that she and the count were stranded on a boat for hours and finally rescued. She calmly refuses to elaborate on what might have happened in the interval between the rescue and her return home.

Although Harold accepts the explanation and Count Leuville no longer visits Sacountala, the husband forever is tormented with thoughts of what may have occurred between his wife and the count. He also wonders about the sincerity of her love. "Est-elle amoureuse comme autrefois?" (*DE* 293). The story ends with a description of Harold's distressed preoccupation with this wife's attitude. He realizes that, in other cultures, a wife suspected of infidelity would have been severly punished by her husband or even killed. However, he is left only to agonize over his uncertainty about her feelings and to speculate that the root of the problem may well have been his own preoccupation with ambition. "Ce soupçon s'effacera-t-il de mon amour et de ma vie? J'ai peut-être été un mari trop distrait, trop occupé de la philosophie, de la nature . . . et de la paix du monde" (*DE* 294).

Harold does not serve merely as a latent vehicle for Allart's musings on the kind of fate that she felt a caracature of Henry Bulwer-Lytton might merit. It is also an essay that analyzes the institution of marriage in Western Europe and in various other cultures; that is, what is acceptable behavior of husbands and wives in certain ethnic groups, what is tolerated and what is not. For example, at one point, Sacountala tells Harold he is free to enter into a polygamous marriage with Louise (even though she, his first wife, would not like the arrangement), since Sacountala's own maternal culture accepts such unions. "Elle me dit que si je voulais rétablier chez moi la polygamie de son pays, elle ne s'y opposait pas, que j'étais son maître . . . [mais]

que cette française ne serait pas son amie" (*DE* 281).

At another point, Harold speaks of how he has been amused at how moralists in Paris discuss marriage and fear for its future because of the infidelities and audacity of rich wives and other spirited young women. In reality, the institution of marriage is rock-solid, Harold insists, and its existence will never be in danger because of any changing mores.

> Vraiment le mariage a des bases si solides, qu'il ne dépend en rien du tout des mœurs des villes ni des mœurs des riches. Le mariage est le sort du genre humain tout entier. Qu'importent quelques infractions, le plus souvent très-motivées et très-justes, car les villes et les richesses amènent des complications que le peuple ignore? L'universalité, *l'indispensabilité* du mariage saute aux yeux, et les mœurs de Paris, ni de Londres, ni de l'Italie, ni de l'Espagne, n'y feront jamais rien. En Chine j'ai vu les paysans n'avoir qu'une femme à cause de la dépense, et leurs mœurs sont celles des paysans d'Europe (*DE* 261-62, Allart's italics).

Once again , even in her old age and some 30 years after her own heartfelt attempt at marriage had ended in disaster, Hortense defends the basic solidarity of the institution and, with her inveterate optimism, foresees its transcendence over and endurance in the face of inevitable human foibles.

Le Jeune Comte Henri ou l'Education, which originally was written in 1867 at Montlhéry just a few years after the death of 23-year-old Henri Allart, is one of the author's most simplistic works in terms of plot development. The rather thin story of young Henri, his rapport with his wise, but self-effacing mother, Alexandrine, and the superficial adventures in love that lead happily to his marriage to a young French-Greek beauty has the markings of the author's ponderings about what might have been had her younger son lived and had she been able to guide him to a loving union with a young lady of whom she could approve.

The young Count Henri l'Espine was born and raised in Italy of a noble, but penniless French family that had settled in Germany, then Naples. When his father died, his French mother took him back to her native Fontainbleu and began seeing to his education with a erudite tutor, Miltiade Botzaris, an expert in Greek, who also has an affinity for the writings of Bernardin Saint-Pierre.

The light-minded Henry studies half-heartedly because his real passions are running about the Fontainbleu woods by day and enjoying his telescope by night. He goes through a flurry of brief courtships with Adelaïde, Germaine, Céleste, and Amélie, all local young ladies of various charms. Eventually, Miltiade introduces him to the comely Charlotte de Myrte, whose mother was Greek. The two young people, who both speak Greek, have an instant rapport. Charlotte's formerly languid demeanor quickly becomes vivacity as she revels in Henry's charms. "Cette languer qui n'était qu'une flamme violée, prit feu dans les regards envirés du jeune homme" (*DE* 343). With encouragement from Alexandrine, Miltiade, and Charlotte's father, the young lovers joyfully plan their wedding.

In a letter to his friend, the Princess of Solms, written Oct. 27, 1860, Sainte-Beuve wrote praises of Hortense's character, but not such kind words about her works. "C'est une femme loyale, un honnête homme, très instruite, spirituelle dans ses lettres, mais *très décousue* dans ses livres dont aucun n'a eu un véritable succès" (quoted by Billy 251, and Séché 16, n. 1, my italics). Though one may make an argument against her other works being called *décousu*— a word that translates as "unraveling," but more specifically, means jumbled, incoherent and without liaison—this term can be applied rather accurately to *Le Jeune Comte Henri*.

The simplistic plot about the title character weaves in and out of philosophical ruminations that Allart presents through conversations between Alexandrine and Miltiade. More important than the storyline about young Henri's quest for love and self-discovery is the Platonic and intellectual rapprochement between the two older characters. They discuss the writings of Chateaubriand, Bernardin Saint-Pierre and religious matters, and Miltiade counsels Alexandrine toward ancient-style spiritual meditation. At one point, the tutor speaks about death—which probably played somewhat on the mind of the aging Allart—and states that society should celebrate, rather than fear, the passage from earthly life into eternity. "Mais les prêtres ont inventé l'effroi, l'appareil lugubre; moi je voudrais qu'on célébrât la mort par des fêtes. On oublie trop l'amour sur la terre, et, dans la mort, l'immoralité; ce qui fait qu'on ne sait ni vivre, ni mourir" (*DE* 320).

Hortense's last years were spent in tranquillity with Marcus, her daughter-in-law, and her grandchildren. In 1876, three years before her death, she published her *Timide essai sur la Correspondance sublime de Cicéron,* an examination of the Roman statesman whom she had long studied and admired.

Hortense Allart died Feb. 28, 1879, at Montlhéry at the age of 77 years and five months. She had gone about the previous day engaged in her usual activity with no sign of anything being abnormal, and had spoken that evening with a neighbor woman about some plans they had for the next day. However, the next morning, she did not respond to a knock at her bedroom door. Marcus entered the room to find his mother stretched out on her bed, fully clothed, but showing no sign of life. She had died from the rupture of an aneurysm, the same condition that had claimed her mother at a much earlier age as she was pinning up her long, heavy hair.

After his mother's death, Marcus burned a large part of her remaining correspondence. This was according to Hortense's wishes, since in her last few years, she was still troubled by what d'Aurevilly had said about *Les Enchantements de Prudence*, and wished for no more arbitrary criticism of her personal writings. (Séché notes that in the margin of George Sand's 1872 letter that praised *Les Enchantement de Prudence* and later became its preface, Hortense had penned a note to Marcus: "A jeter au feu!" [75]).

Fortunately, Marcus retained a certain amount of her letters. However, the largest debt of gratitude for preserving her correspondence goes to Sainte-Beuve, who kept most of her letters written to him between 1841 and 1848. "On saura un gré infini à Sainte-Beuve de les avoir conservées" (Séché 76).

Hortense was buried not at Montlhéry, but rather at Bourg-la-Reine, which, although it is now a large, urban suburb of Paris, still had a countryside quality about it at that time. Her tomb in the small cemetery there was placed, according to her wishes, next to that of her son Henri who had preceded her in death in 1862 at age 23.

The common gravestone reads, "Ici Reposent Henri Diodati Allart et Sa Mère." On the left are carved words bearing a short tribute to Henri. "Né le 1er jour du printemps, le 21 mars 1839, mort dans son printemps à Montlhéry, à 23 ans, le 19 juillet 1862. Après une vie trop courte, mais très indépendante et très heureuse." Underneath the words is carved a small coat of arms in the middle of four stars.

On the right side of the tomb, one reads Hortense's birth and death dates, then a short paragraph about her faith in an eternal afterlife: "Madame Hortense Allart de Méritens, femme de lettres, née le 7 septembre 1801, morte à Montlhéry, à 78 ans, le 28 février 1879. Elle a voulu reposer auprès de son jeune fils; mais, morte dans la foi réformée, elle disait bien que les corps seuls seraient ici et l'esprit ailleurs." Despite her Protestant faith, Hortense may have died not believing in the literal divinity of Jesus Christ. There is no cross on her tomb (Billy 266).

Marcus, who died in Lunéville on Jan. 12, 1901, at age 74, was buried, according to his wishes, next to his mother and half-brother. His name appears at the bottom of the same tombstone: Marcus-Napoléon Allart, 1826-1901.[3]

Although Allart's Romanticism and her feminism often seemed at odds, they ultimately came together to illustrate a lifetime fulfillment of her most cherished ideals— unbridled self-expression, the complete emancipation of women, the right of women to the same liberty in love that men have, the preservation of one's personal and professional identity, courageous self-esteem in the face of society's prejudice against professional women and unwed mothers, and the right to hope for a happy eternal life based on an earthly life of good works and the assertion of one's natural human rights.

Her novels are more than mere samples of Romantic fiction of the period, for the intensity of the sentimentality is buffered by her heroines' courage in the face of a society that often is hostile to their best interests. Her novels also abound with her insistence that living bravely and sincerely according to one's own conscience is not only vital, but also is ultimately sufficient to transcend cruel laws that subjugate women and deny their right to full expression of creativity, sexuality, and personal fulfillment.

Sainte-Beuve once called Allart *"femme à la Staël,"* (letter dated July 12, 1863, quoted by Billy 252), an epithet she always refused to take with any seriousness or egotism.   She never was the kind of writer who postured and nursed illusions about her own greatness. Her modesty as well as her generous admiration for others were both indeed rare.

> Ce qui plaît, chez Hortense, c'est qu'elle est aussi peu femme, ou homme, de lettres que possible; il est exceptionnel qu'on tienne une plume avec si peu de pose et qu'on ne s'illusionne pas davantage sur sa valeur, mais il est rarissime de voir un auteur conserver une telle fraîcheur d'admiration et de modestie. Elle trouvait tout naturel qu'on l'oubliât et que Marie [d'Agoult] . . . . occupât une place d'honneur (Vier 22).

Her lifetime testified to this sincerity and unpretentiousness as well as to her hope for a better world and her belief in a fraternity of mankind verified by a sisterhood among women. As she opened her heart to George Sand and her home to Marie d'Agoult, refusing to let their simultaneous attractions to the same men taint the friendship she felt for each one, she hoped that all women some day could strive to be less competitive and more sincere with one another.   "Je ne sais pourtant pourquoi les femmes n'y mettent pas plus de loyauté et ne veulent pas au moins servir d'exemple et d'excuse pour les autres," she wrote Sainte-Beuve on Oct. 18, 1845 (*L.I. à S.-B.* 135).

In a subsequent letter, she told Sainte-Beuve that she always would counsel young women to follow nature and to pursue love and fulfillment according to their own desires, for to seek oneself through love and passion for another is to give oneself to the dictates of divine law. To accept anything less is tantamount to self-destruction.

> Si je rencontrais sur mon chemin une fille délicate, spirituelle et forte, je lui dirais de faire comme j'ai fait, de suivre noblement la nature. Il vaut mieux combattre au sein des passions que de combattre les passions, car la fille qui a un amant, même inférieur, vit, existe, respire, est dans la vérité, verse des larmes, en jouit, cède à la loi divine. Mais la fille qui combat la nature ne connaît que des tourments: affreuse, ténébreuse, toute sa machine se détraque, c'est un ébranlement universel, et il vaut mieux mourir" (*L.I. à S.-B.* 247).

Although Allart's name inevitably is linked to those of Chateaubriand, Sainte-Beuve, Sand, and d'Agoult, her merit stems not so much from her association with them and with other writers of the time, as it does from her own intelligence, charm, unselfishness, productivity, and the value of her novels, essays, histories and letters. André Billy, perhaps her most perceptive critic and sensitive champion, wrote that Sand and d'Agoult may have surpassed her in fiction-writing talent, but their superiority over her was in this talent and in this quality only.[4] In every other aspect, Hortense equaled them or triumphed. Billy's book ends with praise for Hortense's positive influence on some of the writers who have overshadowed her. " . . . éclairé du rayonnement de deux hommes de génie [Chateaubriand and Sainte-Beuve] apparentés en plus d'un point, elle leur a renvoyé sa propre lumière et ils ne s'en sont pas mal trouvés" (275). He concludes his article "L'Enchanteur Délaissé" with a supplication for a reexamination of her works, and, in particular, a new critical edition of *Les Enchantements de Prudence* (223).

In his book *Portrait des Femmes d'Héloïse à Cathérine Mansfield*, Emile Henriot also claims that Allart's works deserve a closer examination and insists that a volume of her letters should have an honored place on shelves of correspondence. "Quand le temps sera venu d'imprimer ce qui en vaut la peine, il y aura un très joli volume à publier, avec un choix de ses lettres, qui la classera sûrement, en bonne place, dans le premier rang de nos épistolières" (238).

This book was created as a testimony to the value of Allart's novels and as an admonition for increased modern-day appreciation for Allart as *romancière*, as well an urgent appeal for the publication of new editions of *Gertrude, Jérôme, Sextus, L'Indienne, Settimia, Clémence, Les Petits Livres,* and all three volumes of her *Enchantements.*

Although this spiritual *"femme à la Staël"* does not yet occupy a large place in either history or literature, the writings of Hortense Allart de Méritens testify to her status as a serious *femme de lettres* as well as a viable Romantic and feminist voice of her era. The surface has been merely tapped as to defining the role of her life and works in galvanizing the development of modern feminist literature.

Notes

[1] Séché does not give the source of the writing from which he quotes, but prefaces the lengthy citation with the paragraph, "J'avais fait appel aux souvenirs de ceux qui pouvaient l'avoir connue dans ses dernières années. Une de ses petites-filles a bien voulu rédiger à mon intention la note suivante:" 73.

[2] Mme P. de Saman. *Derniers Enchantements. Gertrude. Harold. Le Jeune Comte Henri. Lettres de Béranger.* (Paris; Michel Lévy frères, 1874)   247.   (Subsequent references to this work will appear in partentheses after the quotation and will be indicated by the abbrievation *DE.*)

[3] Séché's book contains a typed reproduction of the words as they appear on the tombstone, 77.

[4] "Ses deux amies George Sand et Marie d'Agoult, supérieures à elles par le talent, mais par le talent seulement, ne lui ont pas ménagé les témoingnages de leur estime et de leur sympathie" (Billy, "Chateaubriand et Hortense Allart: L'Enchanteur Délaissé," *La Revue des Deux Mondes,* 223).

Bibliography

Works of Hortense Allart

Allart, Hortense. *Lettres sur les Ouvrages de Mme de Staël.* Paris; Bossange Père, Libraire, 1824.

—. *Nouvelles Lettres à Sainte-Beuve.* Lorin A. Uffenbeck, ed. Geneva: Librairie Droz S.A., 1965.

Allart, Hortense de Méritens. *Lettres inédites à Sainte-Beuve (1841-1848).* Léon Séché, ed. Paris: Société du mercure de France, 1908.

Allart, Madame Hortense . *Settimia,* 2 vols. Paris : Arthus Bertrand, Libraire-Éditeur, 1836.

Méritens, Madame Hortense de . *Clémence.* Paris; Sceaux, Typographie de E. Dépée, 1865.

Meritens, Hortense Allart de . *Etudes Diveres, Premier Petit Livre.* Paris: Chez M. Renault, Librairie, 1850.

—. *Etudes Diverses, Second Petit Livre.* Paris: Chez Renault, Librairie, 1850.

— . *Etudes Diverses, Troisième Petit Livre.* Paris; Chez Renault, Librairie, 1851.

Séché, Léon. *Hortense Allart de Méritens dans ses Rapports avec
Chateaubriand, Béranger, Lamennais, Sainte-Beuve, George Sand,
Mme d'Agoult.* Paris: Société du Mercure de France, 1908.

Simon, Jules. *L'Ouvrière.* Paris; Librairie Hachette, 1891.

Uffenbeck, Lorin A. *Index: Chateaubriand et son Groupe Littéraire sous
l'Empire.* Chapel Hill, NC: North Carolina University Press, 1973.

Walker, Alan *Franz Liszt: The Virtuoso Years,* 2 vols. New York: Alfred A.
Knopt, 1983.

Winegarten, Renée. *The Double Life of George Sand.*   New York: Basic
Books, Inc., Publishers, 1978.

Periodicals

Bertelà, Maddelena: "*Gertrude,* Un roman qui plaisait à Stendhal,"
Francophonia   VI.11 (autunno 1986): 87-109.

Billy, André. "La femme qui a aimé Sainte-Beuve," *Revue de Paris* 61.1
(janvier 1961): 16-29.

---. "Chateaubriand et Hortense Allart: L'Enchanteur Délaissé," *La Revue
des Deux Mondes.* 3 (1 Nov . 1960): 207-23.

Ciureanu, P., "Lettere di Hortense Allart à Gino Capponi," *Studi Francesi* 1
(1957): 242-52.

---. "Stendhal e Hortense Allart," *Quaderni di filologia e lingue romanze ,* 1
(1985): 185-207.

Desanti, Dominique.   "George, Marie, Pauline, Flora et les Autres," *Friends
of George Sand Newsletter* 6: 1 & 2 (Fall and Winter 1983):21.

"Lettere di Hortense Allart a George Sand," *Studi Francesi* 6:2 (September-
December 1958): 420-26.

Pailleron, Marie-Louise. "Hortense Allart et Chateaubriand," *La Revue des
Deux Mondes* CX (Jan 1, 1940): 66-84; (Jan. 14, 1940): 261-79.

---. "Hortense Allart et Sainte-Beuve," *La Revue des Deux Mondes* CX (1
Jun 1940):458-83.

--- . "La Comtesse d'Agoult et Hortense Allart sous le Seconde Empire," *Lettres Modernes.* Paris, 1960.

Vier, Jacques. "La Comtesse d'Agoult et Allart sous le Seconde Empire, d'après une correspondence inédite," *Archives des Lettres Modernes* 33 (1960): 2-30.

Zimmerman, Dorothy. "George Sand and the Feminists of the 1830's and 1840's in France," *Friends of George Sand Newsletter.* (Fall-Winter 1981): 20-24.

Conference   Proceedings

Garnett, Mary Anne. "La Reine noire et la reine blanche." Proc. of Eighth International George Sand Conference. Tours, 1989. 255-68.

Unpublished   materials

Uffenbeck, Lorin A. *The Life and Writings Hortense Allart (1801-79).* Diss. U of Wisconsin, 1957.

Rabine, Leslie. *The Other Side of the Ideal: Women Writers of Mid-Nineteenth-Century France (George Sand, Daniel Stern, Hortense Allart, and Flora Tristan)* Diss. Stanford U, 1973.

About the author

Helynne Hollstein Hansen received her Ph.D. in French from the University of Utah in Salt Lake City. Her dissertation was entitled "Marriage and the Feminist Spirit in Two Female Novelists of the Romantic Era: Madame de Staël and George Sand."

She is an assistant professor of modern languages at Western State College of Colorado in Gunnison, Colo., and a former visiting professor of French at Brigham Young University in Provo, Utah.